WJEC/Eduqas

Religious Studies
for A Level Year 2 & A2

Religion
and Ethics

Richard Gray with Peter Cole

Series Editor: Richard Gray

Illuminate
Publishing

Published in 2020 by Illuminate Publishing Ltd, PO Box 1160, Cheltenham, Gloucestershire GL50 9RW

Orders: Please visit www.illuminatepublishing.com
or email sales@illuminatepublishing.com

© Richard Gray, Peter Cole

British Library Cataloguing-in-Publication Data

A catalogue record for this book is available from the British Library

ISBN 978-1-911208-66-2

Printed by Standartų Spaustuvė, Lithuania

02.20

The publisher's policy is to use papers that are natural, renewable and recyclable products made from wood grown in sustainable forests. The logging and manufacturing processes are expected to conform to the environmental regulations of the country of origin.

Every effort has been made to contact copyright holders of material reproduced in this book. If notified, the publishers will be pleased to rectify any errors or omissions at the earliest opportunity.

This material has been endorsed by WJEC/Eduqas and offers high quality support for the delivery of WJEC/Eduqas qualifications. While this material has been through a WJEC/Eduqas quality assurance process, all responsibility for the content remains with the publisher.

Series editor: Richard Gray
Editor: Geoff Tuttle
Design and Layout: EMC Design Ltd, Bedford

Acknowledgements

Thanks go to Dr Greg Barker for the endless trails of emails, phone calls and face-to-face meetings to journey through the Specification – 'You ROCK man!' Thanks to 'Philosophy Ninja' Clare Lloyd for her support and feedback on drafts. Appreciation to Andrew Pearce WJEC for reading proofs and Peter Cole for stepping in to help me. Thanks cannot do justice to the understanding and support of editor Geoff Tuttle and our personal journeys over the last two years. Thanks to Peter Burton and Illuminate for bearing with my many imperfections. Last, but not least, to my family for struggling through with me.

Richard Gray 2020

Cover Image: Mellimage / Shutterstock.com

Photo acknowledgements

p. 1 Mellimage; **p. 6** Thomas Soeliner; **p. 8** Imrans Photography; **p. 10** Alexandru Nika; **p. 11** (top) Lebrecht Music and Arts Photo Library / Alamy Stock Photo; **p. 11** (bottom) Natata / Shutterstock.com; **p. 12** (top) Glock / Shutterstock.com; **p. 12** (bottom) Associated Newspapers / REX / Shutterstock; **p. 14** Fizkes; **p. 16** Public domain; **p. 17** MSSA; **p. 19** Ron Ellis; **p. 20** gualtiero boffi; **p. 21** Elnur;

p. 26 neneo / Shutterstock.com; **p. 29** Pictorial Press Ltd / Alamy Stock Photo; **p. 30** Rawpixel.com; **p. 31** Hanna Kuprevich; **p. 33** Luis Molinero; **p. 35** Elnur; **p. 37** marekuliasz; **p. 39** sripfoto; **p. 45** (top) Mario Breda; **p. 45** (bottom) Courtesy Dover Publishing; **p. 46** Mark Gerson / National Portrait Gallery, London; **p. 48** Photographee.eu; **p. 49** Monkey Business Images; **p. 50** Astrid Demeillier / Shutterstock.com; **p. 51** University of Michigan; **p. 52** WAYHOME studio; **p. 53** (top) Andrey_Kuzman; **p. 53** (bottom) Joe Gough; **p. 58** Andrey_Popov; **p. 60** docstockmedia; **p. 62** (left) Andrejs Marcenko; **p. 62** (right) Tupungato; **p. 64** Inspiring; **p. 65** EvrenKalinbacak; **p. 66** sasha2019; **p. 69** (left) Iakov Filimonov; **p. 69** (right) Blablo101; **p. 70** (top) Peshkova; **p. 70** (bottom) Hibrida; **p. 71** (top) antoniodiaz; **p. 71** (bottom) Monkey Business Images; **p. 72** rogistok; **p. 73** ViSnezh; **p. 75** (top) Anton Shaparenko; **p. 75** (bottom) Debby Wong / Shutterstock.com; **p. 76** (top) Dim Tik; **p. 76** (bottom) Olga Gold; **p. 77** Orla; **p. 79** (top) corgarashu; **p. 79** (bottom) lassedesignen; **p. 80** Macrovector; **p. 89** giulio napolitano; **p. 90** Courtesy Georgetown University Press; **p. 91** Zvonimir Atletic / Shutterstock.com; **p. 93** rock-the-stock; **p. 95** Derenskaya; **p. 97** Andrei Shumskiy; **p. 99** Public domain; **p. 103** Leremy; **p. 105** Kathleen Johnson; **p. 107** cge2010; **p. 111** Maxim Apryatin; **p. 119** Sven Hansche; **p. 121** MicroOne; **p. 123** OSTILL is Franck Camhi; **p. 126** CALSC; **p. 129** Marcin Kadziolka / Shutterstock.com; **p. 130** jorisvo / Shutterstock.com; **p. 133** crbellette / Shutterstock.com; **p. 135** rudall30; **p. 137** guruXOX; **p. 139** Corona Borealis Studio; **p. 141** fizkes; **p. 143** Becky Stares; **p. 147** Andrey_Popev; **p. 154** Zvoimir Atletic / Shutterstock.com; **p. 155** (top) Courtesy Darton Longman & Todd; **p. 155** (bottom) Renata Sedmakova / Shutterstock.com; **p. 156** Everett – Art; **p. 157** Fiberg Fedor; **p. 158** RomrodPhoto; **p. 159** Everett Collection Historical / Alamy Stock Photo; **p. 160** Public domain; **p. 161** Public domain; **p. 162** Everett Historical; **p. 163** (top) Public domain; **p. 163** (bottom) Renata Sedmakova / Shutterstock.com; **p. 164** MarinaGrigorivna; **p. 165** ProStockStudio; **p. 166** Heritage Image Partnership Ltd / Alamy Stock Photo; **p. 167** (top) Pouwel Weyts / Public domain; p167 (bottom) Exclusively; **p. 168** (left) Public domain; **p. 168** (right) Public domain; **p. 170** (top) kapona; **p. 170** (bottom) The Print Collector / Alamy Stock Photo; **p. 175** Billion Photos; **p. 176** Public domain; **p. 178** (top) Anton27; **p. 178** (bottom) Courtesy: National Human Genome Research Institute, genome.gov; **p. 179** (top) Adapted from learngenetics.com; **p. 179** (bottom) The Curious Travelers / Shutterstock.com; **p. 180** (top) Boris 15 / Shutterstock.com; **p. 180** (bottom) desdemona72; **p. 181** Public domain; **p. 183** (top) Georgios Kollidas; **p. 183** (bottom) Ryan Kempster; **p. 184** Geoff A Howard / Alamy Stock Photo; **p. 186** (right) Anton_Ivanov / Shutterstock.com; **p. 186** (left) RedlineVector; **p. 189** Master1305; **p. 191** Granger Historical Picture Archive / Alamy Stock Photo; **p. 193** Public domain; **p. 195** (top) Public domain; **p. 195** (bottom) hikrcn / Shutterstock.com; **p. 196** vlastas; **p. 201** Padmayogini / Shutterstock.com; **p. 203** Chapel of Grace; **p. 207** PRISMA ARCHIVO / Alamy Stock Photo; **p. 208** buchan; **p. 209** Renata Sedmakova / Shutterstock.com; **p. 210** Paolo Paradiso / Shutterstock.com; **p. 211** Anita Ponne; **p. 212** artmig; **p. 213** Everett – Art; **p. 215** The Picture Art Collection / Alamy Stock Photo; **p. 216** ixpert; **p. 217** PopTika; **p. 218** Vlad_Chornley; **p. 220** dmitry_islentev; **p. 222** Gerrit Veldman / Shutterstock.com; **p. 230** Natata / Shutterststock.com; **p. 232** Dean Drobot; **p. 234** Gorodenkoff; **p. 235** BlueRingMedia; **p. 237** holaillustrations; **p. 239** stoatphoto; **p. 246** Wozzie / Shutterstock.com; **p. 248** Designsoul; **p. 251** Vectorpocket; **p. 254** agsandrew; **p. 257** PranThira; **p. 260** Tony Baggett / Shutterstock.com; **p. 263** Jayakumar; **p. 265** Tashatuvango; **p. 266** Valery Rybakow; **p. 268** Sony Herdiana; **p. 269** diy 13; **p. 270** (left) Mashosh; **p. 270** (right) Everett Historical / Shutterstock.com

Contents*

*The contents page follows the Eduqas Specification v4 September 2019. For WJEC the contents are the same but the Theme labelling is slightly different. Ethical thought is Theme 1ABC; Deontological ethics is Theme 2ABC; Theme 4ABC is Theme 3ABC; Theme 4DEF is Theme 4ABC.

About this book

With the new A Level in Religious Studies, there is a lot to cover and a lot to do in preparation for the examinations at A Level. The aim of these books is to provide enough support for you to achieve success at A Level, whether as a teacher or a learner, and build upon the success of the Year 1 and AS series.

Once again, the Year 2 and A2 series of books is skills-based in its approach to learning, which means it aims to continue combining coverage of the Specification content with examination preparation. In other words, it aims to help you get through the second half of the course whilst at the same time developing some more advanced skills needed for the examinations.

To help you study, there are clearly defined sections for each of the AO1 and AO2 areas of the Specification. These are arranged according to the Specification Themes and use, as far as is possible, Specification headings to help you see that the content has been covered for A Level.

The AO1 content is detailed but precise, with the benefit of providing you with references to both religious/philosophical works and to the views of scholars. The AO2 responds to the issues raised in the Specification and provides you with ideas for further debate, to help you develop your own critical analysis and evaluation skills.

Ways to use this book

In considering the different ways in which you may teach or learn, it was decided that the books needed to have an inbuilt flexibility to adapt. As a result, they can be used for classroom learning, for independent work by individuals, as homework, and they are even suitable for the purposes of 'flipped learning' if your school or college does this.

You may be well aware that learning time is so valuable at A Level and so we have also taken this into consideration by creating flexible features and activities, again to save you the time of painstaking research and preparation, either as teacher or learner.

Features of the books

The books all contain the following features that appear in the margins, or are highlighted in the main body of the text, in order to support teaching and learning.

Key terms of technical, religious and philosophical words or phrases

> **Key terms**
>
> Empirical: knowledge gained through the senses

Quickfire questions simple, straightforward questions to help consolidate key facts about what is being digested in reading through the information

quickfire

> 1.1   What is the peripatetic axiom?

Key quotes either from religious and philosophical works and/or the works of scholars

> **Key quote**
>
> The concept of 'My Station and its Duties' is the core of Bradley's moral theory. (Warnock)

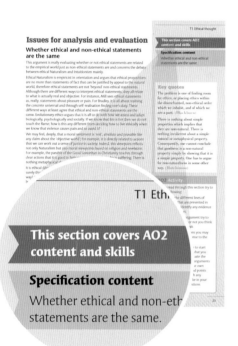

Study tips advice on how to study, prepare for the examination and answer questions

Study tip

In answering a question on ethical Naturalism, it may be helpful to mention the two different examples studied here, Utilitarianism and Bradley's *My Station and its Duties*, to demonstrate that you are aware that there are different expressions of ethical Naturalism.

AO1 Activities that serve the purpose of focusing on identification, presentation and explanation, and developing the skills of knowledge and understanding required for the examination

AO1 Activity

There has been a lot to comprehensively digest with the work of F. H. Bradley and so try to design a flow diagram that indicates the key aspects of each section, e.g. Hegel's dialectical, Bradley's developed Naturalism, *My Station and its Duties*, advantages, moral guidance, science.

AO2 Activities that serve the purpose of focusing on conclusions, as a basis for thinking about the issues, developing critical analysis and the evaluation skills required for the examination

AO2 Activity

As you read through this section try to do the following:
1. Pick out the different lines of argument that are presented in the text and identify any evidence given in support.

Glossary of all the Key terms for quick reference.

Specific feature: Developing skills

This section is very much a focus on 'what to do' with the content and the issues that are raised. They occur at the end of each section, giving 12 AO1 and 12 AO2 activities that aim to develop particular skills that are required for more advanced study at Year 2 and A2 stage.

The Developing skills for Year 2 and A2 are grouped so that each Theme has a specific focus to develop and perfect gradually throughout that Theme.

AO1 and AO2 answers and commentaries

The final section has a selection of answers and commentaries as a framework for judging what an effective and ineffective response may be. The comments highlight some common mistakes and also examples of good practice so that all involved in teaching and learning can reflect upon how to approach examination answers.

Richard Gray
Series Editor
2020

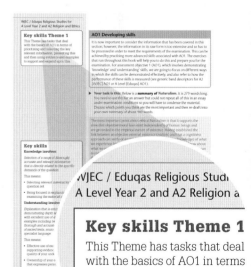

5

T1 Ethical thought

Specification content

Objective moral laws exist independently of human beings; moral terms can be understood by analysing the natural world; ethical statements are cognitivist and can be verified or falsified; verified moral statements are objective truths and universal.

Key terms

Empirical: knowledge gained through the senses

Epistemology: philosophy of knowledge derived from the Greek episteme (knowledge) and logos (words or discussion), i.e. 'discussion about knowledge'

Peripatetic axiom: philosophical view found in Ancient Greek philosophy that 'Nothing is in the intellect that was not first in the senses'

Tabula rasa: literally means 'a clean slate' and refers to the peripatetic axiom

D: Meta-ethical approaches – Naturalism

Naturalism: objective moral laws exist independently of human beings

The best way to approach Naturalism is to begin with re-visiting a concept from Year 1. In philosophy, the terms 'empirical' and 'empiricism' were used. These terms are usually quite heavily associated with philosophers Locke and Berkeley but especially with the Scottish philosopher David Hume. The empirical philosophical view is particularly pertinent when it comes to considering the philosophical discipline of epistemology; that is, the study of how and what we 'know'. The word **epistemology** is derived from the Greek episteme (knowledge) and logos (words or discussion), i.e. 'discussion about knowledge'.

Key quotes

Naturalism is an approach to philosophical problems that interprets them as tractable through the methods of the empirical sciences or at least, without a distinctively *a priori* project of theorising. (**Jacobs**)

Ethical Naturalism is the idea that ethics can be understood in the terms of natural science. One way of making this more specific is to say that moral properties (such as goodness and rightness) are identical with 'natural' properties, that is, properties that figure into scientific descriptions or explanations of things. (**Rachels**)

The epistemological position empiricism takes is that all knowledge is derived from the senses; that is, what we see, hear, touch, smell and feel is responded to by our intellect, which gives the experiences meaning. David Hume advocated that we are born in a state of **tabula rasa**, which literally means 'a clean slate'. In other words, we are born with an absence of preconceptions, predetermined views, or indeed anything in our minds. Everything that we know and learn has its origins in the world of sense experience. This is not a new idea; indeed, it affirms the **peripatetic axiom** of Ancient Greek philosophy and it is also referred to in Aquinas' writings: 'Nothing is in the intellect that was not first in the senses.'

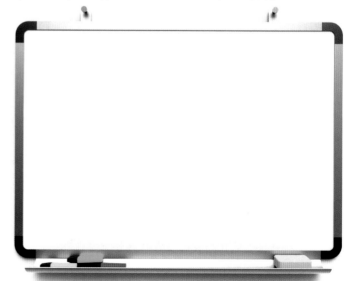

David Hume argued that we were born tabula rasa.

According to empiricism, when a proposition (statement) is put forward it is first of all assessed by our cognitive faculties for meaning based upon what we know to be the case from our past experience of the world around us. The world of sense-experience is then appealed to as the basis for establishing the truthfulness of the statement, proposition or theory that is currently presented. Once meaning is established by cognition, the truth value of a proposition can be assessed and verified.

Key quote

According to the naturalist, there is only the natural order. If something is postulated or claimed to exist but is not described in the vocabulary that describes natural phenomena, and not studied by the inquiries that study natural phenomena, it is not something we should recognise as real. (Jacobs)

Cognitivism and realism

Linked to this are the ideas of cognitivism and realism.

In philosophy, cognitivism is very much related to how our mental faculties process information and terms, and you will meet this again when studying religious language. Cognitivism holds that a statement or proposition must be related to our experience in order to verify whether or not it is meaningful. Cognitivism is the linguistic aspect of the empirical approach, that is, it establishes primarily whether or not a proposition has valid empirical meaning. The resulting validation test against our experience was crucially important to those philosophers that belonged to what was called the Vienna Circle, or Logical Positivists.

Often, an underlying assumption of cognitivism is that the world around us is objective or real, that is it exists independently of us and our minds and so can be used to establish knowledge and truth. This philosophical position is referred to as realism; however, there are many different discussions within philosophy as to how a realist understanding or interpretation of the world is derived, how this relates to cognitivism, and indeed, what the result of that implies for our knowledge of the world. This is not our concern here. For our studies we take realism to mean that the world around us is simply 'there' and it is not just our imagination, a delusion or psychological projection. In other words, it is a real existence that is mind-independent of us and therefore judgements about moral behaviour are 'real' because they relate directly to objective facts of existence.

For example, take the statement: 'The kind neighbour takes out my bins to the road every Monday morning.' In cognitive terms this makes sense as it concurs with our world of experience and what we know – our minds recognise the notions of kindness, neighbour, taking, etc. Realism acknowledges that this is true when we experience, through our sense of sight, the neighbour physically taking out the bins and realism acknowledges that we did not just imagine it.

The 'kindness' aspect is the final assessment. Therefore, a cognitive, realist approach affirms that a judgement as to the neighbour's moral character can be found through the experience of this being a helpful act and bringing happiness to others involved (from experience we can see that a 'kind' act is that which brings

Key terms

Cognition: the mental action or process of acquiring knowledge and understanding through thought, experience, and the senses

Cognitivism: the philosophical view that sentences express meaningful propositions

Logical Positivists: famous group of philosophers interested in logical philosophy, also known as the Vienna Circle

Proposition: statement

Realism: view that an object exists in reality independently of our mind (mind-independent)

quickfire

1.1 What is the peripatetic axiom?

quickfire

1.2 What does the word epistemology mean?

happiness). The language is meaningful, and the moral judgement relates directly to the consequences of the physical act. A cognitive, realist approach, then, sees a moral or ethical proposition as being related directly to the empirical world, truthful and valid.

An act as simple as taking out another's bin for collection can be seen in ethical terms.

Key quotes

According to moral realists, statements about what actions are morally required or permissible and statements about what dispositions or character traits are morally virtuous or vicious (and so on) are not mere expressions of subjective preferences but are objectively true or false according as they correspond with the facts of morality – just as historical or geographic statements are true or false according as they fit the historical or geographic facts. (Hale)

Naturalism was supposed to explain away ethics altogether by associating ethical concepts such as goodness or duty with non-ethical concepts such as pleasure or utility or the desire that society should be preserved. (Warnock)

Empiricism, cognitivism and realism are all inter-related; however, as with realism, that inter-relationship is much debated within epistemology, and different philosophers take different positions on the subtleties of what this inter-relationship actually is. This is where it gets really complex but fortunately, again, it is not our concern. Suffice to say that an empirical, cognitivist and realist approach is one that recognises that the world around us can provide answers to our philosophical questions and that we do not need to go beyond the realm of the senses for an explanation.

In short, this position described above is the position of philosophical Naturalism. What, then, of ethical debate about the nature of good, bad, right or wrong? What does this all mean for ethics?

Naturalism and analysis of the natural world

From this foundation of philosophical Naturalism it is proposed that ethical knowledge can be reduced to, and explained through, empirical means. **Ethical Naturalism**, then, argues that we can know whether something is good, bad, right or wrong by deference to the world around us, an experience of which imparts this ethical knowledge.

quickfire

1.3 What does the term 'proposition' mean?

quickfire

1.4 Which group of philosophers were associated with the Vienna Circle?

Key term

Ethical Naturalism: the view that ethical propositions can be understood by analysing the natural world

This means that ethical Naturalism proposes:

That moral terms can be understood by analysing the natural world (empirical)

In other words, ethical language can be understood by referring to, and closely analysing, what we experience from the natural world around us. For example, we all understand that to experience the kindness of another is a 'good' experience and that to experience cruelty from another is a 'bad' experience.

That ethical statements are cognitivist and can be verified or falsified (cognitivist)

Taken further, this then means that our experiences have meaning because we can verify, from our experiences, that kind acts are 'good' and cruel acts are 'bad' due to the happiness or suffering that these experiences produce. We can all verify this and it means the same for everyone.

That verified moral statements are objective truths and universal

If the ethical descriptions and statements about our world have meaning for everyone then it also follows that they are objective truths and universal. If the world around us is objective or real, that is it exists independently of us, then it can be used to establish knowledge and truth. We can then discuss ethics meaningfully and establish certain propositions about good and bad ethical behaviour, for example that kindness is good, because our experience of the world verifies this.

That objective features of the world make propositions true or false (moral realism)

If these experiences are mind-independent, uniform and universal then this also means that the statements 'kindness is an ethically good act' and 'cruelty is an ethically bad act' are true because these experiences are grounded in the objective features of the world around us. That is, we can actually see how kindness works. From this, we all can agree that kindness is good because the experiences in the world around us establish that this is true.

The classical example of ethical Naturalism as an ethical theory is that of **Utilitarianism** as proposed by Mill. A Utilitarian approach is typically naturalistic in that it applies ethical reasoning from the basis of the experience of happiness and that the most useful ethical action is seen as that which brings the maximum levels of 'happiness or pleasure'. Utilitarians argue that everyone should do the most useful thing. The most useful thing is seen as action or actions that result in maximum levels of happiness or pleasure. Therefore, actions that produce the most happiness are seen as good. However, Mill was very interested in establishing an ethical society, not just individual guidance, and therefore the most important contribution by Mill, then, can be argued to be his introduction of the idea of **universalisability**. This proposed that everyone ought to aim at the happiness of everyone, as increasing the general happiness will increase individual happiness. This argument then supports the idea that people should put the interests of the group before their own interests.

Mill's theory of Utilitarianism mirrors the progressive statements in the shaded box above:

- Moral terms can be understood by analysing the natural world in relation to the effects of our actions.
- Ethical statements are cognitivist and can be verified or falsified in relation to what we know about actions and their consequences from the empirical world, namely, the amount of happiness or pain they create.

Key quote

According to the naturalist, there are no Platonic forms, Cartesian mental substances, Kantian noumena, or any other agents, powers, or entities that do not (in some broad sense) belong to nature.
(Jacobs)

Key terms

Universalisability: Mill's utilitarian principle that that everyone ought to aim at the happiness of everyone, as increasing the general happiness will increase individual happiness

Utilitarianism: theory first systematically outlined by Jeremy Bentham stating that we ought to aim to produce the greatest amount of pleasure and the least amount of pain

Key terms

Descriptive: term used as a criticism of Naturalism that it can only describe and not be prescriptive

Normative: to do with 'norms' of behaviour used in ethics to describe theories stating what we should do or how we should behave

quickfire

1.5 How does Utilitarianism define the word 'good'?

- Verified moral statements are objective truths and universal so we can establish that everyone ought to aim at the happiness of everyone, as increasing the general happiness will increase individual happiness.
- The objective features of the world, namely the impact of acts that create happiness and acts that create suffering, make our ethical propositions about the nature of such action true or false.

The most important point about ethical Naturalism is that it supports the view that objective moral laws exist independently of human beings and are grounded in the empirical nature of existence. Having established the link between an objective external existence (realism) and that a cognitivist approach can verify or establish the validity of what we experience (empiricism), then it follows logically that what we know about what we experience makes our ethical statements objective. Therefore, we can recognise objective moral laws that exist independently of human beings and that are located firmly in the world around us.

As Naturalism places great emphasis on the empirical then it opens itself up to the realm of the sciences and so we find we have social Naturalism, biological Naturalism, evolutionary ethics, psychological Naturalism and philosophical materialism. However, there is also the whole debate about whether or not Naturalism is a purely **descriptive** theory or, whether it is also a **normative** theory that can direct ethical obligation.

For the purpose of this Specification, ethical Naturalism should be understood as set out here, that is, as empirical, cognitive and realist, and also in relation to the contribution to philosophy of F. H. Bradley to which we now turn.

Mill's argument that the interests of the group should come before the interests of the individual is the underlying feature of democracy.

AO1 Activity

Think of an everyday scenario and write a paragraph describing it with reference to some of the key terms above.

Study tip

Start to create a glossary of key terms but make sure that you have a separate column for the definitions so that it makes it easy to cover them up and test yourself.

F. H. Bradley's *Ethical Studies* and idealist moral philosophy

F. H. Bradley, a famous British philosopher, belonged to the tradition of British Idealism, a group of thinkers heavily influenced by Hegel's philosophical methodology. Technically, Bradley is not regarded as a naturalist philosopher; his major work on ethics, *Ethical Studies*, is a highly polemical work so typical of the Hegelian tradition.

However, although Bradley was by no means a naturalist philosopher, his essay in chapter five of *Ethical Studies* entitled *My Station and its Duties*, does present us with a unique form of ethical Naturalism. What Bradley attempts to do in this chapter is to conflate the contrasting meta-ethical ideas found within Utilitarianism and Kantian ethics by applying Hegel's dialectical synthesis, therefore developing a unified ethical theory without any deficiencies. Ultimately, Bradley considered this new unified theory also deficient due to the incompleteness of its **metaphysical** end (self-realisation). With great irony, at the end of his book *Ethical Studies*, Bradley had again shifted position back towards a metaphysical, idealist position and concluded that the best explanation of morality was through religion!

F. H. Bradley (1846–1924)

The philosopher Hegel (1770–1831)

Specification content

F. H. Bradley – ethical sentences express propositions; objective features of the world make propositions true or false; meta-ethical statements can be seen in scientific terms.

quickfire

1.6 What philosopher did Bradley use to develop a naturalistic notion of duty?

Key Person

Francis Herbert Bradley was born in Clapham, Surrey, England. In 1865, Bradley entered University College, Oxford and in 1870 was awarded a lucrative fellowship with no teaching duties at Merton College, Oxford. Bradley's most influential book on ethics, *Ethical Studies* 1876, contains a series of related essays which applied a Hegelian approach (dialectical method) working through a series of defective theories towards a better understanding of ethics.

Key Person

Georg Wilhelm Friedrich Hegel was a German philosopher who tried to overcome the problems of dualistic ideas or contrasting ideologies, e.g. the distinctive separation of the meta-physical and the physical. Hegel did this by considering one view (thesis) and then the contrary view (antithesis) and then combining what he thought were the unifying truth factors (synthesis) – this method was known as dialectical synthesis.

Key terms

Dialectical synthesis: Hegel's view that two opposite views (hypothesis, antithesis) can be united (synthesis) through philosophical analysis. One simple example would be: hypothesis 'the universe began with the Big Bang'; antithesis 'God created the world'; synthesis 'God was the first cause and is compatible with the Big Bang'

Idealism: a philosophical school associated with Hegel that proposes that there must be an identity of thought and existence as a complete whole (das Absolute)

Polemical: philosophical argument of or involving strongly critical writing or speech

Self-realisation: Bradley's view that the self wanders through a philosophical course of discovery, interacts with society and nature and, ends with a realisation of one's identity and ethical role within the world

Key quote

The concept of 'My Station and
its Duties' is the core of Bradley's
moral theory. (Warnock)

Key term

Transcendental idealism: Kant's
complex philosophy found in the
Critique of Pure Reason (1781, 1787)
that rejects the notion of objective
empiricism and argues that our
experiences of things are only 'sensible
forms of our intuition'

*The philosopher Emmanuel Kant
(1724–1804)*

*Aldous Huxley the British author
(1894–1963)*

Bradley's ethical Naturalism in *My Station and its Duties*

As outlined above, the book *Ethical Studies* is a progressive work that contains
seven different proposals about, and positions on, ethical theories. Each chapter
is seen as superior to the previous chapters and yet at the same time retaining
some of their validity. Therefore, Bradley's new Naturalism is seen to be an
advancement of one type of Naturalism (ethical Hedonism and Utilitarianism)
and an **improvement** on the transcendental idealism of Kant. Bradley was
attracted by the naturalistic approach of Utilitarianism but also interested in
Kant's transcendental notion of duty. In true Hegelian fashion, Bradley sets out to
combine the empirical basis of Naturalism with the idea of universal obligation
from Kant's idealist ethical theory.

Two illustrations from English literature may help us explain Bradley's
understanding of ethics in his essay in *My Station and its Duties*. In *Devotions Upon
Emergent Occasions*, written by the metaphysical poet John Donne, he writes the
following:

> *No man is an island,*
> *Entire of itself,*
> *Every man is a piece of the continent,*
> *A part of the main …*
> *Therefore never send to know for whom the bell tolls;*
> *It tolls for thee.*

Although not originally meant as a poem, it expresses extremely well the empirical
fact that within nature a human being is a social creature that interacts with and is
dependent upon other human beings. In terms of philosophy, Bradley wanted to
demonstrate that the deficiency of Hedonistic Utilitarianism was that although it
claimed to be universal in outlook, it was in fact too egotistical and did not really
acknowledge the 'self' as part of the whole.

A contrasting passage from *The Doors of Perception*, written by Aldous Huxley,
contains the following passage:

> *We live together, we act on, and react to, one another; but always and
> in all circumstances we are by ourselves. The martyrs go hand in hand
> into the arena; they are crucified alone … By its very nature every
> embodied spirit is doomed to suffer and enjoy in solitude. Sensations,
> feelings, insights, fancies – all these are private … from family to
> nation, every human group is a society of island universes.*

In contrast to Donne's 'no man is an island', Huxley's work depicts the idea of self
as an isolated entity, agonising in its own ultimate loneliness. Bradley rejected
Kant's transcendental idealism that viewed the world we experience as a world
through appearances and not substance. He also rejected the 'self' as some form
of independent, intuitive faculty that was simultaneously able to interact with
experience. Bradley's position in *My Station and its Duties* was to demonstrate that
the 'isolated' metaphysical self was 'concretely' part of the 'island' of the whole
social organism.

Therefore, Bradley aimed at an ethical theory that would satisfy these issues: a
theory that was both naturalistic and yet simultaneously into which, the idea of
a metaphysical self was fully integrated. He wished to unite Huxley's separated
self with the holistic humanity of Donne and so bring together the theories of
Utilitarianism with the ideas of Kant: Bradley writes, 'when he can separate himself
from that world, and know himself apart from it, then **by that time his self**, the
object of his self-consciousness, **is penetrated, infected, characterised by the
existence of others**.'

Station and duty through self-realisation

For Bradley, the whole point of ethics was concerning the 'self' but not in abstract alone with no relation to the physical world, like metaphysical philosophers would suggest. Instead, the realisation should be that the 'self' could be fully appreciated when understood within, and not to be seen as separate from, the whole and the best way to understand oneself, one's purpose and one's duty was to find one's niche, or '**station**' as Bradley expresses:

'To know what a man is (as we have seen) you must not take him in isolation. He is one of a people, he was born in a family, he lives in a certain society, in a certain state. What he has to do depends on what his place is, what his function is, and that all comes from his station in the organism.'

Bradley's solution was that through a process of 'self-realisation' that identifies the location, role and function of a human being in the social organism of the world: 'we, in fact do, put ourselves forth and see ourselves actual in outer existence'. That is, it is through enactment and inter-action with the world around us that the self discovers an ethical sense of **duty**. This is the process of self-realisation. Such self-realisation eradicates the sense of self-isolation that is merely a delusion. Bradley is clear that the true idea of 'self' is integral to the society within which it operates.

The nature of ethical statements as part of the concrete universal

For Bradley, then, true ethical statements depict interactions with our world and recognise that we are part of a whole. For Bradley, it is because an agent's 'station' and 'duty' are to be found within the empirical realm that the nature of ethical statements expressed are both verifiable (cognitive) and relate to the facts of the world in which we live (Bradley follows Hegel and refers to this as the '**concrete universal**'). Our goal is to realise our true self, which we learn (through observation) in the family and community, adapting the values of our society – and those of other societies that offer sound criticisms of our society.

Bradley's starting point with ethics, according to Mary Warnock, is that he acknowledges a certain set of 'facts': 'the fact that we often feel ourselves to be under some obligation' or the fact that 'we have morally failed in some way'. This foundation, for Bradley, was the fact of 'moral consciousness' that united everyone and each goal of self-realisation served the end of what he calls the self as a whole, that is, society. Bradley's notion of self-realisation, according to Mary Warnock, is 'directed over a period of time to a way of life, a system of interconnected actions'. That is, a person's moral acts are judged over a period of time and as part of their actions overall. Morality becomes an act of self-assertion or self-expression.

Bradley's view of morality is general at best. However, any moral act destroys the illusion that we are isolated from the world and instead embraces reality. Therefore, the ultimate aim or end of morality is not just to remove the illusion of separateness from the world but actually it is to bring any sense of separateness to an end. In other words, through self-realisation, Bradley's naturalistic ethic went beyond simply identifying what 'is'; it also identified what a person ought to be. Bradley states: 'How does the contradiction disappear? It disappears by me identifying myself with the good will that I realise in the world, by my refusing to identify myself with the bad will of my private self.' For Bradley, a person's individual station of duty accomplishes a universal work; through self-sacrifice the self is restored. In other words, through realising one's station and its duties within the whole moral organism, we realise who we are and what behaving ethically is.

quickfire

1.7 What was Bradley's problem and what was the solution he proposed?

Key terms

Concrete universal: Bradley's view that the self is not isolated but is derived from dialectical relations with the world

Duty: Bradley's explanation of ethical awareness through a process of self-realisation brought about by interaction with society and nature and acknowledgement of one's station

Station: Bradley's term to acknowledge the location, role and function of a human being in the social and natural world

Key quotes

There is here no need to ask and by some scientific process find out what is moral, for morality exists all round us, and faces us, if need be, with a categorical imperative, while it surrounds us on the other side with an atmosphere of love. **(Bradley)**

This is the Hegelian morality which stresses the social character of the individual, and finds the content of moral life in the actions which derive from particular social relations and functions. **(Norman)**

There is nothing better than my station and its duties, nor anything higher or more truly beautiful. **(Bradley)**

In my station my particular duties are prescribed to me, and I have them whether I wish to or not. **(Bradley)**

Morality is 'relative', but nonetheless real. At every stage there is the solid fact of a world so far moralised. There is an objective morality in the accomplished will of the past and present, a higher self worked out by infinite pain, the sweat and blood of generations, and now given to me by free grace and in love and faith as a sacred trust. **(Bradley)**

The universal which is the end, and which we have seen is concrete and does realise itself, does also more. It gets rid of the contradiction between duty and the 'empirical' self; it does not in its realisation leave me forever outside and unrealised. **(Bradley)**

Key term

Non-sensuous moral ideal:
Bradley's term for Kant's general theory of duty

Bradley believed that through realising one's station and its duties within the whole moral organism we realise who we are and what behaving ethically is.

Bradley's conclusions about *My Station and its Duties*

According to Bradley, the ethical theory found in the essay *My Station and its Duties* improves on Utilitarianism and Kant's idea of duty:

- *My Station and its Duties* combines objectivity (empirical fact) with the **'non-sensuous moral ideal'** (duty or moral obligation). Bradley's theory is that all sense of conflict between duty and individual sensuality is resolved as all these elements become part of the wider external world that is the concrete universal.

- *My Station and its Duties* is philosophically 'objective' because it brings together subject (individual) and object (the world around us). It is this 'bringing together' that is the completing of the whole and the justification of absolute objectivity for Bradley. In other words, the 'whole' works and functions as it should do when everyone discovers and works within their particular station.

- It is also to do with the 'concrete' and considers actual empirical ethical facts that derive from, and are prescribed from, 'the whole'. Such prescriptions are not chosen but given: 'I and everyone else must have some station with duties pertaining to it, and those duties do not depend on our opinion or liking.' Ethical statements (propositions about our 'duty') are therefore empirically verified and seen in scientific terms as true or false in relation to objective features of the world (our 'station' as part of the concrete universal).

Bradley summarises his theory beautifully when he writes:

'It is a concrete universal because ... It is an organism and a moral organism, and it is a conscious self-realisation, because only by the will of its self-conscious members can the moral organism give itself reality. It is the self-realisation of the whole body, because it is one and the same will which lives and acts in the life and action of each. It is the self-realisation of each member because each member cannot find the function which makes him himself, apart from the whole to which he belongs.

Bradley and normative ethics

Since Bradley's exploration is meta-ethics, he does not outline any normative ethical guidance but simply explains the origins of our sense of goodness, badness, rightness and wrongness. For Bradley, it is in the empirical world (the concrete universal) that the philosopher can find verification for ethical statements (objective features of the world make propositions true or false). However, although meta-ethical statements can be seen in scientific terms, he argues that 'there cannot be a moral philosophy which will tell us what in particular we are to do, and also that it is not the business of philosophy to do so'. Indeed, for Bradley such an idea was 'simply ludicrous'.

Despite this, throughout his essay, Bradley does offer statements such as:

- 'I am what I ought to be ...'
- 'Its duties teach us to identify others and ourselves with the station we fill ...'
- 'It teaches us that a man who does his work in the world is good ...'
- 'The work of the individual for his needs is a satisfaction of the needs of others as much as of his own ...'

Bradley's moral Naturalism 'breaks down the antithesis of despotism and individualism' but at the same time as denying them separately 'preserves the truth of them both'; to be an individual recognises the whole and in return the whole determines a person's individuality. Bradley's ultimate moral injunction is to be aware of the morality that is all around us, that 'faces us, if need be with a categorical imperative, while it surrounds us on the other side with an atmosphere of love'.

So the question remains, 'how do we know and come to identify what our duty is?' Bradley's solution in *My Station and its Duties* was that this 'knowledge' had a physical basis and a clear scientific explanation but the specifics of this appear to be in accepting whatever social and moral norms upon which one's station is based. Bradley quotes Hegel in support: 'the wisest men of antiquity have given judgement that wisdom and virtue consist in living agreeably to the Ethos of one's people'.

AO1 Activity

There has been a lot to comprehensively digest with the work of F. H. Bradley and so try to design a flow diagram that indicates the key aspects of each section, e.g. Hegel's dialectical, Bradley's developed Naturalism, *My Station and its Duties*, advantages, moral guidance, science.

Study tip

In answering a question on ethical Naturalism, it may be helpful to mention the two different examples studied here, Utilitarianism and Bradley's *My Station and its Duties*, to demonstrate that you are aware that there are different expressions of ethical Naturalism.

quickfire

1.8 What are the three advantages of *My Station and its Duties* according to Bradley?

Key quote

The view which thinks moral philosophy is to supply us with particular moral prescriptions confuses science with art. (Bradley)

quickfire

1.9 Did Bradley agree with having normative ethics?

Key terms

Categorical imperative: Kant's view of an unconditional moral obligation which is binding in all circumstances and is not dependent on a person's inclination or purpose

Despotism: Bradley's understanding of absolute power or the ultimate controlling all

Specification content

Challenges: Hume's Law (the is-ought problem); Moore's Naturalistic Fallacy (moral language is indefinable); the Open Question Argument (moral facts cannot be reduced to natural properties).

The Scottish philosopher David Hume (1711–1776)

Key term

Hume's Law: that an 'ought' cannot be derived from an 'is'

Challenges to Naturalism

There have been many challenges to Naturalism as an adequate explanation for the nature of ethics. The challenges are not restricted to those listed in this part of the Specification, as challenges also include alternative theories that have been proposed, such as Intuitionism and Emotivism. Indeed, as this theme progresses, you will see how each theory interacts and responds to another with challenges. In terms of Naturalism itself, immediately there are three.

Hume's Law (the is-ought problem)

Possibly the most famous objection to Naturalism is that in maintaining that ethical propositions can be identified from natural phenomena, this then reduces ethical propositions to observational or descriptive meaning or a mere explanation of what is happening. For example, when a person gives money freely to another who is less fortunate, we can see that it has brought more comfort to the life of the less fortunate and had no real material detriment for the giver. However, to draw from this a conclusion that 'it is good for the more fortunate person to give money to a less fortunate person' has nothing at all to do with the actual actions. A new layer of knowledge has been introduced that is not part of the original state of play. This new layer, according to critics of Naturalism, is NOT part of the actions but something quite separate. Logically, one cannot draw out from the argument an element that was not included in the first place. That is, to say what *is* happening does not logically lead to the conclusion of what *ought* to happen. The observation was first put forward by David Hume and is sometimes referred to as **Hume's Law** or Hume's Guillotine and states that it is not a logical step to derive an 'ought' from an 'is'. Hume writes:

'In every system of morality, which I have hitherto met with, I have always remarked, that the author proceeds for some time in the ordinary way of reasoning, and establishes the being of a God, or makes observations concerning human affairs; when of a sudden I am surprised to find, that instead of the usual copulations, is, and is not, I meet with no proposition that is not connected with an ought, or an ought not. This change is imperceptible; but is, however, of the last consequence. For as this ought, or ought not, expresses some new relation or affirmation, it is necessary that it should be observed and explained; and at the same time that a reason should be given, for what seems altogether inconceivable, how this new relation can be a deduction from others, which are entirely different from it.'

In terms of moral propositions, Hume's view is debated and is related to another one of his principles, often referred to as **Hume's Fork** (see diagram). This sees the principles of *a priori* knowledge (conceptual and prior to experience) and *a posteriori* knowledge (relating to experience) as completely separate types of knowledge, and just as the prongs on a fork cannot converge, neither can the types of knowledge. For Hume, a moral proposition is neither stating a propositional, that is, an *a posteriori* empirical 'fact', nor is it an *a priori* truth and so does not really belong to the world of logic or empiricism; such a statement is a statement of value or judgement that cannot be deduced logically or demonstrated empirically from a series of events. The philosophers Bertrand Russell and Alfred Ayer made Hume's Fork a basis for further development of their own empiricist philosophies, and especially in the case of Ayer, had a marked influence on their moral philosophy.

Professor Philip Stratton-Lake of Reading University explains the 'is/ought' challenge to Naturalism with reference to cooking a lobster!

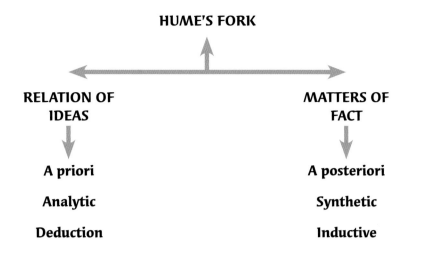

HUME'S FORK

RELATION OF IDEAS	MATTERS OF FACT
A priori	A posteriori
Analytic	Synthetic
Deduction	Inductive

Key quotes

Naturalism in ethics, like attempts to square the circle and to 'justify induction', will constantly recur so long as there are people who have not understood the fallacy involved. (Hare)

Naturalism provides a view from the outside, and from that perspective, it provides all sorts of interesting information. But it misses something that can be experienced only from the inside, namely the normative force of the reasoning. (Rachels)

'Empirical investigation can tell us many things about the world, but it does not seem that it can tell whether certain acts are right or wrong, good or bad ... For instance, if science told us that a lobster's neurological system is sufficiently advanced for it to feel pain, we'd revise our view about the permissibility of boiling them alive. But all that science would have told us is that lobsters feel pain when boiled alive. Science does not inform us that boiling them alive is wrong. That seems to be something that cannot be known empirically.'

This is a good analogy but it also reveals something else about Hume's argument when Stratton-Lake states, 'we'd revise our view about the permissibility of boiling them alive'. To illustrate this, we can return to the example first put forward:

- A person gives money freely to another who is less fortunate.
- We can see that it has brought more comfort to the life of the less fortunate.
- The action also had no real material detriment for the giver.
- A conclusion is drawn that 'if it causes us no material detriment we **ought** to give money to a less fortunate person'.

The matter of fact, following Hume's analysis, is that the conclusion drawn has nothing at all to do with the actual actions themselves and that we have introduced an extra element of judgement or value that is not inherent in the actions themselves. The example has merely demonstrated that one thing has led to another. The conclusion is not valid.

We observe the actions but unless we have, say, a premise that 'comfort and not creating financial difficulties for oneself = good', and that we 'ought to pursue this' then we cannot induce the conclusion we 'ought'. In other words, if we want this conclusion to be derived from the reasoning, then we must reveal the hidden premise that could suggest it.

Even then, this premise is incorrect because it has equated 'good' with 'comfort' and 'financial health' but the question still remains, how has this been established? Can this be demonstrated? We cannot do this without first defining what 'good' is. If not then we must reject the premise and without a premise we see that it has failed again.

Key term

Hume's Fork: sees the principles of *a priori* knowledge (conceptual and prior to experience) and *a posteriori* knowledge (relating to experience) as completely separate types of knowledge

Key quote

The most important objection to ethical Naturalism is that it leaves out the normative aspect of ethics. Since the whole point of ethics is to guide action, there could hardly be a more serious complaint. The objection can be expressed in various ways. One way, which we have already considered, is to say that we cannot derive 'ought' from 'is'. Another is to say that ethical assertions are prescriptive, whereas their naturalistic translations are merely descriptive. Or it may just be said: look at the whole naturalistic account and you will find nothing that tells you what to do. (Rachels)

quickfire

1.10 By which term is Hume's Law also known?

quickfire

1.11 What do the two prongs of Hume's Fork represent?

So precisely what was Hume meaning in the extract above when he comments on the relationship between 'is' and 'ought'? There is disagreement amongst philosophers here and this is significant not just for Naturalism but also for philosophers such as John Finnis in his revised Natural Law theory. There are two possible interpretations:

(1) Traditionally, it has been understood that Hume meant that **ethical propositions can never be considered as empirically valid, nor can they be logically deduced from a series of events** since, as value judgements, they are significantly different from empirical events and *a priori* truths.

(2) However, some philosophers question this conclusion and argue that Hume was simply pointing out that **the logic in the argument was inconsistent and nothing more**. This will be explored in Theme 2D with John Finnis.

Challenges: Moore's Naturalistic Fallacy

We will be looking at the work of G. E. Moore in the next section on Intuitionism. Indeed, it was Moore's critique and rejection of Naturalism that was a crucial element in the development of his own theory of ethics. Moore's contention was very simple. He began his ethical enquiries with what he considered the most obvious question to ask: 'what is good?'

Moore argued that if we are to discuss ethics meaningfully then we need to establish the most basic of questions: 'what do we mean by "good"?' Moore writes,

'... this question, how good is to be defined, is the most fundamental question in all Ethics ... Its definition is, therefore, the most essential point in the definition of Ethics ... Unless this first question be fully understood, and its true answer clearly recognised, the rest of Ethics is as good as useless from the point of view of systematic knowledge.' (Moore)

By this, Moore is concerned with what he calls the 'intrinsic value' of good as an end in itself. He sees this as a peculiar use of the word good that differentiates it from good or right actions that are a means to an end in bringing about good. Ethics, then, is based entirely on the underpinning notion of what good 'is'.

Moore writes:

'Let us, then, consider this position. My point is that **good is a simple notion**, just as yellow is a simple notion; that, just as you cannot, by any manner of means, explain to anyone who does not already know it, what yellow is, so you cannot explain what good is. Definitions of the kind that I was asking for, definitions which describe the real nature of the object or notion denoted by a word, and which do not merely tell us what the word is used to mean, are only possible when the object or notion in question is something complex.'

Moore is not saying that things can't be 'good'; indeed, there are many things that can be identified by their 'goodness', for example pleasure, love, happiness, health and so forth. What Moore was pointing out was that a particular quality that is described as 'good' cannot be used to define 'good'; in other words, we cannot identify a single property or quality that explains what goodness in itself 'is'. We can say a door is yellow so that it is a yellow door, but when we ask what yellow is, we do not reply 'it is door or dooriness'. A yellow door would help us understand the notion of yellow but the door does not define what yellow 'is'. In the same way with 'good', we can identify pleasure as good but to answer that 'goodness' is pleasure, that is – pleasure alone – does not satisfy our quest for a definition as there are many other things that are also good or a means to goodness. There is no shortage of possible definitions: naturalness, virtue, wisdom, love, peace, duty, etc.

This means that good in itself cannot be a natural property and to identify it with a particular natural property does not define good. Good in itself is 'unanalysable'. Moore called this the Naturalistic Fallacy and just as Hume argued you cannot derive an ought from is, Moore argued you cannot define goodness through nature and experience. Good is simply good.

Another way Moore tried to explain it was in relation to 'parts'. He argued that things are often defined in relation to their constituent parts, for example, a horse, namely four legs, etc., or a chariot, four wheels, etc. The problem with good is that it has no constituent parts itself, it is just a simple notion or concept. He writes:

'Good, then, if we mean by it that quality which we assert to belong to a thing, when we say that the thing is good, is incapable of any definition, in the most important sense of that word. The most important sense of definition is that in which a definition states "what are the parts which invariably compose a certain whole?"; and in this sense good has no definition because it is simple and has no parts. It is one of those innumerable objects of thought which are themselves incapable of definition, because they are the ultimate terms of reference to which whatever is capable of definition must be defined.'

In particular, Moore was keen to attack the principles of Utilitarianism that clearly equated the definition of good with pleasure. However, ethics is about discovering any property that defines goodness that is potentially part of other properties – a sort of common denominator. For example, pleasure, happiness and love may be analysed to see whether or not we can identify the 'goodness' elements within them. Since we cannot discover this, we cannot say that they are all exactly the same as good as they are all very different; this would be nonsense. However, that is exactly what theories such as Utilitarianism do in identifying goodness as happiness.

Moore writes:

'Yet a mistake of this simple kind has commonly been made about good ... Ethics aims at discovering what are those other properties belonging to all things which are good. But far too many philosophers have thought that when they named those other properties they were actually defining good; that these properties, in fact, were simply not other, but absolutely and entirely the same with goodness. This view I propose to call the Naturalistic Fallacy and of it I shall now endeavour to dispose.'

Therefore, Moore concluded that:

- Good is a simple concept or notion that cannot be broken down;
- Good, in itself, it is not relational, nor dependent upon any other constituent part and neither is it a constituent part itself;
- The term 'good' is therefore indefinable;

and that not to recognise this would render any pursuit of ethics as 'useless' as he confirms: 'Unless this first question be fully understood, and its true answer clearly recognised, the rest of Ethics is as good as useless from the point of view of systematic knowledge.'

The door cannot define yellow in the same way an action cannot reveal what 'good' means.

Key quotes

If I am asked, 'What is good?' my answer is that good is good, and that is the end of the matter. Or if I am asked 'How is good to be defined?' my answer is that it cannot be defined, and that is all I have to say about it. (Moore)

It does not matter what we call it provided we recognise it when we meet it. (Moore on the Naturalistic Fallacy)

Moore makes it perfectly clear that what he thinks you cannot legitimately do to 'good' is to analyse it. It is impossible to name its parts because it has no parts. (Warnock)

Key term

Naturalistic Fallacy: Moore's view that it is a logical error to explain that which is good reductively in terms of natural properties such as 'pleasant' or 'desirable'

Key quote

It is an enquiry to which most
special attention should be directed;
since this question, how good is to
be defined, is the most fundamental
question in all Ethics. That which
is meant by good is, in fact, except
its converse bad, the only simple
object of thought which is peculiar
to Ethics. Its definition is, therefore,
the most essential point in the
definition of Ethics; and moreover
a mistake with regard to it entails
a far larger number of erroneous
ethical judgements than any other.
Unless this first question be fully
understood, and its true answer
clearly recognised, the rest of Ethics
is as good as useless from the point
of view of systematic knowledge.
(Moore)

A closed question always invites a definitive answer.

G. E. Moore also then relates the implications of this to his second question 'what ought we to do?' Whilst Hume's Law made an observation about logical process and inducing an inappropriate conclusion from what 'is' the case, Moore focuses on the linguistic process of meaning and the nonsensical conclusions that had to be drawn if one identifies good with a natural quality.

He looks at Mill's Utilitarianism and explains the linguistic contradiction in trying to find an 'ought' from something that is unanalysable. He finds simply that in setting out to find out what one 'ought' to do from identifying the meaning of good with pleasure, one only arrives at the end of not what we ought to do, but of what we do already do. Moore's reasoning is as follows:

- If we think that we can define good by a natural quality such as 'what is desired' we are mistaken. Then to argue that we 'ought to pursue desire because it is good' is another fallacy.

  'That fallacy, I explained, consists in the contention that good means nothing but some simple or complex notion, that can be defined in terms of natural qualities. In Mill's case, good is thus supposed to mean simply what is desired; and what is desired is something which can thus be defined in natural terms.' (Moore)

- We are mistaken because it creates a **tautology**. That is, if 'desire' is good then we ought to seek desire. Unfortunately, this then means that we ought to seek what we do in fact seek.

  'Mill tells us that we ought to desire something (an ethical proposition), because we actually do desire it; but if his contention that "I ought to desire" means nothing but "I do desire" were true, then he is only entitled to say, "We do desire so and so, because we do desire it"; and that is not an ethical proposition at all; it is a mere tautology.' (Moore)

- Moore's contention is that since good is indefinable we cannot identify it as a natural quality because when we consider what this implies ethically in terms of duty, obligation and 'ought' (normative proposition) all we are doing is describing what we are already doing and not a normative proposition.

  'The whole object of Mill's book is to help us to discover what we ought to do; but in fact, by attempting to define the meaning of this "ought", he has completely debarred himself from ever fulfilling that object: he has confined himself to telling us what we do do.' (Moore)

Key term

Tautology: saying the same thing twice over in different words

quickfire

1.12 When Moore stated 'good is a simple notion' what did he mean?

Challenges: the open question argument

The open question argument, as it is called, is really a demonstration of the futility of defining good within the parameters of empiricism; quite simply, all attempts will fail because they still leave an unanswered question about 'good'. In other words, if we can define the ethical notion of good then we can state precisely what that good is in relation to psychological, biological or sociological truths. This would be a simple 'closed question' with a definitive answer. For example, 'Have you done your homework?' or 'Shall we have tea at 6pm?' or 'is the sum of 2 + 2 equal to 4?'. The answer to such questions can be a straight, 'yes' or 'no'. The problem is that this does not work with 'good'.

The main issue is that in attempting to define good by natural properties (e.g. pleasure) we are actually precipitating an open question, that is, a question with no definitive answer. This is because we still can legitimately ask 'is pleasure good?' once we have defined good as pleasure. It would not be a meaningless question to ask. But if we have succeeded in defining good then we should not need to ask this further question because it would be illogical.

- For example, if 'pleasure is the same as good' then we could say 'whatever promotes pleasure is good' but this would be really an unnecessary statement equivalent to 'whatever promotes pleasure promotes pleasure!'
- Also, if we ask whether or not the promotion of pleasure is good, then we will in effect be asking 'are good things good?' which is, of course, nonsense.
- ***Since it is never absurd to ask of natural properties 'is this good?'***, we know that we can logically ask the question 'is the promotion of pleasure good?' and, in fact, it is ***not nonsense*** because pleasure is a complex notion and not a simple notion.
- Therefore, if that is the case, then good cannot be identified as, or defined by, natural properties which are by their very nature complex notions.

Moore writes:

'The hypothesis that disagreement about the meaning of good is disagreement with regard to the correct analysis of a given whole, may be most plainly seen to be incorrect by consideration of the fact that, whatever definition may be offered, it may always be asked, with significance, of the complex so defined, whether it is itself good.'

AO1 Activity

Go through the three challenges again and try to summarise them yourself so that you can deliver a quick presentation to someone else that will last no longer than one minute.

Study tip

Try to think of your own challenges to Naturalism or make a list of what you consider to be its strengths and what you consider to be its weaknesses.

Key quotes

Moore claims that we can test any naturalistic definition of goodness by asking whether something that has those natural properties is good, and then seeing whether this question is open or closed. If the definition is true, then the question must be closed, so if it is open, the definition must be false. (Stratton-Lake)

Suppose, for instance, someone proposes that goodness can be defined in terms of causality and pleasure. To be good, they claim, is just to cause pleasure. Moore's view is that if this definition were correct, it would be a closed question whether something that causes pleasure is good. For in effect one would be asking whether something that causes pleasure causes pleasure, and that is clearly a closed question. But, Moore insists, the question 'is something that causes pleasure good?' is an open question. One could, without conceptual confusion, debate whether something that causes pleasure is good. So goodness cannot be defined as that which causes pleasure. (Stratton-Lake)

quickfire

1.13 What is a closed question?

It is a tautology to say, 'The wealthy person had a lot of money.'

Key skills Theme 1

This Theme has tasks that deal with the basics of AO1 in terms of prioritising and selecting the key relevant information, presenting this and then using evidence and examples to support and expand upon this.

Key skills

Knowledge involves:

Selection of a range of (thorough) accurate and relevant information that is directly related to the specific demands of the question.

This means:

- Selecting relevant material for the question set
- Being focused in explaining and examining the material selected.

Understanding involves:

Explanation that is extensive, demonstrating depth and/or breadth with excellent use of evidence and examples including (where appropriate) thorough and accurate supporting use of sacred texts, sources of wisdom and specialist language.

This means:

- Effective use of examples and supporting evidence to establish the quality of your understanding
- Ownership of your explanation that expresses personal knowledge and understanding and NOT just reproducing a chunk of text from a book that you have rehearsed and memorised.

AO1 Developing skills

It is now important to consider the information that has been covered in this section; however, the information in its raw form is too extensive and so has to be processed in order to meet the requirements of the examination. This can be achieved by practising more advanced skills associated with AO1. The exercises that run throughout this book will help you to do this and prepare you for the examination. For assessment objective 1 (AO1), which involves demonstrating 'knowledge' and 'understanding' skills, we are going to focus on different ways in which the skills can be demonstrated effectively, and also refer to how the performance of these skills is measured (see generic band descriptors for A2 [WJEC] AO1 or A Level [Eduqas] AO1).

▶ **Your task is this:** Below is a **summary of Naturalism**. It is 279 words long. You need to use this for an answer but could not repeat all of this in an essay under examination conditions so you will have to condense the material. Discuss which points you think are the most important and then re-draft into your own summary of about 140 words.

The most important point about ethical Naturalism is that it supports the view that objective moral laws exist independently of human beings and are grounded in the empirical nature of existence. Having established the link between an objective external existence (realism) and that a cognitivist approach can verify or establish the truth or not (objective knowledge) of what we experience (empiricism), then it logically follows that what we know about what we experience makes our ethical statements objective. Therefore, we can recognise objective moral laws that exist independently of human beings and that are located firmly in the world around us.

In other words, ethical language can be understood by referring to, and closely analysing, what we experience from the natural world around us. For example, we all understand that to experience the kindness of another is a 'good' experience and that to experience cruelty from another is a 'bad' experience. Taken further, this then means that our experiences have meaning because we can verify with others that kind acts are 'good' and cruel acts are 'bad' because of the happiness or suffering that these experiences contain. We can all recognise this and this means the same to everyone. If the ethical descriptions and statements have meaning for everyone then it also follows that they are objective truths and universal. We can discuss ethics meaningfully and establish certain propositions about good and bad ethical behaviour. If these experiences are uniform and universal then this also means that the statements 'kindness is an ethically good act' and 'cruelty is an ethically bad act' are true because these experiences are grounded in the objective features of the world around us.

When you have completed the task, refer to the band descriptors for A2 (WJEC) or A Level (Eduqas) and in particular have a look at the demands described in the higher band descriptors towards which you should be aspiring.

Work through each bullet point and check that you have met the demands.

Issues for analysis and evaluation

Whether ethical and non-ethical statements are the same

This section covers AO2 content and skills

Specification content
Whether ethical and non-ethical statements are the same.

This argument is really evaluating whether or not ethical statements are related to the empirical world just as non-ethical statements are and concerns the debate between ethical Naturalism and Intuitionism mainly.

Ethical Naturalism is empiricist in orientation and argues that ethical propositions are no more than statements of fact that can be justified by appeal to the natural world, therefore ethical statements are not 'beyond' non-ethical statements. Although there are different ways to interpret ethical statements, they all relate to what is actually real and objective. For instance, Mill sees ethical statements as, really, statements about pleasure or pain. For Bradley, it is all about realising the concrete universal and through self-realisation finding one's duty. These different ways at least agree that ethical and non-ethical statements are the same. Evolutionary ethics argues that it is all to do with how we assess and adapt biologically, psychologically and socially. If we know that fire is hot then we do not touch the flame; how is this any different from deciding how to live ethically when we know that violence causes pain and so avoid it?

We may feel, deeply, that a moral sentiment is 'real', absolute and provable like any claim about the 'objective world'; for example, it is directly related to actions that we can work out a sense of justice in society. Indeed, this viewpoint reflects not only Naturalism but also moral viewpoints based on religion and revelation. For example, the parable of the Good Samaritan in Christianity teaches through clear actions that it is good to help someone in need or who is suffering. There is nothing metaphysical about that.

It is ethical dilemmas and problems that cause debate and disagreement but surely this is all part of learning how to best adapt to life in a collaborative way? One of the most famous statements of naturalist ethics has been made by Richard Dawkins who argued that 'selfish genes' can explain the behaviour of humanity by using evidence of the evolution of certain behaviour traits in apes. Dawkins identifies different ways in which 'selfish genes' may bring about altruistic behaviour in individuals. Kin selection is no more than genes replicating themselves by creating individuals who are prone to nurture and defend; we see this in parental love and family affections. Dawkins explains collaboration and sharing but most importantly what he calls the Handicap Principle: Here, Dawkins demonstrates that some animals take on the most dangerous jobs of watching for predators and providing for the less fortunate. For Dawkins, this all explains the general capacity for normative judgement and guidance, and the tendency to exercise this capacity in social life. Animals also demonstrate sentiments and are able to detect them in others, can be motivated by others, make simple judgements and exhibit certain particular systems of norms or types of practice. This all shows that morality is actually embedded in the process of evolution and has a purely naturalistic explanation.

Key quotes

The problem is one of finding room for ethics, or placing ethics within the disenchanted, non-ethical order which we inhabit, and of which we are a part. (Blackburn)

There is nothing about simple properties which implies that they are non-natural. There is nothing incoherent about a simple natural or metaphysical property. Consequently, one cannot conclude that goodness is a non-natural property simply by showing that it is a simple property. One has to argue for non-naturalness in some other way. (Hutchinson)

AO2 Activity

As you read through this section try to do the following:

1. Pick out the different lines of argument that are presented in the text and identify any evidence given in support.

2. For each line of argument try to evaluate whether or not you think this is strong or weak.

3. Think of any questions you may wish to raise in response to the arguments.

This Activity will help you to start thinking critically about what you read and help you to evaluate the effectiveness of different arguments and from this develop your own observations, opinions and points of view that will help with any conclusions that you make in your answers to the AO2 questions that arise.

Key questions

Is empiricism (or Logical Positivism) all that there is to our knowledge of the world?

Does the fact that there are different naturalist theories weaken this meta-ethical view?

Does the fact that we 'feel' an ethical viewpoint is prove-able or objective mean that it really is?

Is it true that you cannot derive values from facts?

If good is indefinable, as Moore says, why then do so many still persist in offering definitions of this term?

AO2 Activity

List some conclusions that could be drawn from the AO2 reasoning from the above text; try to aim for at least three different possible conclusions. Consider each of the conclusions and collect brief evidence to support each conclusion from the AO1 and AO2 material for this topic. Select the conclusion that you think is most convincing and explain why it is so. Try to contrast this with the weakest conclusion in the list, justifying your argument with clear reasoning and evidence.

However, there are clear challenges to Naturalism. Moore argued that contrary to ethical Naturalism, ethical statements are *a priori* matters of truth just as with mathematics and can be identified through use of one's intuition. In this sense ethical propositions are very different from non-ethical propositions. Firstly, Hume's 'is-ought problem' can be used to show that Naturalism is wrong – you cannot derive a value from a fact. Therefore, ethical statements are not the same as non-ethical statements. Secondly, the ethical term 'good' is indefinable because it is a simple notion like the word yellow but it is also self-evident; non-ethical statements are not self-evident and so not the same as ethical statements. Thirdly, the term good always raises an open-ended question when we attempt to define its meaning with reference to a natural or non-ethical property. All these arguments present ethical propositions and language as very different from non-ethical statements.

It could be argued that ethical language is value laden in a different way from non-ethical language. For example, the statement 'this is a good door' is not an ethical statement and yet uses the word good. The judgement made may be down to its specific purpose, such as opening easily, looking good, retaining heat in a house or to its durability. However, when we make the statement, 'this is a good person', the goodness element is not entirely about 'purpose' if we did have one but is more about the person's moral qualities. It is something very different and so linguistically, ethical statements are very different from non-ethical statements.

So what possible conclusions could we arrive at?

We could maintain that ethical and non-ethical statements are the same, as maintained by ethical Naturalism. ethical Naturalism would reject Moore's linguistic analysis for a more pragmatic and empirical approach to ethics. Ethics is about action and not about *a priori* concepts. Evidence abounds to support this and also the fact that contemporary science (biology and psychology) are working towards a suitable, empirical explanation.

Alternatively, we could conclude that ethical and non-ethical statements are entirely different matters. This could be by arguing that ethical understanding of good is innate and accessed through our intuition. The support of ethics being about values, debates and judgements adds strength to this position. The evaluative nature of ethics, however, is not confined to ethics alone and does have some relevance in non-ethical statements.

There may be somewhere where the two converge. Bradley attempted to do this but he, himself admitted that he had failed to unite the conceptual with the empirical and had to find an alternative answer to Hume's Fork.

Study tip

It is vital for AO2 that you actually discuss arguments and not just explain what someone may have stated. Try to ask yourself, 'was this a fair point to make?', 'is the evidence sound enough?', 'is there anything to challenge this argument?', 'is this a strong or weak argument?' Such critical analysis will help you develop your evaluation skills.

The extent to which ethical statements are not objective

Specification content

The extent to which ethical statements are not objective.

Ethical Naturalism in some sense promotes the views that ethical propositions are objective because they can be evidenced through empirical means. So, for example, Mill (Utilitarianism) and Bradley (*My Station and its Duties*) felt that their respective ideals such as happiness and duty were perfectly objective.

However, this may not be the case at all. Even David Hume recognised the fact that ethical statements were value statements and meant something very different from empirical 'facts.' Hume was the first philosopher to suggest that they do not have meaning but are just expressions of emotions or approval and disapproval. If this is accepted as the case then empiricism cannot accept the claims to objectivity of an ethical Naturalism as proposed by Mill (Utilitarianism) and Bradley (*My Station and its Duties*). In fact, values suggest personal views, and personal views differ. This makes ethical statements more subjective. Mackie suggested this when he argued: 'In short, this argument from relativity has some force simply because the actual variations in the moral codes are more readily explained by the hypothesis that they reflect ways of life than by the hypothesis that they express perceptions, most of them seriously inadequate and badly distorted, of objective values.'

This line of argument asks that if morality were objective, why are there so many arguments about morality throughout the world? Indeed, the very fact that this course considers Divine Command Theory, Virtue Theory, Ethical Egoism, Naturalism, Intuitionism and Emotivism presents a fundamental challenge to the claim that ethical statements are objective given the great variety and difference in how ethical statements are explained. How does a person distinguish between something actually being right and it merely seeming right to that person? It still may be concluded by that person that their view is right, but someone like Moore or Prichard, who appeal to duty and intuition, can only respond in a moral argument by saying, 'I know I am right' when there is a disagreement over an ethical issue or a challenge to their ethical theories.

One strength of Naturalism is that it makes morality objective, and this has the strength of raising morality above personal opinion. Through Naturalism you can arrive at absolutes (such as murder is wrong) and this matches a common-sense view of ethics. We have seen this work in Natural Law theory, and the Roman Catholic Church, amongst others, accept this view. Indeed, Naturalism entails scientific testing of degrees of morality, for example, as we have seen through the application of Utilitarianism to the needs of society. This approach also reflects a modern worldview that we need to test statements (scientific, empirical approach) and not just accept blindly a claim to objective knowledge, especially when it has been pointed out that such knowledge is to do with 'feelings.'

Despite this, one could still argue for objectivity by arguing that it is possible to identify common elements of morality that span across the globe, through culture, language and geography. This is a demonstration, not only that a particular naturalistic ethical theory is founded in objectivity, but that morality in general is as well.

There are some important issues to consider here. What do we mean by 'objective'? Do we mean that ethical statements are consistent and are applied consistently? Do we mean they are *a priori* objective as with mathematical formulae? Is objectivity just an abstract concept that has no real appropriation for the real world? Do we mean they are beyond question or challenge? Or, do we mean that they mean the same for all and can be recognised and followed by all? Is objectivity perceived by all? To each question we may get a different answer as to whether or not ethical statements are objective.

Key quote

Disagreements about moral codes seems to reflect people's adherence to and participation in different ways of life. The causal connection seems to be mainly that way round: it is that people approve of monogamy because they participate in a monogamous way of life. (Mackie)

AO2 Activity

As you read through this section try to do the following:

1. Pick out the different lines of argument that are presented in the text and identify any evidence given in support.

2. For each line of argument try to evaluate whether or not you think this is strong or weak.

3. Think of any questions you may wish to raise in response to the arguments.

This Activity will help you to start thinking critically about what you read and help you to evaluate the effectiveness of different arguments and from this develop your own observations, opinions and points of view that will help with any conclusions that you make in your answers to the AO2 questions that arise.

There is also the question as to whether ethical statements can really be objective if there are so many theories, or that one theory develops from another; for example, Bradley's claim that through the dialectical methodology we can arrive at an ultimate answer.

In general, although not always, the concept of objectivity is associated with the meta-physical and deontological systems, that are *a priori*, conceptual, whereas ethical systems that are more empirically based do recognise some form of subjectivity.

Key quote

In short, this argument from relativity has some force simply because the actual variations in the moral codes are more readily explained by the hypothesis that they reflect ways of life than by the hypothesis that they express perceptions, most of them seriously inadequate and badly distorted, of objective values. (Mackie)

There are several possible conclusions. The most obvious is that ethical statements do reflect objective and absolute truths. Alternatively, ethical statements are merely a 'sign of the times', that is, products of human culture. Overall, however, it appears that many people accept that all we can ascertain is that some ethical statements and positions are objective whereas others are contingent and reflect the need for human interpretation and creativity.

Study tip

It is vital for AO2 that you actually discuss arguments and not just explain what someone may have stated. Try to ask yourself, 'was this a fair point to make?', 'is the evidence sound enough?', 'is there anything to challenge this argument?', 'is this a strong or weak argument?' Such critical analysis will help you develop your evaluation skills.

There are debates within the Roman Catholic Church that have raised questions about the objectivity of ethical statements.

Key questions

In terms of Moore's claim for objectivity based on Intuitionism, what prevents this from simply being Moore's own subjectivity?

Do statements of value really not have any factual meaning?

Does the reality of so many different ethical systems really mean that ethics is relative? Can't there be 'more' or 'less' true ethical approaches?

If something is common sense and/ or true across cultures (don't commit murder), does that really mean it is objective and absolute?

Can scientific testing really establish what should constitute moral behaviour?

AO2 Activity

List some conclusions that could be drawn from the AO2 reasoning from the above text; try to aim for at least three different possible conclusions. Consider each of the conclusions and collect brief evidence to support each conclusion from the AO1 and AO2 material for this topic. Select the conclusion that you think is most convincing and explain why it is so. Try to contrast this with the weakest conclusion in the list, justifying your argument with clear reasoning and evidence.

AO2 Developing skills

It is now important to consider the information that has been covered in this section; however, the information in its raw form is too extensive and so has to be processed in order to meet the requirements of the examination. This can be achieved by practising more advanced skills associated with AO2. The exercises that run throughout this book will help you to do this and prepare you for the examination. For assessment objective 2 (AO2), which involves 'critical analysis' and 'evaluation' skills, we are going to focus on different ways in which the skills can be demonstrated effectively, and also refer to how the performance of these skills is measured (see generic band descriptors for A2 [WJEC] AO2 or A Level [Eduqas] AO2).

▶ **Your task is this:** Below is a **summary of two different points of view concerning ethical Naturalism**. It is 150 words long. You want to use these two views and lines of argument for an evaluation; however, to just list them is not really evaluating them. Present these two views in a more evaluative style by firstly condensing each argument and then, secondly, commenting on how effective each one is (weak or strong are good terms to start with). Allow about 200 words in total.

1. Moral Naturalism, while attractive, has been dismissed by many in the light of G. E. Moore's Open Question Argument (Moore 1903, 5–21). Moore's thought is as follows. Suppose 'N' to abbreviate a term expressing the concept of some natural property N, maximally conducing to human welfare perhaps [2], and suppose a naturalist proposes to define goodness as N-ness. We swiftly show this to be false by supposing someone were to ask of something acknowledged to be N, whether it was good. This, Moore urges, is an open question. The point is, essentially, that it is not a stupid question in the sort of way, 'I acknowledge that Lenman is an unmarried man but is he, I wonder, a bachelor?' is a stupid question: if you need to ask it, you don't understand it. Given what the words concerned mean, the question of whether a given unmarried man is a bachelor is, in Moore's terminology, closed. So goodness and N-ness, unlike bachelorhood and unmarried-man-hood, are not one and the same.

2. For Bradley, it is because an agent's 'station' and 'duty' are to be found within the empirical realm that the nature of ethical statements expressed is both verifiable (cognitive) and relates to the facts of the world in which we live (realism). However, it is with the duty element that Bradley clearly sees as beyond the Kantian notion of *a priori* knowledge but grounded firmly in the experience of the real world. Our place and role in the historical community provide us with a measurable observable basis for a satisfying life. Our goal is to realise our true self, which we learn (through observation) in the family and community, and adapt the values of our society – and those of other societies that offer sound criticisms of our society.

When you have completed the task, refer to the band descriptors for A2 (WJEC) or A Level (Eduqas) and in particular have a look at the demands described in the higher band descriptors towards which you should be aspiring.

Work through each bullet point and check that you have met the demands.

Key skills Theme 1

This Theme has tasks that deal with the basics of AO2 in terms of developing an evaluative style, building arguments and raising critical questions.

Key skills

Analysis involves:

Identifying issues raised by the materials in the AO1, together with those identified in the AO2 section, and presents sustained and clear views, either of scholars or from a personal perspective ready for evaluation.

This means:

- That your answers are able to identify key areas of debate in relation to a particular issue
- That you can identify, and comment upon, the different lines of argument presented by others
- That your response comments on the overall effectiveness of each of these areas or arguments.

Evaluation involves:

Considering the various implications of the issues raised based upon the evidence gleaned from analysis and provides an extensive detailed argument with a clear conclusion.

This means:

- That your answer weighs up the consequences of accepting or rejecting the various and different lines of argument analysed
- That your answer arrives at a conclusion through a clear process of reasoning.

Specification content

Objective moral laws exist
independently of human beings;
moral truths can be discovered by
using our minds in an intuitive way.

Key quote

G. E. Moore's *Principia Ethica*
was first published in 1903. It
has become the custom to regard
it as the source from which the
subsequent moral philosophy of the
century has flowed. (Warnock)

Key terms

A priori: prior to the senses

Ethical non-Naturalism: an
alternative term for Intuitionism

Non-metaphysical moral realism:
an alternative term for Intuitionism

E: Meta-ethical approaches: Intuitionism

Intuitionism: objective moral laws exist independently of human beings and moral truths can be discovered by using our minds in an intuitive way

The best way to approach Intuitionism is to begin with re-visiting a concept from Year 1. In philosophy, the term *a priori* was used. This term is usually quite heavily associated with areas of philosophy such as logic and rationalism. Remember that *a priori* refers to knowledge that we may have prior to experience; that is, an innate, conceptual awareness of principles, for example, those associated with mathematics like shapes and numbers. G. E. Moore had proposed that 'good' was a simple concept and indefinable other than in relation to itself. Then, just as with mathematics, the principles of ethics are *a priori* and exist independently of human beings. In addition, these are self-evident truths and therefore truths that do not need to be 'established' and known through some kind of rationalism.

It is important to note that Moore did not explain how a recognition of good was to be implemented, processed or caused; it just 'is.' Just as 'good' is undefinable, or at best defined as 'good', in the same way we just recognise 'goodness' through 'intuition' and it does not need any working out. He wrote:

'Again, I would wish it observed that, when I call such propositions Intuitions, I mean merely to assert that they are incapable of proof; I imply nothing whatever as to the manner or origin of our cognition of them. Still less do I imply (as most Intuitionists have done) that any proposition whatever is true, because we cognise it in a particular way or by the exercise of any particular faculty: I hold, on the contrary, that in every way in which it is possible to cognise a true proposition, it is also possible to cognise a false one.'

In other words, once we begin to apply reason or suggest something is worked out through reason, error becomes possible.

In the preface to his book *Principia Ethica* Moore also suggests that there are two key questions for moral philosophy: (1) what kind of things ought to exist for their own sake? and (2) what kind of actions ought we to perform? His answer to the first question was that such things that ought to exist for their own sake were intrinsically good. We can see these things even though they are indefinable, and we cannot present any evidence to support this other than simply recognising this. The answer to the second question was that we ought to perform actions that bring about this intrinsic goodness and this can be supported by empirical evidence.

The term 'Intuitionism' is also referred to as 'ethical non-Naturalism' because it removes itself from the idea that objective moral laws can be induced from the empirical world. However, this does not mean it is a 'metaphysical' approach to ethics as it also clearly asserts that moral principles are 'there' in the same way concepts such as numbers 'exist.' Intuitionism has also been referred to as a 'non-metaphysical moral realism.'

Moore sees no connection between meta-ethics and metaphysics since meta-ethics is concerned with the very first question about ethics, namely, the nature of goodness. As we have seen from the Naturalistic Fallacy, no exploration, examination nor enquiry into the innate properties of the empirical and physical world could provide insight into what 'goodness' **is**.

G. E. Moore

Key quotes

Principia Ethica actually downplayed the metaphysical side of its non-Naturalism, saying that goodness has 'being' but does not 'exist', as numbers too do not exist, and in particular does not exist in any 'supersensible reality', because there is no such reality. (Hurka)

Intuitively the intuitionists seem right. Empirical investigation can tell us many things about the world, but it does not seem that it can tell whether certain acts are right or wrong, good or bad … That seems to be something that cannot be known empirically. (Stratton-Lake)

Our first conclusion as to the subject-matter of Ethics is, then, that there is a simple, indefinable, unanalysable object of thought by reference to which it must be defined. By what name we call this unique object is a matter of indifference, so long as we clearly recognise what it is and that it does differ from other objects. (Moore)

Mary Warnock states: 'Moore concedes that it is possible that metaphysics might have some relevance to the question of what we ought to do, though it could have none to the question of what is good. For what we ought to do is determined by some practical and causal questions about the consequences of our acts.'

Intuitive ability is innate and the same for all moral agents

The word 'good' is not meaningless even though it cannot be defined; it is simply that to say something is 'good' is saying something that cannot be paraphrased by another word. The term that is often used for this by intuitionists is that good is sui generis, meaning that it is without comparison and unique (from the Latin 'of its own kind'). This understanding and ability to recognise 'good' is innate and the same for all moral agents. Moreover, the 'goodness' that we perceive is not some relative truth based upon empirical perception; it is objective and the same self-evident truth for all.

Moore writes:

'Everyone does in fact understand the question 'Is this good?' When he thinks of it, his state of mind is different from what it would be, were he asked, 'Is this pleasant, or desired, or approved?' It has a distinct meaning for him, even though he may not recognise in what respect it is distinct. Whenever he thinks of "intrinsic value," or "intrinsic worth," or says that a thing "ought to exist," he has before his mind the unique object – the unique property of things – that I mean by "good". Everybody is constantly aware of this notion, although he may never become aware at all that it is different from other notions of which he is also aware. But, for correct ethical reasoning, it is extremely important that he should become aware of this fact; and as soon as the nature of the problem is closely understood, there should be little difficulty in advancing so far in analysis.'

Key Person

George Edward Moore was born on November 4, 1873, and grew up in South London. He was schooled at Dulwich College, where he studied the classics in Greek and Latin. Moore studied at Cambridge University at the age of 18 and became interested in the study of philosophy, becoming good friends with fellow student Bertrand Russell, and in later life Ludwig Wittgenstein, who was a student under Russell. Moore graduated with a first-class philosophy degree and won a fellowship to continue his studies. He returned to Cambridge in 1911 after a seven-year break from studies and taught and lived there for the rest of his life. As well as professor of philosophy, Moore was editor of Mind and was well respected by friends and colleagues, renowned for being a man of impeccable moral character. Moore died in Cambridge in 1958.

quicKfire

1.14 If moral terms are not identified with natural qualities then why are they not metaphysical?

Specification content
Intuitive ability is innate and the same for all moral agents.

Key terms
Innate: part of, integral to
Sui generis: unique

Something that is self-evident does not require proof.

Key term

Self-evident: a proposition that needs no verification and remains a truth independently of whether or not we perceive it as so

quickfire

1.15 Can something exist that is self-evident even if we are not aware of it?

Specification content

Intuition allows for objective moral values.

Key quotes

The first thing to note is that a self-evident proposition is not the same as an obvious truth … What is obvious to you may not be obvious to me. But self-evidence is not relative in this way. Although a proposition may be evident to one person but not to another, it could not be self-evident to one person, but not to another. A proposition is just self-evident, not self-evident to someone. (Stratton-Lake)

The individual should rather guide his choice by direct consideration of the intrinsic value or vileness of the effects which his action may produce. (Moore)

Moore was careful to differentiate between intuition and things that are **self-evident**. Intuition is the process by which we arrive at the 'knowledge' and recognition of the things that are self-evident. Intuition is a conscious mental state that recognises what is self-evident. The self-evident concept of good, however, is not a mental state at all.

In other words, conscious intuition reveals objective truths, self-evident truths and not things that may be common sense, an obvious fact or truth relating to a particular empirical context. What is obvious, or evident, to one person may well not be to another; however, an objective proposition is self-evident, which means it is evident in itself and does not depend upon normal, natural perception. For example, the number 4 is a self-evident truth; it may well be the case that it is not evident to some and yet evident to others. However, it still remains a truth independently of whether or not we perceive it as so. A proposition may be evident *to* someone but a self-evident proposition is just there in itself in the first instance and known through intuition. Intuition does not provide justification for a self-evident proposition; intuition just accesses that self-evident proposition.

Richard Norman points out that Moore is keen to define the type of 'intuitionist' philosopher that he is because his Intuitionism is different in two respects: (1) intuition it is not about belief in what actions are right, but about things that are good in themselves, and (2) he does not want to imply that there is some special way in which we can know them to be true, as Norman writes, 'He means only, he says, that we can know them to be true, and that we cannot give any further reasons why they are true … It is simply a belief which one knows to be true, but for which one has no reasons.'

Intuition allows for objective moral values

The last two chapters of Moore's *Principia Ethica* are concerned with two questions:

- What should we do?
- What things are good?

Firstly, Moore's answer to the first question is very simple: any moral obligation has inherent within it the obligation to do good and produce the greatest amount. Moore states:

'Our "duty," therefore, can only be defined as that action, which will cause more good to exist in the Universe than any possible alternative. And what is "right" or "morally permissible" only differs from this, as what will not cause less good than any possible alternative. When, therefore, Ethics presumes to assert that certain ways of acting are "duties" it presumes to assert that to act in those ways will always produce the greatest possible sum of good.'

This is our duty, to perform actions that cause more good to exist than any possible alternative. We do this by calculating and weighing up of the consequences of actions.

This sounds surprisingly familiar if we consider that it is a similar proposition to what utilitarian philosophers may proclaim. Indeed, Warnock observes, 'on the question of conduct Moore is in far closer agreement with the utilitarians than with any other moral philosophers … They differ only about the question of how to assess the value of the consequences.' Moore's Intuitionism has therefore come to be seen by philosophers as a form of consequentialist Intuitionism.

Indeed, Moore had already argued as to why there are disagreements in ethical debate and in particular with his own view when he states:

'Though, therefore, we cannot prove that we are right, yet we have a reason to believe that everybody, unless he is mistaken as to what he thinks, will think the same as we do. It is as with a sum in mathematics. If we find a gross and palpable error in the calculations, we are not surprised or troubled that the person who made this mistake has reached a different result from ours. We think he will admit that his result is wrong, if his mistake is pointed out to him. For instance, if a man has to add up 5 + 7 + 9, we should not wonder that he made the result to be 34, if he started by making 5 + 7 = 25. And so in Ethics, if we find, as we did, that "desirable" is confused with "desired," or that "end" is confused with "means," we need not be disconcerted that those who have committed these mistakes do not agree with us. The only difference is that in Ethics, owing to the intricacy of its subject matter, it is far more difficult to persuade anyone either that he has made a mistake or that that mistake affects his result.'

In other words, the reason people do not see what Moore is arguing about intuition and ethical debate is because their different answer is down to their mistake in methodology or working out the problem. Somewhere along the line we can identify the mistakes of others. However, Moore argues that if they have made that mistake initially, it is very difficult in ethical debate to point out that the rest of the argument, which may seem sound, is actually built upon an error.

At the end of *Principia Ethica* Moore identifies some intrinsic moral goodness (chapter 6 *The Ideal*). His method for identification of such goods is to propose such things that if they were to exist independently and abstractly they would still be considered good. Moore writes: 'Indeed, once the meaning of the question is clearly understood, the answer to it, in its main outlines, appears to be so obvious, that it runs the risk of seeming to be a **platitude**. By far the most valuable things, which we know or can imagine, are certain states of consciousness, which may be roughly described as the pleasures of human intercourse and the enjoyment of beautiful objects.'

For Moore, the purity of human friendship and aesthetic beauty were intrinsic goods on the basis that we can perceive them as existing in isolation from everything else and still class them as good. Moore did not deny that there were other goods, but just that sometimes they are mixed due to the complexity of the natural world. He writes: 'It is necessary to consider what things are such that, if they existed by themselves, in absolute isolation, we should yet judge their existence to be good; and, in order to decide upon the relative degrees of value of different things, we must similarly consider what comparative value seems to attach to the isolated existence of each.' In general, Moore's goods are similar to Aristotle's virtues and his recognition of their mixed nature is in line with his initial analysis of simple and complex in relation to establishing 'what is good?'

Moore's evils are divided into three groups:

1. The first class consists of those evils, which seem always to include an enjoyment or admiring contemplation of things which are themselves either evil or ugly ...

2. The second class of great evils are undoubtedly mixed evils; but I treat them next, because, in a certain respect, they appear to be the converse of the class last considered ...

3. The third class of great positive evils appears to be the class of pains.

Moore argued that disagreements in ethical debate were mainly down to an underpinning methodology that a person accepted as true.

Key term

Platitude: a moral comment that has been used too often to be meaningful, cliché

Key quotes

All moral laws, I wish to shew, are merely statements that certain kinds of actions will have good effects. (Moore)

The utmost, then, that Practical Ethics can hope to discover is which, among a few alternatives possible under certain circumstances, will, on the whole, produce the best result. It may tell us which is the best, in this sense, of certain alternatives about which we are likely to deliberate ... it may thus tell us which of the alternatives, among which we can choose, it is best to choose. If it could do this it would be sufficient for practical guidance. (Moore)

Key quote

In *Principia Ethica* he defended his claim that beauty on its own is good by appealing to intuitions about a very specific beautiful world … Moore likewise insisted that before we make judgements of self-evidence we must make sure that the propositions we are considering are clear; failure to do so, he claimed, explained much of the disagreement about ethics. (Hurka)

AO1 Activity

Try to list some examples of virtues that can be seen to be good that arise from personal relationships and think of ways in which these virtues can become mixed or distorted. For example, agapeic love (see Situation Ethics topic from AS / Year 1 book) can be spoiled by poor intention. Honesty is good but can be affected by the situation that calls for discretion.

Study tip

Moore's theory of intuition needs to be carefully explained so that you know exactly what Moore is referring to. It may help by thinking of things that it is not, rather than what it is, to help you.

quickfire

1.16 What two things did Moore suggest were self-evidently good?

Specification content

Intuition needs a mature mind so not infallible.

Key quotes

What then is it for a proposition to be self-evident? Locke says that a self-evident proposition is one that 'carries its own light and evidence with it, and needs no other proof…' Price tells us that a self-evident proposition is immediate, and needs no further proof…. Ross writes, a self-evident proposition is 'evident without any need of proof, or of evidence beyond itself'. (Stratton-Lake)

If nothing is self-evident, nothing can be proved. (C.S. Lewis)

Key term

Infallibility: without error

Intuition needs a mature mind so not infallible

Intuition in itself as a foundation of knowledge is the belief that at some point there must be a framework, basis, anchor or starting point from which all other judgements can be made. Aristotle recognised this in his book *Metaphysics* when he stated: 'Some, indeed, demand to have the law proved, but this is because they lack education; for it shows lack of education not to know of what we should require proof, and of what we should not. For it is quite impossible that everything should have a proof; the process would go on to infinity, so there would be no proof.' What Aristotle is arguing is that knowledge always rests upon something, for example, evidence or something that is relative to it to help explain it (e.g. hot and cold). If we continue looking retrospectively upon knowledge then there must be a 'first cause' (see the Cosmological argument topics from AS/Year 1) otherwise knowledge would be infinite. The basis for knowledge had to begin with something. The key question is whether this begins with our education (nurtured) or whether or not it is simply *a priori* and innate within us. In other words, Moore suggests that this process of intuition by which we have access to self-evident knowledge is *a priori*.

For Intuitionists, then, knowledge of good is innate and *a priori* knowledge. However, although not subject to rational proof in the same way empirical knowledge is, the implications of what is recognised as intuitively good does reveal a sense of **infallibility** to the idea of 'self-evident' truths when it comes to consideration of acting upon this knowledge. Moore, as we have seen, conceded that what could be intuitively recognised as good was not to do with actions and consequences but a recognition of the thing that was good in itself. Therefore, any fallibility of intuition is directly related not to the *a priori*, self-evident awareness and recognition of good, but rather in how we practically put this knowledge into action.

Key quote

A self-evident proposition is one of which a clear intuition is sufficient justification for believing it, and for believing it on the basis of that intuition … but this is not because understanding provides justification; rather, it is because it is needed to get the proposition clearly in view, and so enables a clear intuition of it. But it is the intuition that justifies, not the understanding. (Stratton-Lake)

For Moore, the 'what ought I do?' was his secondary question to which his answer was to pursue those actions that produce more good. The identification of such actions was directly related to his self-evident awareness of intrinsic goodness found in aesthetic beauty and personal friendship relationships. He also recognised that there were mixed goods of less purity, in the same way the empirical world is made up of mixed, complex phenomena. However, the goal to pursue acts that produce the greatest amounts of good are not shared by all Intuitionists. We will see that H. A. Prichard argued that it was not the 'good' (i.e. Moore's first question that revealed the sui generis of moral knowledge) but rather the obligation to act, that is, the duty innate in the idea of 'what we ought to do', that was the basis, the sui generis, for all moral thinking. We will explore this more later. Likewise, W.D. Ross, like Prichard, rejected Moore's proposal that to pursue the acts that produced the greatest amount of good was the best application of the self-evident, intuitive ethical knowledge. Indeed, in his book *The Right and the Good*, Ross argued that some actions are not dependent upon their consequences in order to be considered right or wrong. He claimed that intuition could be used to establish what he called 'prima facie duties' such as fidelity, justice and keeping a promise. They are prima facie because they could be prioritised over another when a conflict of interest arises.

However, according to Ross, there is need for a gradual awakening towards a revelation of this innate intuitive awareness and suggests that self-evident insights are: 'not in the sense that it is evident from the beginning of our lives, or as soon as we attend to the proposition for the first time, but in the sense that when we have reached sufficient mental maturity and have given sufficient attention to the proposition it is evident without any need of proof, or of evidence beyond itself.' In a similar fashion, another philosopher who advocated ethical Intuitionism, H. A. Prichard, also felt strongly that the revelation of such ethical intuitions was not evenly distributed amongst people and that some had a more developed, or more mature 'sense' of intuition that others.

Key quotes

How do we acquire moral and axiological knowledge? Ross maintains that 'both in mathematics and in ethics we have certain crystal-clear intuitions from which we build up all that we can know about the nature of numbers and the nature of duty'. (Skelton)

But despite what has been said above, critics of Intuitionism can claim that the fact that there is disagreement between moral philosophers and even intuitionists themselves undermines the view that certain propositions are self-evident … Persistent disagreement amongst reflective, thoughtful, and comprehending moral philosophers may cast doubt on the view that any of these propositions are self-evident. (Stratton-Lake)

Moore held that intuition of good was infallible, but how we translate this and act upon intuition may well be in error.

Key term

Prima facie duties: first impression; accepted as correct until proved otherwise

quickfire

1.17 Why does an application of intuitive thought need a mature mind?

Specification content

H. A. Prichard, 'ought to do' has no definition; recognise what we 'ought to do' by intuition.

Key Person

H. A. Prichard was a very distinguished moral philosopher who taught at Oxford during the first half of last century. Born in London in 1871, Harold Prichard attended Clifton College in Bristol and was admitted to New College, Oxford to study mathematics. After receiving a First Class Honours in mathematics in 1891, he then studied Greats (ancient history and philosophy) receiving First Class Honours in 1894. He returned to Oxford in 1895 where he spent the rest of his life, first as Fellow of Hertford College (1895–98) and then of Trinity College (1898–1924).

Key quote

Knowledge is not knowledge of the ground of the obligation, but is itself the ground of the obligation. (Warnock)

Key terms

Irreducible: cannot be broken down into further parts

sui generis: unique, from the Latin 'of its own kind'

Underivative: is not dependent on or derived from something else, a simple concept

Ought is indefinable but can be recognised by intuition

Like Moore, Prichard argued that moral knowledge was indefinable, but it was not the 'good' that was the basis of intuitive moral insight. Moore's distinction was that 'goodness' (i.e. that which is good in itself) is the basis of our intuitive recognition and that 'rightness' or 'oughtness' was the outworking of this. As we have seen, this created some possible incoherence when considering how Moore suggested this was pursued and the consequentialism that followed did not sit comfortably with other Intuitionists.

For Prichard (and Ross) it was the 'rightness' or sense of obligation or duty that was the intuitive element of our moral thinking. Their approach became more deontological. That is, when there are actual moral conflicts we learn to decide upon the greater obligation, and over time, develop a more advanced, intuitive sense of right and wrong. Despite empirical evidence, it was still the sense of duty and moral Intuitionism that was the driver in deciding what to do and NOT a goal of creating the most possible good. Prichard and, later, Ross, were philosophers who had a slightly different approach to Moore in that they were concerned about the sense of 'oughtness' and 'duty' as a key element of intuition and defining the way we think morally rather than it being a consequence of our moral insight as Moore had attested.

For Prichard moral knowledge was unique, **sui generis** and also was clearly separated from reason and empirical influence. Prichard rejected Moore's intuitive consequentialism that argued that 'what we ought to do' is to act so that we produce the greatest amount of good through our actions. Prichard argued that since our moral intuition can be found in our sense of obligation or duty when we recognise what we 'ought' or 'should' do, then any reasoning about 'what should we do?' or 'how should we act?' has already been answered. Moral truth is contained within the sense of obligation that we intuitively feel when confronted with a situation. This truth, however, is not subject to reason and since this is the case, the way to behave morally is equally not the result of rational analysis and debate. We just 'know' what we ought to do.

Duty remains **underivative**, indefinable and an **irreducible** concept just like Moore's 'good' and yellow in three ways:

1. In the normative realm it maintains the non-naturalist view that normative truths of duty are sui generis, neither reducible to nor derivable from empirical investigation. They are self-evident.
2. Neither are the truths of duty extracted from moral judgements, normative truths or values that have a non-moral origin.
3. The duties are specific (e.g. to keep promises and not to harm others) and do not derive from a more general consequentialist duty to promote good consequences. As Thomas Hurka writes, 'The main reason we ought to keep our promises or not harm others is just that we ought to; those duties, like the normative realm as a whole and moral duty in general, are self-standing.'

Although the specific duties may conflict, the fact is that they are not reducible to one basic duty like consequentialism and are indeed independent of consequentialist thinking. As Thomas Hurka explains, 'The various duties can conflict, but when they do there are no rules for deciding between them: we can only make a direct intuitive judgement about which duty is stronger.'

How this process is activated is the subject of the next section on general and moral reasoning.

Key quotes

The improper question is supposed to be the demand for reasons why something which has the characteristic of being obligatory, has this characteristic. All demands, Prichard says, for proof that something is a duty are mistaken. (Warnock)

In 1909 Prichard published his only book, Kant's *Theory of Knowledge*, which was an account of Kant's transcendental idealism … The book's main conclusion is that 'knowledge is sui generis and therefore a "theory" of knowledge is impossible. Knowledge is knowledge, and any attempt to state it in terms of something else must end in describing something which is not knowledge.' (Dancy)

Two ways of thinking (general and moral)

The last section ended with considering the fact that duties can conflict when an ethical decision needs to be made. In one sense, this is illogical if there is only one right way to act. It may be that we respond that 'the real world is not as simple as that and moral issues are complex' but this response is very much based in what Prichard calls the world of general reasoning.

General reasoning is basically using the empirical evidence around us to present logical argument. For any moral decision, the appreciation of certain facts concerning the circumstances involved is referred to as 'preliminaries'. However, such preliminaries, no matter how strong, do not hold any obligation. In addition, Prichard speaks not of conflicting duties but of the fact that general reasoning may throw up different 'claims' and the ultimate 'claim' may well be the ultimate moral duty but it does **not necessarily have to be**. Prichard was careful to point out that an appeal to general reasoning must not let it become the driver for recognising one's proper moral duty; only intuition can do this.

Moral reasoning is the recognition and assertion of one's duty by intuitive thought. It is present in our unreflective consciousness according to Prichard.

quickfire

1.18 How did Prichard disagree with Moore about what we 'ought' to do?

Specification content

H. A. Prichard: two ways of thinking (general and moral).

Key terms

Claims: Prichard's term for an argument put together from general reasoning

General reasoning: using the empirical evidence around us to present logical argument

Moral reasoning: application of intuition

Preliminaries: gathering of claims

Unreflective consciousness: Prichard's explanation that intuition is not determined by philosophical reflection

quickfire

1.19 How is general reasoning different from moral reasoning, according to Prichard?

Although it is usual to consider evidence and circumstances of a moral decision, these preliminaries do not provide us with any moral obligation according to Prichard.

Key quotes

Prichard makes clear, being in a position to grasp the self-evidence of an obligation may require appreciating certain facts about one's circumstances that are 'preliminaries' in the process of thinking about ethical issues … part of a process that Prichard calls 'general' in contrast to moral thinking. (Timmons)

If we ask ourselves what this something else is, we seem driven to say that … what is called a conflict of duties is really a conflict of claims on us to act in different ways, arising out of various circumstances of the whole situation in which we are placed. (Timmons)

Prichard is not suggesting that nothing can get us to feel an obligation – for example, seeing something or hearing something or learning about something. What he is denying is that any description of such facts, no matter how complete, entails or otherwise implies any particular obligation. (Kaufman)

The sense that we ought to do certain things arises in our unreflective consciousness, being an activity of moral thinking occasioned by the various situations in which we find ourselves. (Prichard)

Key term

Eudaimonia: Aristotle's term for happiness of well-being

Moral reasoning subsumes general reasoning. The danger in this relationship between the two types of reasoning is that general reasoning will not take a subordinate role. Indeed, to focus on the complexity of a moral issue is in itself an appeal to the consequentialist position. However, to be guided by this alone would be tantamount to surrendering moral intuition.

Prichard was fearful of the consequential nature of general thinking and pointed out that it is here where the potential for distortion of duty can be found. For example, although he agreed that a moral duty must always mention its explanatory ground; however, in trying to derive the obligation to keep promises from a duty to promote the good, consequentialism could turn the obligation to keep promises into a quite different obligation that promote other values, i.e. discretion, honesty and trust. We have the same problem here as with the open question argument because we can then ask, 'but is honesty good?' In effect consequentialism turns the duty to keep promises into something it is not, and thereby distorts the moral phenomena. As Thomas Hurka writes, 'in trying to explain the duty to keep promises, consequentialism destroys it.'

Key quote

This idea of distorting the moral phenomena was central to Prichard's argument that moral duty in general is underivative. (Hurka)

Moral thinking must not work like that because it is intuitive and self-evident. Prichard does acknowledge that whilst issues can appear complex, we must not let general reasoning distort moral phenomena and turn it into consequentialism. Prichard refers to another example from Aristotle to demonstrate how identification of an intuitive ultimate good such as eudaimonia (well-being) can be distorted in a different way when duties are derived from it. For instance, concerning the duty to relieve pain if it is for someone else, is it that doing so will make our own lives better? Or, is it that doing so will make the other person's life better? If the answer is that it will make our own lives better, by contributing, given the right motives, to our own eudaimonia, we can object that this is not the right explanation. This is because the obvious and right explanation is that relieving another's pain will make his or her life better, so the duty is fundamentally other-regarding and not directed towards our own well-being.

Key quotes

Even when consequentialism yields the right verdict about which act is right, he held, it oversimplifies the explanation of the act's rightness … and in ignoring it consequentialism distorts the moral phenomena. (Hurka)

Even when consequentialism yields the right conclusion about how we ought to act, it gives the wrong reason for it … According to Prichard, we ought to pay our debt because we incurred it, and not because (or only because) of any good that will result. (Hurka)

Ross also argued that 'even when consequentialism is right about which acts are right, it is wrong about why they are right. If we think we ought to keep a promise, he insisted, the reason is not that this will have good consequences; it is simply that we promised.' (Hurka)

So we have now established that general reasoning can be dangerous if it is given too much emphasis. However, the question still remains, 'how can we ensure that moral duty succeeds?'

Prichard's Intuitionism is very clever in the way it proposes its methodology for this and it is linked closely to epistemology. Indeed, Prichard uses **Descartes' principle of skepticism** to demonstrate that moral reasoning is that which is 'confirmed by doubt.' In other words, general reasoning is used to support and confirm what we originally recognised through intuition. We sometimes need to check the addition of our maths, even though we know our method is correct; we sometimes confirm our initial observations with a 'second glance'. Prichard writes:

'Just as the recognition that the doing of our duty often vitally interferes with the satisfaction of our inclinations leads us to wonder whether we really ought to do what we usually call our duty, so the recognition that we and others are liable to mistakes in knowledge generally leads us, as it did Descartes, to wonder whether hitherto we may not have been always mistaken. And just as we try to find a proof, based on the general consideration of action and of human life, that we ought to act in the ways usually called moral, so we, like Descartes, propose by a process of reflection on our thinking to find a test of knowledge, i.e. a principle by applying which we can show that a certain condition of mind was really knowledge, a condition which **ex hypothesi** (according to the hypothesis proposed, i.e. intuition) existed independently of the process of reflection.

In other words, the way general thinking is used is for reflective purposes in relation to the intuition and not for evaluative purposes to build an argument or case as for what is right. In a given situation we should be intuitively aware of what the right course of action should be. We are presented with plenty of alternatives and arguments but they are there not to convince us; they are there to deflect the doubt that what we originally thought of was the correct course of action. Hurka observes that, 'The stage of being moved by such skepticism is not pointless; it is an essential part of philosophical reflection. But its end-result should be a return to our original convictions, and so it is with moral duty.' Therefore, the purpose of general reasoning is to shore up our initial intuition and not to distort it.

Key quotes

Modern epistemology, which begins with Descartes, is a response to the fact that we can doubt many of the things that we think we know to be true, and the theorising that follows is an effort to find a procedure by which we can demonstrate that we really do know what we think we know ... Prichard thinks that similarly, modern moral philosophy's primary aim is to find a way by which to demonstrate that what we think is our duty, really is obligatory. (Kaufman)

We might, he thinks, come to doubt the truth of such insights, but the mistake of moral philosophy is to assume that such doubts can be assuaged by argument. The only appropriate response, in the moral as in the mathematical case, is that the doubts themselves are illegitimate. Reflection can serve a useful purpose only insofar as it returns us to a place in which we can recognise the self-evidence of the claims we began by doubting. (Le Bar)

Descartes was the famous philosopher who coined the term 'I think, therefore I am' (French: je pense, donc je suis / Latin: cogito ergo sum) and introduced the principle of doubt to confirm a truth.

Key terms

Descartes' principle of skepticism: that doubt can be resolved through challenge

Ex hypothesi: according to the hypothesis proposed

That is, general reasoning is not used independently to arrive at some sort of conclusion by presenting and manipulating evidence and argument. Absolutely not. These are the 'illegitimate' claims Prichard speaks of. Instead, general reasoning is used to shore up the knowledge already gained through intuition as to what our obligation is. It is useful to see what Prichard actually writes:

The sense that we ought to do certain things arises in our unreflective consciousness, being an activity of moral thinking occasioned by the various situations in which we find ourselves. At this stage our attitude to these obligations is one of unquestioning confidence. But inevitably the appreciation of the degree to which the execution of these obligations is contrary to our interest raises the doubt whether after all these obligations are really obligatory, i.e., whether our sense that we ought not to do certain things is not illusion. We then want to have it proved to us that we ought to do so, i.e., to be convinced of this by a process which, as an argument, is different in kind from our original and unreflective appreciation of it. **This demand is, as I have argued, illegitimate**.

Hence in the first place, if, as is almost universally the case, by **Moral Philosophy is meant the knowledge which would satisfy this demand, there is no such knowledge, and all attempts to attain it are doomed to failure because they rest on a mistake, the mistake of supposing the possibility of proving what can only be apprehended directly by an act of moral thinking**.

Extract from H.A. Prichard Does Moral Philosophy Rest on a Mistake? (1912)

quickfire

1.20 Why was Descartes an important philosopher for Prichard?

quickfire

1.21 How can moral reasoning be distorted according to Prichard?

Key quote

Just as we try to find a proof, based on the general consideration of action and of human life, that we ought to act in the ways usually called moral, so we, like Descartes, propose by a process of reflection on our thinking to find a test of knowledge, i.e. a principle by applying which we can show that a certain condition of mind was really knowledge, a condition which ex hypothesi existed independently of the process of reflection. (Kaufman)

AO1 Activity

What key words would you use if you were going to write your own essay on the topic of H. A. Prichard? Choose four to six terms and write a few sentences justifying why each of these terms is critical for this discussion.

Study tip

It is popular to think that Prichard uses evidence to support and determine a moral decision in line with intuition. Make sure that you understand that evidence is there to deter doubt with regard intuition and to shore up that intuitive thought.

No proof of moral intuition exists: the argument from queerness

Possibly the most famous of challenges to the proposal of Intuitionism was that of J. L. Mackie in his book, *Ethics: Inventing Right and Wrong*, published in 1977 (pages 38–42). Mackie's position is that there are no objective ethical values, that is, values that can be known, verified and part of the empirical world and yet at the same time independent of us.

Mackie argues that what Intuitionism does is present us with implausible oddities and strange suggestions that ultimately make the whole theory queer; hence, he refers to it as '**the argument from queerness**.' Mackie writes:

> 'Even more important, however, and certainly more generally applicable, is the argument from queerness. This has two parts, one metaphysical and the other epistemological. If there were objective values, then they would be entities or qualities or relations of a very strange sort, utterly different from anything else in the universe. Correspondingly, if we were aware of them, it would have to be by some special faculty of moral perception or intuition, utterly different from our normal ways of knowing everything else.'

Firstly, it is this very 'queerness' of moral properties that makes it implausible that they exist. Mackie's is a very heavily empirically based objection and no different from Kant's challenge against the cosmological argument for the existence of God that if a God did exist, this 'first cause' would be so very different from anything that we experience or know and so would not be able to recognise or know about it. This is because our knowledge is limited to the phenomenal world of space and time and it is not possible to speculate about what may or may not exist independently of space and time. Secondly, Mackie refers to Hume when considering how knowledge can never provide an 'influencing motive of the will' and that any ethical term that does this has to add the element of queerness to a particular description. In the end, Mackie summarises the proposal that moral judgements are made and issues solved by an ethical intuition 'is a travesty of actual moral thinking'.

Specification content

Challenges: no proof of moral intuition exists; intuitive 'truths' can differ widely; no obvious way to resolve conflicting intuitions.

Key term

The argument from queerness: Mackie's view that Intuitionism is too odd to accept

Knowledge that cannot be verified by empirical means has the same queerness as metaphysical entities that 'exist' beyond all that we know of existence within our physical universe, according to J. L. Mackie.

Key quotes

John Mackie maintained that moral properties, understood broadly along intuitionist lines, are queer because they are inherently motivational, in the sense that when we come to see that some act is good, we are motivated to do it. No other property we know of has such inherent motivational force. (Stratton-Lake)

Of course the suggestions that moral judgements are made or moral problems solved by just sitting down and having an ethical intuition is a travesty of actual moral thinking. (Mackie)

quickfire

1.22 Why did Mackie consider Prichard's Intuitionism 'queer'?

Key quote

Finally, Ethical Intuitionists allowed that various other factors can lead to disagreement. Clarke, for instance, allowed that stupidity, corruption, or perverseness ... John Balguy also acknowledges that self-evident moral principles ... have been, doubted, 'even by philosophers and men of letters' ... And Price maintained that all forms of knowledge, including intuitive knowledge, may be evident in different degrees. Intuition may be clear and perfect but may sometimes be faint and obscure. Such variance in degrees of clarity allows that a self-evident proposition may be imperfectly and obscurely grasped, and this may lead someone to deny its truth ... Given all these ways in which the truth of a self-evident proposition may be missed, it is no surprise that there is no universal assent. But the absence of universal assent is quite consistent with self-evidence, as long as one does not regard 'self-evidence' to mean, or imply, obviousness. (Stratton-Lake)

Intuitive 'truths' can differ widely and there is no way to resolve conflicting intuitions

The main problem with Intuitionism for many philosophers is that because there is no real, established list of 'duties' or 'obligations' then not only are people unaware of what they should do, what they think they should do will also differ widely. Ross and Prichard did make reference to some suggested 'duties', Prichard in his various essays through illustration and Ross through a more systematic presentation of what he called 'prima facie' duties. However, the fact that duties vary from person to person and situation to situation means that the wide difference is potentially unavoidable. Stratton-Lake concurs, 'if intuitions are intellectual seemings, one might ask why certain moral propositions seem true whereas others do not'. For example, if two people met the same moral dilemma and yet had different intuitions about what was the right thing to do then how would this be resolved? Rather than solving moral problems it appears to make them more complex to actually work out.

More pertinently, even the intuitionist philosophers cannot agree on what duties and obligations are universal. This may be due to the fact that they have slightly different approaches as we have seen – Moore is more consequentialist and yet Prichard and Ross are more deontological – yet the fact still remains that they disagree. As Richard Norman observes, 'Clearly Ross's experience may be different from Moore's, for what is self-evidently true for one of them is self-evidently false for the other.'

Linked to the idea of conflicting duties is the criticism that differences occur because an individual is more or less left to their own devices and no amount of logical discourse could deter a decision because Intuitionism is not based on nor answerable to the process of logical reasoning. As Norman writes again, 'Moreover, since the truths which are supposed to be self-evident are, by definition, ones for which no reasons can be given, there can be no way of resolving the disagreement or of showing which of the views in question is really the apprehension of a self-evident truth.'

In response, the deontological intuitionists would argue that although there may be conflicts and claims to self-evident truths, this does not mean that the truths themselves are conflicting as in any given situation there is one single intuitive truth – it is a case of distinguishing between true intuition and those guided by consequentialism and empirical evidence towards a very different goal.

Key quotes

Philosophers who claim that fundamental value-judgements are self-evident are not necessarily committed to claiming that their truth is always apparent to everyone. (Norman)

It is not surprising, then, that other philosophers have concluded that these fundamental value-judgements are really not the expression of self-evident truths at all; they are merely the expressions of personal preferences, of feelings and emotions, of individual likes and dislikes. (Norman)

As Stratton-Lake argues, 'It is worth noting that moral disagreement does not imply that people have different intuitions ... Similarly, it is plausible to suppose that many act consequentialists still have the intuition that it is wrong to harvest organs from a healthy but non-consenting donor to save five other lives. But because they have persuaded themselves of the truth of act consequentialism, they would not believe this act is wrong.'

Overall there are many philosophers who see moral disagreement as throwing doubt over the claim that moral propositions are self-evident. If specific moral propositions are known and correctly understood, then, everyone who had an understanding would accept them and there would be universal agreement and acknowledgement between these people. Therefore, since there is not such universal agreement, then there can be no self-evident moral propositions.

AO1 Developing skills

It is now important to consider the information that has been covered in this section; however, the information in its raw form is too extensive and so has to be processed in order to meet the requirements of the examination. This can be done by practising more advanced skills associated with AO1. For assessment objective 1 (AO1), which involves demonstrating 'knowledge' and 'understanding' skills, we are going to focus on different ways in which the skills can be demonstrated effectively, and also refer to how the performance of these skills is measured (see generic band descriptors for A2 [WJEC] AO1 or A Level [Eduqas] AO1).

▶ **Your next task is this:** Below is a **summary of Mackie's argument from queerness**. You want to explain this in an essay but they are your teacher's notes and so to write them out is simply copying them and not demonstrating any understanding. Re-write your teacher's notes but you need to replace the words used (apart from key religious or philosophical terminology) with different words so that you show that you understand what is being written and that you have your own unique version.

Mackie argues that what Intuitionism does is present us with implausible oddities and strange suggestions that ultimately make the whole theory queer; hence, he refers to it as 'the argument from queerness'. Firstly, it is this very 'queerness' of moral properties that makes it implausible that they exist. Mackie's is a very heavily empirically based objection and no different from Kant's challenge against the cosmological argument for the existence of God that if a God did exist, this 'first cause' would be so very different from anything that we experience or know and so would not be able to recognise or know about it. This is because our knowledge is limited to the phenomenal world of space and time and it is not possible to speculate about what may or may not exist independently of space and time. Secondly, Mackie refers to Hume when considering how knowledge can never provide an 'influencing motive of the will' and that any ethical term that does this has to add the element of queerness to a particular description. In the end, Mackie summarises the proposal that moral judgements are made and issues solved by an ethical intuition 'is a travesty of actual moral thinking.'

When you have completed the task, refer to the band descriptors for A2 (WJEC) or A Level (Eduqas) and in particular have a look at the demands described in the higher band descriptors towards which you should be aspiring. Ask yourself:

- Does my work demonstrate thorough, accurate and relevant knowledge and understanding of religion and belief?
- Is my work coherent (consistent or make logical sense), clear and well organised?
- Will my work, when developed, be an extensive and relevant response which is specific to the focus of the task?
- Does my work have extensive depth and/or suitable breadth and have excellent use of evidence and examples?
- If appropriate to the task, does my response have thorough and accurate reference to sacred texts and sources of wisdom?
- Are there any insightful connections to be made with other elements of my course?
- Will my answer, when developed and extended to match what is expected in an examination answer, have an extensive range of views of scholars/schools of thought?
- When used, is specialist language and vocabulary both thorough and accurate?

Key skills

Knowledge involves:

Selection of a range of (thorough) accurate and relevant information that is directly related to the specific demands of the question.

This means:

- Selecting relevant material for the question set
- Be focused in explaining and examining the material selected.

Understanding involves:

Explanation that is extensive, demonstrating depth and/or breadth with excellent use of evidence and examples including (where appropriate) thorough and accurate supporting use of sacred texts, sources of wisdom and specialist language.

This means:

- Effective use of examples and supporting evidence to establish the quality of your understanding
- Ownership of your explanation that expresses personal knowledge and understanding and NOT just a chunk of text from a book that you have rehearsed and memorised.

Specification content
Whether moral terms are intuitive.

Issues for analysis and evaluation

Whether moral terms are intuitive

One line of argument would be that many people would say that they experience things as intuitively 'right' or 'wrong' and some people may refer to it as 'instinct'. In other words, they take it for granted that it is 'the way it is or should be' and that it is an 'objective feature of the world' or 'a fact'. Intuitionism supports this common experience of morality even for those who do not believe in God. For those who believe in God, they may argue that intuitive ethical thinking is very similar to religious experience, revelation or an awareness of objective moral codes that exist independently of the empirical world.

From a philosophical perspective, Prichard argued that moral knowledge was unique, sui generis and also was clearly separated from reason and empirical influence. This line of thinking did not see 'what we ought to do' is produce the greatest amount of good through our actions, like Moore advocated. Instead, to guard against the accusation that ethical thinking is empirical, Prichard argued that our moral intuition can be found in our sense of obligation or duty. In other words, moral truth is contained within the sense of obligation that we intuitively feel when confronted with a situation. Prichard made sure that there could be no empirical challenge to Intuitionism by stating that this truth, however, is not subject to reason. If this is the case, the way to behave morally is also not a result of empirical analysis or rational debate. His argument concluded that we just 'know' what we ought to do. This is a very difficult argument to counter.

In support of Prichard, many religions, philosophers and societies could argue that the world is an 'ordered' place. This order is shown in the laws of nature, the laws of mathematics, the laws of ethics and the fact that there is a common sense of morality in many cultures. Intuitionism supports this view of the world by presenting moral terms as intuitive (underived and true apart from analysis). Indeed, approaching moral terms as intuitive avoids the Naturalistic Fallacy – definitions reduce or limit the ideas of 'good' and 'bad'.

Key quote

Prichard maintains that our feelings of obligation are basic and immediate – prima facie, to borrow an expression from fellow 'intuitionist' W. D. Ross – and for anyone who has ever felt morally obligated, this seems pretty hard to deny. (Kaufman)

However, one could argue that if moral terms were intuitive, then we would expect morality to be uniform the world over or at least we would expect there to be uniformity (a common intuition) between those who consider and reflect seriously on morality. However, anthropology can give examples where this is not the case! Psychologists and sociologists can demonstrate that what appear to be intuitive approaches to morality are really the result of conditioning from family, tribe and/or culture.

The typical response may be that some are not using intuitive thinking and are being guided by general reasoning and this would account for any differences. Indeed, we are back to square one with Prichard's definition of duty as both intuitive and self-evident. Within just our own culture there are widely different views on specific ethical issues amongst those who have reflected deeply, but are we to consider that these people are not listening to their intuition? There is no way to verify Intuitionism! There is no empirical evidence for it and there is no agreement on the origin of Intuitionism. Even the Intuitionists disagree amongst themselves on what morality consists of, for example Moore's version is different from that of Prichard and from that of Ross.

AO2 Activity

As you read through this section try to do the following:

1. Pick out the different lines of argument that are presented in the text and identify any evidence given in support.

2. For each line of argument try to evaluate whether or not you think this is strong or weak.

3. Think of any questions you may wish to raise in response to the arguments.

This Activity will help you to start thinking critically about what you read and help you to evaluate the effectiveness of different arguments and from this develop your own observations, opinions and points of view that will help with any conclusions that you make in your answers to the AO2 questions that arise.

This is the very basis of the challenge to the proposal of Intuitionism that J .L. Mackie proposed in his book, *Ethics: Inventing Right and Wrong*, published in 1977 (pages 38–42). Mackie argues that what Intuitionism does, in hiding behind the explanation of self-evident truths, is to present us with implausible oddities and strange suggestions that ultimately make the whole theory queer; hence, he refers to it as 'the argument from queerness'. Mackie argues: 'If there were objective values, then they would be entities or qualities or relations of a very strange sort, utterly different from anything else in the universe … Correspondingly, if we were aware of them, it would have to be by some special faculty of moral perception or intuition, utterly different from our normal ways of knowing everything else.'

This is similar to Kant's challenge against the cosmological argument for the existence of God that if a God did exist, this 'first cause' would be so very different from anything that we experience or know and so would not be able to recognise or know about it. This is because our knowledge is limited to the phenomenal world of space and time and it is not possible to speculate about what may or may not exist independently of space and time.

Another argument was presented by David Hume. David Hume argued that knowledge can never provide an 'influencing motive of the will' and that any ethical term that does this has to add the element of queerness to a particular description. This also supports Mackie's argument that Intuitionism is 'is a travesty of actual moral thinking'.

It appears we can adopt different conclusions as follows: Moral terms are intuitive; or, moral terms come from testing our views over and over again in different situations; or, moral terms are both given by our intuition and develop in response to real-life situations. Ultimately, it would seem, the problem of 'testing' and evaluating whether moral terms are intuitive all reduces to the principle that intuition is self-evident. Therefore, even if we demonstrated that ethical terms were not intuitive, we would be wrong according to intuitivists and that we simply have not used our intuitions correctly!

Key quote

Moreover, since the truths which are supposed to be self-evident are, by definition, ones for which no reasons can be given, there can be no way of resolving the disagreement or of showing which of the views in question is really the apprehension of a self-evident truth. (Norman)

Study tip

It is vital for AO2 that you actually discuss arguments and not just explain what someone may have stated. Try to ask yourself, 'was this a fair point to make?', 'is the evidence sound enough?', 'is there anything to challenge this argument?', 'is this a strong or weak argument?' Such critical analysis will help you develop your evaluation skills.

Key questions

Is our intuition really a trustworthy guide to ultimate truth? What about my intuition that there is a ghost in my closet?

Is there really one true order to the universe, or is that viewpoint merely an interpretation of reality?

Is there really no uniformity amongst the various moralities the world over?

Do people in our own culture really disagree on the most important aspects of morality?

Do you need to have empirical evidence to know if an action should be judged as moral or immoral?

AO2 Activity

List some conclusions that could be drawn from the AO2 reasoning from the above text; try to aim for at least three different possible conclusions. Consider each of the conclusions and collect brief evidence to support each conclusion from the AO1 and AO2 material for this topic. Select the conclusion that you think is most convincing and explain why it is so. Try to contrast this with the weakest conclusion in the list, justifying your argument with clear reasoning and evidence.

AO2 Developing skills

It is now important to consider the information that has been covered in this section; however, the information in its raw form is too extensive and so has to be processed in order to meet the requirements of the examination. This can be done by practising more advanced skills associated with AO2. For assessment objective 2 (AO2), which involves 'critical analysis' and 'evaluation' skills, we are going to focus on different ways in which the skills can be demonstrated effectively, and also refer to how the performance of these skills is measured (see generic band descriptors for A2 [WJEC] AO2 or A Level [Eduqas] AO2).

▶ **Your next task is this:** Below is a **brief summary of two different points of view concerning the validity of the theory of Intuitionism**. You want to use these two views and lines of argument for an evaluation; however, they need further reasons and evidence for support to fully develop the argument. Re-present these two views in a fully evaluative style by adding further reasons and evidence that link to their arguments. Aim for a further 100 words.

> Many people would say that they experience things as intuitively 'right' or 'wrong' – in other words as 'objective features of the world' or 'facts'. Intuitionism supports this common experience of morality – even for those who do not believe in God.
>
> There is no way to verify Intuitionism! There is no empirical evidence for it and there is no agreement on the origin of Intuitionism (God? Gut feelings? Genetics?). Even the Intuitionists disagree amongst themselves on what morality consists of!

When you have completed the task, refer to the band descriptors for A2 (WJEC) or A Level (Eduqas) and in particular have a look at the demands described in the higher band descriptors towards which you should be aspiring. Ask yourself:

- Is my answer a confident critical analysis and perceptive evaluation of the issue?
- Is my answer a response that successfully identifies and thoroughly addresses the issues raised by the question set?
- Does my work show an excellent standard of coherence, clarity and organisation?
- Will my work, when developed, contain thorough, sustained and clear views that are supported by extensive, detailed reasoning and/or evidence?
- Are the views of scholars/schools of thought used extensively, appropriately and in context?
- Does my answer convey a confident and perceptive analysis of the nature of any possible connections with other elements of my course?
- When used, is specialist language and vocabulary both thorough and accurate?

Key skills

Analysis involves identifying issues raised by the materials in the AO1, together with those identified in the AO2 section, and presents sustained and clear views, either of scholars or from a personal perspective ready for evaluation.

This means:

- That your answers are able to identify key areas of debate in relation to a particular issue
- That you can identify, and comment upon, the different lines of argument presented by others
- That your response comments on the overall effectiveness of each of these areas or arguments.

Evaluation involves considering the various implications of the issues raised based upon the evidence gleaned from analysis and provides an extensive detailed argument with a clear conclusion.

This means:

- That your answer weighs up the consequences of accepting or rejecting the various and different lines of argument analysed
- That your answer arrives at a conclusion through a clear process of reasoning.

F: Meta-ethical approaches: Emotivism

Emotivism as an ethical theory

The theory of **Emotivism** is usually associated with the British philosopher A. J. Ayer and, quite independently of Ayer's work, the American philosopher Charles L. Stevenson. Whilst Ayer was more influenced by the Logical Positivists and the ideas of the **verification principle**, Stevenson was influenced more by the later ideas of Wittgenstein on the meaning of language.

However, prior to the popularisation of the theory of moral language as emotive, this had been already raised by empiricists such as David Hume and then by one of Moore's closest friends at Cambridge, Bertrand Russell. Ayer acknowledges this in his first edition preface: 'The views which are put forward in this treatise derive from the doctrines of Bertrand Russell and Wittgenstein, which are themselves the logical outcome of the empiricism of Berkeley and David Hume.'

Key quote

The sense of the world must lie outside the world. In the world everything is as it is and happens as it does happen. In it there is no value – and if there were it would be of no value. (Wittgenstein)

A year prior to the publication of Ayer's book, *Language, Truth and Logic* (1936) Bertrand Russell had published a book called *Religion and Science* (1935) and argued that moral judgements of right and wrong were justified if they promote good but in terms of whether or not an act is a good act he states: 'there is no evidence either way; each disputant can only appeal to his own emotions'. He also argued that moral statements were a form of rhetoric to rouse the emotions of others. Russell writes: 'Questions as to "value" lie wholly outside the domain of knowledge. That is to say, when we assert that this or that has "value", we are giving expression to our own emotions, not to a fact which would still be true if our personal feelings were different.' He concluded the contrary to Moore when he argued that for something to have intrinsic value is a matter, not of objectivity as Moore claimed, but of pure subjectivity. For example, the classic case is with the goodness of beauty, which, as we know from the common phrase that 'beauty is in the eye of the beholder', is totally a matter for debate and personal perspective.

Alfred Ayer's book Language, Truth & Logic *generated a lot of debate amongst moral philosophers when first published in 1936.*

In other words, whilst Moore indicated that 'self-evident' truths did not need justification, Russell drew a different conclusion that for something to be 'self-evident' just means that it cannot be deemed true or false and, in that case, in the words of Richard Norman, 'They make no statements and they convey no knowledge.'

This section covers AO1 content and skills

Specification content

Theory that believes objective moral laws do not exist; a non-cognitivist theory; moral terms express personal emotional attitudes and not propositions.

It was the philosopher Bertrand Russell who first really challenged Moore's views and suggested that ethical language was emotive.

Key terms

Emotivism: theory that ethical propositions are simply expressions of approval or disapproval

Verification principle: methodology of the Logical Positivists that only statements that are empirically verifiable (i.e. verifiable through the senses) are cognitively meaningful

Key quote

Moore would agree that moral judgements are neither analytic nor empirically verifiable. But he believed that they are nevertheless true or false, because they are about non-natural properties. But Ayer responds that our 'intuitions' are simply our feelings of approval or disapproval. Feelings are not cognitions of value, and value does not exist independently of our feelings. (Lacewing)

1.23 According to Russell, where did question of value belong?

Alfred Ayer was influenced by Hume's empiricism and also the scientific approach of the Logical Positivists.

Key quote

On Hume's account, our ethical nature is characterised by the capacity for sympathy, or the ability to feel with (empathise with) others. On such an account any variation in moral codes must be a consequence of differing social conditions, while ultimately all such codes must express some fundamentals which humanity shares. (Hayward)

Key quote

Questions as to 'value' lie wholly outside the domain of knowledge. That is to say, when we assert that this or that has 'value', we are giving expression to our own emotions, not to a fact which would still be true if our personal feelings were different. (Russell)

This principle of non-verification was taken up by Alfred Ayer in relation to his work with the Logical Positivists who were all mainly from mathematical, scientific or engineering backgrounds. The Logical Positivists were interested in types of knowledge and language that could be verified through either analytical or synthetic means by appeal to logic or empiricism (see the Philosophy topic on Religious Language from AS / Year 1). This in itself relates back to Hume's Fork.

Warnock summarises his position well when she writes:

'Ayer's general contention is, briefly, that any statement that has meaning must fall into one of two categories. Either, it must be analytic, that is necessarily true but not concerned with empirical matters of fact; or it must be empirical. If it is empirical, it can never be more than probable; it is, in fact, a hypothesis. Both the meaning and the probability of the hypothesis are established by empirical verification. That is to say, if a statement is to qualify for the second category, it must be capable of verification by sense experience.'

The problem for ethical propositions is that to be verified they must fit into one of the two categories of Hume's Fork (see earlier diagram and explanation). Either, they fit into the category of logic, mathematics and symbols as analytic propositions; or, they fall into the second category of the empirical experience of science and propositions of empirical matter of fact.

Key quote

Even the most enthusiastic intuitionist would never maintain that one literally saw or heard the goodness of an action. (Warnock)

There are no other categories of knowledge and language.

The problem is, as Hume, Russell and Ayer analysed, ethical propositions do not fall into either category. Furthermore, as Hume had observed years earlier, 'when you pronounce any action or character to be vicious, you mean nothing, but that from the constitution of your nature you have a feeling or sentiment of blame from the contemplation of it'. Hume points out that such feelings are 'not qualities in objects, but perceptions in the mind'. Reason cannot find a motive for an action and neither can an ethical proposition be grounded in anything else other than our own 'experience'.

Whilst Hume gave a typical naturalist account of such feelings by linking them 'objectively' to biological heritage and social conditioning, Russell and Ayer drew a very different conclusion.

In order to discover precisely what Ayer concluded, it would be beneficial to refer closely to his argument presented in chapter 6 of his seminal work, *Language, Truth and Logic (LTL)*. At the outset, however, Ayer never proposed that ethical propositions were of no value or worth or that ethical debate was not worthy of pursuit, as he states clearly in later writings, but simply that they are not factual or that it is not possible to verify them. However, although for Ayer religious language or ethical religious language such as 'God is good' were rendered as meaningless by the Logical Positivist approach, for ethical language per se it was clear that it did have some purpose. Whereas the verification principle renders religious language as meaningless, the verification principle simply recognises that ethical language is different and should not be the object of meta-ethical philosophical enquiry.

For Ayer, ethical language was not about communicating specific meaning and definition but it did have a different purpose. However, since this was not a meta-ethical enquiry into defining meaning then his interest in ethical language was very limited. In LTL he writes that his task is: 'to show what people are doing when they make moral judgements' and no more.

quickfire

1.24 What was Ayer's purpose in his analysis of ethical language?

Key quote

If someone still wishes to say that ethical statements are statements of fact, only it is a queer sort of fact, he is welcome to do so. So long as he accepts our grounds for saying that they are not statements of fact, it is simply a question of how widely or loosely we want to use the word 'fact'. My own view is that it is preferable so to use it as to exclude ethical judgements, but it must not be inferred from this that I am treating them with disrespect. The only relevant consideration is that of clarity. (Ayer)

A.J. Ayer: Ethical statements are neither verifiable nor analytic

Ayer sets off with the recognition that whilst ethical statements are of value, 'significant' (he does not explain how) and 'scientific' in one sense (he does not explain how), in another sense because they are simply emotions they become unscientific, insignificant and unverifiable. Ayer seems to acknowledge that ethical statements do have some meaning and relevance but he does not elaborate because his investigation is all about how language works in the literal sense and what is happening when we use it. He writes:

'We shall set ourselves to show that in so far as statements of value are significant, they are ordinary "scientific" statements; and that in so far as they are not scientific, they are not in the literal sense significant, but are simply expressions of emotion which can be neither true nor false.'

Ayer sees four categories existing within ethical philosophy:

1. Propositions which express definitions of ethical terms.
2. Propositions describing the phenomena of moral experience, and their causes.
3. Exhortations to moral virtue.
4. Ethical judgements that attempt to ascribe value.

Ayer argues that philosophers do not always differentiate between these classes: 'It is unfortunately the case that the distinction between these four classes, plain as it is, is commonly ignored by ethical philosophers; with the result that it is often very difficult to tell from their works what it is that they are seeking to discover or prove.' Indeed, Ayer sees only sees the first class, that of meta-ethics and definitions of ethical terms as the area that could be considered to constitute ethical philosophy.

According to Ayer, the second category belongs to the scientific disciplines of psychology and sociology. The exhortations are really commands and have the intention and purpose of provocation and do not belong to any branch of philosophy or science. The fourth category certainly does not belong to moral philosophy according to Ayer, as it is simply a matter of personal approval or disproval. However, Ayer does raise the question as to whether or not it is possible that such value judgements could be somehow 'translated to ethical fact'?

Specification content

A.J. Ayer – ethical statements are neither verifiable nor analytic; made to express joy or pain (emotion); expressed to be persuasive; Emotivism is not subjectivism.

Key quote

We are not now concerned to discover which term, within the sphere of ethical terms, is to be taken as fundamental ... We are inquiring whether statements of ethical value can be translated into statements of empirical fact. (Ayer)

quickfire

1.25 How many classes of philosophical ethical investigation did Ayer outline?

Ayer felt that ethical language and its use and meaning belonged to the subject area of psychology rather than philosophy.

Emotivism is not subjectivism

The position held by subjectivism is that values arise out of the different attitudes that a person or society/culture has towards things. In other words, our emotions about the things that we see ascribe some sort of value to them. For example, we may feel that corporal punishment is bad, but is it really our feelings about the action the very thing that makes the action a 'bad' thing? For Ayer, emotions and attitudes towards issues that elicited an ethical proposition in no way affect the moral value of the object of such a proposition.

Ayer writes:

'If we say this, we are not, of course, denying that it is possible to invent a language in which all ethical symbols are definable in non-ethical terms, or even that it is desirable to invent such a language and adopt it in place of our own; what we are denying is that the suggested reduction of ethical to non-ethical statements is consistent with the conventions of our actual language. That is, we reject Utilitarianism and subjectivism, not as proposals to replace our existing ethical notions by new ones, but as analyses of our existing ethical notions. Our contention is simply that, in our language, sentences which contain normative ethical symbols are not equivalent to sentences which express psychological propositions, or indeed empirical propositions of any kind.'

Rejection of Intuitionism

As we have already seen, Ayer overtly rejects Intuitionism. His reasons are not the same as those of Russell, who, if we remember, rejected intuition because it was purely subjective and not a basis for knowledge. For Ayer it was a simple matter of verification. This occurs especially where there is a debate about establishing which value is true when there are different intuitions. Since there is no way to solve this then its value cannot be determined and thus demonstrates that an appeal to intuition is pointless. Ayer writes:

'In admitting that normative ethical concepts are irreducible to empirical concepts, we seem to be leaving the way clear for the "absolutist" view of ethics – that is, the view that statements of value are not controlled by observation, as ordinary empirical propositions are, but only by a mysterious "intellectual intuition". A feature of this theory, which is seldom recognised by its advocates, is that it makes statements of value unverifiable. For it is notorious that what seems intuitively certain to one person may seem doubtful, or even false, to another. So that unless it is possible to provide some criterion by which one may decide between conflicting intuitions, a mere appeal to intuition is worthless as a test of a proposition's validity.'

In addition, Ayer points out that any ethical element in a proposition adds nothing to its factual content. He uses stealing as an example and demonstrates that to say 'You acted wrongly in stealing that money' is no different from saying 'You stole that money'. There is no further statement being made about 'stealing money' that can be evaluated as true or false. It is simply a moral disapproval.

Key quotes

I do in fact suspect that the experiences which some philosophers want to describe as intuitions, or as quasi-sensory apprehensions, of good are not significantly different from those that I want to describe as feelings of approval. (Ayer)

We begin by admitting that the fundamental ethical concepts are unanalysable, inasmuch as there is no criterion by which one can test the validity of the judgements in which they occur. (Ayer)

Key quote

For in saying that a certain type of action is right or wrong, I am not making any factual statement, not even a statement about my own state of mind. I am merely expressing certain moral sentiments. And the man who is ostensibly contradicting me is merely expressing his moral sentiments. So that there is plainly no sense in asking which of us is in the right. For neither of us is asserting a genuine proposition. (Ayer)

Ethical statements can be persuasive

Despite all this, Ayer did give one concession to ethical propositions. In a sense it was a great shame that he did not elaborate further on this aspect; however, it appears that since ethics is only one aspect of his whole theory about LTL, then he dealt with it within the framework of the purposes of his book and the simple notion of verification. As Mary Warnock observed, 'Ayer, perhaps unwisely, presents his case for Emotivism as though it rested primarily on a desire to find an ethical theory which would not conflict with the verification doctrine.'

The area he conceded that ethical propositions may have some worth was as means of persuasion. He writes: 'It is worth mentioning that ethical terms do not serve only to express feeling. They are calculated also to arouse feeling, and so to stimulate action. Indeed some of them are used in such a way as to give the sentences in which they occur the effect of commands. Thus the sentence "It is your duty to tell the truth" may be regarded both as the expression of a certain sort of ethical feeling about truthfulness and as the expression of the command "Tell the truth".'

Key quote

The sentence 'You ought to tell the truth' also involves the command 'Tell the truth', but here the tone of the command is less emphatic. In the sentence 'It is good to tell the truth' the command has become little more than a suggestion … In fact we may define the meaning of the various ethical words in terms both of the different feelings they are ordinarily taken to express, and also the different responses which they are calculated to provoke. (Ayer)

In conclusion, there is no way that we can find a criterion for determining the validity of ethical judgements according to Ayer. Ethical statements have no objective validity whatsoever. If, as established above, the ethical element says nothing more about the statement then it is illogical to then ask whether that additional element is true or false. According to Ayer, ethical statements are 'pure expressions of feeling and as such do not come under the category of truth and falsehood'. We cannot verify them just as we cannot verify a cry of pain!

Therefore, ethical propositions are simply what Ayer called 'pseudo-concepts' and unanalysable. Ayer saw this as falling within the discipline of psychology. They are also to do with the moral habits of a given person or group of people, and a study of what causes them to have precisely those habits and feelings. This was an area of study for sociology and anthropology. Even the discipline of casuistry (applying an ethical rule to solve a given moral situation) is not a scientific discipline but rather one of analytical investigation as to how a moral system is structured.

Once again, if ethical arguments were formal logic or scientific procedure then the concept of goodness and rightness would be demonstratively different from the actions or situation. Since these concepts have been shown to add nothing to the action or situation then they are not independently verifiable. As Ayer puts it, 'There is no procedure of examining the value of the facts, as distinct from examining the facts themselves.'

Key quote

In every case in which one would commonly be said to be making an ethical judgement, the function of the relevant ethical word is purely 'emotive'. It is used to express feeling about certain objects, but not to make any assertion about them. (Ayer)

Key term

Pseudo-concepts: something treated as a concept but can only be mentally apprehended and not empirically verified

quickfire

1.26 What did Ayer compare the verification of an ethical proposition to?

For Ayer ethical language was nothing more than personal approval or disapproval.

Key quotes

Ethical argument is not formal demonstration. And not in a scientific sense either. For then the goodness or badness of the situation, the rightness or wrongness of the action, would have to be something apart from the situation, something independently verifiable, for which the facts adduced as the reasons for the moral judgement were evidence. *(Ayer)*

There is no procedure of examining the value of the facts, as distinct from examining the facts themselves. We may say that we have evidence for our moral judgements, but we cannot distinguish between pointing to the evidence itself and pointing to that for which it is supposed to be evidence. Which means that in the scientific sense it is not evidence at all. *(Ayer)*

Again, when I say that moral judgements are emotive rather than descriptive, that they are persuasive expressions of attitudes and not statements of fact … I am not saying that nothing is good or bad, right or wrong, or that it does not matter what we do. *(Ayer, On the Analysis of Moral Judgements)*

In conclusion, Ayer revisits what he stated in the first place. He had not set out to demonstrate that 'morals are trivial or unimportant, or that people ought not to bother with them' and nor did he conclude this. Ayer would consider this a value judgement of his own and so by his own method, unverifiable, as there would be no logical justification for this conclusion. His conclusion is that 'all moral theories, intuitionist, naturalistic, objectivist, emotive, and the rest, in so far as they are philosophical theories, are neutral as regards actual conduct'. In other words, they tell us nothing about the actions themselves but simply may inform us what people are doing when they make moral judgements. Ayer then distinguishes between ethics proper, that is the first three of his four categories listed above (namely, experience, virtue and value) to which no true moral philosopher should be 'presumptuous' enough to engage, and meta-ethics. He sees meta-ethics as the true realm of philosophy, and indeed, the subject with which he has himself been engaging with in attempting to define and analyse ethical propositions.

Anthropology studies the evolution of human behaviour and Ayer felt that this was best suited to assess moral behaviours.

It would be beneficial here to present his conclusion:

I hope that I have gone some way towards making clear what the theory which I am advocating is. Let me now say what it is not. In the first place, **I am not saying that morals are trivial or unimportant, or that people ought not to bother with them**. For this would itself be a judgement of value, which I have not made and do not wish to make. And even if I did wish to make it, it would have no logical connection with my theory. For the theory is entirely on the level of analysis; it is an attempt to show what people are doing when they make moral judgements; it is not a set of suggestions as to what moral judgements they are to make. And this is true of all moral philosophy, as I understand it. All moral theories, intuitionist, naturalistic, objectivist, emotive, and the rest, in so far as they are philosophical theories, are neutral as regards actual conduct. To speak technically, they belong to the field of meta-ethics, not ethics proper. That is why it is silly, as well as presumptuous, for any one type of philosopher to pose as the champion of virtue. And it is also one reason why many people find moral philosophy an unsatisfying subject. For they mistakenly look to the moral philosopher for guidance.

AO1 Activity

Why not research the Logical Positivists on the Internet to find out more about what they thought regarding ethics.

Study tip

It is good to see a link between philosophers/philosophical ideas, for example, how Hume, Russell and Ayer follow a particular empiricist tradition.

Ethical terms are just expressions of personal approval (hurrah) or disapproval (boo)

Now that we have covered Ayer's argument in LTL there are two areas of the Specification left to cover in relation to Emotivism as a theory. Since Emotivism extends beyond Ayer, it would be beneficial to look at these two areas briefly in relation to the work of Charles L. Stevenson as well as Ayer. Stevenson was an American philosopher noted for his work on Emotivism and is seen as the philosopher who developed it into a full-bodied, systematic theory. In 1937 he published in the *Mind* Journal an article entitled, *The Emotive Meaning of Ethical terms*. He followed this up with two later papers and then produced his book, *Ethics and Language*, published in 1944 by Yale University Press, which is seen to be a classic systematic presentation of the theory.

For some reason, at a point in time that the current author cannot accurately locate, there emerged in response to Ayer's proposals a nickname for his theory of Emotivism. This was because Ayer insisted that ethical propositions were simply emotive and feelings of either approval or disapproval. Emotivism therefore became known also as the **'Hurrah-boo!' theory** as it was felt that Ayer proposed that ethical terms are just expressions of personal approval (hurrah) or disapproval (boo). To be fair to Ayer, his role was simply to indicate what was happening with language when we use ethical propositions in line with his overall theory of verification. When something could not be verified, Ayer offered a simple reason and explanation but to explore further the thing that could not be verified was not his intention. As we have seen, he saw this as the role of sciences.

Nonetheless, the one glimpse of an alternative to ethical terms only being expressions of personal approval (hurrah) or disapproval (boo), was when he suggested that there was an alternative purpose of persuasion.

It is with this glimpse that we see an alternative approach that was taken by Charles Stevenson. Surprisingly, Stevenson developed his work at the same time as Ayer quite independently and in a different direction.

For Stevenson, his interest was not really in verifying ethical language but he did accept that if we seek scientific verification, then this was not the most helpful way to view the theory of Emotivism. He started with the word 'good' and argued that to make ethical questions clear any definition should: (1) enable disagreement about goodness; (2) have a certain magnetism or appeal to act in its favour; (3) not be subject to verification by scientific method.

He saw this as understanding the true nature of Emotivism but preferred the term **'interest theory.'** Stevenson was interested in how ethical propositions were used in two ways: (1) how they acquired power; and, (2) how **dynamic power** in using an ethical proposition influenced its meaning.

Stevenson realised that we actually use ethical propositions, or in fact any words, for a variety of purposes, e.g. arouse sympathy, persuade, drop hints, approve, disapprove, command, etc. He referred to this as the 'causal or dispositional property' of a word or proposition.

He writes, 'The emotive meaning of a word is the tendency of a word, arising through the history of its usage, to produce (result from) affective responses in people.' In other words, there are certain ethical words that are very well suited to an emotive meaning because they have a dynamic use. To leave an emotive element of such words out would mean we are misled to believe that it is purely descriptive when in actual fact this ignores its dynamic usage and so its actual meaning is distorted. The reason that the term 'good' is indefinable is because in any definition of it the emotive element will be distorted. Stevenson argued that good has a pleasing emotive meaning and that 'this is a rough description of meaning and not a definition'; however, it is adequate enough.

Key terms

Dynamic power: the sense in which language is best analysed to determine meaning according to Stevenson

'Hurrah-boo!' theory: another term for the theory of Emotivism

Interest theory: Stevenson's theory of Emotivism

quickfire

1.27 Which philosopher developed a more systematic approach to Emotivism?

The American philosopher Charles L. Stevenson thought that the answer to 'verifying' ethical language could be found by studying its use.

Key quote

While Stevenson granted that moral language didn't have factual or cognitive content, he argued that it had emotive meaning. Moral propositions aren't true or false, but they aren't meaningless either – moral language allows us to express emotions. (Messerly)

Stevenson saw persuasion as a key purpose of ethical discourse.

quickfire

1.28 For a clear ethical definition, what three things needed to be present according to Stevenson?

Key terms

Propositions about belief: statements of fact or verifiable by empirical means

Propositions about attitude: views or value judgements about statements of belief

Key quote

In normative ethics any description of what is the case is attended by considerations of what is to be felt and done about it; the beliefs that are in question are preparatory to guiding or redirecting attitudes. (Stevenson)

Specification content

Challenges: no basic moral principles can be established; ethical debate becomes a pointless activity; there is no universal agreement that some actions are wrong.

Stevenson suggested that the emotive aspects of ethical propositions were used in a variety of different ways although he tended to see persuasive definitions as a common use. His research is vast, and the book *Ethics and Language* is 336 pages long but these initial observations serve to show that there is much more to ethical propositions than just being expressions of personal approval (hurrah) or disapproval (boo).

Emotivism explains why people disagree about morality

The obvious conclusion to be drawn from Emotivism is that if ethical propositions are really just expressions of approval or disapproval then it follows that people inevitably will disagree about morality because we are all simply expressing our own opinions.

Moreover, it may then be suggested that there can never be any agreement in ethical debate and also that maybe ethical debate becomes pointless. Ethical debate would just become our emotional response to facts that we all agree on; since emotions are not verifiable and cannot contribute to meaningful logical discourse, ethics becomes meaningless.

However, for Stevenson ethical debate was meaningful and to demonstrate this he made a distinction between propositions, distinguishing between **propositions about 'belief'** and **propositions about 'attitude'**. Attitudes are statements that reflect the emotive use of ethical language in debate; they reveal how the person feels and sees things. Beliefs are more to do with facts that can be verified such as the 'nature of light transmission' to use Stevenson's example, or, something like the date that you last met somebody. Beliefs are not about ethical convictions.

- War is the last resort, and abortion is the legal termination of a foetus, are examples of beliefs.

- War/abortion is always wrong and war/abortion is sometimes wrong are attitudes.

According to Stevenson, what happens in ethical debate is that people are trying to change others' attitudes not their beliefs. It would be valid to say that these attitudes are just describing the feelings of the individuals involved; however, if we account for emotive meaning we can see that each is trying to affect the others' feelings and influence them. The disagreement is a disagreement not **about** attitudes – the debate concerns not a focus on how one attitude is better than another – but rather it is a disagreement **in** attitudes towards the issue in hand. Therefore, Emotivism can explain why people disagree about morality without making ethical debate meaningless. In fact, Emotivism makes ethical debate meaningful.

Challenges to Emotivism

Mary Warnock points out that Emotivism is too broad a theory for ethical language. It is not precise enough because it does not differentiate between ethical and non-ethical emotive use of language. For example, if Emotivism attempts to influence someone's attitude then how exactly is an advertisement for donations to Water Aid different from advertising a McDonald's burger as 100% pure beef with nothing added in order to suggest it is healthy food?

Other general challenges include the fact that ethical language and debate is not always 'emotive', sometimes we use it to distance ourselves from others' views or indeed display indifference and not moral judgement and some see morality and ethical debate as a rational and logical process of reasoning.

We now look at three more specific challenges.

No basic moral principles can be established

A general criticism of Emotivism is that the theory only values meta-ethics. Ayer used meta-ethics to reduce ethical statements to mere sentiments that express no factual information whatsoever. If this is the case then no basic moral principles can be established. Likewise, Stevenson confined his approach to meta-ethics in that he looked specifically at the meaning and use of language. Even when he applied this to ethical statements there was no real insight offered into meta-ethical definitions or normative principles.

As Hayward writes, 'One conclusion that can be drawn from Emotivism is that value judgements are not rational and so no rational agreement is possible on ethical matters and no knowledge can be had of them.'

Differences in opinion only heighten this problem and complicate matters. Emotivism suggests no way in which differences of opinion can be resolved; it can only observe that they happen. However, history demonstrates that clear decisions have been made for the better and to say that it was simply down to emotions ridicules these important ethical decisions.

Finally, the fact that it reduces morality to emotions which have no rational basis nor justification, means that the whole idea of basic moral principles is unfounded and suggests that they do not exist anyway. The other extreme is that there is no limit on moral principles that can be identified through emotions but that they are so conflicting that no sense of coherence can be found amongst them all.

Ethical debate becomes a pointless activity

Related to the above challenge, if there are no basic moral principles then ethical debate becomes a pointless activity because we need to ask, 'what are we debating?' If we cannot differentiate 'good' from 'bad' and 'right' from 'wrong' and only have feelings to revert to then why bother at all?

If ethical debate is not pointless it would certainly not be rational and could provide no definitive answers. By reducing ethical debate to trying to influence each other's' attitudes then it becomes no more than an exercise in propaganda. Surely this cannot be the case if an argument is presented with sufficient evidence?

The problem is that if one does follow the inclination of Emotivism then it does not address why many feel that whether or not the basis of 'good' and 'bad' is established it is also possible to present ethical debate. Ethical debate is not just about emotions but also to do with a process of reasoning using evidence to support an argument. It can be acknowledged that the outcome of the argument may be explained as personal opinion but the argument itself is still important. Indeed, how is that any different from Prichard's Intuitionism? Therefore to suggest that ethical debate is pointless appears 'to be throwing the baby out with the bathwater'.

There is no universal agreement that some actions are wrong

Although it could be argued that there is some value still in moral debate, even if it just about persuasion, it will never be able to establish a unanimous, universal agreement on those actions that are considered as wrong. There is no sense of authority to appeal to.

Mackie has also pointed out that we are not clearly differentiating between the things we disapprove of when he writes: 'The emotivist is unable to distinguish between my dislike of curries and my dislike of genocide. But the difference between the two is profound. I dislike curry because I don't like its taste. I abhor genocide because it's immoral.'

In addition, what would happen in ethical debate? History has proven that minority interests and 'emotions' (to use Ayer's perspective) have actually been the correct way forward. Look at slavery, homosexuality and women's rights not as moral issues but as relating to basic human rights and the law. The outcome has shown that basic principles of what is wrong can be established through ethical argument. Emotivism does not seem to reflect what has actually happened through ethical debate.

Key quotes

It is disagreement in attitude, which imposes a characteristic type or organisation on the beliefs that may serve indirectly to resolve it, that chiefly distinguishes ethical issues from those of pure science. (Stevenson)

One advantage of this theory is that it easily explains how and why it is that moral judgements motivate us. If moral language were just descriptive, stating how things are, why would that get us to act in certain ways? We need to care. And what we care about is captured in our attitudes to the world. (Lacewing)

Remembering that the chemical composition of water is H_2O and that the atoms are joined by covalent bonding is a proposition about belief according to Stevenson.

Not liking the taste of a certain food is a very different expression of disapproval from disagreeing about whether one approves of cruelty to animals.

AO1 Developing skills

It is now important to consider the information that has been covered in this section; however, the information in its raw form is too extensive and so has to be processed in order to meet the requirements of the examination. This can be done by practising more advanced skills associated with AO1. For assessment objective 1 (AO1), which involves demonstrating 'knowledge' and 'understanding' skills, we are going to focus on different ways in which the skills can be demonstrated effectively, and also refer to how the performance of these skills is measured (see generic band descriptors for A2 [WJEC] AO1 or A Level [Eduqas] AO1).

▶ **Your next task is this:** Below is a **brief summary of one challenge to Emotivism**. You want to explain this in an essay but as it stands at present it is too brief. In order that you demonstrate more depth of understanding, develop this summary by providing examples that will help you explain it further. Aim for 200 words in total.

> Moral debate, even if it just about persuasion, will never be able to establish a unanimous, universal agreement on those actions that are considered as wrong. There is no sense of authority to appeal to. In addition, what would happen in ethical debate? History has proven that minority interests and 'emotions' (to use Ayer's perspective) have actually been the correct way forward. The outcome has shown that basic principles of what is wrong can be established through ethical argument. Emotivism does not seem to reflect what has actually happened through ethical debate.

When you have completed the task, refer to the band descriptors for A2 (WJEC) or A Level (Eduqas) and in particular have a look at the demands described in the higher band descriptors towards which you should be aspiring. Ask yourself:

- Does my work demonstrate thorough, accurate and relevant knowledge and understanding of religion and belief?
- Is my work coherent (consistent or make logical sense), clear and well organised?
- Will my work, when developed, be an extensive and relevant response which is specific to the focus of the task?
- Does my work have extensive depth and/or suitable breadth and have excellent use of evidence and examples?
- If appropriate to the task, does my response have thorough and accurate reference to sacred texts and sources of wisdom?
- Are there any insightful connections to be made with other elements of my course?
- Will my answer, when developed and extended to match what is expected in an examination answer, have an extensive range of views of scholars/schools of thought?
- When used, is specialist language and vocabulary both thorough and accurate?

Key skills

Knowledge involves:

Selection of a range of (thorough) accurate and relevant information that is directly related to the specific demands of the question.

This means:

- Selecting relevant material for the question set
- Be focused in explaining and examining the material selected.

Understanding involves:

Explanation that is extensive, demonstrating depth and/or breadth with excellent use of evidence and examples including (where appropriate) thorough and accurate supporting use of sacred texts, sources of wisdom and specialist language.

This means:

- Effective use of examples and supporting evidence to establish the quality of your understanding
- Ownership of your explanation expressing personal knowledge and understanding, NOT just a chunk of text from a book that you have rehearsed and memorised.

Issues for analysis and evaluation

The extent to which moral terms are just expressions of our emotions

This section covers AO2 content and skills

Specification content
The extent to which moral terms are just expressions of our emotions.

The first argument could be that moral terms do not attempt to define what terms like 'right' or 'wrong' mean, they are just an individual's emotional response to situations. Alfred Ayer suggested this.

Indeed, viewing moral terms as expressions of emotion would explain the diversity of moral opinion that we see across cultures and within our own culture. Any intuitionist response that seeks to explain these differences by positing that there are different intuitive abilities at work, cannot be substantiated with any evidence at all other than 'we know this is the case'.

Again, another argument could be that we can measure emotions and even explore the biological foundations of emotions. There has been no similar claim when it comes to Intuitionism. Instead of empirical evidence for Intuitionism there are conflicting and unsubstantiated claims that intuitions come from God, the 'gut' or genetics.

One could argue that the Emotivism view is very logical and scientific. Emotivism recognises the importance of the scientific approach to language and that words have particular meanings. These meanings must be empirically verified and, as they cannot be verified, Emotivism rejects, therefore, the abstract use of words in previous philosophical discussion.

Also, Emotivism does not necessarily mean that moral terms have no value. For example, Stevenson pointed out that what happens in ethical debate is that people are trying to change others' attitudes and if we account for emotive meaning we can see that each is trying to affect the others' feelings and influence them. Therefore, Emotivism can explain why people disagree about morality without making ethical debate meaningless. In fact, Emotivism makes ethical debate meaningful and is, according to Stevenson, more than just an expression of emotion.

However, if moral terms were only expressions of emotions then there would be no point in real moral debate. The emotional responses people give are based on some inner belief or conscience and surely something more deeply rooted than mere emotions. Any ethical naturalist would obviously disagree and argue that moral terms express propositions, which can be seen as true or false by considering objective features of the world.

You could also argue that asserting moral statements as mere expressions of emotions is a way of defining moral terms. This leads us back to Moore's Naturalistic Fallacy and the rationality of not defining moral terms.

It is also held by some that emotional debates are needed to engage with what ethics is all about. What Emotivism does is just look at meta-ethics but not ethics proper. Indeed, one could argue that Ayer was wrong because his exclusion of three of his four categories of ethical philosophy was simply due to the fact that all he was interested in was meta-ethics.

If Emotivism were true, there would be no point to moral discussions. This runs counter to the instincts of many who feel that these discussions are valid. Also, if Emotivism is true, it must reduce a moral statement to the same level as all other statements that do not come from a source that is logically verifiable; moral statements are therefore at the same level as statements used in advertising, bribes and blackmail. An intuitionist would say that this cannot possibly be the case!

Key quote

And therefore we should, I think, conclude that the validity of ethical judgements is not determined by the felicific tendencies of actions, any more than by the nature of people's feelings; but that it must be regarded as 'absolute' or 'intrinsic', and not empirically calculable. (Ayer)

AO2 Activity

As you read through this section try to do the following:

1. Pick out the different lines of argument that are presented in the text and identify any evidence given in support.

2. For each line of argument try to evaluate whether or not you think this is strong or weak.

3. Think of any questions you may wish to raise in response to the arguments.

This Activity will help you to start thinking critically about what you read and help you to evaluate the effectiveness of different arguments and from this develop your own observations, opinions and points of view that will help with any conclusions that you make in your answers to the AO2 questions that arise.

Key quote

Stevenson analyses emotive meaning by connecting meaning to use. The purpose of moral judgements is not to state facts, but to influence how we behave through expressions of approval and disapproval. Words with emotive meaning do just that. If moral language is just descriptive, how can moral truths motivate us? Emotivism, by contrast, connects caring, approving, disapproving, with the very meaning of ethical words. (Lacewing)

AO2 Activity

List some conclusions that could be drawn from the AO2 reasoning from the above text; try to aim for at least three different possible conclusions. Consider each of the conclusions and collect brief evidence to support each conclusion from the AO1 and AO2 material for this topic. Select the conclusion that you think is most convincing and explain why it is so. Try to contrast this with the weakest conclusion in the list, justifying your argument with clear reasoning and evidence.

Another argument would be that if moral statements are nothing more than a creation of family/culture/society, why are people able to 'stand outside' of their culture/family/society and challenge them morally? Therefore, there must be a basis for morality other than human emotion.

In addition, how do we differentiate 'right' between two people's moral opinions? Nothing can be resolved, and therefore some would see this as unworkable. Stevenson argues that ethical language has a dynamic nature and magnetism but it could be suggested that rational ethical statements are not judged on the basis of emotional response but assessed by the nature of their argument. Mary Warnock has clearly pointed out that a claim that 'murder is wrong' is not simply about seeking approval! Such a serious ethical proposition is to be challenged, questioned, debated and deliberated with caution. If ethical statements were really just down to emotions then our moral obligations would not be consistent at all and there would be chaos.

It could be argued, however, this is one of the strengths of Stevenson's views in that it does allow Emotivism to move beyond a simple exchange of voices; it allows for persuasion, challenge and the clear expression of reasons. Why is it considered a bad thing for moral debate to be based upon gaining others' approval or avoiding their disapproval; this appears to have been most of the practice in applied ethics throughout history.

Key quote

While Stevenson granted that moral language didn't have factual or cognitive content, he argued that it had emotive meaning. Moral propositions aren't true or false, but they aren't meaningless either – moral language allows us to express emotions. Thus he could easily account for our differences regarding ethics – we have different emotions. And when we disagree, Stevenson said we have a disagreement in attitude. But reasons or arguments will not change other people's attitudes. (Messerly)

One conclusion could be that moral terms are expressions of emotions but there is more to moral language than just approval, as Stevenson has demonstrated. Alternatively, moral terms are not at all the expressions of emotion, they are objective and absolute features in the world and this would be the conclusion of ethical Naturalism. It could also be concluded, however, that moral terms may have both an emotional pole and an objective pole and that it is difficult or impossible to untangle one from the other.

Whether one of Naturalism, Intuitionism or Emotivism is superior to the other theories

One line of argument would be that Emotivism, like Naturalism, does not ask us to simply believe that morality exists/is a given (as does Intuitionism). It appeals to our scientific minds. However, rather than saying (with naturalists) that morality can be measured or observed in the natural world, Emotivism has a robust presentation of morality as a social and psychological creation.

One could suggest that it is egalitarian! All moral expressions can be explained by this theory, from 'thou shalt not kill' (as a 'boo!' to killing) to 'be nice and help everyone' ('hurrah' for nice people!). Even the seemingly emotionless moral idea that 'principles should rule over feelings' can itself be seen as a creation of an emotional society!

In addition, Emotivism saves you from pointless conversations! It advises you that you can discuss matters of fact (i.e. what happens to a foetus in the abortion process); but warns you from thinking you can have a discussion of moral values (rightness/wrongness of abortion) since these are merely expressions of emotion.

On the one hand, it could be argued that Intuitionism has the virtue of corresponding with the sense that many of us have that certain actions are just 'right and good' or 'wrong and bad'. Indeed, Emotivism reduces a moral statement to the same level as all other statements that do not come from a source that is logically verifiable; moral statements are therefore at the same level as statement used in advertising, bribes and blackmail. It becomes no more than propaganda. An intuitionist would say that this cannot possibly be the case. For Prichard, moral reasoning was far superior to general reasoning when it came to ethical decisions and that Intuitionism was a clear differentiator between ethical and non-ethical propositions. In this case, moral statements are not reduced but actually stand firm. Naturalism, on the other hand, sees itself as the solution because it argues that we can have an objective set of moral values that can be established through empirical means. Indeed, they would argue that Utilitarianism is their champion in that we can clearly see how this works in society, for example, with our political system and aspects of law.

Naturalism may be seen as superior as it encourages moral discussion and debate. After all, if Emotivism were true, there would be no point to moral discussions. This runs counter to the instincts of many who feel that these discussions are valid.

Intuitionism has the virtue of corresponding with the sense that many of us have that certain actions are just 'right and good' or 'wrong and bad' – Emotivism reduces a moral statement to the same level as all other statements that do not come from a source that is logically verifiable; moral statements are therefore at the same level as statements used in advertising, bribes and blackmail. An intuitionist would say that this can't possibly be the case!

Intuitionism and Rationalism can be seen as superior to Emotivism because if, as Emotivism demands, moral statements are nothing more than a creation of family/culture/society, why are people able to 'stand outside' of their culture/family/society and challenge them morally? Therefore, there must be a basis for morality other than human emotion.

Specification content

Whether one of Naturalism, Intuitionism or Emotivism is superior to the other theories.

Key quote

'Moral judgements express feelings or attitudes' it is said. 'What kind of feelings or attitudes?' we ask. 'Feelings or attitudes of approval' is the reply. 'What kind of approval?' we ask, perhaps remarking that approval is of many kinds. It is in answer to this question that every version of Emotivism either remains silent, or by identifying the relevant kind of approval as moral approval – that is, the type of approval expressed by a specifically moral judgement – becomes vacuously circular. (MacIntyre)

AO2 Activity

As you read through this section try to do the following:

1. Pick out the different lines of argument that are presented in the text and identify any evidence given in support.

2. For each line of argument try to evaluate whether or not you think this is strong or weak.

3. Think of any questions you may wish to raise in response to the arguments.

This Activity will help you to start thinking critically about what you read and help you to evaluate the effectiveness of different arguments and from this develop your own observations, opinions and points of view that will help with any conclusions that you make in your answers to the AO2 questions that arise.

Key questions

Is it really true that moral discussions really have no point?

If societies create morality how does one account for people in those societies challenging moral norms?

Are moral statements really at the same level as statements used in advertising and other forms of persuasion?

Are there not certain activities that are simply 'bad' or 'wrong' or, alternatively, 'good' or 'right'?

Can't we prove that there are moral absolutes by looking at common moral themes shared by societies across the world?

Key quote

The central ethical terms – 'right', 'wrong', 'good' and 'bad' – only have emotive meanings, of expressing approval or disapproval. But many moral terms ('steal', 'honesty', 'respect') have both descriptive and emotive meanings. To be told that someone is 'honest' is to learn something about them. For instance, they can't be honest while lying frequently! And whether someone lies frequently is a matter of fact. But the term 'honest' isn't just a description; it also has an emotive meaning of approval. (Lacewing)

All three theories have their strengths and their weaknesses. It could be suggested that they look at different aspects of ethics. For instance, Emotivism tends to focus on how the propositions are used (Stevenson) whereas Naturalism tends to calculate decisions based upon evidence and experience. Intuitionism is unique in that it considers the obligatory nature and how ethical awareness compels us to behave. Would there be any use trying to adopt Bradley's Hegelian dialectical methodology and synthesise through combining all aspects and seeing them as different ways of achieving the same goal?

Depending on which line of argument is accepted one could conclude that there is no real answer and that any of Naturalism (or Emotivism, or Intuitionism) is superior to the other theories. Indeed, since there is no way, ultimately, to prove what is the source of our morality, judging that one of these meta-ethical positions is superior is not possible. In addition, it could be concluded that there is no proof that there is an objective or absolute source of morality, then Naturalism or Emotivism has to be superior to the other theories.

Since there is no way, ultimately, to prove what is the source of our morality, can we make judgment over which one of these meta-ethical positions is superior?

AO2 Activity

List some conclusions that could be drawn from the AO2 reasoning from the above text; try to aim for at least three different possible conclusions. Consider each of the conclusions and collect brief evidence to support each conclusion from the AO1 and AO2 material for this topic. Select the conclusion that you think is most convincing and explain why it is so. Try to contrast this with the weakest conclusion in the list, justifying your argument with clear reasoning and evidence.

The extent to which the different meta-ethical theories encourage moral debate

Specification content

The extent to which the different meta-ethical theories encourage moral debate.

One line of argument could be that Emotivism definitely discourages moral debate, as disagreement is not about 'rightness' 'or 'wrongness' but about different emotional stances. The only debate you can have is about facts (defined via Logical Positivism), not the moral positions that are apparently based upon these facts. In other words, whilst it may appear that a debate is actually taking place it is no more than an exchange of emotions and is not a meaningful debate. Emotivism tends to reduce ethical debate to a very basic level according to this line of thinking.

In addition, it could be argued that Intuitionism discourages moral discussion as it says morality is known intuitively. There can never be an explanation of why we should act morally as we always know that we ought to. The key to Prichard's Intuitionism is that it is moral thinking that determines the outcome and not general reasoning. Therefore, we are technically encouraged not to engage too much in debate.

Nevertheless, in response to this, Prichard does consider it necessary to consider all 'claims' and 'preliminaries' before confirming (through Descartes' skeptical doubt) that our intuition was the correct recognition of duty. Since, intuitive thinking does develop and need a mature approach of thought, it could be argued that, in fact, Intuitionism according to Prichard does encourage moral debate.

For those who follow absolutist and objective approaches to ethics (i.e. Intuitionism, Divine Command Theory, etc.), there is no point of having dialogue with the natural and social sciences. This is because added insights cannot change one's moral stance. However, again, quite to the contrary, there is the whole debate about the application of Natural Moral Law, for example, the 'principle of double effect' and indeed the position taken by Revisionists such as those who are linked with Proportionalism. This whole area has been a minefield as the great depth and breadth of Roman Catholic moral theology will attest to over the past 50 years.

The various approaches that align with naturalist ethics can certainly encourage debate since they encourage observation and measurement – you can debate the validity of the observations and the measurements (i.e. is activity X causing more pleasure than pain?'). Utilitarianism is the classic example for encouraging engagement with social and political issues, both of which have an underlying ethical basis. The greatest happiness principle and the principle of universalisability are pertinent examples in relation to law and democracy. Even Bentham's Hedonic Calculus is relevant to how Utilitarianism developed through ethical debate and created Act and Rule versions.

Also, it is the whole purpose of moral debate according to Stevenson's version of Emotivism. Indeed, Emotivism explains why people do engage in debate about morality for persuasion and affirmation of attitudes. Indeed, Emotivism itself, as a theory, has encouraged much debate about morality as it is so extremely reductive! It provokes discussion about the essence of ethics as few other approaches can.

Also, if we follow Ayer's Emotivism then it does not address why many feel that whether or not the basis of 'good' and 'bad' is established, ethical debate is not just about emotions but also to do with a process of reasoning using evidence to support an argument. It can be acknowledged that the outcome of the argument may be explained as personal opinion but the argument itself is still important. Indeed, how is that any different to Prichard's Intuitionism? Therefore, to suggest that ethical debate is pointless appears 'to be throwing the baby out with the bathwater'.

Key quote

There is no particular Socratic or Dimechian or Kantian way to live your life. They don't offer ethical codes and standards by which to live your life. (Stephen Fry)

AO2 Activity

As you read through this section try to do the following:

1. Pick out the different lines of argument that are presented in the text and identify any evidence given in support.

2. For each line of argument try to evaluate whether or not you think this is strong or weak.

3. Think of any questions you may wish to raise in response to the arguments.

This Activity will help you to start thinking critically about what you read and help you to evaluate the effectiveness of different arguments and from this develop your own observations, opinions and points of view that will help with any conclusions that you make in your answers to the AO2 questions that arise.

Key questions

Is it really true that the only meaningful discussion one can have is about facts rather than values?

Does Intuitionism with its insistence on morality as a 'given' really discourage any ethical discussion?

If the social sciences can inform our ethical choices, doesn't this mean that ethics is not objective and absolute?

Is it not possible to speak of measurements of pain and pleasure in terms of the results of moral decisions?

Does Emotivism really end all discussion since it reduces morality to emotional expression?

Key quote

In matters of conscience, the law of the majority has no place. (Gandhi)

Study tip

It is vital for AO2 that you actually discuss arguments and not just explain what someone may have stated. Try to ask yourself, 'was this a fair point to make?', 'is the evidence sound enough?', 'is there anything to challenge this argument?', 'is this a strong or weak argument?' Such critical analysis will help you develop your evaluation skills.

One conclusion could be that meta-ethical approaches do encourage moral debate even though some of these encourage more debate than others. Another alternative conclusion could be that one of the meta-ethical approaches actually encourages debate: Emotivism rules it out, Intuitionism prevents any discussion on the source of morals, and in Naturalism there are only calculations and no real debate about morality. Finally, there could also be a conclusion that suggests there will always be debates regardless of these theories. Since these are 'meta' ethical approaches rather than normative ethical theories, their intention is not to focus on debating particular issues but outlining a general approach to ethics. We will still have to discuss particular moral decisions.

If we are to study ethics effectively and have meaningful moral debate, do we have to weigh up what is right in theory against what actually works in practice?

AO2 Activity

List some conclusions that could be drawn from the AO2 reasoning from the above text; try to aim for at least three different possible conclusions. Consider each of the conclusions and collect brief evidence to support each conclusion from the AO1 and AO2 material for this topic. Select the conclusion that you think is most convincing and explain why it is so. Try to contrast this with the weakest conclusion in the list, justifying your argument with clear reasoning and evidence.

AO2 Developing skills

It is now important to consider the information that has been covered in this section; however, the information in its raw form is too extensive and so has to be processed in order to meet the requirements of the examination. This can be done by practising more advanced skills associated with AO2. For assessment objective 2 (AO2), which involves 'critical analysis' and 'evaluation' skills, we are going to focus on different ways in which the skills can be demonstrated effectively, and also refer to how the performance of these skills is measured (see generic band descriptors for A2 [WJEC] AO2 or A Level [Eduqas] AO2).

▶ **Your next task is this:** Below is an argument concerning **whether Naturalism, Intuitionism or Emotivism is superior to the other theories**. You need to respond to this argument by thinking of three key questions you could ask the writer that would challenge their view and force them to defend their argument.

On the one hand, it could be argued that Intuitionism has the virtue of corresponding with the sense that many of us have that certain actions are just 'right and good' or 'wrong and bad'. Indeed, Emotivism reduces a moral statement to the same level as all other statements that do not come from a source that is logically verifiable; moral statements are therefore at the same level as statements used in advertising, bribes and blackmail. It becomes no more than propaganda. An intuitionist would say that this cannot possibly be the case. For Prichard, moral reasoning was far superior to general reasoning when it came to ethical decisions and that Intuitionism was a clear differentiator between ethical and non-ethical propositions. In this case, moral statements are not reduced but actually stand firm. Naturalism, on the other hand, sees itself as the solution because it argues that we can have an objective set of moral values that can be established through empirical means. Indeed, they would argue that Utilitarianism is their champion in that we can clearly see how this works in society, for example, with our political system and aspects of law.

When you have completed the task, refer to the band descriptors for A2 (WJEC) or A Level (Eduqas) and in particular have a look at the demands described in the higher band descriptors towards which you should be aspiring. Ask yourself:

- Is my answer a confident critical analysis and perceptive evaluation of the issue?
- Is my answer a response that successfully identifies and thoroughly addresses the issues raised by the question set?
- Does my work show an excellent standard of coherence, clarity and organisation?
- Will my work, when developed, contain thorough, sustained and clear views that are supported by extensive, detailed reasoning and/or evidence?
- Are the views of scholars/schools of thought used extensively, appropriately and in context?
- Does my answer convey a confident and perceptive analysis of the nature of any possible connections with other elements of my course?
- When used, is specialist language and vocabulary both thorough and accurate?

Key skills

Analysis involves identifying issues raised by the materials in the AO1, together with those identified in the AO2 section, and presents sustained and clear views, either of scholars or from a personal perspective ready for evaluation.

This means:

- That your answers are able to identify key areas of debate in relation to a particular issue
- That you can identify, and comment upon, the different lines of argument presented by others
- That your response comments on the overall effectiveness of each of these areas or arguments.

Evaluation involves considering the various implications of the issues raised based upon the evidence gleaned from analysis and provides an extensive detailed argument with a clear conclusion.

This means:

- That your answer weighs up the consequences of accepting or rejecting the various and different lines of argument analysed
- That your answer arrives at a conclusion through a clear process of reasoning.

This section covers AO1 content and skills

Specification content

John Finnis' development of Natural Law.

D: John Finnis' development of Natural Law

John Finnis: *Natural Law and Natural Rights*

John Finnis' *Natural Law and Natural Rights* was published in 1980. A professor of Law, Finnis' aim was to present a modern version of Natural Law that had a clear focus on human law. Aristotle had presented Natural Law from a philosophical perspective and Aquinas from a specifically religious perspective, but their audiences were either, on the whole, academic or more interested in living a life in keeping with Christian ethics.

Finnis' premise was that a universal application of the human goods identified in Natural Law 'can be secured only through the institutions of human law' since governments are in a unique position, having the potential to present the 'requirements of practical reasonableness' effectively. He writes:

> 'It is the object of this book to identify those goods, and those requirements of practical reasonableness, and thus to show how and on what conditions such institutions are justified and the ways in which they can be (and often are) defective.'

Despite receiving critical acclaim, Finnis' book also created controversy amongst some scholars, for example Stephen Buckle, who saw it as an attempt to justify Roman Catholic morality through a legal framework. Brigita White suggested that his work was heavily influenced by 'personal conceptions' deriving from his own social context. She protested that: 'His account is not grounded in social realities but in abstractions. The result is a law imbued with a morality that essentially serves the interests of the elite.'

Key quotes

From the publication in 1980 of *Natural Law and Natural Rights*, Finnis has been deservedly recognised as the leading proponent of Natural Law theory within the Anglo-American legal academy. (Greenawalt)

Finnis attempts to formulate a rational basis for moral action. His central thesis is that the act of making law is an act which can and should be guided by moral principles which are a matter of objective reasonableness. (White)

The collapse of Christianity and other religious cultures, as the matrix for contemporary legal and political orders, has posed a challenge to those who wish to affirm that there is a Natural Law. (Finnis)

Statues of the great philosophers Aristotle and Aquinas both of whom have made a significant contribution to the theory of Natural Law.

The reasons for the criticisms can be found in how Finnis understands the significance of the basic goods when applied through his principles of practical reasonableness. For example, the basic good of life incorporates the idea of family, and although it avoids the more specific but contentious term 'procreation', it is clear from other writings of Finnis, precisely what the notion of family involves. In an academic paper entitled *Law, Morality and Sexual Orientation* Finnis states: 'The commitment of a man and a woman to each other in the sexual union of marriage is intrinsically good and reasonable, and is incompatible with sexual relations outside marriage.' Therefore, Finnis rejects homosexual acts as intrinsically unreasonable and non-marital, a view that does not sit well with many people today and many have focused on this to criticise Finnis. Nonetheless, this must not be taken out of context for several reasons:

(1) Finnis is adamant that there should be no discrimination, nor should laws encroach upon **personal freedom** of consenting adults. Moral evil and sin are not necessarily the same as a crime.

(2) Although Finnis does argue that homosexual activity is always a moral evil, it should be noted that the word 'evil' is often misunderstood by those beyond the parameters of Roman Catholic theology. For Finnis, the term clearly refers to an act that is not in line with Natural Law and threatens a 'fundamental human good'.

(3) That being said, it must also be noted that this is also the case for **any form** of non-unitive, non-marital sexual activity.

(4) Finnis, then, presents the traditional Roman Catholic teaching that marital union between man and woman for the purpose of procreation as the ideal basis, and **only** notion, of what the basic good of family involves as integral to the good of life: as Finnis states, 'desire and decision is a pursuit of the good of life, in this case life-in-its-transmission'.

Despite criticisms, the intended universal nature of Finnis' Natural Law means that the basic goods can be accessible for all societies. Natural Law transcends social, political, racial, gender and religious boundaries. Finnis' system has no overall metaphysical or religious governance, unlike Aquinas' Beatific Vision, but this does not mean that religion has no place in his Natural Law; it is simply that the idea of what the word religion means takes on a more universally embracing definition. Finnis clarifies this:

> 'The fact that Natural Law can be understood, assented to, applied, and reflectively analysed without adverting to the question of the existence of God does not of itself entail either (i) that no further explanation is required for the fact that there are objective standards of good and bad and principles of reasonableness (right and wrong), or (ii) that no such further explanation is available, or (iii) that the existence and nature of God is not that explanation.'

Instead, Finnis' attempts to set out a Natural Law for society that is grounded in **jurisprudence**, that is, a legal framework. The way to do this is not by establishing moral laws primarily, as for Finnis these are already made known to us, but by creating a legal system within which the moral principles can operate. There is no doubt that Finnis is religious, and as a Roman Catholic himself, his moral grounding is revealed when he himself applies Natural Law to moral

Key term

Jurisprudence: the philosophy of law as presented by a normative legal system issues. However, such matters are for Finnis quite incidental to the application of Natural Law at the level of human jurisprudence. At the same time, however, Finnis' presentation of Natural Law does demonstrate clearly that there is a genuine central case for religion which is both revealed through Natural Law and compatible with sound philosophy.

quickfire

2.1 What criticism did Stephen Buckle make about John Finnis' form of Natural Law?

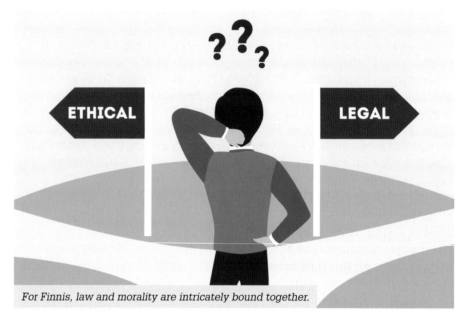

For Finnis, law and morality are intricately bound together.

The relationship between Finnis' Natural Law theory and the theories of Plato, Aristotle and Aquinas

The foundation of Finnis' Natural Law is grounded in earlier ideas of Plato, Aristotle and Aquinas. Finnis avoids Aquinas' divine and eternal levels of law and the teleological goal of the Beatific Vision. Instead Finnis returns to the teleological premise of Aristotle, that the aim of the good life is to 'flourish' or achieve eudaimonia. Finnis understands the term eudaimonia as a complete 'well-being' of the person in society. For Finnis, the purpose of a Natural Law that determines human laws is to create a state of social well-being and to inform and guide everyone towards this for the common good. Human law is for the benefit of each and every citizen. Finnis argues that the role of ethics is to answer the question 'what are the basic aspects of my well-being?'

quickfire

2.2 What does Finnis ground his framework for society in?

He acknowledges his debt to Plato, Aristotle and Aquinas in his introduction and it is clear to see the elements from each in his theory of Natural Law. Indeed, one can see the Socratic search for justice found in Plato's *Republic* and also the political ideology of Plato in justifying the Law. The Law for Finnis is the application of Natural Law that is manifest in the blueprint of legislation that supports human jurisdiction and judicial law and serves to ensure justice for the common good of all.

quickfire

2.3 What conclusion did Finnis reach about the relationship between morality and law?

Finnis 'develops', or, strictly speaking, revisits Natural Law with a heavy dependence upon the philosophical approach of Aristotle as opposed to the theology of Aquinas and yet, crucially, reformulates Aquinas' primary precepts into 'basic goods' that have a more contemporary feel and relevance.

Key quote

Near the very beginning of the tradition of theorising about natural right, we find Aristotle quite explicit that ethics can only be usefully discussed with experienced and mature people, and that age is a necessary but not a sufficient condition for the required maturity. (Finnis)

Finnis' presentation of Natural Law assumes three things:

(1) There are 'goods' that are self-evident truths. Finnis regards the basic goods as the 'pre-moral principles of practical reasonableness'. The basic goods are known through reason but not from speculation, that is, a kind of 'working them out'. They are just there to be known. The basic goods are accessible to all but underived, self-evident and indemonstrable. Finnis writes: 'They are not inferred or derived from anything.' They are similar to Aristotle's concept of philosophical wisdom (**sophia** Greek, σοφία).

(2) The process of establishing Natural Law and identifying what 'should be' or how we 'ought to act' was not what is in accordance with human nature, but what is ***in accordance with reason***. When we identify the goods, we are using reason but in a different (but ***not*** inferior) way from history, science or metaphysics. Finnis writes, 'When discerning what is good, to be pursued, intelligence is operating in a different way, yielding a different logic, from when it is discerning what is the case (historically, scientifically, or metaphysically); but there is no good reason for asserting that the latter operations of intelligence are more rational than the former.' This process of practical reasoning is central to Finnis' understanding of Natural Law.

(3) Practical (ethical) reasoning is the process identified by the requirements of practical reasonableness and similar to Aristotle's practical wisdom (**phronesis** Greek φρόνησις). Practical wisdom, for Aristotle, was the applied wisdom of knowing how to behave and act for the best but not everyone is mature enough, not only restricted by age, but also by virtue of deficient intellect. Finnis agrees and argues that the 'well-informed, etc., simply are better-off (other things being equal) than someone who is muddled, deluded, and ignorant... Knowledge is better than ignorance.' This forms the basis of Finnis' crucial notion of practical, or ethical, reasoning.

The personification of wisdom (Sophia)

Key quotes

… Aquinas asserts as plainly as possible that the first principles of Natural Law, which specify the basic forms of good and evil and which can be adequately grasped by anyone of the age of reason (and not just by metaphysicians), are per se nota (self-evident) and indemonstrable. They are not inferred from speculative principles. They are not inferred from facts. (**Finnis**)

Now it is thought to be the mark of a man of practical wisdom to be able to deliberate well about what is good and expedient for himself, not in some particular respect, e.g. about what sorts of thing conduce to health or to strength, but about what sorts of thing conduce to the good life in general. (**Aristotle**)

Key terms

Phronesis: practical wisdom

Sophia: philosophical wisdom

quickfire

2.4 According to Finnis, what is the starting point for Ethics?

quickfire

2.5 Name two types of wisdom that Aristotle made reference to.

Specification content

Distinction between theoretical and practical reason.

Key quotes

Practical philosophy is a discipline and critical reflection on the goods that can be realised in human action and the requirements of practical reasonableness. (Finnis)

This is a book about Natural Law. It expounds or sets out a theory of Natural Law, but is not about that theory. Nor is it about other theories. It refers to other theories only to illuminate the theory expounded here, or to explain why some truths about Natural Law have at various times and in various ways been overlooked or obscured. (Finnis)

Now each man judges well the things he knows, and of these he is a good judge. And so the man who has been educated in a subject is a good judge of that subject, and the man who has received an all-round education is a good judge in general. (Aristotle, *Nichomachean Ethics*)

Practical wisdom, then, must be a reasoned and true state of capacity to act with regard to human goods. (Aristotle, *Nichomachean Ethics*)

Reasoning is a process not a concept.

quickfire

2.6 What does Finnis mean by theoretical reasoning?

The distinction between theoretical and practical reason

We have seen that the entire exposition of Finnis' Natural Law rests upon an understanding of an ethical reasoning that is very specific. For Finnis, it is imperative that this particular process of reasoning, known as practical reasoning, is clearly differentiated as distinct from theoretical or speculative reasoning. This distinction is so important for Finnis that is takes up much of the first part of Finnis' book before discussion of the basic goods and the requirements of practical reasonableness.

Finnis argues that past interpretations of Natural Law have ascribed to Aquinas and Aristotle an inadequate understanding of the role of theoretical reasoning and have failed to distinguish between theoretical reasoning and practical reasoning. He also argues that ethical methodologies of the past have also wrongly conflated the two types of reasoning.

The great advantage and strength of Finnis' exposition and sharp distinction between the two types of reasoning are that it ensures two things:

(1) That no form of Naturalism can be ascribed to Natural Law, so it is not subject to the Naturalistic Fallacy.

(2) That, at the meta-ethical level, Ayer's observations – made by theoretical, speculative reasoning – are rejected and Natural Law reasoning is possible.

Aristotle distinguished between philosophical wisdom (roughly equating to Finnis' basic good of knowledge) and practical wisdom (roughly equating to Finnis' practical reasonableness). So we can see that Finnis follows Aristotle's understanding of this distinction but he inter-weaves this into his overall framework of the basic goods.

Practical reasonableness is a basic good that is crucial for ethical philosophy and involves two things:

(1) An **awareness** of the basic goods together with the collected treasury of distilled knowledge from experience.

(2) The rational **ability to apply** such knowledge through practical reasoning to real life in the best way possible to achieve the eudaimonic goal of overall well-being.

Finnis' basic goods and requirements of practical reasonableness are philosophical **concepts** and all fall within the discipline of practical reasoning.

Practical reason, then, is what we would call normative reasoning. Typically, we have a set of different options for potential action and we want to discover what we 'ought' to do. Practical reasoning is more person oriented. The process of practical reasoning is, in relationship to Finnis' concept of practical reasonableness, the actual **application** of practical reasonableness to a moral issue in working out what we ought to do. Practical reasoning reveals, through the application of the principles of practical reasonableness, the obligatory force of the self-evident basic goods.

In contrast, theoretical reason is to do with what Finnis calls knowledge that is sought out instrumentally in the pursuit of some objective (i.e. to find out where you can find the cheapest item between supermarkets) and not the knowledge associated with the basic good. Theoretical reason deals with what we have in front of us and tries to make sense of questions of explanation and prediction, very much like scientific analysis and attempts to determine what is going to happen. It is concerned with matters of fact and explanation. It incorporates both the empirical and the *a priori* in matters of speculation (even theoretical reasoning is based upon self-evident principles at times, such as mathematical logic but they are the self-evident truths of theoretical reasoning and not practical reasoning).

This distinction can seem very confusing because a number of ethical theories tend to merge theoretical and practical reasoning. In such instances, theoretical reasoning includes both an explanation of events as they are now or predictions of what will happen **and** helping to decide how we should act. For instance, Utilitarianism takes the view that moral propositions can be induced from what is the case (theoretical reasoning). However, it also has an element of practical reasoning in that its starting point involves associating 'good' with pleasure or happiness.

Finnis' Natural Law has a much more normative basis of practical reasoning. This means it is not guided by what we experience before us, or an analysis of what our world can tell us, but from a more reflective base. It firstly identifies the basic goods that are self-evident. These basic goods are not dependent on empirical analysis or rational argument (theoretical reasoning), but at the same time they are accessed through the process of practical reasoning.

Although the confusion began a long time before Hume (later developed by Moore's Naturalistic Fallacy), Finnis uses Hume as a point of departure in clarifying the difference between theoretical reasoning and practical reasoning.

- For Finnis, Hume's point that moral obligations (practical reasoning) cannot be deduced from empirical observations (a form of theoretical reasoning) is consistent with Natural Law and that Aristotle and Aquinas would agree. Natural Law certainly does not derive 'ought' from 'is'.

- Hume, according to Finnis, was not arguing that an interpretation of what is beneficial, advantageous or good cannot be drawn from empirical observations – indeed Utilitarianism does this – but Hume saw a logical error in the unfounded leap in reasoning that suggests we 'ought' to pursue the goods. This is where alleged naturalistic theories such as Utilitarianism fail. Theoretical reasoning cannot induce obligation; theoretical reasoning merely directs towards the speculative of what will happen if …

- Also incorrect is the naturalistic assumption that Natural Law derives its sense of ethical duty from an observation of the nature of a human being or the empirical world. This has often been an assumed understanding by critics of Natural Law but this does not make the distinction between theoretical and practical reasoning.

- Therefore, Natural Law overcomes the Naturalistic Fallacy because the origin of moral duty is grounded in practical reasoning as demonstrated by the application of the self-evident basic goods.

- Practical reasoning is therefore something quite different from theoretical reasoning. Practical reasoning is based upon self-evident ethical principles and deals with the normative, that is, 'what am I obliged to do to be moral?'

- The key difference between theoretical reasoning and practical reasoning is that theoretical reasoning does not and cannot deal with ethical decisions of obligation.

- For Finnis, the practical reasoning of Natural Law is the realm of ethical debate: 'the principles of Natural Law **explain the obligatory force** (in the fullest sense of 'obligation') of positive laws, even when those laws cannot be deduced from those principles'.

- Finnis also argues that the principles of the basic goods would 'hold good' even if some people are unaware of them. He uses the example of modern accounting principles that have always been valid even when unknown or misunderstood, for example, within medieval banking!

Key quotes

Theoretical reason tries to assess the way things are. Practical reason decides how the world should be and what individuals should do. A theoretical proposition is good if it conforms to reality, while a practical proposition has more complicated and debatable standards. **(Stanford)**

Theoretical reason aims at knowledge of how things are, and its activity terminates in belief about how things are. Practical reason aims at realising the good, and its activity terminates in action rather than belief. **(Lamont)**

Practical reason … is thus concerned not with matters of fact and their explanation, but with matters of value, of what it would be desirable to do. In practical reasoning agents attempt to assess and weigh their reasons for action, the considerations that speak for and against alternative courses of action that are open to them. **(Stanford)**

quickfire

2.7 What does Finnis mean by practical reasoning?

Exam tip

To help you remember all the different lists try to use flash cards and use a practical example for each one – you could even draw an image of the example to help you remember and associate it with a certain teaching.

Exam tip

Make sure that you have a clear awareness of the distinction between Finnis' basic forms of good and Aquinas' primary precepts.

AO1 Activity

After reading through each of the key ways in which Finnis developed Aquinas and Aristotle, close the book and write down some key phrases and/or words relating to each philosopher and then try linking them.

Specification content

Development of the seven basic human goods (life, knowledge, friendship, play, aesthetic experience, practical reasonableness and religion).

Key quote

More important than the precise number and description of these values is the sense in which each is basic. First, each is equally self-evidently a form of good. Secondly, none can be analytically reduced to being merely an aspect of any of the others, or to being merely instrumental in the pursuit of any of the others. Thirdly, each one, when we focus on it, can reasonably be regarded as the most important. Hence, there is no objective hierarchy amongst them. (Finnis)

quickfire

2.8 What three things did Finnis insist regarding his seven basic goods?

Development of the seven basic human goods

Finnis' identification of seven basic goods is his appeal to philosophical wisdom. Finnis sees the identification of those goods as 'basic' in that they should be the common denominators of pro-eudaimonic truth. Finnis insists on three things:

(1) They are self-evident.

(2) They are not overlapping or a part of another basic good.

(3) They are all equally important and there is no inherent hierarchy.

However, as it is in life, depending upon one's focus, one basic good may be more relevant to one situation, or more in focus, than another basic good; however, this does not reflect priority or significance overall, it merely reflects that we are shifting from one situation to another, as Finnis puts it so aptly, 'one by one right round the circle of basic values that constitute the horizon of our opportunities'. Conversely, when one particular basic good is more in focus this does not imply that the others are mere frivolity or superficial; they still retain their implicit value by the very nature of being a potential focus elsewhere.

In conclusion Finnis writes:

'Each is fundamental. None is more fundamental than any of the others, for each can reasonably be focused upon, and each, when focused upon, claims a priority of value. Hence there is no objective priority of value amongst them.'

Finnis lists his seven basic goods as:

- Life
- Knowledge
- Friendship
- Play
- Aesthetic experience
- Practical reasonableness
- Religion

Finnis admits that beyond his seven basic goods there are other 'countless objectives and forms of good' and also 'combinations of ways of pursuing ... and realising ... one of the seven basic forms of good, or some combination of them'. In other words, there are many outworkings of the basic goods such as courage, generosity, moderation, gentleness but that these qualities (virtues), in themselves, are not identical with the basic goods, but simply aspects of these goods by different people and at different time and in different places.

The pursuit of the basic goods is not teleological either; it is seen as a 'participation' in that particular basic good by way of the commitments, projects and actions undertaken. Hence, knowledge is not pursued as an end but participated in for its own good. Behaviour and courses of action that an individual decides upon that encourage and nurture a participation in the basic goods are, for Finnis, 'the first principles of Natural Law' simply because 'they lay down for us the outlines of everything one could reasonably want to do, to have, and to be'.

Life

Finnis defines life as corresponding to Aquinas' precept of self-preservation but interprets this more broadly as signifying 'every aspect of the vitality (vita, life) which puts a human being in good shape for self-determination'. Finnis lists several examples:

- Bodily health
- Mental health
- Freedom from the pain of organic malfunctioning or injury
- Personal survival instincts when in trouble, e.g. when drowning
- All services and laws that work towards this (e.g. medicine, road safety, famine relief and resuscitation of suicides, etc.)
- The act of procreation as 'an intelligently grasped form of good' (distinct from bearing, cherishing and educating a child) and as 'a pursuit of the good of life, in this case life-in-its-transmission'.

Although procreation may be included in this category Finnis is careful to separate out the idea from what he refers to as, a 'single anthropological cluster of sexuality, mating, and family life'.

Bodily health – an example of Finnis' definition of life

Mental health – an example of Finnis' definition of life

Knowledge

Finnis distinguishes between two types of knowledge: (1) knowledge that is sought out because it is good in itself; and (2) knowledge that is sought out instrumentally in the pursuit of some objective. The first type is a basic good, and, being a basic good, is self-evident.

For example, if I want to discover which supermarket sells an item I require at the lowest price, I am pursing knowledge, not in itself, but in relation to an end. This is the second type of knowledge and not a basic good. The basic good that Finnis is talking about is the general concept of aiming to seek out, and reveal, the truth of the matter at all times and in all things. In short, it is the ability to see things clearly and as 'they really are'. It is the type of knowledge that betters ourselves because we are better educated to establish a general awareness of what 'is' the case. Finnis refers to this type of knowledge as an 'achievement-word'; it is nothing to do with belief. Therefore, this type of knowledge is a basic good that constantly aims for the truth.

quickfire

2.9 List the seven basic goods.

Key quotes

The basic practical principle that knowledge is good need hardly ever be formulated as the premise for anyone's actual practical reasoning. (Finnis)

Such a course of reflection is, in a way, an attempt to understand one's own character, or nature. The attempt thus parallels attempts made, in quite another way, by those anthropologists and psychologists who ask (in effect) whether there is a human nature and what are its characteristics. (Finnis)

A first basic value, corresponding to the drive for self-preservation, is the value of life. The term 'life' here signifies every aspect of the vitality (vita, life) which puts a human being in good shape for self-determination. (Finnis)

Now 'knowledge', unlike 'belief', is an achievement-word ... we want the truth when we want the judgments in which we affirm or deny propositions to be true judgments. (Finnis)

Finnis identifies two types of knowledge

Key quotes

The principle that truth is worth pursuing, knowledge is worth having, is thus an underived principle. Neither its intelligibility nor its force rests on any further principle. **(Finnis)**

The third basic aspect of human well-being is play ... each one of us can see the point of engaging in performances which have no point beyond the performance itself, enjoyed for its own sake. **(Finnis)**

Key term

Aesthetic: pleasing to the eye

Play covers a variety of activities.

Finnis makes seven observations about knowledge (truth):

(1) Valuing knowledge does not imply that every investigation is equal.

(2) The value of knowledge is not the same for every person.

(3) Knowledge has no priority of value between one person and another.

(4) It is not the only good nor is 'knowledge is to be pursued by everybody, at all times, in all circumstances'.

(5) Knowledge is not the same as moral obligation –the reflective analysis of practical reasonableness determines morality.

(6) Knowledge is an intrinsic good desirable for its own sake.

(7) Knowledge helps guide human activity by making it intelligible.

Finally, it is knowledge that sets us on our way into practical reasonableness, that is, applying this basic good, or 'value' as Finnis calls it, to the different approaches that we have by making it an underpinning principle.

Play

Finnis sees 'play' as a vital aspect of life that is easily overlooked by moral philosophers. He points out that 'an anthropologist will not fail to observe this large and irreducible element in human culture'. But what is meant by 'play'? Finnis' definition is: 'engaging in performances which have no point beyond the performance itself, enjoyed for its own sake'. This does not mean that they are pointless but simply that they are a self-contained unit of human activity with its own intrinsic value. Play covers many activities in life with different elements of satisfaction, taking many different forms, for example:

- Individual play
- Social play
- Intellectual play
- Physical play
- Play that is strenuous
- Play that relaxes
- Formal play
- Informal play
- Organised and highly structured play
- Play that is ad hoc and spontaneous.

Play incorporates all types of hobbies, interests, arts and skills performed for their own sake. Although play is in itself a self-contained unit, it can be part of any human activity, for example, a sense of humour whilst working. However, play is always 'analytically distinguishable' in that it can be clearly identified and also differentiated from more serious aspects of life.

Aesthetic experience

Finnis acknowledges that this is closely related to play in that play can initiate **aesthetic** experience but it is 'not an indispensable element of play'. Many other things can also initiate an aesthetic experience such as natural features. The important distinction is that play originates with one's own actions whereas aesthetic experience can be beyond this by simple appreciation of an object of art form, natural beauty and entails an inner experience of this. Likewise, one would appreciate theatre and although there is an element of play (leisure) for oneself, the participation and applause of an audience appreciate the artful beauty of the performance of others and the play, musical, genre of talent or opera in itself.

Painting is a form of play but can end with an aesthetic experience (art)!

Friendship (sociability)

The shortest description of Finnis' basic goods can be found in 'friendship'. For Finnis, friendship is something beyond simple sociability. As human beings we have to interact with each other and communicate on a daily basis. Obviously, we have learned, on the whole, to interact sociably and peacefully. Where there are conflicts it is always the aim to resolve these. However, this is not friendship. Sometimes the collaboration between one person and another is simply to realise an end determined by one's own need. It is not narrowly other-regarding, but more a mutual cooperation so that each person is satisfied.

Following Aristotle, Finnis also sees friendship is the flourishment, or 'flowering' as he puts it, of the strongest form of sociability. In other words, whilst sociable collaboration for self-interest is one end of the spectrum, friendship is at the other end. Friendship is all about 'acting for the sake of one's friend's purposes, one's friend's well-being', according to Finnis.

> 'There is the value of that sociability which in its weakest form is realised by a minimum of peace and harmony amongst persons, and which ranges through the forms of human community to its strongest form in the flowering of full friendship.'

Some of the collaboration between one person and another is no more than instrumental to the realisation by each of his or her own individual purposes.

Practical reasonableness

If we compare the two quotes below, one from Aristotle's *Nichomachean Ethics* and the other from Finnis' book *Natural Law and Natural Rights*, we can see that the concept of practical reasonableness is in fact the same as Aristotle's concept of practical wisdom (phronesis) as we have noted from the start.

> 'Now it is thought to be the mark of a man of practical wisdom to be able to deliberate well about what is good and expedient for himself, not in some particular respect, e.g. about what sorts of thing conduce to health or to strength, but about what sorts of thing conduce to the good life in general.' (Aristotle, *Nichomachean Ethics*).

quickfire

2.11 What is the difference between play and an aesthetic experience?

Friendship – a basic good

Wisdom is more than just knowledge.

quickfire

2.12 In what way is practical reasonableness more than just distilling knowledge?

Key quotes

Knowledge of contingent facts that are useful to living well is required in Aristotle's practical wisdom. For Aristotle, practical wisdom requires knowing, in general, how to live well. (Stanford)

For amongst the basic forms of good that we have no good reason to leave out of account is the good of practical reasonableness, which is participated in precisely by shaping one's participation in the other basic goods, by guiding one's commitments, one's selection of projects, and what one does in carrying them out. (Finnis)

'There is the basic good of being able to bring one's own intelligence to bear effectively (in practical reasoning that issues in action) on the problems of choosing one's actions and lifestyle and shaping one's own character.' (Finnis)

To be 'wise' is usually associated with a high quality of knowledge, but the kind of knowledge that is not abstract, or one that you may learn from a text book. The high quality of knowledge that wisdom entails is one supported by experiences, but not just the basic experiences themselves. Wisdom incorporates the outcomes and deliberations of behaviour in life that have been duly assessed, filtered and purified to create a benchmark of anticipation for the potential outworkings of the contingent facts that face us. It is like a mature treasury of advice and guidance.

One usually associates wisdom with age, as both Aristotle and Finnis argue, but they also agree that this is not necessarily so. The essence of wisdom, however, is its practical ability to make sound decisions. Reasonableness is a word that suggests fairness, soberness, soundness, trustworthiness, moderation, logical, sensible, practical, decent and all these synonyms can be found in any dictionary. Practical reasonableness is not just being aware of the treasury of distilled knowledge but it is also simultaneously includes the ability to exercise that knowledge effectively. Aristotle compared philosophical wisdom (sophia) to health and practical wisdom (phronesis) to medicine.

This is absolutely crucial for Finnis and it is why, in itself, practical reasonableness is a basic good and the framework for the nine requirements of practical reason, namely, that 'The good of practical reasonableness structures our pursuit of goods'. Practical reasonableness is the key to the healthy and balanced management and application of the basic goods in the real world.

The process by which one develops practical reasonableness and cultivates soundness of behaviour and character is to 'bring an intelligent and reasonable order into one's own actions and habits and practical attitudes' according to Finnis. This has two aspects:

(1) Internal control that is not biased, emotional or the product of drugs or indoctrination but that is in line with 'the harmony of an inner peace of mind' that is not passive.

(2) External, application of 'genuine realisations of one's own freely ordered evaluations, preferences, hopes, and self-determination'.

Religion

The final basic good identified by Finnis is religion. This is important for Finnis himself, as his main aim is to demonstrate that as a system, Natural Law works perfectly well and is philosophically sound when grounded in religion. Finnis argues that the term 'religion' is lame in defining this basic good because it is more to do with awareness of some cosmic order that is 'other' and that is part of being human.

Therefore, the other side of the coin is that Finnis' Natural Law can also work perfectly well in a non-religious context providing there is an underlying notion of a cosmic order in relation to ultimate questions. Finnis' Natural Law, although justifiably grounded in religion, is then opened up for all to access, even non-believers. It is possible in theory, therefore, for Finnis' Natural Law to be considered as a secular philosophy.

The term 'religion' can equate to 'an intelligent grasp of worthwhile forms' that 'is itself somehow subordinate to something which makes that human freedom, human intelligence, and human mastery possible'. What is vital for Finnis is that 'to have thought reasonably about these questions of the origins of cosmic order and of human freedom and reason – whatever the answer to those questions turns out to be, and even if the answers have to be agnostic or negative'.

The term religion is to do with questions that arise out of the appreciation of the basic goods as a means to an end that bring an 'order that is to be brought into one's character and activity through inner integrity and outer authenticity'. Two questions are significant:

(i) How does this ordering found in the mortality of a human being relate to the lasting order of the cosmos?

(ii) Is human freedom subordinate to something that makes this freedom possible, something that is 'sovereign' overall?

The traditional answer to these questions, namely a relationship between humanity and the divine, can be accepted, doubted or rejected. This does not matter. The answers are not important; it is the questions that are **significant in themselves** without any definitive answers. The fact these are **the** key questions demonstrates for Finnis a 'transcendent origin of the universal order-of-things and of human freedom and reason'.

However, it is this 'sense of "responsibility", in choosing what one is to be and do', recognising and thinking about an irreducibly distinct form of order, that which we term as 'religious'.

Key quotes

But is it reasonable to deny that it is, at any rate, peculiarly important to have thought reasonably and (where possible) correctly about these questions of the origins of cosmic order and of human freedom and reason … even if the answers have to be agnostic or negative? **(Finnis)**

Although in modern times, belief in Natural Law is strongly correlated to belief in God … Natural Law theorists have consistently asserted that individuals can discover the Natural Law, independent of their particular religious beliefs. **(Greenawalt)**

Buddhist mandala (a symbol of cosmic order); Finnis uses the word 'religion' in the sense of awareness of some cosmic order.

quickfire

2.13 Why is the basic good of 'religion' a confusing description?

AO1 Activity

Create a mind map that summarises facts about (a) Finnis' basic goods and (b) the principles of practical reasonableness, in relation to his version of Natural Law. This helps with the ability to select and present the key, relevant features of the material you have read.

Specification content

Nine Requirements of Practical Reason (view life as a whole, no arbitrary preference amongst values, basic goods apply equally to all, do not become obsessed with a particular project, use effort to improve, plan your actions to do the most good, never harm a basic good, foster common good in the community and act in your own conscience and authority); the common good and the need for authority.

Key quotes

Moral virtue comes about as a result of habit, whence also its name (ethike) is one that is formed by a slight variation from the word ethos (habit). (**Aristotle, Nichomachean Ethics**)

It is so wonderful to be a rational animal, there is a reason for everything that one does … (**Franklin**)

quickfire

2.14 How many principles did Finnis identify that are grounded in the morality found in the basic goods?

The Nine Requirements of Practical Reason

We have already defined clearly what Finnis means by practical reasoning. Practical reason (practical reasoning or, as Finnis terms it, 'practical reasonableness') is the process through which there is a mutual collaboration of the basic goods with wisdom and an application of these goods to the ethical life to achieve a state of social well-being and, through law, to inform and guide everyone towards this for the common good. From insight into the basic goods what we 'ought' to do, our moral obligations, is rationally applied to life and from this our laws evolve. Finnis suggests that to 'participate thoroughly in any basic value calls for skill'. The skill of practical reasoning demands that the good of practical reasonableness is participated in 'precisely by shaping one's participation in the other basic goods, by guiding one's commitments, one's selection of projects, and what one does in carrying them out' according to Finnis. There are nine requirements of practical reasonableness in shaping and structuring such participation. Finnis points out that similar to the basic goods, each requirement is 'fundamental, underived, irreducible' and that 'each of these requirements concerns what one must do, or think, or be if one is to participate in the basic value of practical reasonableness'.

(1) The WJEC/Eduqas Specification lists Finnis' nine requirements. With the exception of [2], the Specification list is not Finnis' actual statements but rather one interpretation of them. There are some subtle differences. To help teachers and students, this table below matches up Finnis' actual wording used in his book to those phrases found in the Specification.

(2) The headings in the book are from the Specification but have Finnis' words in brackets.

Specification headings	Finnis' headings
[1] View life as a whole	[1] A coherent plan of life
[2] No arbitrary preferences amongst values	[2] No arbitrary preferences amongst values
[3] Basic goods apply equally to all	[3] No arbitrary preferences amongst persons
[4] Do not become obsessed with a particular project	[4] Detachment
[5] Use effort to improve	[5] Commitment
[6] Plan your actions to do the most good	[6] The (limited) relevance of consequences: efficiency within reason
[7] Never harm a basic good	[7] Respect for every basic value in every act
[8] Foster common good in the community	[8] The requirements of the common good
[9] Act in your own conscience and authority	[9] Following one's conscience

Key quote

For amongst the basic forms of good that we have no good reason to leave out of account is the good of practical reasonableness, which is participated in precisely by shaping one's participation in the other basic goods, by guiding one's commitments, one's selection of projects, and what one does in carrying them out. (**Finnis**)

Finnis' list of requirements is 'structured' by practical reasonableness. The methodology of practical reasonableness is the methodology of what we call 'ethics'. Finnis is simply stating that to participate in ethics well one has to be structured by the requirements that make ethics 'work'.

Finnis is precise in his choice of words. His requirement is not talking about achieving the greatest good for all or just arbitrarily doing good actions. He refers to the phronimos of Aristotle. We have seen that the term phronesis (Greek φρόνησις) refers to practical wisdom; for Aristotle the phronimos was the ethical expert. Likewise, for Aquinas, prudentia is the noun that describes the person who has wisdom, good sense and discretion; namely, the virtue of prudence that brings with it impeccable judgment. Finnis writes: 'Someone who lives up to these requirements is thus Aristotle's phronimos and has Aquinas' prudentia; they are requirements of reasonableness or practical wisdom, and to fail to live up to them is irrational'.

Finnis also points out that the structure of practical reasonableness enables participation in 'all the (other) basic aspects of human well-being'. For Finnis, this amounts to what he calls 'fullness of well-being', that is, the maximum or full potential of life.

(1) View life as a whole ('A coherent plan of life')

Finnis' requirement of practical reasonableness here is all to do with focus and perspective. When it is established what is wanted from life, namely, to live life in accordance with the pursuit of the basic goods, then according to Finnis, only if 'one intelligently directs, focuses, and controls one's urges, inclinations, and impulses', can this be achieved.

Finnis compares this to a general commitment towards this goal rather than a detailed 'blueprint' because life throws up 'all manner of unforeseeable contingencies'. On the whole, it is not just about how we respond to the particulars of life but it is to do with our vision for what our lives should be like and what our priorities are. Sometimes we need to step back to see our progress in life and reflect on the bigger picture. This is the 'coherence' Finnis is speaking of; to have the general game plan of realising the basic goods and harmonising our personal commitments with them.

Key quote

Implicitly or explicitly one must have a harmonious set of purposes and orientations, not as the 'plans' or 'blueprints' of a pipe-dream, but as effective commitments. (Finnis)

Finnis quotes Ecclesiasticus, 'in whatever you do remember your last days' (7:36) with the purpose of not being morbid and thinking about one's death but rather establishing the 'proper perspective for choosing how to live one's present life'. Finnis also gives an example of misdirected goals and refers to Jesus' parable of the Rich Fool (Luke 12:13–20) who makes wealth his goal in life only for it to be taken in an instant when his life is taken that night.

F. Scott Fitzgerald's fictional character Jay Gatsby played by Leonardo DiCaprio.

Key quote

Each of these requirements concerns what one must do, or think, or be if one is to participate in the basic value of practical reasonableness. (Finnis)

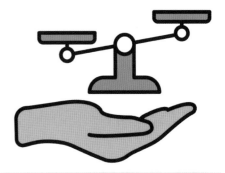

The good of practical reasonableness structures our pursuit of goods.

quickfire

2.15 What two things are necessary to achieve the point of Finnis' theory (i.e. eudaimonia – well-being)?

Key quotes

It is unreasonable to live merely from moment to moment, following immediate cravings, or just drifting. (Finnis)

Even a happy life cannot be without a measure of darkness, and the word happy would lose its meaning if it were not balanced by sadness. It is far better to take things as they come along with patience and equanimity. (Carl Jung)

Life is much more successfully looked at from a single window. (F. Scott Fitzgerald, *The Great Gatsby*)

Key quote

Gatsby believed in the green light, the orgastic future that year by year recedes before us. It eluded us then, but that's no matter – tomorrow we will run faster, stretch out our arms farther. (F. Scott Fitzgerald, *The Great Gatsby*)

The pursuit of wealth for its own sake does not bring about 'good'.

Key quote

Any commitment to a coherent plan of life is going to involve some degree of concentration on one or some of the basic forms of good, at the expense, temporarily or permanently, of other forms of good. (Finnis)

The Golden Rule of Christianity

(2) No arbitrary preferences amongst values

Finnis' next requirement is that there must be no 'leaving out of account, or arbitrary discounting or exaggeration', of the basic goods. It has already been stated that there is no priority amongst the goods as all are equally important; however, they may not have equal emphasis in one person's life compared to another. That is, one should ensure that as much balance is maintained in life between goods **as far as is possible**. However, this is **not** about making sure that certain goods are prioritised over others; this is just a misunderstanding of Finnis. Indeed, 'no arbitrary preferences' means exactly the opposite and Finnis makes it explicitly clear that all goods work together collectively and do not compete in any hierarchical structure. This requirement is all to do with accepting that sometimes in life, depending upon who we are, we give emphasis to a certain good or goods.

Therefore, Finnis is realistic with this requirement in that he is well aware that our lives are all different and that individually this can only make sense if we accept that such an overall balance is based upon 'one's assessment of one's capacities, circumstances, and even of one's tastes'. This will inevitably involve emphasis on some goods rather than others. This emphasis, however, needs to be on 'the basic forms of human excellence' and not on 'merely derivative and supporting or instrumental goods as wealth'. In other words, the shift of emphasis from one good must not be in favour of a non-good such as pursuit of wealth for its own sake (greed), or as with Fitzgerald's *The Great Gatsby*, the pursuit of wealth as a delusion of achieving happiness and love. Finnis refers to John Rawls, an American moral and political philosopher, who described such an error as the 'thin theory of the good'.

Finnis' own example in his book is a tongue-in-cheek observation about scholars: 'Some scholars may have little taste or capacity for friendship, and may feel that life for them would have no savour if they were prevented from pursuing their commitment to knowledge.' In other words, scholars (or teachers!) may not have many friends, or value friendship as much as the pursuit of knowledge, yet at the same time they should not make the mistake of denying that friendship is good in itself. Finnis' friends, then, are clearly in proportion to his extensive knowledge!

Other examples he uses are the emphasis of a politician, for the sake of democracy, who may focus on justice and liberty and not particularly on friendship, play or aesthetic experience. Also, a parent would never neglect the search for truth, play or friendship as they would, in effect, be 'mutilating' both themselves and their children.

(3) Basic goods apply equally to all ('No arbitrary preferences amongst persons')

The phrase, 'basic goods apply equally to all' is a suitable description of what Finnis means by 'no arbitrary preferences amongst persons'. Finnis himself states: 'Next, the basic goods are human goods, and can in principle be pursued, realised, and participated in by any human being.'

Although we may not be aware of what formula of goods makes other people flourish or even make it our concern, we are still to acknowledge that the goods are also for the benefit of others and not just ourselves – as Finnis describes them, 'partakers of those goods'. Finnis explains that to be other-aware is important even though we focus on ourselves. Ironically, it is only by making our own focus right that we can help others. Therefore, there is 'reasonable scope for self-preference', although Finnis does point out that

'This third requirement remains a pungent critique of selfishness, special pleading, double standards, hypocrisy, indifference to the good of others … and all the other manifold forms of egoistic and group bias.'

The pursuit of this in ethics or for the phronimos (ethical expert) is often seen in the quest for universalisation. In a religious context, Finnis compares it to the Golden Rule of Christianity: 'In everything do to others as you would have them do to you; for this is the law and the prophets.' (Matthew 7:12)

(4 and 5) Do not become obsessed with a particular project and use effort to improve. ('Detachment and commitment')

The fourth and fifth requirements of practical reasonableness are all about balancing. This time it is not about balancing the goods and making sure all goods are pursued at least to some extent. Here it is about balancing projects; that is, in the changing circumstances of life one is inevitably involved in different things whether it be groups, jobs, hobbies, politics, etc. These are what Finnis calls 'limited projects' and not life-long projects. Indeed, one must maintain detachment from them. However, detachment is not the same as indifference. Detachment is all about being able to see perspective and viewing the project as just part of the grand scheme of things. In other words, if the project was removed, then one's life should not fall apart or be meaningless. Finnis writes: 'There is no good reason to take up an attitude to any of one's particular objectives, such that if one's project failed and one's objective eluded one, one would consider one's life drained of meaning.'

The opposite of detachment is fanaticism. This is why detachment is so important and to be able to have a perspective on life as a whole and not be obsessed with particular projects. Finnis states:

'Moreover, there are often straightforward and evil consequences of succumbing to the temptation to give one's particular project the overriding and unconditional significance which only a basic value and a general commitment can claim: they are the evil consequences that we call to mind when we think of **fanaticism**. So the fourth requirement of practical reasonableness can be called detachment.'

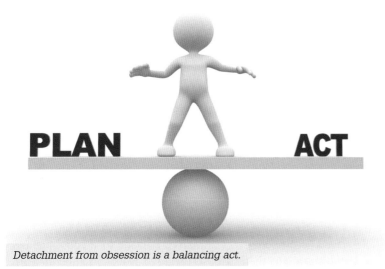

Detachment from obsession is a balancing act.

Commitment, the fifth requirement of practical reasonableness, is the balanced approach between fanaticism and indifference. Finnis states:

'The fifth requirement establishes the balance between fanaticism and dropping out, apathy, unreasonable failure, or refusal to 'get involved' with anything. It is simply the requirement that having made one's general commitments one must not abandon them lightly (for to do so would mean, in the extreme case, that one would fail ever to really participate in any of the basic values).'

Key quote

It is one thing to have little capacity and even no 'taste' for scholarship, or friendship, or physical heroism, or sanctity; it is quite another thing, and stupid or arbitrary, to think or speak or act as if these were not real forms of good. (Finnis)

Key quotes

'Do to (or for) others what you would have them do to (or for) you.' Put yourself in your neighbour's shoes. Do not condemn others for what you are willing to do yourself. Do not (without special reason) prevent others getting for themselves what you are trying to get for yourself. These are requirements of reason, because to ignore them is to be arbitrary as between individuals. (Finnis)

And this requirement of fidelity has a positive aspect.

One should be looking creatively for new and better ways of carrying out one's commitments, rather than restricting one's horizon and one's effort to the projects, methods, and routines with which one is familiar. (Finnis)

Key quote

The sixth requirement has obvious connections with the fifth, but introduces a new range of problems for practical reason, problems which go to the heart of 'morality'. (Finnis)

Key quotes

In short, no determinate meaning can be found for the term 'good' that would allow any commensurating and calculus of good to be made in order to settle those basic questions of practical reason which we call 'moral' questions… it is senseless to try to sum up the quantity of the size of this page, the quantity of the number six, and the quantity of the mass of this book. (Finnis)

A first formulation is that one should not choose to do any act which of itself does nothing but damage or impede a realisation or participation of any one or more of the basic forms of human good. (Finnis)

Reason requires that every basic value be at least respected in each and every action.

To choose an act which in itself simply (or primarily) damages a basic good is thereby to engage oneself willy-nilly (but directly) in an act of opposition to an incommensurable value (an aspect of human personality) which one treats as if it were an object of measurable worth that could be outweighed by commensurable objects of greater (or cumulatively greater) worth. (Finnis)

(6) Plan your actions to do the most good ('The (limited) relevance of consequences: efficiency within reason')

This requirement is all about choosing the most efficient response to moral questions. Finnis does acknowledge that in life 'there is a wide range of contexts in which it is possible and only reasonable to calculate, measure, compare, weigh, and assess the consequences of alternative decisions'. However, the impact of such factors should be as limited as possible. It is like applying Occam's razor to such features. The most efficient response is that which limits the weighting of consequences and maximises the application of the goods through reason. Finnis refers to this as producing actions that have a 'fitness for purpose' and he offers the following guidance as examples:

In situations of choice

- It is reasonable to prefer human good to the good of animals.
- It is reasonable to prefer basic human goods (such as life) to merely instrumental goods (such as property).

In cases of inevitable damage

- It is reasonable to prefer stunning to wounding, wounding to maiming, maiming to death: i.e. lesser rather than greater damage to one-and-the-same basic good in one-and-the-same instantiation.

In situations of suffering

- It is reasonable to prefer a remedy that both relieves pain and heals, to the one that merely relieves pain.

Finnis does gives more examples, but such examples are hardly extensive. However, Finnis recognises that this is a 'real requirement, with indefinitely many applications in "moral" (and hence in legal) thinking'.

(7) Never harm a basic good ('Respect for every basic value in every act')

This is another requirement that directly touches upon ethical methodology and in particular, a more traditional Natural Law approach. It focuses on not contravening a basic good. Finnis states: 'The basic values, and the practical principles expressing them, are the only guides we have. Each is objectively basic, primary, incommensurable with the others in point of objective importance.' In a sense this is the essence of Natural Law in that it refers directly to the goods (just as in Aquinas' primary precepts) and considers actions that potentially affect them in the following ways:

1. Directly promote a basic good.
2. Directly promote a basic good and indirectly damage a different good.
3. Directly damage a basic good and indirectly promote another basic good.
4. Directly damage a basic good.

Finnis argues that we aim for (1) always. However, he also recognises that 'unavoidable side-effects accompany every human choice, and their consequences are incalculable'. In which case he then suggests (again to avoid consequentialism) 'it is always reasonable to leave some of them, and often reasonable to leave all of them, out of account'. Finnis ranks (2) above (3) but concludes that (4) 'can never be justified in reason'. The crux of it all is to be able to identify and pre-empt the impact on the basic goods overall but Finnis gives no further specific criteria for making such a decision. He simply justifies the approach as an alternative to the dangers of consequentialism. This is one of Finnis' most controversial requirements and some, for example Professor Stephen Buckle, have accused him of limiting consequentialism in order to promote Roman Catholic values.

(8) Foster common good in the community ('The requirements of the common good')

For Finnis, the idea of any system of community regulation must be endowed with a sense of ownership. A cooperative and collaborative understanding of the basic goods ensures that four elements are vindicated:

- Justice
- Human rights
- Authority
- The law.

In other words, Finnis is proposing that favouring and fostering everyone's best interests in relation to the basic goods is the foundation of these four elements of society. This in itself validates the roles of justice, human rights, authority and the law; it is their vindication. This means that it is essentially a demonstration that for these four elements to exist is right, reasonable, or fully justified. These relate to his overall ideology of human law and authority.

(9) Act in your own conscience and authority ('Following one's conscience')

Finnis sees his whole chapter on the structure of practical reasonableness as 'in effect a reflection on the workings of conscience'. For Finnis, conscience is the development of an 'inclination' that is in touch with the requirements of practical reasonableness vis-à-vis the other eight requirements. His argument is that if one is in touch with these and they are working within one's 'personal full-being', then conscience 'flows' from this finely tuned reason that is basic-goods aware and practical reasonableness.

The alternative is simple. The alterative state is to be unfortunate 'in one's inclinations or upbringing' and one is simply misled by one's conscience. Finnis appeals to Aquinas for verification of his definition in line with Natural Law but the fact of the matter is just this: you are either in tune or you are not!

Finnis does not see this as the basic argument it first appears to be, simply because it logically follows from the eight previous requirements of practical reasonableness. It is therefore not an argument that stands alone, but more of a conclusion drawn from the eight previous requirements of practical reasonableness. Conscience, for Finnis is the sign of fullness of being and is an apt end to the obligations of the requirements of practical reasonableness in that together they form a 'deep structure of practical thinking, more particularly, of moral thought'.

Finnis concedes that for each individual moral judgement there are different shades of application for the nine requirements due to the fact that each requirement is not necessarily drawn upon in every instance. However, every moral judgment does bear the mark of one or more of the requirements. The requirements of practical reasonableness therefore form the basis of all moral obligation or responsibility.

AO1 Activity

Try and think of some more practical examples for each of the nine principles of practical reasonableness. This will help you to develop your answers explaining aspects of Finnis' Natural Law theory.

Law is all about the 'common good' and human rights.

Key quotes

Very many, perhaps even most, of our concrete moral responsibilities, obligations, and duties have their basis in the eighth requirement. We can label this the requirement of favouring and fostering the common good of one's communities. The sense and implications of this requirement are complex and manifold.

Finnis argues that unless law is grounded in what it is to be human and relates to a moral code, then human beings will not see that following the law is morally right and will obey it only out of habit or fear whilst the tools of civic education and enforcement endure. (P. Vardy)

The ninth requirement might be regarded as a particular aspect of the seventh (that no basic good may be directly attacked in any act), or even as a summary of all the requirements. But it is quite distinctive. It is the requirement that one should not do what one judges or thinks or 'feels'-all-in-all should not be done. That is to say one must act 'in accordance with one's conscience'.

Conscience, for Finnis, is the sign of fullness of being.

The common good and the need for authority

We have touched upon Finnis' appeal to the common good and the need for authority both at the beginning of the section and in the requirements of practical reasonableness. Brigita White observes, 'Aristotle saw the state, or more correctly, the Greek polis, as a natural entity', and also that Aquinas saw Natural Law as purposeful for 'people to live in society' and also 'ensured the compliance of those of "evil disposition".' In the tradition of both Aristotle and Aquinas, Finnis presents his Natural Law theory as 'a necessary medium for the expression of natural principles and for the development of a communal environment in which the "goods" are attainable'. In other words, the need for the authority of the law is driven by the need to support the common good of all, 'for those principles justify the exercise of authority in community'. The authority of Natural Law originates with the needs of the common good and is a framework of support. Any laws in any society should promote the basic goods and guide citizens away from error.

So, what about changes in law? What about the different laws around the world? What about the fact that there have been and still are unjust laws? How does Finnis address this? His response is simple: he is not writing about 'doctrines' of Natural Law that **have been** applied but rather indicating the principles of Natural Law that **should be** applied. The variations in understandings and application of Natural Law theories are simply examples of how people and societies have attempted to apply Natural Law principles. Just because they may have failed in some ways does not mean that the Natural Law principles have failed. Natural Law principles, unlike discourse and theories, are good in themselves; as Finnis has argued earlier, 'the mathematical principles of accounting "hold good" even when, as in the medieval banking community, they are unknown or misunderstood'. In other words, the different theories about Natural Law cannot change the unchangeable principles of Natural Law; all they can do is obscure them. He writes, 'Natural Law could not rise, decline, be revived, or stage "eternal returns", it could not have historical achievements to its credit. It could not be held responsible for disasters of the human spirit or atrocities of human practice.'

The law supports the common good.

AO1 Developing skills

It is now important to consider the information that has been covered in this section; however, the information in its raw form is too extensive and so has to be processed in order to meet the requirements of the examination. This can be achieved by practising more advanced skills associated with AO1. The exercises that run throughout this book will help you to do this and prepare you for the examination. For assessment objective 1 (AO1), which involves demonstrating 'knowledge' and 'understanding' skills, we are going to focus on different ways in which the skills can be demonstrated effectively, and also, refer to how the performance of these skills is measured (see generic band descriptors for A2 [WJEC] AO1 or A Level [Eduqas] AO1).

▶ **Your next task is this:** Below is an **outline of Finnis' explanation of a coherent plan of life**. At present it has no quotations at all to back the points made. Underneath the outline are two quotations that could be used in the outline in order to improve it. Your task is to re-write the outline but make use of the quotations. Such phrases as 'for example', 'according to ...', 'the scholar ... argues', or, 'it has been suggested by ...' may help.

We all have dreams of what our lives could be like if we only had certain things or if we only achieved certain things. It may be wealth, health, laughter, love or peace. Finnis' requirement of practical reasonableness here is all to do with focus and perspective.

Finnis compares this to a general commitment towards this goal rather than a detailed 'blueprint' because life throws up 'all manner of unforeseeable contingencies'. On the whole, it is not just about how we respond to the particulars of life but it is to do with our vision for what our lives should be like and what our priorities are. Sometimes we need to step back to see our progress in life and reflect on the bigger picture. This is the 'coherence' Finnis is speaking of; to have the general game plan of realising the basic goods and harmonising our personal commitments with them.

'It is unreasonable to live merely from moment to moment, following immediate cravings, or just drifting.' (Finnis)

'Life is much more successfully looked at from a single window.' (F. Scott Fitzgerald, *The Great Gatsby*)

When you have completed the task, try to find another quotation that you could use and further extend your answer.

Key skills Theme 2

The second Theme has tasks that concentrate on a particular aspect of AO1 in terms of using quotations from sources of authority and in the use of references.

Key skills
Knowledge involves:

Selection of a range of (thorough) accurate and relevant information that is directly related to the specific demands of the question.

This means:

- Selecting relevant material for the question set
- Being focused in explaining and examining the material selected.

Understanding involves:

Explanation that is extensive, demonstrating depth and/or breadth with excellent use of evidence and examples including (where appropriate) thorough and accurate supporting use of sacred texts, sources of wisdom and specialist language.

This means:

- Effective use of examples and supporting evidence to establish the quality of your understanding
- Ownership of your explanation that expresses personal knowledge and understanding and NOT just reproducing a chunk of text from a book that you have rehearsed and memorised.

Specification content

Whether Finnis' Natural Law is
acceptable in contemporary society.

Issues for analysis and evaluation

Whether Finnis' Natural Law is acceptable in contemporary society

In a sense, any system of Natural Law has an undeniable strength in appealing to our common human nature because it is universal in that the regulations and punishments are the same for all and this then makes it objective. Finnis' work is recognised as 'the leading proponent of Natural Law theory within the Anglo-American legal academy' according to Greenawalt. Indeed, the close relationship between morality and legal jurisdiction makes Finnis' theory applicable to all aspects of life that befall a citizen.

Another strong argument in support of its contemporary relevance for society is that it is grounded in reason. White argues, 'Finnis attempts to formulate a rational basis for moral action. His central thesis is that the act of making law is an act which can and should be guided by moral principles which are a matter of objective reasonableness.' Indeed, Finnis' system allows for a safe and secure community based on clear principles that can be used to carefully formulate laws. It also protects society morally since, like all Natural Law theories, it establishes clearly which acts are always bad. It is therefore acceptable in contemporary society.

However, although this may be presented as an argument that this gives us clear guidance and values, some have rejected this. For instance, Finnis is known widely to be very 'right wing' in terms of politics and his conservative principles in applying Natural Law have been criticised. For example, he has made controversial observations about immigration, equating it with 'reversed colonisation' and causing 'a trajectory of demographic and cultural decay'. He has also been criticised for his views on homosexual acts, any non-marital unitive acts, contraception and abortion; however, these views are in line with the Roman Catholic magisterium and therefore will appeal to some in contemporary society.

An article from the *Guardian* newspaper reports that 'during a speech at Harvard University in April (1994), Finnis was reportedly booed by campus protesters who labelled him a "hate monger" and a "homophobe" and compared his invitation to lecture to giving the grand wizard of the Ku Klux Klan a platform.' This is clearly over exaggeration but it does highlight that he has firm views about how Natural Law should be applied. Nonetheless, as Finnis himself points about, there is a difference between what he actually writes and states and what the media reports.

Vardy cites Stephen Buckle who criticises Finnis, accusing him of using his Natural Law theory to 'support the moral viewpoint of the Catholic Church on a range of controversial issues, including contraception and masturbation'. Indeed, Finnis himself argues that 'The collapse of Christianity and other religious cultures, as the matrix for contemporary legal and political orders, has posed a challenge to those who wish to affirm that there is a Natural Law.' This may well mean that Finnis' Natural Law has a tendency to appeal mainly to the contemporary Roman Catholic community.

Despite this, it does not mean that Finnis' basic goods and principles of practical reasonableness will not work. One major strength is the encouragement for individuals to engage with society by embracing the common goods which are not presented as a list of 'don'ts'. Instead they encourage purpose in life which is to be enjoyed and full of activity. The rules where there are rules seem to appeal to common sense and the law is positive in defending human rights. This all makes for an attractive, thriving modern society. His emphasis on aesthetics, play and sociability makes a vital contribution towards the 21st-century discussions about shared values, citizenship and tolerance. This is definitely relevant for all in contemporary society.

AO2 Activity

As you read through this section try to do the following:

1. Pick out the different lines of argument that are presented in the text and identify any evidence given in support.

2. For each line of argument try to evaluate whether or not you think this is strong or weak.

3. Think of any questions you may wish to raise in response to the arguments.

This Activity will help you to start thinking critically about what you read and help you to evaluate the effectiveness of different arguments and from this develop your own observations, opinions and points of view that will help with any conclusions that you make in your answers to the AO2 questions that arise.

One of the main attractions for Finnis' Natural Law is that it does not need consideration of a God. Whilst it does not deny the importance of 'religion' as a basic good, unlike Aquinas, there is no need to ground his theory in divinity. In this way it appeals to both religious and non-religious peoples as a common social foundation. As Einwechter writes, 'Since Natural Law is part of the nature of things the knowledge of it is accessible to all men through reason apart from any supernatural revelation.' This, then, adds to the force of its relevance today.

Finnis' Natural Law could be argued to be a clear, common-sense replacement for Proportionalism. Proportionalism has been accused of being vague, too complex and full of disparate views so as not to be of any use. Finnis' system does not depend so much on individual interpretation as he argues that his goods are self-evident and the same for all. In the same way and because of this, his system could be seen to be more relevant in contemporary society than some other ethical theories.

Some key questions that may arise could be: do we face problems in contemporary society to which the basic goods do not apply? What kind of things do we value in contemporary society? Would modern society have an argument for prioritising some goods over others? In some ways it could be argued that Finnis' Natural Law will not always appeal to some in contemporary society.

Indeed, it is also possible to deny that Finnis' model of Natural Law is relevant to all in society. For instance, we could reject the assumption that humans share a common human nature and also suggest that the basic goods are incomplete. In fact why are there seven? Why not more or less? Are the goods fully representative and meaningful? Brigita White suggests, 'A self-evident principle is only self-evident to the subject, in this case Finnis, and then only to the extent that it has become self-evident and not challenged by that subject's experience. It is quite conceivable that different people would come up with entirely different formulations of goods to be attained.' This argument questions the very basis of Finnis' theory. For example, the good of life ignores any consideration of death and the right to die and so immediately evades difficult debate about suicide and euthanasia. Indeed, Brigita White comments, 'Although, Finnis indeed posits a place for morality in the law, the type of morality Finnis has in mind is questionable.'

Another question of its relevance would be the fact that it is a inflexible; we can never challenge the basic goods as they are self-evident. For example, to not be able to go against a basic good does not recognise the fact that some ethical dilemmas are significantly complex, whereas at least a proportionalist recognises the complexity of moral issues and has the willingness to challenge the absolute application of basic goods in a practical context.

In fact, this brings us onto another line of argument that would suggest that there are other, more relevant and flexible systems of ethical theory that may be better for contemporary society. These include both religious and non-religious. Indeed, our society is built upon democracy and the law and our political system has had much utilitarian influence. People may prefer this because it is more flexible and applicable in a variety of ways and see Finnis' Natural Laws as simply inflexible.

There are clearly ways in which Finnis' Natural Law is acceptable in society but this does not mean that it will always work, that there are no problems, or indeed, that another alternative ethical theory may be better in serving contemporary society.

Study tip

It is vital for AO2 that you actually discuss arguments and not just explain what someone may have stated. Try to ask yourself, 'was this a fair point to make?', 'is the evidence sound enough?', 'is there anything to challenge this argument?', 'is this a strong or weak argument?' Such critical analysis will help you develop your evaluation skills.

AO2 Activity

List some conclusions that could be drawn from the AO2 reasoning from the above text; try to aim for at least three different possible conclusions. Consider each of the conclusions and collect brief evidence to support each conclusion from the AO1 and AO2 material for this topic. Select the conclusion that you think is most convincing and explain why it is so. Try to contrast this with the weakest conclusion in the list, justifying your argument with clear reasoning and evidence.

Specification content

The strengths and weaknesses of
Finnis' Natural Law.

The strengths and weaknesses of Finnis' Natural Law

Evaluating the strengths and weaknesses of Finnis' Natural Law incorporates many of the strengths and weaknesses of traditional Natural Law itself. For instance, one traditional strength is that it is based on what it means to be human. To be human means acting in line with one's true nature and following our natural inclinations. It could be argued that this strength is common to versions put forward by Aristotle, Aquinas and Finnis.

It could be argued that Finnis' version also appeals to common sense and rationality in embracing the goals of 'happiness' and 'fulfilment' whether through the Beatific Vision of Aquinas or the 'eudaimonia' of Aristotle by way of his notion of 'well-being'. Either can be embraced by Finnis' Natural Law. In addition, when Finnis' theory is applied, it assumes the special status of human beings and some see this as a strength of all forms of Natural Law that distinguishes it from a more cold, factual and descriptive accounts, say for example, from science and evolution. The basic goods are common to all people in Finnis' theory just as those identified in Aristotle's virtues and Aquinas' precepts.

Again, it could be contended that another strength is that it is about following natural inclinations, which means that the application to a moral issue is always the same, wherever you are and whoever you are. Indeed, this has proven very popular in developing a deontological system with Roman Catholicism. It is, arguably, clear how Finnis' Natural Law is applied, for example through an awareness of the basic goods and their realisation through the principle of practical reasonableness. It is therefore clear for all to see why some actions are in line with the goods and why some are not. This is very useful for ethical debate.

Therefore, the application of Finnis' Natural Law, just like the justice of Aristotle's system of Natural Law and the secondary precepts in Aquinas' Natural Law, seems clear. All Natural Law systems advocate a rational process, rather than an intuitional or emotive one, and unlike consequential or situational based systems, Finnis' Natural Law in particular together with the magisterium's interpretation of Aquinas' version, judge the intrinsic value of actions regardless of the outcomes; it is the action itself, not the outcomes, that decides whether an act is moral. Accordingly, rationality also forms the basis of the problem of real and apparent goods and the possibility of reasoning wrongly often based on the intrinsic value of a good; indeed, Finnis strengthened these with the development of the principles of practical reasonableness and upholds Aquinas' doctrine of double effect which allows for a possible conflict of the goods.

Finally, one could argue that Finnis' Natural Law does have its unique advantages over and against Aristotle's version and that developed by Aquinas. First of all, Finnis presents the concept of 'religion' with a view to establishing that there is rational support, vindication and credibility in grounding Natural Law in a belief in God. Aristotle's version is unclear about this connection and in Aquinas one could argue that it is assumed by faith rather than established through reason as Finnis does. Nonetheless Finnis goes further and establishes what one could call the 'other side of the coin' in that his version is also open to systems of thought and worldviews that may be different, agnostic or atheistic but that nonetheless have some overall appreciation of ultimate questions. Finnis' system has the beauty of not needing God for its authority but simultaneously establishing the rational and philosophical credibility of a creator God.

Secondly, another way in which it could be argued that Finnis strengthens the case of Natural Law over against its more traditional versions is that it unpacks Aquinas' 'ordered society' by including friendship, play, and aesthetic experience and explains how they contribute to the goal of human well-being. Finally, although

AO2 Activity

As you read through this section try to do the following:

1. Pick out the different lines of argument that are presented in the text and identify any evidence given in support.

2. For each line of argument try to evaluate whether or not you think this is strong or weak.

3. Think of any questions you may wish to raise in response to the arguments.

This Activity will help you to start thinking critically about what you read and help you to evaluate the effectiveness of different arguments and from this develop your own observations, opinions and points of view that will help with any conclusions that you make in your answers to the AO2 questions that arise.

one of the strengths of traditional Natural Law is that it is a universal moral law that is not relative to culture or a religion, Finnis' theory formulates a clear relationship between that of the moral laws and the social legislation that serves to create an environment conducive to the common good. This gives a clear basis for societal law, underpinned by morality, and there is an authority and a clear justification of why this would work on an international stage.

One of the weaknesses ascribed to Natural Law in terms of morality is that Hume and Moore demonstrated clearly that it falls foul of the Naturalistic Fallacy. It is argued that describing the facts of any situation never leads to making a value judgement. What 'is' (fact) does not imply what 'ought to be' (value). In other words there seems to be a mistake in reasoning (fallacy) in identifying morality with another concept (i.e. nature). Nonetheless, Finnis' version does counter this claim by observing that Hume objected to the logical leap and did not deny that 'ought' could not be identified, only not by normal empirical reasoning; this is the strength of Finnis' explanation of practical reasoning based upon the goods.

Nevertheless, central criticisms such as the question as to whether or not an action is 'natural' have been posited. Does it just mean that it refers to the action that is common to a particular group? Is there a common human nature? Surely the fact that cultures have different values challenges the idea of a common nature; for example, the Spartan 'nature' was to kill weak or defective children. Indeed, some would still deny there was any such thing as a human nature. This has always been a critical area for Natural Law to address and Finnis' system is no exception.

Indeed, Darwinism sees natural selection as the source of human nature rather than any divine or rational source and guidance. This certainly damages the justification and authority of any Natural Law theory. If there is a constant unchanging human nature and a Natural Law that stems from it, how is it that so many through the centuries have got human nature so wrong. (e.g. slavery and apartheid considered natural). Despite this, Finnis has re-iterated that it is not a process of establishing Natural Law by identifying what 'should be' or how we 'ought to act' in accordance with human nature, but what is in accordance with reason. This is arguably the most crucial aspect for Finnis' system.

Another criticism is that human nature seems to change. For instance, the debate about homosexuality has raised questions about what is natural and the system of marriage and family life have been redefined. Finnis' response and defence of the traditional interpretation of Natural Law is well known but is it acceptable for all today?

Despite the criticisms, and despite the fact that Natural Law is a major component of Roman Catholic doctrine, its legalistic might seem to some to be in conflict with a Christian stance. It is action centred rather than people and consequence centred. This is particularly evidenced in Natural Law approaches to abortion and euthanasia. Although the doctrine of double effect assumes that a sharp distinction can be drawn between directly intending a result and merely foreseeing it, there are still many alternative consequentialist systems that some may argue are preferable because they are more flexible in today's world.

In conclusion, the main issue seems to be that although there are clearly many strengths, the crux of the matter appears to be whether its weaknesses are enough to question the validity and authority of Natural Law. Perhaps an awareness of weaknesses, criticisms, and the dangers of imposing underlying specific religious views will help maintain its effectiveness in the future?

Key questions

Does it just mean that it refers to the action that is common to a particular group?

Is there a common human nature?

Can we define what is 'natural' so easily?

Does Finnis effectively counter the Naturalistic Fallacy?

Key quote

There is no reason to doubt that each of the basic aspects of human well-being is worth seeking to realise. (Finnis)

Study tip

It is vital for AO2 that you actually discuss arguments and not just explain what someone may have stated. Try to ask yourself, 'was this a fair point to make?', 'is the evidence sound enough?', 'is there anything to challenge this argument?', 'is this a strong or weak argument?' Such critical analysis will help you develop your evaluation skills.

AO2 Activity

List some conclusions that could be drawn from the AO2 reasoning from the above text; try to aim for at least three different possible conclusions. Consider each of the conclusions and collect brief evidence to support each conclusion from the AO1 and AO2 material for this topic. Select the conclusion that you think is most convincing and explain why it is so. Try to contrast this with the weakest conclusion in the list, justifying your argument with clear reasoning and evidence.

Key skills Theme 2

The second Theme has tasks that concentrate on a particular aspect of AO2 in terms of using quotations from sources of authority and in the use of references in supporting arguments and evaluations.

Key skills

Analysis involves:

Identifying issues raised by the materials in the AO1, together with those identified in the AO2 section, and presents sustained and clear views, either of scholars or from a personal perspective ready for evaluation.

This means:

- That your answers are able to identify key areas of debate in relation to a particular issue

- That you can identify, and comment upon, the different lines of argument presented by others

- That your response comments on the overall effectiveness of each of these areas or arguments.

Evaluation involves:

Considering the various implications of the issues raised based upon the evidence gleaned from analysis and provides an extensive detailed argument with a clear conclusion.

This means:

- That your answer weighs up the consequences of accepting or rejecting the various and different lines of argument analysed

- That your answer arrives at a conclusion through a clear process of reasoning.

AO2 Developing skills

It is now important to consider the information that has been covered in this section; however, the information in its raw form is too extensive and so has to be processed in order to meet the requirements of the examination. This can be achieved by practising more advanced skills associated with AO2. The exercises that run throughout this book will help you to do this and prepare you for the examination. For assessment objective 2 (AO2), which involves 'critical analysis' and 'evaluation' skills, we are going to focus on different ways in which the skills can be demonstrated effectively, and also, refer to how the performance of these skills is measured (see generic band descriptors for A2 [WJEC] AO2 or A Level [Eduqas] AO2).

▶ **Your next task is this:** Below is an **evaluation of the relevance of Finnis' Natural Law theory**. At present it has no quotations at all to support the argument presented. Underneath the evaluation are three quotations that could be used in the outline in order to improve it. Your task is to re-write the outline but make use of the quotations. Such phrases as 'according to ...', 'the scholar ... argues', or, 'it has been suggested by ...' may help.

John Finnis' Natural Law theory is very relevant for today. Finnis is himself a legal scholar and the whole purpose of his writings is to establish a legal framework that respects certain basic goods.

It is also relevant because he has updated Aquinas' precepts into more modern, approachable concepts.

However, it is not always relevant as many who advocate it are religious people with strong support for the values and teachings of Roman Catholic theology, including ethical and social values in particular.

Nonetheless it is based in reason and has very much a common-sense feel about it according to many. In this way it is easily applicable.

Against this, it does not necessarily represent everyone's sense of value or, in particular, the underpinning sense of morality similar to that belonging to the Roman Catholic Church.

From the publication in 1980 of *Natural Law and Natural Rights*, Finnis has been deservedly recognised as the leading proponent of Natural Law theory within the Anglo-American legal academy. (Greenawalt)

Finnis attempts to formulate a rational basis for moral action. His central thesis is that the act of making law is an act which can and should be guided by moral principles which are a matter of objective reasonableness. (White)

Although, Finnis indeed posits a place for morality in the law, the type of morality Finnis has in mind is questionable. (White)

When you have completed the task, try to find another quotation that you could use and further extend your evaluation.

E: Bernard Hoose's overview of the Proportionalist debate

This section covers AO1 content and skills

Specification content
Bernard Hoose's overview of the Proportionalist debate.

What is 'Proportionalism'?

The problem in defining 'Proportionalism' is that although its origins are clear, the 'movement' itself is difficult to pin down to one particular view. There are so many scholars involved and each has a slightly different perspective. In addition, whether or not it is a full-blown ethical 'theory' in itself is also debated. Proportionalism, then, is not a single entity as such.

Although, the term Proportionalism has been used by the Pope, a more familiar term used within Roman Catholic theology to describe the thinkers that take this approach to ethics is 'revisionists'. Indeed, the term 'revisionists' is preferred by most who take the proportionalist line as they see their work as a simple revision of Natural Law rather than a new theory that replaces it. However, despite the slightly different presentations of Proportionalism by revisionist scholars, most scholars share the same common view that it is based upon Aquinas' understanding of the 'principle of double effect'.

The Specification content deals with Hoose's discussion of major debates within Proportionalism that emerged in its early years. Hoose does not opt for a clear definition of Proportionalism because it is not a unified 'theory', 'methodology' or 'movement'. However, once the issues have been covered in this section there is a timeline at the end that may be useful to give an understanding of trends within Proportionalism as a whole up until the present day. From this, the next section on application of the 'theory' will begin by identifying three different ways in which Proportionalism can be applied to help teachers and pupils in differentiating between some key differences in understanding the debate.

Study tip

This section of the textbook includes some background material, although hopefully this will be of use in explaining aspects of the Proportionalism debate. This is because Proportionalism has not been taught as a major part of any specification until now. Targeted resources have been slender at best, and short summaries are difficult to find. This is an attempt to provide a context of the debate as well as a specification-specific presentation.

Hoose's book *Proportionalism* was published in 1987, 22 years after the debate began and 29 years before this Specification was written. Proportionalism as a phenomenon, then, pre-dates Hoose's book but the Specification post-dates Hoose's book by 30 years, and there have been significant contributions to the debate since then. These significant contributions also need to be considered in addition to Hoose's book in order to represent Proportionalism accurately.

In 1991, a convention was held at The Jesuit School of Theology at Berkeley University in the USA that listened to and debated various definitions of Proportionalism and its strengths and weaknesses. It was clear from the debates that there is no single definition that satisfies everyone involved in the debate. Indeed, Richard McCormick pointed out that 'the "ism" term conveys the deceptive impression of an ideologically unified movement' although elsewhere in his writings he has observed that 'most theologians share similar perspectives'. Professor Christopher Kaczor in his *Proportionalism and the Natural Law tradition* (2002) wrote that a definition of Proportionalism cannot 'definitively capture all the variations and different formulations of proportionalist theory'. Professor Philip Foubert presented a definition that 'Proportionalism is a family of

Key terms

Jesuit: someone belonging to the Roman Catholic religious order the Society of Jesus

Proportionalism: an approach to Natural Law that focuses in particular on the fourth condition of the principle of double effect as outlined by Thomas Aquinas

Revisionists: those scholars who support Proportionalism

Key terms

Commensurate reason: justifying appropriate compensation, another term used for proportionate reason

Hermeneutical: the science of interpretation

Principle of double effect: a term to describe an ethical method of interpretation first identified in Aquinas' treatment of killing in self-defence

Proportionate reason: reasoning that ensures evil that occurs is compensated and subsumed by a greater good

Summa Theologica: Thomas Aquinas' main theological writing

approaches based on the traditional "three fonts of morality" (that is, the judgment is based on the act in itself, the agent's intention, and relevant circumstances)'. His observation that Proportionalism was a 'family of approaches' indicates similarity through some underlying principle without being identical.

In 1995, James Walter defined Proportionalism in *The HarperCollins Encyclopaedia of Catholicism* as 'a type of analysis for determining the objective moral rightness and wrongness of actions in conflict situations and procedure for establishing exceptions to behavioural norms. It began in the mid 1960s as a revision of both the 'principle of double effect' and the doctrine of intrinsic moral evil.'

A very important distinction has also been made by an ardent advocate of Proportionalism, Father Garth Hallett, a Professor of Philosophy and Jesuit priest. He argues that Proportionalism itself is not a methodology since there are a variety of ways in which scholars have argued that proportionate reason needs to be applied. Hallett instead argues that it is an ethical norm; that is, the norm that everyone agrees that proportionate reason should be used in ethical decision making but that there are different methodologies of how this should be done that have been put forward. Proportionalism, then, is a norm and directive of what ought to be applied to an ethical dilemma but not one that exemplifies or instructs how to do this and therefore not a full-blown ethical theory.

Key quotes

Philosophically, revisionism formulates a norm or criterion grounded in reason and experience for determining the objective rightness or wrongness of acts. This criterion is called proportionate reason and designates the school of thought known as Proportionalism. **(Salzman)**

The distinction between a norm or criterion, on the one hand, and a method or procedure, on the other, is often noted but as often ignored with unfortunate consequences. **(Hallett)**

In terms of identifying the heart of the debate, perhaps the following could be used as a working definition:

> Proportionalism is an acceptance of the norm or criterion that Aquinas' fourth condition of the principle of double effect is the fundamental basis for dealing with ethical issues involving conflict situations. From this position, a proportionalist thinker attempts to determine the correct way to apply proportionate reason.

Obviously, it is much more complicated than this and in order to provide further depth and insight, this chapter will go beyond the work of Bernard Hoose to the wider proportionalist debates.

Proportionalism can be traced back to an article first published by a German Jesuit scholar, Peter Knauer, entitled 'The **Hermeneutical** Function of the '**principle of double effect**'' (French 1965; translated into English 1967) in which he challenges traditional understandings of Aquinas' 'principle of double effect'. Knauer's main argument was that the most important factor in considering the 'principle of double effect' was the notion of '**commensurate reason**' or as it has since been translated '**proportionate reason**'. It is from this that 'Proportionalism' got its name. Indeed, Proportionalism, fundamentally, is all about the 'principle of double effect'. It is simply a debate about how we should interpret and apply Aquinas' 'proportionate reason' that is expressed in his *Summa Theologica II-II 64, 7* in which Aquinas discussed the issue of killing in self-defence.

Knauer's article was pertinent at the time since society was debating the moral issues of contraception, divorce, remarriage and abortion. These issues were also being identified as key contemporary issues by Roman Catholic moral theologians and this focus generated much ethical debate in the years that followed. However, professor Christopher Kaczor points out that although the publication of *Humanae Vitae* (**papal encyclical** that clarified the Roman Catholic tradition's teachings about contraception) arose at the same time as Proportionalism, there is no logical link with Knauer's work. In *Humanae Vitae* the Pope condemns any use of 'artificial means' to regulate fertility. This meant that 'each and every marital act [sexual intercourse] must remain open to the transmission of life' (*Humanae Vitae* 11). Despite the papal declaration, Kaczor writes, 'In fact, it is logically possible to accept Proportionalism and still hold that all acts of contraception are wrong'. In other words, Proportionalism was originally not a response to the debate about contraception, although early writers did comment on this issue.

Indeed, the origins of Proportionalism probably have more to do with the post-Vatican II constitution of *Glaudium et Spes* (Hope and Glory), sections 12–22 of which focus on the notion of human dignity in promoting moral goodness in the world through freedom, intelligence, wisdom and conscience as created 'in the image of God' would suggest. The aim and focus of the constitution was clearly 'how do we live as Christians in the contemporary world and respond to the increasingly complex social and moral issues that are arising?'

In addition, although Joseph Fletcher's work 'Situation Ethics' was influential in Protestant circles, this '**New Morality**' had already been denounced by the Pope and, as we shall later see, Fletcher's ideas had very little impact within Roman Catholic theology. Indeed, proportionalists were very critical of Fletcher. For example, in describing Fletcher's work, Richard McCormick writes: 'Fletcher has not made up his mind on how moral judgements are made. As long as this remains unclear, he can squeeze out of any epistemological corner, because he has none he calls his own.'

A papal encyclical delivers official doctrine and teachings of the Roman Catholic Church.

McCormick also cites James Gustafson, a distinguished Protestant theological ethicist, who wrote: '"love" like "situation" is a word that runs through Fletcher's book like a greased pig.'

However, just like within Protestant Christianity, in the 1960s there was the same sense of uneasiness within Roman Catholic moral theology in response to the changing social and moral views within society, some of which contradicted traditional Roman Catholic teaching.

Key quote

The task of authentically interpreting the word of God, whether in its written form or in that of Tradition, has been entrusted only to those charged with the Church's living magisterium, whose authority is exercised in the name of Jesus Christ. (*Veritatis Splendor*)

quickfire

2.16 Who are the opponents of Proportionalism?

Key quotes

Always summoning him to love good and avoid evil, the voice of conscience when necessary speaks to his heart: do this, shun that … fulfilled by love of God and neighbour. In fidelity to conscience, Christians are joined with the rest of men in the search for truth, and for the genuine solution to the numerous problems which arise in the life of individuals from social relationships. (**Glaudius et Spes Chapter 1:16**)

The name 'proportionalism' was coined by those who opposed this approach; the 'ism' term conveys the deceptive impression of an ideologically unified movement. In fact, it is not a method but a way of examining received moral norms according to a conflict model of reality. (**McCormick**)

quickfire

2.17 From where does Proportionalism get its name?

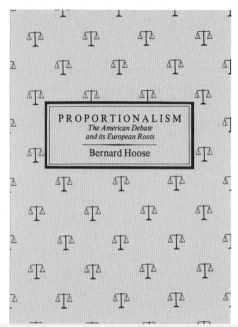

Hoose's book was an attempt to summarise what early proportionalists were arguing.

Key terms

Carmelites: a religious mendicant order of the Roman Catholic tradition that focuses on contemplation, prayer, community and service

Magisterium: the authority of the Roman Catholic Church in maintaining authentic interpretation of the Bible and sacred Roman Catholic tradition headed by the Pope and Bishops and supported by a body of scholars

Traditionalists: those scholars who support the magisterium, traditional authority of the Roman Catholic Church

Unequivocal: used to refer to something that is beyond doubt

Univocal: used to refer to a word that has only one possible and unambiguous meaning

Bernard Hoose's overview

'Bernard Hoose's Proportionalism' refers to a specific book written by Bernard Hoose, a British-Italian moral theologian, university lecturer and former member of the Order of the **Carmelites**. The book, *'Proportionalism: The American Debate and its European Roots'* (1987) was a published version of Hoose's PhD thesis and it was a commentary on and evaluation of Proportionalism.

The term 'Hoose's Proportionalism', then, refers to the theory of Proportionalism itself that is identified within his book. Hoose's book does not present a theory of Proportionalism as developed by Hoose; Hoose is a commentator on Proportionalism and not a direct contributor. Instead, his book contains references to a variety of scholars who have contributed to the debate and Hoose's aim was to evaluate their contributions. Hoose's book *Proportionalism*, as a commentary on the Proportionalism debate, was therefore more objective and indirect than having a direct involvement in the debate.

Hoose identifies Proportionalism as a 'fiery debate' within moral theology and his book is an attempt to survey and tease out the theological and moral debates about Proportionalism that had emerged over the previous 20 years (1967–87). The main purpose of Hoose's book is to identify the key debates between the revisionists in the Roman Catholic tradition (sometimes referred to as proportionalists) and the more traditional supporters of the **magisterium** (the authority of the Roman Catholic Church), or, as they were known, **traditionalists**. Although Hoose begins with the origins of Proportionalism and how it became a topic for debate from a historical perspective, from chapter three onwards he moves on to consider Proportionalism from a more thematic approach with a view to clarifying some 'misunderstandings' that had arisen in the debate during the early years (1967–87).

The first two chapters of Hoose's book are devoted to the origins of the debate in both Europe and the USA. Hoose clarifies some 'misunderstandings' and explains that the earliest problem for Proportionalism was due to the nature of the various words and terms that the scholars involved were using. Early writers on Proportionalism tended to use specific words in debate and, although sometimes they referred to the same notion, they could also refer to different notions. For example, words such as good, bad, right, wrong, sin, evil, intrinsic evil, ontic evil, pre-moral evil, immoral, moral, values and disvalues and so forth were all used in a way that was neither **univocal** nor **unequivocal**.

This was because early contributors to the Proportionalism debate were Roman Catholic theologians from different parts of (mainly) Europe and the USA and they were writing about Proportionalism from their own particular faith position. This meant that they used language that sometimes had a common understanding with others, or, sometimes used specific language that had a different meaning for them, or, even sometimes, they introduced new words to discuss concepts that were already part of the debate in different wording. It was all very confusing. Indeed, for Hoose, the main problem was that the Proportionalism debate was within ***theology*** and did not begin as a philosophical exercise. In other words, there was no universal basis to begin from like a set of pre-agreed definitions such as 'good means ...' and 'ontic refers to ...'. Hoose identifies the various elements of this confusion and also points out that it was some time into the debate before such misunderstandings were ironed out.

Following this, Hoose focuses on three specific areas of the early debate that are crucial for Proportionalism:

1. The **distinction between moral goodness and rightness** in which he discusses the theological perspective of 'good' as being inaccurate because it invariably incorporates the conflation of good with right. This distinction between good and right is vital for understanding Proportionalism.

2. The **teleological** and **deontological** **distinctions** in which Hoose considers both teleological and deontological features of Natural Law and Proportionalism.

3. The **direct and indirect distinction** demonstrated in the 'principle of double effect' that is at the very heart of the debate about Proportionalism.

Although Hoose does evaluate and draw conclusions, on the whole, he does remain neutral; however, despite seeing both strengths and weaknesses on each side of the debate, his sympathy with the revisionists comes out in his conclusion that 'our analysis has, I think, demonstrated clearly enough the coherence and validity of Proportionalism'. Nonetheless, Hoose does point out that although there was general agreement amongst proportionalists that proportionate reason is the fundamental norm or criterion to use for ethics, there was no real suggestion as to how this was to be applied as a methodology: 'a careful examination of the writings of proportionalists reveals that they do not in fact propose a method'.

Therefore, the main issue for the Roman Catholic tradition, according to Hoose, is that 'If we are satisfied that Proportionalism is what must be taught, we must now ask how it is to be taught.' Since Hoose's book, the debate has continued as fiercely as before as can be seen from the timeline at the end of this chapter.

Key quote

If we are satisfied that Proportionalism is what must be taught, we must now ask how it is to be taught. (**Hoose**)

Study tip

It is vital that you are able to make thorough and accurate use of specialist language and vocabulary in context in your answers; therefore, check your spelling carefully, and ensure that you have used specialist terms in the correct way.

AO1 Activity

As you read through this theme, note down significant dates and/or their corresponding events. When you have done so, create a chronological timeline so that you have a clear idea of what happened when and why.

Key terms

Deontological: used to refer to a rule-based system of ethics

Direct and indirect distinction: used to refer to an act that is directly intended and an indirect consequence of a direct action

Teleological: used to refer to an ethical system that has a final goal or 'end'

quickfire

2.18 Why was the early debate about Proportionalism so confusing according to Hoose?

Thomas Aquinas first introduced the ideas behind the principle of double effect.

Key terms

Apparent goods: an act that may seem good but is really not

Indifferent: another word for neutral

Intrinsic evil: an act that is always evil no matter what the circumstances

Intrinsic good: an act that is always good no matter what the circumstances

Maxim: a general rule

Real goods: an act that is truly good

Reasoning wrongly: to follow the wrong line of reasoning based on error

Key quotes

What then are we to say? Should we continue in sin in order that grace may abound? By no means! How can we who died to sin go on living in it? (Romans 6:1–2)

What then? Should we sin because we are not under law but under grace? By no means! (Romans 6:15)

Proportionalism and the 'principle of double effect'

Since Proportionalism is a debate in Roman Catholic moral theology concerning the application of Natural Law to ethical issues, it is therefore also based on established ethical rules determined by precepts (or goods). These goods are 'intrinsic goods'; an act that directly and purposefully violates an intrinsic good is therefore an 'intrinsic evil'. The Roman Catholic tradition has long held to the principle that there are certain acts that are considered as intrinsically evil and therefore ethically wrong. For instance, rape, masturbation, lying and contraception have been highlighted by the Catechism of the Roman Catholic Church (2356, 2352, 1753, 2370) as intrinsically evil. Torture also heads the list of topics that have been debated.

This idea of certain actions being intrinsically evil and ethically wrong then, is the first part of the proportionalist maxim that 'It is never right to go against a principle …' as it is grounded firmly in Natural Law. It refers to those situations whereby a precept is compromised by a decision which can never be 'right' or 'good'.

Following this logic, one would equally expect war and capital punishment to be intrinsic evil acts; however, this has not been the case according to the history of Natural Law. Indeed, it is clear that although Aquinas struggled to justify the legitimacy of war and capital punishment, he did not use 'proportionate reasoning'. Aquinas' justifications for these conclusions were grounded in different methods within practical reasoning.

Understanding the whole debate about Proportionalism requires an understanding of what the 'principle of double effect' is and how it works. Therefore, to understand Proportionalism and its origins we need to go right back to Aquinas. This is because Aquinas first used the phrase 'proportionate reason' when dealing with a specific problem in applied ethics, in Aquinas' example, the issue of self-defence that presents a 'conflict situation'. The heart of Proportionalism can, therefore, be found in the writings of Aquinas and the 'principle of double effect'.

The 'principle of double effect' is applied when an act that brings evil because it violates a precept or good, is a permissible or acceptable course of action to take in both circumstances and effects. Aquinas argued that to defend oneself against an aggressor when one's life is in danger it is acceptable to defend life; however, what happens when the only way to do this is to kill the aggressor (which is also an evil act)? This is where Aquinas argued that some sound philosophical reasoning needs to be applied. He argued that the self-defence needs to be proportionate. Today it could be equated with the concept of reasonable force to counter a violent aggressor. We will explore the full extent of the meaning of this word 'proportionate' when we look at the 'maxim' identified in the Specification.

As we have seen from Aquinas' Natural Law from year one of the course, 'actions' can be directly intended but have indirect consequences that are unintended. In addition to this there are 'real goods' and 'apparent goods' and cases of reasoning wrongly. As for the issue of self-defence and the 'principle of double effect', Aquinas famously outlines his arguments in *Summa Theologica* II.II 64,7 and 103,8. It is here that Aquinas identifies four key conditions for justifying killing in self-defence:

(1) The actions are good or indifferent

(2) The intention is good

(3) Evil does not flow directly from the action performed

(4) Any evil that occurs is compensated and subsumed by a greater good, that is, it is proportionately reasoned.

In explaining condition (3), Joseph Selling argues that (3) is distinct from (2) in that (3) is more to do with ensuring that evil does not flow directly from the **action** performed. If this is the case then the integrity of the intention (2) is not in question. In other words, the good effect needs to flow directly from the action so that any evil is 'accidental' (indirect), not traceable to (2) intention and thereby not integral to the act-in-itself.

To sum up, the third point is crucial for many who use the 'principle of double effect' in that it ensures that there is no evil intent and that any evil that occurs does so indirectly. It also means that each condition is clearly independent of the other:

(1) The **act** is good/neutral

(2) The **intention** is good and direct

(3) Any evil **effect** is indirect

(4) Any evil resulting is secondary and compensated by a primary (greater) good (commensurate/**proportionate reason**).

Aquinas' analysis of self-defence according to the principle of double effect.

Precept (good)	preservation of life
Ontic evil	death
Evil act-in-itself (the means – finis operis)	killing i.e. introducing a pre-moral evil
Intention (the end – finis operantis)	self-defence, self-preservation of life
Effects / outcome	self-preservation but death of the oppressor
Ethical judgements possible	(1) this is morally right as death of oppressor was an unintended or 'indirect' consequence **or** (2) immoral and therefore wrong as the death of oppressor was an intended or direct consequence

Scenario A

The intention/circumstance (the end) is purely for self-defence with an intent to preserve one's life by diminishing aggression (proportionate reason may dictate that this act is morally right even though it may not be 'completely' or 'holistically' morally good) and not seeking to kill in order to diminish aggression and preserve one's life.

Verdict

Aquinas agreed that this was correct use of principle of double effect. All four conditions of principle of double effect are met. It is the morally right thing to do because although killing introduces pre-moral evil, ultimately there is a clear distinction between the **act of killing in self-defence** and the **act of killing as murder**.

Scenario B

Intention/circumstance (the end) = self-defence with excessive force

Intention/circumstance (the end) = self-defence with intent to harm or kill

Intention/circumstance (the end) = death of the attacker

Verdict

Aquinas could not accept these because this scenario has broken the conditions associated with principle of double effect: (1) it is **not indifferent** (2) **intention is not good** and (3) the **direct evil effect** that therefore flows from this is death through murder (4) evil is unnecessary / is not compensated/subsumed by a greater good and therefore **not commensurate or proportionate reasoning**. There are of course other permutations of this.

Key terms

Act-in-itself: the simple action without consideration of intention of circumstances

Finis operis: the act-in-itself

Finis operantis: the intention behind the act

Ontic evil: physical natural evil such as the fact of death, disease, pain and suffering

quickpire

2.19 Give two examples of intrinsically evil acts that have been highlighted by the Catechism of the Roman Catholic Church.

Aquinas' example of killing in self-defence is crucial for understanding proportionate reasoning.

Key quote

'Proportionate reason' is a moral principle used to determine concretely and objectively the rightness or wrongness of acts and various exceptions to behavioural norms. (Walter)

Key term

Ectopic pregnancy: a pregnancy where the embryo embeds itself 'out of place' (ectopic), most often in the fallopian tube endangering the life of both foetus and mother

In considering Aquinas, Peter Knauer, however, argued that the fourth condition of proportionate reason, or as he translated it 'commensurate reason', was the key to understanding 'principle of double effect' and that, in fact, it incorporated all three previous conditions.

This was a new interpretation of 'principle of double effect'. This perspective meant that although elements of an ethical act could be dissected and analysed, it was the complete ethical act that needed to be considered as a whole with all elements together. The 'indirect' and 'direct' aspects of an ethical act, then, are not separate causal effects but more simultaneous aspects or elements of the concrete act. As Kaczor writes, 'for Knauer, the evil brought about by an act was justified if, and only if, one had a proportionate reason'. Knauer writes that 'the expression "commensurate reason" determines the meaning of all the other concepts'. At the same time Willem Van der Marck, a Dutch Roman Catholic scholar, wrote an article on the issue of artificial contraception and proposed that the traditional understanding of 'principle of double effect' did not exist and that 'only the concrete human act is good or bad'.

This is a particular area of contention between the proportionalist position and that of the magisterium. Proportionalists acknowledge 'evil' but do not universally accept the blanket term 'intrinsic evil' because (i) it understands this to mean that any intrinsically evil act is evil no matter when, where or how performed (ii) it implies that the ethical act-in-itself needs no consideration of any other elements when making an ethical decision such as intention, and, (iii) an understanding of ontic evil means that every ethical event contains an aspect of imperfection as it originates in the human person. The magisterium, as we know, consider intrinsic evil to be an act-in-itself and therefore evil, regardless of the circumstances.

However, another new and defining argument arose from Knauer's understanding of 'principle of double effect'. He proposed that 'Every human act brings evil effects with it', and that 'Evil may be accepted in exchange if, in relation to the whole, the smallest possible evil is exchanged for the highest possible gain'. This interpretation and understanding of the 'principle of double effect' was a clear departure from the traditional understanding of both ontic evil and intrinsic evil.

The best illustration of this new approach to 'principle of double effect' can be seen in looking at the issue of an ectopic pregnancy. In the 1960s, a traditional approach to an ectopic pregnancy would be to permit the removal of the fallopian tube directly, which also indirectly involves the removal of the foetus, but to **not** permit the cutting of the tube (mutilation) and direct removal of the foetus from the tube to then repair the tube. This uses a strict application of 'principle of double effect' that considers the direct intention and act of aborting the foetus through mutilation of the tube as failing the four criteria. Knauer instinctively observed that the procedure of removing the tube created most evil. As Selling writes, 'He concluded that the 'principle of double effect' was not only being abused in this situation but that the core meaning of the principle itself was being ignored'. Since the development and use of a drug called methotrexate, which targets the most rapidly growing cells of the embryo (first used in the 1980s), the method of removing both part of the tube and the foetus dilemma was replaced with a different 'direct' act that raised an equal dilemma. Needless to say, the only licit act in line with the 'principle of double effect' remained the option to remove a section of the fallopian tube directly, indirectly removing the foetus but also reducing the fertility of the woman.

In practice, for proportionalists, this means that the direct act of removal of the foetus can be preferred to the removal of both tube and foetus, because 'commensurate' or 'proportional reasoning' has removed the sharp distinction between direct and indirect actions and intentions and based the ethical decision upon deontology, teleology, intentions, and considered the overall balance between resulting ontic and pre-moral evils and ontic and pre-moral goods, **values and disvalues**. Is, then, the removal of just the foetus a 'good' act? The answer is 'no', since 'every human act brings evil effects with it' according to Knauer; however, it is an ethically correct decision or 'right act' that simultaneously acknowledges an evil act (abortion) but one that incorporates both the saving of the mother's life and the possibility of future life.

Theologians such as John Finnis and all those scholars involved in producing *Veritatis Splendor* see the proportionalist methodology as directly contradicting the divine principle found in Romans 3:8, 'And why not say (as some people slander us by saying that we say), "Let us do evil so that good may come"? Their condemnation is deserved!' This biblical verse (condition 3 associated with the 'principle of double effect') is crucial for those who reject the proportionalist methodology and it is the principal reason for rejection by the magisterium. The declaration by the Pope in *Veritatis Splendor* is clear that those who follow proportionalist thinking are those who contravene this verse and use good ends to justify evil means. However, this interpretation of Romans 3:8 is contested by revisionist theologians.

The traditionalists argue that Proportionalism gives too much emphasis to the fourth condition of 'principle of double effect' (proportionate reasoning) and ironically takes it out of all proportion! Revisionists/proportionists respond that the fourth condition of 'principle of double effect' is not the last condition to be tested but is actually the most important issue in the 'principle of double effect' for Aquinas and is a summary of the first three conditions. Grisez and Finnis, the New Natural Law thinkers hold that a basic good can never be commensurate or proportionate. Selling argues that "principle of double effect' is a fine example of the Catholic tradition being able to "compare" sometimes very different "goods" with each other.'

Therefore, both traditionalists and proportionalists use the 'principle of double effect' with reference to Aquinas and apply proportionate reasoning as one of the conditions; however, it is in **how** they understand Aquinas' four conditions, and in particular the fourth condition of proportionate reason, where they differ widely. This separates them and aptly justifies the revisionists who follow Knauer's interpretation as 'proportionalists'.

NORMAL PREGNANCY   ECTOPIC PREGNANCY

EMBRYO   EMBRYO

In an ectopic pregnancy the embryo embeds itself in the fallopian tube.

AO1 Activity

Write down five key points you have learned about the principle of double effect. This will help in selecting relevant information for an answer to a question that expects knowledge and understanding of Proportionalism.

Key quotes

We may never directly take the life of an innocent human being, though we may sometimes tolerate the indirect and unintended loss of life that comes with trying to properly address a life-threatening medical situation. **(Catholic Education Resource Centre)**

Some say that cutting out a section of the tube with a baby inside is no different than using methotrexate because, in either case, the baby ends up dying. Yet the difference in how the baby dies is, in fact, critical. There is always a difference between killing someone directly and allowing someone to die of indirect causes. **(Catholic Education Resource Centre)**

Key term

Values and disvalues: a proportionalist way of calculating elements of a moral event

quickfire

2.20 What happened during the 1980s to assist with ectopic pregnancies?

Study tip

Make sure that you are familiar with the details of the principle of double effect so that you are able to demonstrate thorough, accurate and relevant knowledge and understanding of it in relation to Proportionalism.

Specification content

Proportionalist maxim ('it is never right to go against a principle unless there is a proportionate reason which would justify it').

> **Key terms**
>
> Agape: Christian love
>
> Pre-moral evil: a potential feature of a moral act, e.g. anger, deceit – some proportionalists extend this to all types of imperfection that occur as a result of any action

A proportionalist maxim 'it is never right to go against a principle unless there is a proportionate reason which would justify it'

There are many areas for debate within Proportionalism itself but the Specification focuses on four key aspects of Proportionalism as identified within Bernard Hoose's book:

(1) A 'proportionalist maxim'

(2) Distinction between evil moral act and pre-moral evil/ontic evil

(3) The difference between and good act and a right act

(4) How proportionate reasoning is based upon agape.

We will take each aspect in turn and attempt to relate it to the Proportionalism debate in general.

The first item to consider is what is referred to as 'Hoose's proportionalist maxim'. What this refers to is the fourth rule of the 'principle of double effect'. In the Specification this is presented as '**it is never right to go against a principle unless there is a proportionate reason which would justify it**'.

There are two aspects to the maxim: (1) deontological emphasis; and (2) a proviso (condition) of commensurate (comparable or proportionate) reasoning.

The maxim stated in the Specification is an attempt made by writers to present the basic thesis of Proportionalism; however, this maxim, presented this way, does have its limitations and dangers and we need to be careful how each aspect of the maxim is understood.

The deontological emphasis 'it is never right to go against a principle'

It is vital to remember that Proportionalism falls within both Natural Law and Roman Catholic theology, which identify clear deontological principles that are absolute. Proportionalists do not reject deontological rules, just as Joseph Fletcher did not reject the laws. As stated above, these are always and in all cases to be followed and, despite an apparent contradiction in 'principle of double effect', the four conditions make it clear that it is in situations of a conflict of interest wherein a greater good overturns a lesser evil.

We have already seen that Aquinas' example of the 'principle of double effect', using self-defence, is the classic illustration, whereby even though killing is permitted, the true purpose and intent of the action is preservation of life. For proportionalists, therefore, and in terms of Romans 3:8 '... Let us do evil so that good may come ...' the 'principle of double effect' transforms this to 'Let us do the greater good in preserving life even though this may result in unavoidable, but proportionately lesser, evil'. In this way, it is argued that the maxim 'it is never right to go against a principle' – that is the willing acceptance of death through evil means that conflicts with the preservation of life – is still upheld despite the accidental and unavoidable act of killing. It is this idea of **conflict** within a precept or between precepts that is the key to 'principle of double effect'. Accordingly, for proportionalists, deontological values behind the precepts are maintained.

The proviso of 'unless there is a proportionate reason which would justify it'

An understanding of what the phrase 'proportionate reason' means precisely, and accurately, is vital for Proportionalism. Any misunderstanding of this at the outset would mean a total misunderstanding of Proportionalism and this has occurred on many occasions. James Walter states: 'If proportionate reason is misunderstood as something added over and above an act already defined, e.g., either as "intention" in the classical manualist tradition or as some "serious reason", then one will continue to misrepresent the theory of proportionate reason at a very fundamental level, i.e., at the level of definition.' Proportionate reason is synonymous with practical reason (ethical reasoning) only as far as its context allows (the 'principle of double effect') and so is a very specific type of practical reasoning.

Accordingly, Knauer has argued that defining 'proportionate reason' as some serious reason which one might offer in order to justify pre-moral evil in any action as 'the most evil form of ethical relativism'. It may well be worth heeding the words of Aquinas himself: 'though proceeding from a good intention, an act may be rendered unlawful if it be out of proportion to the end'.

The term 'proportionate' refers to the focus of that reasoning for the 'final condition for the determination of morality' according to James Walter because it establishes a formal structural relationship between the pre-moral value(s) and disvalue(s) in the act. In other words, each and every aspect of the moral act is considered as valid without being dismissed through any form of direct/indirect distinction.

Proportionalists uphold the absolute need for rules (deontology).

Study tip

There are many opportunities in this topic to show that you can use an extensive range of scholarly views/schools of thought. It is important, however, that you are accurate in their usage. Rather than just learning names, test yourself further by writing a short paragraph in connection with each one that summarises the viewpoint/argument that they have made.

AO1 Activity

After reading through each of the key aspects of the proportionalist maxim, close the book and write down some key phrases and/or words relating to each aspect.

Misinterpretation of the maxim

Unfortunately, sometimes the maxim is interpreted glibly as 'yes rules are important but **if there is good reason** to break them …'. This is precisely the sort of presentation that has angered proportionalists and also led to associations of Proportionalism with consequentialism and teleological approaches. In *Veritatis Splendor* the magisterium accuses proportionalists of abusing the verse in

Key quotes

One should not mean by 'reason' some serious reason which one might offer in order to justify the pre-moral evil in the act. (Walter)

Positively, most proponents of the contemporary theory mean by 'reason' a concrete value which is at stake in the act of an agent. (Walter)

Proportionate reason means three things: a) a value at stake at least equal to that sacrificed; b) no other way of salvaging it here and now; c) its protection here and now will not undermine it in the long run. (McCormick)

Though proceeding from a good intention, an act may be rendered unlawful if it be out of proportion to the end. (Aquinas)

quickfire

2.21 Why is the first part of the proportionalist maxim so important?

Key term

Veritatis Splendor: a papal encyclical published in 1993

Key quotes

The proportionality condition is usually understood to involve determining if the extent of the harm is adequately offset by the magnitude of the proposed benefit. (McIntyre)

Reason does not mean some serious reason, or even a good intention that would justify the pre-moral disvalues in an act… Similar to the misinterpretation of reason, proportionate is frequently considered 'a mathematical measurement' or 'weighing'. (Salzman)

Specification content

Distinction between a good act (an act that follows the moral rule) and a right act (an act that is not necessarily a good act but creates the lesser of two evils).

Romans 3:8. In other words, the concern of the encyclical and the Roman Catholic magisterium is that proportionalists are justifying evil in order to arrive at a greater good. However, proportionalists would respond that they are concerned with justifying what is right and are considering seriously the 'principle of double effect' and commensurate reason not because they wish to justify evil but rather because they wish to evaluate the grave consequences of breaking a precept against the holistic unit of the moral action including various elements (act-in-itself, intention, moral character, effect, pre-moral goods and evils or values, etc.).

It is therefore not so much they wish to justify evil as they feel they are obliged to explain why the moral act in its entirety produces more that is good which renders the evil as necessary, but at the same time, subsumed by a greater good. This does not mean the action in itself is good, or to put it bluntly not evil, but rather, that it is morally 'right', which is an entirely different matter altogether. For example, it is difficult to see how anyone, anywhere would think that an abortion is a 'good' act-in-itself, or that mutilation of the body is a 'good' act-in-itself, or that killing in self-defence is a 'good' act-in-itself; however, many would agree that sometimes they are the 'right' course of action to take and this is down to commensurate and proportionate reasoning.

The message is clear and the maxim 'never right to go against a principle' delivers the deontological force of this. The proviso is of reasoning that is of such force, gravity and intensity that it is comparable in ethical status to that of the deontological rule it attempts to challenge. These are simply the first three conditions of the 'principle of double effect' and they must not be forgotten. As McCormick writes in his essay *Ambiguity in Moral Choice*, proportionate reason means 'a value at least equal to that sacrificed' and that there is 'no less harmful way of protecting the value here and now' so that such proportionate reason would not 'undermine it in the long run'. This is no mere or simplistic hermeneutical feat but involves a complex series of deliberations involving many aspects of the ethical act such as precepts/goods, ethical rules, intentions, the moral character of the individual, the 'means' (finis operis) and the 'ends' (finis operantis), the values (pre-moral goods) and disvalues (pre-moral evils).

The crucial debate: good and right

As we have seen earlier, Hoose's main observation initially was that there was a different use of vocabulary amongst early writers on Proportionalism. For example, sometimes a scholar would talk about something being bad or evil when meaning 'wrong'. Alternatively, 'sin' would be equated with 'evil' or 'immorality' and different words used for the same concept. For instance, concerning the term 'ontic evil' Peter Knauer wrote of 'physical evil', Josef Fuchs of 'pre-moral evil', whilst Richard McCormick used both 'pre-moral evil' and 'non-moral evil', and whilst Bruno Schiller preferred 'non-moral evil', Louis Janssens varied between 'ontic evil' and also 'pre-moral disvalue'. This was evident from Hoose's survey of the earliest articles published by Knauer, McCormick, Schiller and Janssens to name a few.

In the light of a very complex debate that was emerging, Hoose attempted to clarify the issues of good, evil, right and wrong by looking at a fundamental philosophical distinction that had been made by G. E. Moore in his *Principia Ethica* many years earlier. For Moore, in ethical debate there was a definite distinction between the words good and right, and the words evil and wrong. In short, a good moral action is an action that follows a moral rule and does not deviate; it is a **descriptive** term that highlights the moral qualities of an action and the person involved. However, the question as to whether this is a morally right action to take is an entirely different matter; this is not descriptive, but **evaluative**, and requires a moral judgement and that this moral judgement could be based upon a variety of different determining factors.

Although Moore admitted that a morally good act could depend upon intention, for him, the idea of considering the intention of an act had no value whatsoever in judging whether it was morally right or wrong. He writes regarding the moral praiseworthiness of an act: 'My point is only that this question does sometimes depend on the motive, in some degree; whereas the questions whether his action was right or wrong never depends upon it at all.'

Therefore, an action may be morally good but whether or not it is morally right or wrong depends upon several contextual factors that a philosopher must consider. For the proportionalist, this soon developed into a consideration of an action by looking at the balance of goods and evils that were intrinsic to the whole, concrete ethical decision and action, and achieving this 'calculation' through considering other contributing contextual factors that were integral to this. It is also interesting to note that intention, although part of the proportionalist overall reasoning, only serves to help identify what is good, and, true to Moore's original distinction, it cannot solely, or directly, determine what is right.

Hoose notes that there was some confusion initially amongst Proportionalists about this:

> 'Chirico, like so many other people (not surprisingly at that stage) had failed to grasp the importance of the distinctions between pre-moral evil, the moral wrongness of an act and the moral badness of a person acting. An act is either morally right or morally wrong. It cannot be both. If we talk of morally evil (meaning morally wrong) elements in an act that is morally right and is performed by a morally good person, we confuse the whole issue.'

Hoose was not the only one irritated by the imprecise language used. Frankena, in McCormick's book '*Doing Evil to Achieve Good*', directly criticises the early work of Richard McCormick who does precisely what Hoose had observed and states: 'Like most moral theologians, Catholic and Protestant, he carries his discussion on entirely by the use of words like good, bad, evil, sins, value, moral evil, immoral, morally acceptable; he makes little or no use of right, wrong, ought, duty, obligation or a right. That is, he mainly uses what I call **aretaic** terms and only occasionally **deontic** ones.' For both Hoose and Frankena, in order to debate philosophically, there needed to be made a clear distinction between the predicates of actions and their agents. Aretaic terms say more about the agent than they do the action; deontic terms say more about what is ethical or moral about the action.

Key quotes

We should note the distinction … between a 'natural' good or evil and 'moral' goodness or malice which can only be attributed to the entire moral event, taking its cue from the end which is embraced through intention. (Selling)

And now faith, hope, and love abide, these three; and the greatest of these is love. (1 Corinthians 13:13)

In other words, the Roman Catholic Church had a clear idea of what was 'good'. Aquinas' primary precepts and rightly reasoned secondary precepts were the 'rule', i.e. the deontological norm. When applied to ethical issues these were absolute and there was no need for deviation. Proportionalists agreed that rules were, in general, a good thing; however, when application to ethical issues arises, they rejected the idea of an absolute 'rule' and exploited the loophole of Aquinas' thinking about commensurate, proportionate reasoning. Therefore, the rules, although absolute in one sense – in abstract – that in general, work in practice, should be carefully reasoned in application so that they are in fact the purest form of the rule.

Key terms

Aretaic: Frankena's term to describe words that are to do with goodness and virtue as qualities of a person and act, from the Greek word arete meaning 'virtue'

Deontic: an evaluative term that concludes what one should do and how one should behave

Key quote

Blessed are the merciful, for they will receive mercy.

Blessed are the pure in heart, for they will see God.

Blessed are the peacemakers, for they will be called children of God. (Matthew 5: 7–9)

quickfire

2.22 What does Frankena mean when he says proportionalists mainly used aretaic terms?

Virtues and moral character of a person are important to Christianity.

In this way, proportionalists were seeing themselves as being true to Aquinas' thinking. However, the implications of this are as follows:

A good act for proportionalist thinkers is describing an action that follows and is in accordance with a moral rule and not only produces a good end, also impacts upon the virtuous character of the individual involved.

A right act for proportionalist thinkers does not necessarily have to be a good act or follow a moral rule when conflict arises between obligations; a right act can be a good act or an act that is right because it produces a greater amount of good than evil.

The crux of the debate is:

- Proportionalists '*moral good is not necessarily moral right; moral evil is not necessarily morally wrong*'.
- Traditional Roman Catholic theology '*moral good necessarily is moral right; moral evil is always morally wrong*'.

Hoose concludes, 'This chapter has helped to clarify the main issue for us. It has asked the question: what are the proportionalists talking about? It has answered that some of them are talking about how to ascertain the rightness and wrongness of acts, and it would seem that the others should be discussing the same thing, although it is far from clear that they are in fact doing so.'

Hoose also offers a perceptive explanation for this in his third chapter, '*The Moral Goodness / Moral Rightness Distinction*' when he states that it was 'an inaccurate appreciation of what is contained in the deposit of faith'. By this Hoose means that Roman Catholic theologians and philosophers are concerned with questions of **soteriology**, that is, 'what must I do to be saved?' Integral to any answer is all about moral character, in Hoose's words 'being and becoming morally good'. Christian lifestyle is about virtue as much as it is about rules for living; it is all about becoming a good person, a 'Christian' individual defined by character. Therefore, the morally right thing to do is inextricably bound up with the morally good thing to do. It is all part of the '**salvific reality**' and the end goal of the **Beatific Vision**. In fairness, Josef Fuchs, one revisionist, had already begun to see this at the time of Hoose's research, when Fuchs indicated that morality for the Roman Catholic Christian was not just concerned with the finis operis (act-in-itself) but also with the finis operantis (the intention) of the moral agent, that is, a person's attitude and, therefore, personal virtue, character or 'goodness'. However, this use of the term 'goodness' is not always helpful when considering whether an action is morally right or wrong.

What is clear, however, was that gradually emerging within the debate was the fact that there was a clear distinction between what was a morally good action and what was a morally right action, and that the two were not necessarily synonymous.

This distinction has held through to the debate today and it is the essence of Proportionalism's defence that good and right are not always the same. Traditional Roman Catholic theology, however, would **never** say that a good act is one which considers the lesser of evils, but conversely, it could concede that a good act must also be a right act.

Key terms

Beatific Vision: the teleological end of Natural Law according to Aquinas whereby one is united with God through Christ

Salvific reality: the realisation that the teleological end of life is salvation

Soteriology: a quest to discover what the requirements for salvation are

Key quotes

The motive may be important for a decision about moral goodness or badness (sin) but has no part in decisions about the moral rightness or wrongness of acts. (Hoose)

The conscience cannot mislead one about moral goodness and badness. It always and infallibly calls for moral goodness. However, it can mislead on regarding what is morally right. (Hoose)

Every aspect of the moral event contains some amount of good and evil. For the very fact that it takes place, or as Thomas would say, 'has being', is good, while no human activity is perfect and there is always a deficiency of some sort. (Selling)

Distinction between an evil moral act (an immoral act) and pre-moral/ontic evil

First of all, we have seen that 'an evil moral act' is, within Roman Catholic theology, usually understood as 'intrinsic evil'. An act is intrinsically evil if it is always bad, sinful and wrong in every instance and can never be considered as good or right. Acts such as torture, murder, rape, stealing and lying have been the topics for debate within Proportionalism. However, as we have seen from the distinction between 'good' and 'right', in Proportionalism an evil act may not always be an **immoral act**, as sometimes it may be in line with **commensurate reasoning** and therefore the 'ethically right' course of action to take. For the proportionalist, there is more to an act than just its physical aspect when moral evaluations, judgements and decisions are made.

It is interesting that Professor Joseph Selling, a more contemporary proportionalist, in his book *Reframing Catholic Theological Ethics* (2016) has also distinguished between an 'act' (the moral act-in-itself) and what he calls an 'event' by which he means the various elements that enter the equation upon acting. He writes:

> 'Making moral evaluations and decisions is a complex process. This is why I refer to it as an "event" rather than an "act". The component parts of the moral event are distinct. When a moral event is complete, all the parts form an inseparable unity. However, those component parts may still be addressed individually. This is perhaps most obvious when one considers the ends or reasons why one does anything.'

This is useful when considering what is meant by ontic / pre-moral evil according to proportionalists.

Ontic evil in traditional Roman Catholic thought is physical evil as opposed to moral evil (Aquinas). It belongs to the natural evil fold; **however**, proportionalists have 'stretched' this out to incorporate the complete 'fallenness' of nature. For example, the writings of both Knauer and Janssens include the idea of moral imperfection in humanity as part of ontic evil. Whilst Roman Catholic theology makes a distinction between ontic (e.g. physical fact of death, disease, etc.) and pre-moral evil (factors integral to the human moral disposition, e.g. hatred, jealousy and anger), proportionalists conflate the two.

Professor Paul Quay published an article in 1985 *Theological Studies 46* that criticises this conflation of ontic and pre-moral evils. Quay argues that a physical absence of good (ontic evil) such as 'some damage to ... physical or psychic substance or power of operation' such as sickness of some kind, is very different from the understanding of ontic evil that revisionists such as Louis Janssens propose: 'We call ontic evil any lack of a perfection at which we aim, any lack of fulfilment which frustrates our natural urges and makes us suffer. It is essentially the natural consequence of our limitation.' For Quay, proportionalists have extended the physical aspects of ontic evil into the general shortcomings of moral character evident from human fallen nature such as general lack of perfections, which is, according to Quay, inaccurate. To some extent this was hidden by the chaotic nature of the early debate due to the problematic use of language between those involved in the discussions.

For proportionalists, then, the terms 'ontic' and 'pre-moral' refer to values that underline an action and not the act-in-itself i.e. they are possible **features** of an act and this is why some proportionalists refer to the idea of pre-moral 'values' and 'disvalues'. The act of killing, for example, is an evil act because its ontic / pre-moral features are violation of life, prevents survival, disturbs the good of society, it is unnatural. The problem has been, once again that different proportionalist writers use the term interchangeably or alternative terms like disvalues or nonmoral evil.

Specification content

Distinction between an evil moral act (an immoral act) and pre-moral/ontic evil.

Key quotes

Proportionalism rests on a distinction between physical or pre-moral evil (e.g. killing) and moral evil (e.g. murder). One can do pre-moral evil if there is a proportionate reason. Thus, every killing is not murder. Proportionalism constitutes a middle position objecting on the one hand to neo-Scholastic Natural Law approaches and on the other hand, the newer approaches of Germain Grisez and John Finnis but also objecting to consequentialism and Utilitarianism. (Charles Curran on Richard McCormick's view of Proportionalism)

Concentrating on human behaviour, traditional moral theology tended to exaggerate certain aspects of its analysis ... The phrase 'intrinsic evil' is typical of such exaggeration, for it is never clear whether things are labelled as such in reference to simple physical acts, circumstantiated behaviour, or in fact complete, motivated and intended events. (Selling)

Key terms

Moral event: the term preferred by Professor Joseph Selling to describe an ethical 'act' because it conveys the idea that there is more to an ethical action than just the act-in-itself

Natural evil: used to refer to events in the natural world that cause evil and suffering, e.g. disease and natural disasters

Key quotes

There are many acts that could be called 'intrinsically evil' if their circumstances are exhaustively included in description of the actions. (McCormick)

The agent must take into account not only the so-called welfare values, but also dignity values, expressive actions, institutional obligations, the meaning of the action, the pre-moral evil of breaking a promise, the unfairness of a situation, etc. (Hoose)

Proportionalists argue that no judgement of moral rightness or wrongness of acts can be made without considering all circumstances of the action. (Walter)

Because the human act is a structural unity, no aspect of the act can be morally appraised apart from all the other components. Consideration of the agent's intention, all foreseeable consequences, institutional obligations, and a proportion between the pre-moral values and disvalues are necessary before making moral judgment. (Walter)

The way in which this is relevant for the proportionalist debate is that an ethical act should be evaluated on account of not just the act-in-itself but also considering the various elements that the initiation of that action brings: intention and circumstances, any pre-moral or ontic goods and evils, values/disvalues behind the act (e.g. life/death, health/illness) or our own imperfections and the world around us – the things that we may possess or lack. As Salzman writes: 'Those aspects include consequences (both short and long term, to the extent that these are foreseeable), context or situation, pre-moral values and disvalues, institutional obligations, relational considerations, the traditional circumstances, and any other consideration that would influence an overall analysis of an act's rightness or wrongness.'

For example, killing in self-defence makes the act-in-itself morally right when proportionate reasoning is applied, although not morally good; however, since the pre-moral values and ontic circumstances that outweigh the pre-moral evil inherent/potential in the act of killing, killing in self-defence may be morally right. Remember, any kind of killing can never really be morally good but this is not the same as moral rightness. Rightness is not goodness and this is explored in the next section.

It is this 'compromise' that is the issue for traditional Roman Catholic theology, and this is why there is confusion over an '*intrinsic evil act*'. Proportionalists would reject this in terms of finis operis (i.e. the act-in-itself) because it is abstracted from all the considerations outlined above; however, when such wider considerations are taken into account, it may well **become** an 'intrinsically evil act' in this instance, but only when proportionate reason has been applied (which, in their view, is traditional Roman Catholic theology anyway). As Richard McCormick writes in his *Notes on Moral Theology*: 'There are many acts that could be called "intrinsically evil" if their circumstances are exhaustively included in description of the actions.'

However, by intrinsic evil, not only does the magisterium insist that an intrinsic evil act is always evil; more crucially, an intrinsic evil act is evil by its very nature, that is, the act-in-itself is always wrong.

Proportionalists would reply that the action of killing is evil, and when all elements of the moral action are considered, it may well be evil in that particular case; however, the complete act of killing may not necessarily be **fully and comprehensively** evil when the ontic evils / ontic goods / disvalues/values, motives, intentions and circumstances are factored into account. It may well be the morally right action when the good elements outweigh this evil. Proportionalists here, are making a clear distinction between moral evil/good and moral rightness/wrongness.

Nonetheless, traditional Roman Catholic theology argues that being morally good and acting morally good are more important than the moral 'rightness' as defined by proportionalists which is seen as an ugly compromise to consequentialism. According to both the Pope and traditional Roman Catholic theology, **moral 'rightness' is identical/synonymous with moral goodness** – there can be no separation and compromise! According to the Pope, Proportionalism is just disobeying Romans 3:8, 'And why not say (as some people slander us by saying that we say), **"Let us do evil so that good may come"? Their condemnation is deserved!'**

The crucial point for traditional Roman Catholic theology is that the moral culpability of the individual (especially intention re: virtue) may be affected by the 'extras' that Proportionalism considers. For example, according to traditional theology, to kill in self-defence is both morally bad and a morally wrong action (and would need penance through confession) but the individual may not incur the sins of a pre-meditated murder and so whilst the act is morally bad this does not make the individual morally bad. In other words, as Moore observed, intention can affect moral goodness of a person but never moral rightness and vice versa!

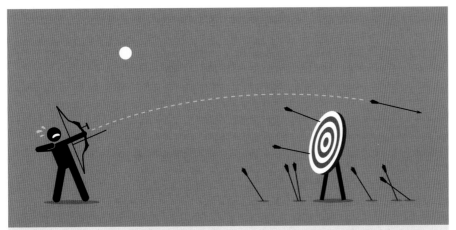

Louis Janssens referred to ontic evil as any lack of a perfection at which we aim, any lack of fulfilment which frustrates our natural urges and makes us suffer.

Study tip

Make sure you understand the crucial difference between 'good' and 'right' for proportionalist theory. Try to think of an example to back up your explanation.

AO1 Activity

Make sure that you know what the key terms used here mean. Make a list of some important concepts and their meaning to recall: ontic evil, immoral act, pre-moral, evil moral act, a good act, a right act, etc.

Key quotes

Human acts are moral acts because they express and determine the goodness or evil of the individual who performs them. They do not produce a change merely in the state of affairs outside of man but, to the extent that they are deliberate choices, they give moral definition to the very person who performs them, determining his profound spiritual traits. (Veritatis Splendor 71)

By contrast, the fruit of the Spirit is love, joy, peace, patience, kindness, generosity, faithfulness, gentleness, and self-control. There is no law against such things. (Galatians 5:22–23)

quickfire

2.23 How do some proportionalists understand ontic evil?

Specification content
Proportionality based on agape.

Proportionality based on agape

As we have seen, Aquinas' Natural Law ethics identifies agape or Christian love as the highest of all virtues. When Natural Law ethics is applied, it must therefore be grounded in agape. In line with the Beatific Vision, Christians will accordingly aim towards the end of developing a 'Godly' and virtuous character as exemplified in the person of Jesus.

During the mid to latter half of the 20th century, philosophers and theologians were questioning a purely deontological approach to ethics. This was especially so with Joseph Fletcher as we have seen from a study of Situation Ethics. Fletcher rejected any absolutist deontological position because, for him, the practical and applied aspect of ethics did not allow this approach to work. He also rejected 'absolute' freedom (libertarianism) as well and his argument that an approach based upon situationism could work if the principle of agape was used. To clarify something that is often misunderstood about Fletcher, however, he rejected a deontological approach to ethics. Fletcher did not, as some have read him, reject moral laws or rules, which is a very different matter altogether. For Fletcher, religious and moral rules served a specific purpose but how he saw them as different to a traditional deontological understanding of them was that they were never intended to be absolutes. This debate took place mainly within Protestant Christianity. However, although Roman Catholic moral theologians were aware of the debate, the idea of proportionality based on agape had nothing at all to do with Situation Ethics.

Indeed, Roman Catholic theologians were united in their response to what they called the 'New Morality' as typified by Fletcher and other thinkers. The Roman Catholic position, as articulated by the Pope in encyclicals and two major documents, namely, *Humanae Vitae* (29 July 1968) and *Veritatis Splendor* (6 August 1993), was a rejection of any teleological ethical position determined solely by 'ends', consequences or situation but also a strong defence of a purely deontological approach grounded firmly in Aquinas' Natural Law. This was the response of the Roman Catholic Church to those **outside of the Roman Catholic tradition**, i.e. the Protestant traditions, that may have supported a more consequential approach to ethics.

Within Roman Catholicism itself, however, despite a united front in statements such as *Humanae Vitae* and *Veritatis Splendor*, there was a **different** internal debate about the approach to applied ethics. This had nothing at all to do with the consequentialist debates going on at the same time within Protestant Christianity and was, as we have seen, centred around the understanding of the 'principle of double effect'.

Hopefully this will deter any form of comparison between Proportionalism and Situation Ethics. The word agape is Christian, biblical and not exclusive to Situation Ethics. In addition, any Christian model of ethics should be based in the teachings of Jesus about love. The fact that a constitution was published by the magisterium in the 1960s that focused on a loving and virtuous Christian response to moral and social issues underlines this. Proportionalism was no different and a central focus on the revealed virtue of love, closest to the Beatific Vision, was stressed together with the idea of being and becoming a 'good' person by developing a 'virtuous' character.

The difference between Proportionalism and Situation Ethics is that Proportionalism is not based upon agape alone and as Hoose writes: 'McCormick accused Fletcher of being ambiguous and of using flamboyant rhetoric as if it were moral reasoning'. Indeed, as we have seen earlier, McCormick saw Fletcher's work as having no methodology, and the scholar Gustafson accused Fletcher of using the revealed virtue of love in an evasive way 'that runs through Fletcher's book like a greased pig'. Needless to say, Roman Catholic moral theologians could not relate to agape as outlined by Joseph Fletcher.

Key quote

The elaboration of Virtue Theory provides a fertile background for developing a richer picture of the virtuous person. It also highlights various human situations that predictably call for a virtuous response. (Selling)

Key term

Consequentialist: any ethical theory that hinges a moral decision upon what the consequences of the action would be (the end or outcome)

For Proportionalism, agape remains the highest virtue, as stated by Paul in 1 Corinthians 13 that 'the greatest of these is love'. Proportionalists still concur with traditional Roman Catholicism that developing the highest of the revealed virtues is the very basis of living a Christian life, which automatically and very appropriately, incorporates ethical behaviour.

Key quotes

'Teacher, which commandment in the law is the greatest?' He said to him, 'You shall love the Lord your God with all your heart, and with all your soul, and with all your mind. This is the greatest and first commandment.' (Matthew 22:36–38)

But I say to you listen, love your enemies, do good to those who hate you. (Luke 6:27)

Beloved, let us love one another, because love is from God; everyone who loves is born of God and knows God. (1 John 4:7)

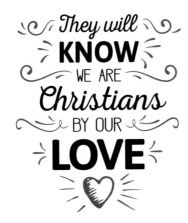

Love should be the basis of any Christian ethical theory.

quickfire

2.24 Why is agape central to Proportionalism?

Key terms

Conflation: the merging of two ideas

Hybrid: of mixed character or composed of different elements

Proportionalism as a hybrid of Natural Law, a deontological / teleological ethic

Specification content

As a hybrid of Natural Law, a deontological / teleological ethic.

A hybrid is a mixture or conflation of two clearly distinct elements or ideas. A deontological / teleological ethic therefore means that it is both rule-based but also dependent upon considering the 'ends' of any rule in order to add further validation.

In some ways this heading can be very misleading as it could lead us to assume that Natural Law, especially that outlined by Aquinas, is either deontological or teleological and not a hybrid itself. It also assumes that Proportionalism, although related to Natural Law, is a different theory in stating 'Proportionalism as a hybrid of Natural Law'. However, in line with the Specification main heading for this whole theme, the focus is on 'recent modern developments' and in this sense Proportionalism is very much a recent modern development within Natural Law moral theology. This is important to note. Indeed, proportionalists argue that Proportionalism is only being true to the fundamentals of Natural Law ethical theory in considering both the deontological and teleological aspects. They argue that the proportionalist position is not a deontological / teleological hybrid of Natural Law but that more importantly, it is vital to see Natural Law itself as a deontological / teleological hybrid! Proportionalists argue that they are preserving the tradition of Aquinas and Natural Law and that Natural Law was never intended as a purely deontological ethic. In the same way, Hoose points out that 'the need for proportionate reason is one of the deeply rooted elements in the tradition of Catholic moral theology'.

Since Natural Law has various ethical aspects that are both deontological (precepts) and teleological (the end of the Beatific Vision and the goal of virtuous behaviour), both the precepts and virtues are essential in Natural Law moral theology. The magisterium of Roman Catholicism has in fairness promoted both aspects of Natural Law; however, there is a general feeling by some scholars that precepts and deontology have been stressed as first and foremost and that virtues have long been neglected. Many therefore see the Roman Catholic understanding of Natural Law, based in Aquinas, as fundamentally deontological. This is not a universally accepted viewpoint within the traditionalist camp. However, there has also been a recent emphasis on establishing norms for moral behaviour through deontological means and the focus has been on maintaining and establishing the precepts and presenting an emphasis on intrinsic evils in order to respond to the social, moral and religious challenges of modern society and alternative ethical theories such as those that are purely consequentially based such as Utilitarianism, Situation Ethics and later, post-modernism.

It is no great surprise that whilst traditionally upholding Aquinas' interpretation of capital punishment as licit, the magisterium has now declared any form of capital punishment illicit. Indeed, the concept of a 'Just War', to which Aquinas has made such an important contribution, is now being debated within Roman Catholic moral theology and the Pope is being urged to refine the traditional teachings on this issue. What is very interesting is that as the proportionalist controversy is centred around an interpretation of 'principle of double effect' as outlined by Aquinas and that these two issues relate directly to this controversy. One could suggest that the magisterium is 'tightening up' the deontological focus of Natural Law.

Joseph Selling's modern presentation of Roman Catholic moral theology looks at the structure of a moral act in its entirety as the basis of Natural Law ethical theory. Hoose's understanding was the same in his book. It would be wrong, argues Hoose, to accuse proportionalists of demanding a shift from deontological to teleological. He writes: 'Catholic moral theology has always been predominantly teleological. However, it must be admitted that there are examples of widely taught deontological norms of behaviour in the formulation of which the teleological aspects have either been ignored or not considered important enough to be taken into consideration.'

In 1993, the papal encyclical *Veritatis Splendor* (Splendour of the Truth) was released by the magisterium, six years after Hoose's book. In it the Pope clearly dismisses Proportionalism as a 'teleological theory' and groups it with Utilitarianism and Situation Ethics. The reasons for its rejection are that it is (a) purely consequentialist and therefore teleological interpretation of Natural Law and (b) it promotes immorality by suggesting that evil means can be used to produce good ends. The biblical verse used is Romans 3:8. Therefore, the magisterium clearly consider Proportionalism as teleological.

There were some interesting responses to *Veritatis Splendor*. Charles Curran, a well-known advocate for Proportionalism, had mixed reactions. On the one hand, he writes: 'I find myself in agreement with many of the Pope's problems with some contemporary ethical thinking, with the positive points he makes against them, and with the applications especially in the area of social ethics.' On the other hand, he also writes: 'I disagree with the position that condemns the revisionist developments in moral theology, but I am even more disturbed by other aspects of the papal document.' It is clear that the elements that 'disturb' Curran are not only the magisterium's insistence on 'intrinsically evil acts' and the condemnation of revisionist theology but mainly to do with the fact that he thinks the magisterium misunderstands and misinterprets revisionist theology at a very basic level by grouping it with other theories: 'As a result of misreading the present state of Catholic moral theology, the Pope apparently sees no difference between Catholic revisionist moral theologians and the proponents of absolute freedom, conscience separated from truth, individualism, subjectivism and relativism.'

Charles Curran's revisionist theology is often referred to as a 'theology of compromise' because it highlights the tensions between strict deontology and consequentialism. He refers to this position as '**prima facie obligationalism**' or 'teleology' (which he interprets, like Hoose, as distinct from forms of consequentialism). The advantage of seeing revisionist theology (Proportionalism) as teleological with prima facie obligations is that its reasoning takes all aspects of the act into account, unlike deontology, which only focuses on a few aspects of the action, and this is true to Natural Law theory.

Hoose agrees with Curran and states that Proportionalism is teleological and in the same way as Curran he rejects misunderstandings of what teleological means (i.e. those who group it with consequentialism). Hoose argues that Natural Law has always been teleological, but just in its insistence on deontological elements it has ignored teleological aspects. Hoose does not refer to Curran but instead surveys the views of Richard McCormick who constructs a very similar argument. Hoose provides an excellent summary of his own views on the teleology / deontology debate which is worth quoting here:

'That Proportionalism is a teleological theory in the general run of Catholic theological tradition seems to be beyond dispute. However, we have seen that the word "teleological", like so many other words in this debate ("good", "bad", "direct", "intention", etc.), can be misleading. In the proportionalist calculation, the telos aimed at is not the only one to be taken into account. The foreseeable consequences not aimed at must also be included, although the telos aimed at will, of course, be the reason for the act ... we must take into account not only the consequences properly so called, but also dignity values, expressive actions, institutional obligations, the very meaning of the action, etc.'

There is still debate as to whether Proportionalism is a distinctive ethical theory within Natural Law with its own specific methodology. That is, is it a 'teleological' methodology within the deontological theory of Natural Law – just as deriving secondary precepts from primary precepts is the basis of reasoning and the art of **casuistry** the basis of traditional Roman Catholic methodology? Or is it more accurate to say that Proportionalism describes a variety of methods in applying proportionate reason; therefore is it not really an ethical theory with a specific methodology, but simply a norm or criterion proposed?

Vatican dome of Saint Peter Basilica, Rome, Italy. The home of the magisterium.

Key quotes

A realistic assessment of the contemporary state of Catholic moral theology differs considerably from the picture painted in *Veritatis Splendor*. The differences between the Pope and revisionist moral theologians are by no means as great as *Veritatis Splendor* states. (Curran)

Veritatis Splendor strongly disagrees with and condemns many of the developments in Catholic moral theology since Vatican II and stands opposed to the revisionist moral theology in general. (Curran)

Key terms

Casuistry: a rational methodology that seeks to resolve moral problems by extracting or extending theoretical rules from one particular case, and reapplying those rules to new instances

Obligationism: an ethical view proposed by Charles Curran based in duty as part of his theology of compromise

Primae facie: accepted until demonstrated otherwise

Key quote

We should note the distinction ... between a 'natural' good or evil and 'moral' goodness or malice which can only be attributed to the entire moral event, taking its cue from the end which is embraced through intention. (Selling)

quickfire

2.25 What is the problem in evaluating Proportionalism as a deontological/teleological hybrid of Natural Law?

Recent developments in the proportionalist debate 1987 to date

As we have seen, the early debates about Proportionalism were trying to establish some kind of common language, methodology and clarify misunderstandings. Since the publication of Hoose's book, there has been the publication of *Veritatis Splendor*, which included the magisterium's condemnation of Proportionalism as a form of consequentialism. There were also responses to this, including one published by British scholars. The Archbishop of York at the time, Dr John Habgood, concluded that it 'should be interpreted as part of the continuing tension between the Roman Catholic Church's scholars and the magisterium'. The response to *Veritatis Splendor* published by American scholars included contributions by James Gaffney on Proportionalism, Stephen Lammers on war and peace and a notable response by Charles Curran from '*A Revisionist Perspective*'.

Since then the debate has continued until the present day, possibly – it could be argued – at a more sophisticated level but with more clarity. Charles Curran edited the book '*Moral Theology*', which is a collection of essays in honour of Richard McCormick, probably the most influential advocate for Proportionalism in the modern debate. Garth Hallett, another proportionalist has published '*Greater Good: The Case for Proportionalism*' (1995) in which he presents the new concept of 'value maximisation' by which he means that 'an action is right if and only if it promises to maximise value as fully, or nearly as fully, as any alternative action'. Professor Christopher Kaczor in 2000 compiled and contributed towards the seminal work '*Proportionalism: For and Against*', which incorporated the views of the key scholars that have contributed to the debate, both for and against Proportionalism and then shortly afterwards his individual work, '*Proportionalism and the Natural Law Tradition*' (2002), which was a comprehensive critique of Proportionalism from a conservative perspective. Just last year Charles Curran has edited a book that represents the diversity of revisionist approaches to Roman Catholic theology (*Diverse Voices in Modern US Moral Theology*).

The timeline below gives an overview of how the phenomenon that is known as Proportionalism developed during the course of the latter half of last century, and since Hoose's book, the year that followed up until the current day. I hope it is useful, mainly for teachers, but possibly for students who wish to get an overview of the subject.

Timeline of the proportionalist debate within the Roman Catholic tradition

Year	Event
1265–1274	**Thomas Aquinas** writes the *Summa Theologica* and in II.II 64,7 and 103,8 outlines what has come to be called the 'principle of double effect' (PDE).
1274–2018	Traditional Roman Catholic teaching accepts Aquinas' teachings on self-defence as justified by PDE and for the issues of war and capital punishment based upon different rational principles from PDE.
1869–70	**Vatican I**. Papal infallibility established.
1965	German Jesuit **Peter Knauer** writes '*The Hermeneutical Function of the 'principle of double effect'*' (French 1965; translated into English 1967) in which he challenges traditional understandings of the 'principle of double effect'.
1965	Traditionalist Roman Catholic scholar **Willem Van der Marck** writes on the issue of artificial contraception and argues that the direct/indirect distinction of double effect does not exist and that 'only the concrete human act is good or bad'.

Year	Event
1965	Abortion, divorce, remarriage and contraception begin to be identified as key contemporary issues by Roman Catholic moral theologians and generate much ethical debate in the years that follow.
1966	**Richard McCormick** reviews Knauer's article. At first critical, within two years McCormick himself was to be persuaded of Knauer's reformulated arguments and become a champion of Proportionalism.
1967–1968	More scholars enter the debate about the 'principle of double effect' such as **Peter Chirico** and **Charles Curran**. The nature of ethical decisions is recognised as complex and suggested that all values of an ethical act need to be considered. Curran argues for a **theology of compromise**.
1968	Papal Encyclical ***Humanae Vitae*** is published following **Vatican II**. The Pope condemns any use of 'artificial means' to regulate fertility. This meant that 'each and every marital act [sexual intercourse] must remain open to the transmission of life' (Humanae Vitae 11).
1965–80	Richard McCormick compiles his critically acclaimed '***Notes on Moral Theology***' which was a compilation of all articles published in ***Theological Studies*** in which McCormick annually surveys and reviews the literature published within moral theology with a strong revisionist approach to contemporary issues.
1969–86	Various academics respond to the writings of Richard McCormick and begin to address the issue of the nature of Christian Ethics including **Josef Fuchs** and **Bruno Schuller**. This in turn directs towards a more forensic analysis of an ethical act by such writers as McCormick and **Louis Janssens** in addition to Fuchs and Schuller. These scholars all put forward their own ideas on Proportionalism.
1978	McCormick edits and contributes to the book '***Doing Evil to Achieve Good***', which is a collection of essays from academics that directly address the strengths and weaknesses of aspects of Proportionalism. Contributors include McCormick, Brody, Ramsey, Frankena and Schuller. McCormick's first essay, '***Ambiguity in Moral Choice***', presents a methodology for Proportionalism using and responding to works by Knauer, Grisez, Van der Marck, Van der Poel, Philippa Foot and Schuller. His 'synthesis' of their work is a proposal that the traditional idea of intrinsic evil together with the 'principle of double effect' should be understood in relation to proportionate reason and that the 'lesser of two evils' is the preferred outcome.
1984	**James Walter** publishes 'Proportionate reason and its Three Levels of Enquiry: Structuring the Ongoing Debate' in *Louven Studies 10*. In the article, Walter aims to create a firm set of criteria for establishing a proportionalist methodology involving: (1) a definition of proportionate reasoning (2) a set of criteria to guide and establish proportionate reason (3) a test for the fulfilment of such criteria.
1987	**Bernard Hoose** publishes his book '**Proportionalism**', which is a survey and evaluation of the significance of the different strands of proportionalist views. Hoose's book establishes the 'coherence and validity of Proportionalism' and concludes that 'proportionate reason is one of the most deeply rooted elements in the tradition of Catholic moral theology'. Hoose sees both strengths and weaknesses to both sides of the debate.
1993	Papal Encyclical ***Veritatis Splendor*** is published. It is a direct response by the magisterium to the debates in moral theology, entitled 'Regarding Certain Fundamental Questions of the Church's Moral Teaching'. In the document the Pope condemns Proportionalism on the basis it is in direct contradiction to Holy Scripture Romans 3:8 which states: 'And why not say (as some people slander us by saying that we say), "Let us do evil so that good may come"? Their condemnation is deserved!' Proportionalism is accused of being a form of consequentialism and grouped with situationism and teleological theories.

Year	Event
1994	A response to *Veritatis Splendor* published by British scholars. The Archbishop of York at the time, Dr John Habgood, remarked that 'despite the claims of *Veritatis Splendor* to be expressing a universal truth, it is addressed primarily to the theological teachers of the Pope's own Church, much of it is written in coded language with criticisms of practices which outsiders may find hard to identify and evaluate'. As such, Habgood concludes that it 'should be interpreted as part of the continuing tension between the Roman Catholic Church's scholars and its magisterium'.
1995	A response to *Veritatis Splendor* published by American scholars. This response was more specifically directed to the issues raised and included contributions by James Gaffney on Proportionalism, Stephen Lammers on war and peace and a notable response by Curran from '*A Revisionist Perspective*'.
1990	Charles Curran edits the book '*Moral Theology*', which is a collection of essays in honour of Richard McCormick.
1995	Garth Hallett publishes '*Greater Good: The Case for Proportionalism*' in which he argues for a proportionalist approach to Christian ethics that he terms 'value maximisation' by which he means that 'an action is right if and only if it promises to maximise value as fully, or nearly as fully, as any alternative action'.
2000	Professor Christopher Kaczor compiles and contributes towards the seminal work '*Proportionalism: For and Against*' – a 500-page volume incorporating the views of the key scholars that have contributed to the debate both for and against Proportionalism. Knauer, Fuchs, Janssens, Schuller and McCormick represent the case for Proportionalism; Quay, Connery, Grisez and Finnis present the case against; Walter, Vacek, Kiely and Kaczor provide overviews and evaluations.
2002	Kaczor publishes '*Proportionalism and the Natural Law Tradition*' that is a comprehensive critique of Proportionalism from a traditional perspective.
2016	11–13 April a special conference was held to consider the Just War theory and the outcome of this was to urge the Pope to write a papal encyclical announcing any form of war as illicit. Joseph Selling publishes, '*Rethinking Catholic Theological Ethics*'.
2018	2 August 2018 section 2267 of the Church Catechism rejects the legitimacy of any form of capital punishment. Charles Curran edits and publishes '*Diverse Voices in Modern US Moral Theology*'.
2018	Prominent scholars, notably John Finnis, publish articles supporting the new directive against capital punishment and justify how the Pope can change tradition without recourse to a challenge to divine authority and papal infallibility. Edward Feser, on behalf of more conservative Roman Catholics, rejects Finnis' arguments and questions the legitimacy of the change.

The significance of the timeline

What is important about the timeline is what it tells us about both the Proportionalism debate and the role of Hoose's book within it. In many ways, Hoose's book was significant and a welcome contribution to the debate when published in 1987; however, as seen from above there is much more that post-dates his work that has both subsumed it and moved beyond it. Hoose's position in the book is one of establishing the 'coherence and validity of Proportionalism'. He is therefore not so much a key contributor to the ongoing debate but more a commentator on the debate from the outside.

The notion of Proportionalism claims to be derived directly from Aquinas' doctrine – the 'principle of double effect' – and as such this principle is focused on specific ethical dilemmas that are usually described by proportionalists as conflict situations.

Following the years of debate between revisionist theology and the magisterium it is interesting to see that traditional Roman Catholic scholars such as Kaczor – and indeed the magisterium itself – are tending towards a tighter position on such issues as war and capital punishment (in 2016 and 2018 respectively), a departure from the process of reasoning associated with Aquinas. The justification for this is not the 'principle of double effect' but rather an adjustment of Aquinas' reasoning in terms of historical context, or, in the case of Kaczor, a shift of objective in relation to primary precepts/goods.

The irony is that the only realistic position for the revisionists/proportionalists would be to arrive at the same outcome with regard to war and capital punishment by following the magisterium and traditional Roman Catholic teaching. It has been in relation to sexual ethics and family life where there are direct conflicts in moral values that disparity between proportionalists and the magisterium is more widespread.

There is mounting pressure for the magisterium to declare war an intrinsic evil.

quickfire

2.26 Who is usually associated with starting Proportionalism?

Study tip

It is popular to think that Proportionalism is just a simple theory about using reason to justify breaking a rule. Make sure that you understand that there was a great deal of debate amongst scholars about what Proportionalism actually was and that the understanding of what proportionalists were actually arguing has taken years of debate to achieve. Use the timeline to help you see how it developed.

AO1 Activity

Try creating your own flow chart or timeline of what you have learned about the debates related to Proportionalism. This will help in selecting relevant information for an answer to a question that expects knowledge and understanding of the development of an answer on Proportionalism.

Key skills Theme 2

The second theme has tasks that concentrate on a particular aspect of AO1 in terms of using quotations from sources of authority and in the use of references.

Key skills

Knowledge involves:

Selection of a range of (thorough) accurate and relevant information that is directly related to the specific demands of the question.

This means:

- Selecting relevant material for the question set
- Being focused in explaining and examining the material selected.

Understanding involves:

Explanation that is extensive, demonstrating depth and/or breadth with excellent use of evidence and examples including (where appropriate) thorough and accurate supporting use of sacred texts, sources of wisdom and specialist language.

This means:

- Effective use of examples and supporting evidence to establish the quality of your understanding
- Ownership of your explanation that expresses personal knowledge and understanding and NOT just reproducing a chunk of text from a book that you have rehearsed and memorised.

AO1 Developing skills

It is now important to consider the information that has been covered in this section; however, the information in its raw form is too extensive and so has to be processed in order to meet the requirements of the examination. This can be achieved by practising more advanced skills associated with AO1. For assessment objective 1 (AO1), which involves demonstrating 'knowledge' and 'understanding' skills, we are going to focus on different ways in which the skills can be demonstrated effectively, and also, refer to how the performance of these skills is measured (see generic band descriptors for A2 [WJEC] AO1 or A Level [Eduqas] AO1).

▶ **Your next task is this:** Below is a **summary of the proportionalist maxim**. At present it has no references at all to support the points made. Underneath the summary are two references to the works of scholars, and/or religious writings, that could be used in the outline in order to improve the summary. Your task is to re-write the summary but make use of the references. Such phrases as 'according to …', 'the scholar … argues', or, 'it has been suggested by …' may help. Usually a reference included a footnote but for an answer in an A Level essay under examination conditions this is not expected, although an awareness of which book your evidence refers to is useful (although not always necessary).

The message is clear and the maxim 'never right to go against a principle' delivers the deontological force of this. The proviso is of reasoning that is of such force, gravity and intensity that it is comparable in ethical status to that of the deontological rule it attempts to challenge. These are simply the first three conditions of the 'principle of double effect' and they must not be forgotten. This is no mere or simplistic hermeneutical feat but involves a complex series of deliberations involving many aspects of the ethical act such as precepts/goods, ethical rules, intentions, the moral character of the individual, the 'means' (finis operis) and the 'ends' (finis operantis), the values (pre-moral goods) and disvalues (pre-moral evils).

> … a value at least equal to that sacrificed … no less harmful way of protecting the value here and now so that such proportionate reason would not undermine it in the long run. (McCormick)
>
> The proportionality condition is usually understood to involve determining if the extent of the harm is adequately offset by the magnitude of the proposed benefit. (McIntyre)

When you have completed the task, try to write another reference that you could use and further extend your answer.

Issues for analysis and evaluation

The extent to which Proportionalism promotes immoral behaviour

The first thing to establish here is what precisely we mean by 'immoral behaviour'. The 'behaviour' has a tendency to highlight the culpability of the moral agent and suggest that Proportionalism not only leads to immoral acts-in-themselves but also has an impact on the character of the individual over a period of time. If it were just 'immoral acts', then this would be a different matter altogether. So in any evaluation made we need to consider (a) what we mean by immoral and (b) whether or not Proportionalism also promotes immoral behaviour in general, that also results in deficiency of moral character of an individual.

Proportionalism clearly distinguishes between that which is 'moral' and that which is 'good'. For example, for proportionalists a right act is a moral act but not necessarily a good act. For traditional Roman Catholic theology, a right act must be a directly good act. Therefore, traditional Roman Catholicism would contend that, at the very least, Proportionalism opens up the opportunity for immoral behaviour when it says that a right act is not necessarily a good act but produces the lesser of evils in line with proportionate reasoning. Indeed, the magisterium see Proportionalism as promoting evil acts (means) to achieve a greater good (ends) which is in direct contradiction to Romans 3:8 which condemns the practice of 'doing evil to achieve good'. In fact, this was the line of argument presented in *Veritatis Splendor*, a papal encyclical published in 1993 that accused proportionalist theologians of doing just that and condemned them as promoting an ethical theory that was directed by the ends of an action (consequentialist) and so purely teleological in essence. For the magisterium, this sort of ethical theory is very dangerous because it opens up the possibility of justifying evil actions through wrong reasoning and not real goods; this, then, inevitably has the effect of producing moral characteristics within a person that are not tenable with the virtues of Christianity. Christians are encouraged to see the 'wider picture' of morality and brush aside tried and tested deontological principles established in the Catechism of the Roman Catholic tradition. This, according to the magisterium, is dangerous and, therefore, inevitably will lead to immoral acts and attitudes that promote individualistic ends which is not at all virtuous.

However, it is precisely this misunderstanding, argue proportionalist theologians, that is very worrying. Charles Curran's response to *Veritatis Splendor* indicated that the most distressing part of the proclamation was that it grouped proportionalists with consequentialist systems of ethics. Richard McCormick in his book, '*Doing Evil to Achieve Good*' takes issue with this and Bernard Hoose's book '*Proportionalism*' also indicates that whilst Proportionalism may be considered teleological in general, this label has to be considered carefully. In fact, proportionalists argue that Natural Law and Roman Catholic theology, for that matter, have always been a mixture of deontology and teleology but just that the deontological focus has been stressed more. This inevitably would mean that unless deontological rules were followed blindly and not *primae facie*, then any deviation would be considered both evil and wrong, or immoral.

In addition to this, proportionalists would argue that on the whole what they identify as moral acts are good acts or produce a greater amount of good than evil, in which case they cannot be described as immoral. Despite this, the magisterium has felt that Proportionalism does promotes immoral behaviour on the basis that it does not condemn any act as intrinsically evil. However, proportionalists would respond by saying that until all elements of the ethical event are considered the judgement as to whether or not it is intrinsically evil is inappropriate. The

This section covers AO2 content and skills

Specification content

The extent to which Proportionalism promotes immoral behaviour.

Key quote

The principle of double effect leads a marginal existence in the handbooks of moral theology and appears to be useful only in making possible a species of hairsplitting. It is in reality, the fundamental principle of all morality. (**Knauer**)

AO2 **Activity**

As you read through this section try to do the following:

1. Pick out the different lines of argument that are presented in the text and identify any evidence given in support.

2. For each line of argument try to evaluate whether or not you think this is strong or weak.

3. Think of any questions you may wish to raise in response to the arguments.

This Activity will help you to start thinking critically about what you read and help you to evaluate the effectiveness of different arguments and from this develop your own observations, opinions and points of view that will help with any conclusions that you make in your answers to the AO2 questions that arise.

Key quote

Precisely on the questions
frequently debated in moral
theology today and with regard to
which new tendencies and theories
have developed, the magisterium,
in fidelity to Jesus Christ and
in continuity with the Church's
tradition, senses more urgently the
duty to offer its own discernment
and teaching, in order to help man
in his journey towards truth and
freedom. (*Veritatis Splendor*)

AO2 Activity

List some conclusions that could be
drawn from the AO2 reasoning from
the above text; try to aim for at least
three different possible conclusions.
Consider each of the conclusions
and collect brief evidence to support
each conclusion from the AO1 and
AO2 material for this topic. Select
the conclusion that you think is most
convincing and explain why it is so.
Try to contrast this with the weakest
conclusion in the list, justifying your
argument with clear reasoning and
evidence.

proportionalist Richard McCormick did not deny that intrinsic evil existed, but
simply stated that 'There are many acts that could be called "intrinsically evil" if their
circumstances are exhaustively included in description of the actions'. They respond
to traditionalists by arguing that Proportionalism still advocates that people should,
in general, follow deontological rules but that Proportionalism merely gives the
opportunity to differentiate between the best, or most moral, of two bad options in
an extreme situation for the greatest good and, therefore, the best possible outcome
in ethical terms.

In reaction, the magisterium argues that Proportionalism offers little concrete
guidance on how to calculate the various elements of a moral event. This could
be very subjective and therefore could make it easy to perform acts that others
would deem to be immoral, with no concrete way to ascertain what is the truth
of the matter. Indeed, this is the purpose and role of the magisterium, to guide
people's moral choices. Nonetheless, in response to this, proportionalists would
argue that a proportionate approach to difficult ethical dilemmas is more in tune
with the Gospel and teachings of Jesus; it is more compassionate. Peter Knauer
recognised immediately that although the 'principle of double effect' was applied
to ectopic pregnancies, the outcome suggested produced more evil than if one
used proportionate reason as the ultimate guide. Proportionalists would argue that
surely this is more the kind of morality that Jesus advocated where laws, or in this
case, moral principles, were for the benefit of humankind rather than the other way
around.

Indeed, Hoose and proportionalists like Curran and McCormick would argue
that their approach gives clear authority to the law, emphasising that in ordinary
situations these laws are inviolable and so moral behaviour is easy to govern and
judge but it is in cases wherein flexibility is required that a strictly deontological
application of moral law creates more evil and immorality than it does good. Indeed,
the basis of their approach is grounded in the writings of Thomas Aquinas and so has
good authority.

This may well be the case; however, it seems that in promoting flexibility and
grouping all the elements of an act as having significant input, it does open up
the system to misuse and misapplication unless there are some agreed criteria. In
essence, this would make it a nice theory but a very impractical one to regulate in
society. Guidance would be so confusing. For instance, in theory, Proportionalism
makes it possible for someone to justify any act, however heinous, if the
circumstances were extreme enough. Many people would argue that child abuse or
rape are always wrong no matter what the situation. It is the threat of moral anarchy
that Proportionalism could lead to that has forced the magisterium to react so
vehemently.

In conclusion, it is clear that what both proportionalists and traditionalists mean
by immoral are clearly different. One could suggest that whilst it is undisputed that
Proportionalism does have much that is attractive, there will always be the threat
of misapplication and abuse through what both camps would consider as immoral
behaviour. Proportionalists would respond that this is simply not proportionate
reasoning; traditionalists would say that Proportionalism may not promote moral
behaviour, or intend it, but there will always be the potential inherent in its approach.

Study tip

It is vital for AO2 that you actually discuss arguments and not just explain what
someone may have stated. Try to ask yourself, 'was this a fair point to make?',
'is the evidence sound enough?', 'is there anything to challenge this argument?',
'is this a strong or weak argument?' Such critical analysis will help you develop
your evaluation skills.

The extent to which Finnis' Natural Law is a better ethic than Proportionalism

Specification content

The extent to which Finnis' Natural Law is a better ethic than Proportionalism.

The main strength of Finnis' Natural Law is that it is firmly established in the works of Aristotle and Aquinas. Although it demonstrates that Natural Law works as an ethical system with religion as its foundation, it also recognises that, as long as there is a coherent worldview underlying the system, it is a system that is open beyond Christianity. Indeed, Finnis, being a legal expert as well as a theological one, demonstrates how Natural Law works in society. In this sense it appears much more comprehensive than Proportionalism. All the basic goods and values promoted through the principles of practical reasonableness are relevant to contemporary society and are rationally argued.

One could argue that Finnis' system of Natural Law has more consistency than that of Proportionalism. There are many different approaches to Proportionalism, and it does not have a comprehensive and systematic normative system developed unlike that of Finnis. In addition, the proportionalist debate is within Roman Catholicism and is very much part of Christianity whereas Finnis' Natural Law appeals to international communities and is not dependent upon creed, culture, race or gender. In contrast, Proportionalism lacks that breadth and depth.

Finnis' Natural Law in this respect does tend to focus on the 'common good' and is less individualistic than Proportionalism. Finnis writes that, 'authority be exercised … for the purpose of promoting a common good in which such respect for rights is a component'. However, Finnis' Natural Law also encourages active citizens in promoting the fulfilment of the common good, giving purpose and encouragement to develop a society that thrives and achieves personal, social and economic well-being through the basic goods. Indeed, Finnis' Natural Law has been widely recognised as making a major contribution to contemporary thought in promoting such values as tolerance, common good and the goal of well-being.

However, there are critics of the way in which Finnis presents his Natural Law. It is clear that despite a promotion of tolerance and the common good, Finnis has been accused of using his system to promote a specifically traditional form of Roman Catholicism. Indeed, Finnis has had major influence upon the magisterium. Scholars like Stephen Buckle and Brigita White have criticised the underlying agenda that Finnis appears to have. In addition to this, Finnis presents what some would see as controversial views in terms of traditional family values, homosexuality and issues such as abortion and contraception. He has responded to uncontrolled immigration over the last few decades as 'reversed colonisation … a trajectory of demographic and cultural decay' and sees this as a challenge to cultural identity and the basis of the shared goods such as family. Although Finnis has the right to assert his views, some see them as offensive. Nonetheless, this should not blemish the system he presents at all, but rather the way some think he presents it. Indeed, Brigita White has written, 'Although, Finnis indeed posits a place for morality in the law, the type of morality Finnis has in mind is questionable.'

However, one could argue that there is an inherent misconception in the statement. Indeed, both Finnis and Proportionalism could be argued to share the exact same ethic. Both follow Aquinas' Natural Law and Finnis, like proportionalist theologians, is a Roman Catholic. Their values are very much the same, they promote the precepts (goods) and the Christian virtues. Both appeal to the 'principle of double effect' when dealing with the appropriate dilemmas. Nonetheless, to some extent their approach to the 'principle of double effect' is very different. Finnis sides with the traditionalists and opposes a proportionalist understanding of the 'principle of double effect'.

AO2 Activity

As you read through this section try to do the following:

1. Pick out the different lines of argument that are presented in the text and identify any evidence given in support.

2. For each line of argument try to evaluate whether or not you think this is strong or weak.

3. Think of any questions you may wish to raise in response to the arguments.

This Activity will help you to start thinking critically about what you read and help you to evaluate the effectiveness of different arguments and from this develop your own observations, opinions and points of view that will help with any conclusions that you make in your answers to the AO2 questions that arise.

In addition to this, proportionalists would say that they have a distinctive ethical methodology but not a distinctive normative ethic as they follow Aquinas' Natural Law. Indeed, one could argue that their approach to ethics is superior to that of traditionalists in that it appeals to a more contemporary way of approaching ethical issues but at the same time has just as much coherence and consistency in their ethic against the background of Aquinas' Natural Law and Roman Catholic tradition. Furthermore, they could argue that theirs is the better Christian ethic, whereas despite Finnis' own interpretation and application of his Natural Law system, it can be used and applied by other religions, cultures and the non-religious alike. In this way, if we are looking for a better religious ethic then maybe Proportionalism is superior. The extension of Finnis' Natural Law to all nations and cultures surely complicates in that it allows for varying interpretations and applications. Of course, Finnis would deny that this is possible as he sees Natural Law as applicable to all, and any misinterpretations and misapplications are simple wrong reasoning. Indeed, he would point to the internal conflicts and inconsistencies within Proportionalism itself.

Key quote

The collapse of Christianity and other religious cultures, as the matrix for contemporary legal and political orders, has posed a challenge to those who wish to affirm that there is a Natural Law. **(Finnis)**

Study tip

It is vital for AO2 that you actually discuss arguments and not just explain what someone may have stated. Try to ask yourself, 'was this a fair point to make?', 'is the evidence sound enough?', 'is there anything to challenge this argument?', 'is this a strong or weak argument?' Such critical analysis will help you develop your evaluation skills.

Despite all the pros and cons of Finnis' system against those of Proportionalism, the statement assumes that we can actually judge what a better ethics is. This must surely depend upon the person evaluating the issue. One person may say that they are both as good or both as bad but then prefer an alternative ethic such as Utilitarianism or Situation Ethics.

It would appear that the matter boils down to either individual preference based upon a critical analysis of what each approach to ethics promotes. In contemporary society it would not be surprising to hear people say that Proportionalism has more in common with the postmodern world of today as it is much more flexible. Then again, proportionalists would say that they have misunderstood and embellished the flexibility of proportionate reason, whereas some Roman Catholics may respond, as possibly would John Finnis, that to have less in common with contemporary society is indeed a strength!

In conclusion, to be fair to both systems there are clearly strengths and weaknesses for each. Each have their critics – Proportionalism from within Roman Catholicism and Finnis' system from beyond Roman Catholicism. Ultimately, it can be graciously acknowledged that the Beatific Vision and the highest virtue of love is their goal when approaching ethical matters and so the intentions behind both ethical systems are genuine and for the 'common good' in the case of Finnis, or, in terms of Proportionalism to aspire to the 'greater good'. It would seem unfair to select one over against the other and perhaps settle for the fact that it definitely seems to work for them.

AO2 Activity

List some conclusions that could be drawn from the AO2 reasoning from the above text; try to aim for at least three different possible conclusions. Consider each of the conclusions and collect brief evidence to support each conclusion from the AO1 and AO2 material for this topic. Select the conclusion that you think is most convincing and explain why it is so. Try to contrast this with the weakest conclusion in the list, justifying your argument with clear reasoning and evidence.

AO2 Developing skills

It is now important to consider the information that has been covered in this section; however, the information in its raw form is too extensive and so has to be processed in order to meet the requirements of the examination. This can be achieved by practising more advanced skills associated with AO2. For assessment objective 2 (AO2), which involves 'critical analysis' and 'evaluation' skills, we are going to focus on different ways in which the skills can be demonstrated effectively, and also, refer to how the performance of these skills is measured (see generic band descriptors for A2 [WJEC] AO2 or A Level [Eduqas] AO2).

▶ **Your next task is this:** Below is an **evaluation of a strength and weakness of Proportionalism**. At present it has no references at all to support the arguments presented. Underneath the evaluation are two references made to the works of scholars, and/or religious writings, that could be used in the evaluation in order to improve it. Your task is to re-write the evaluation but make use of the references. Such phrases as 'in his/her book … (scholar) argues that …', 'an interesting argument in support of this is made by … who suggests that …', or, 'the work of (scholar) has made a major contribution to the debate by pointing out …' may help. Usually a reference included a footnote but for an answer in an A-Level essay under examination conditions this is not expected, although an awareness of which book your evidence refers to is useful (although not always necessary).

It could be argued that Proportionalism shows more compassion than a strict adherence to Natural Law would allow. This is more in line with the kind of morality that Jesus advocated where law was for the benefit of humankind rather than the other way around. Indeed, Natural Law is not just about rules but also about virtues. Some would contend that Proportionalism is a better expression of Natural Law than that which the Roman Catholic magisterium presents simply because the magisterium stresses intrinsic evils and rules more than anything else. However, the magisterium would respond by arguing that the papal encyclicals always highlight Christian character and behaviour and that following the rules is just a way that this can be achieved.

> It is not merely tradition but common sense that dictates the need for a proportionate reason. (Hoose)
>
> Human acts are moral acts because they express and determine the goodness or evil of the individual who performs them … they give moral definition to the very person who performs them, determining his profound spiritual traits. (*Veritatis Splendor* 71)

When you have completed the task, try to write another reference that you could use and further extend your evaluation.

Key skills Theme 2

The second theme has tasks that concentrate on a particular aspect of AO2 in terms of using quotations from sources of authority and in the use of references in supporting arguments and evaluations.

Key skills

Analysis involves:

Identifying issues raised by the materials in the AO1, together with those identified in the AO2 section, and presents sustained and clear views, either of scholars or from a personal perspective ready for evaluation.

This means:

- That your answers are able to identify key areas of debate in relation to a particular issue

- That you can identify, and comment upon, the different lines of argument presented by others

- That your response comments on the overall effectiveness of each of these areas or arguments.

Evaluation involves:

Considering the various implications of the issues raised based upon the evidence gleaned from analysis and provides an extensive detailed argument with a clear conclusion.

This means:

- That your answer weighs up the consequences of accepting or rejecting the various and different lines of argument analysed

- That your answer arrives at a conclusion through a clear process of reasoning.

This section covers AO1
content and skills

Specification content

The application of Finnis' Natural Law
and Proportionalism to immigration
and capital punishment.

Key terms

Immigration: term referring to the
movement of population into a country
for residence (short-term or long-term)

Nationalism: the term used to
describe an insular view of a nation
and an aggressive attitude towards
other nations

Patriotism: the term used to describe
pride in one's country

F: Application of the theories

Immigration

To approach **immigration,** we first need to examine what exactly we mean by
the term. The meaning of the word itself may be simple enough, that is, 'migrating
from another country, usually for permanent residence'; however, the potential
issues involved are extremely complex. To apply an ethical theory to immigration
we need to know why it is a moral issue or why there are moral issues involved. It is
not just a case of whether or not the practice of immigration is right or wrong.

According to various dictionaries, a common understanding of the term 'country'
involves an established geographical region that is self-governed and is recognised
as a distinct national identity. The Montevideo Convention in Uruguay (1933)
declared that a country is a country if it meets the following criteria:

a. A permanent population

b. a defined territory

c. government, and

d. capacity to enter into relations with the other states.

In other words, a country is its own self-contained unit but also one that interacts
with other self-contained units through travel, trade and political negotiations.

According the United Nations Declaration of Human Rights (Articles 13 and 14)
everyone has:

1. 'The right to leave any country, including his own, and to return to his country',
    and

2. 'The right to seek and to enjoy in other countries asylum from persecution'.

Therefore, the notions of travel and residence are integral to basic human rights.
However, this also has to be balanced against a country in turn having the right to
protect its borders from aggressors and ensure the well-being of its population.
Immigration is leaving one country and taking up residence in another with no
intention to return. This is not an immediate human right but is a decision made by
individual governments. In addition, if we are to look at immigration, it may be of
benefit to consider the internal dynamic of what it means to belong to a country.
This is very important because it often determines views held about immigration.

The 20th-century sociologist, Herbert Stewart, writing in the *American Journal
of Sociology* in 1917 explored two understandings of what it means to belong to
a country: **patriotism** and **nationalism**. Stewart identifies the ideal view of a
country as that of Athens in Ancient Greek times. He writes: 'The Athenian loved
Athens, less because it had been the home of his father than because it was the
home of his own ideals. He was a democrat, and he admired a constitution under
which every freeman had an equal chance of rising to public office; he had a taste
for art, and he liked to be in a city where artistic genius was furthered at the public
expense …. He loved his country, not so much because it was his own, as because it
was a superior country.'

However, at the time of writing, Stewart had seen the rise of nationalism that
led to WWI. Nationalism sought to conquer, oppress and control others beyond
itself. This was, according to Stewart, full of inconsistent principles and conveyed
'the conception of every race as antagonistic to every other, of one people's
gain as necessarily another people's loss, of all-inclusive world-dominion as the
destiny of a single stock'. Accordingly, Stewart suggested that patriotism is inward
looking, welcoming and having pride in the positive values a country represents;
nationalism, by contrast, is outward looking, seeking to exploit other countries and
impose upon them its ideology.

Stewart also observed that the Church has throughout history rejected the principles of nationalism in favour of patriotism. According to Stewart, the Church was violently opposed to nationalism because the original meaning of patriotism held by the Athenian had been polluted and twisted. According to Stewart, the patriotism of the person 'who both allows and encourages the foreigner to be patriotic too', is a patriotism that is welcoming and that wishes for one's neighbour what one would wish for oneself. The Christian Church felt it had a duty to welcome and embrace all foreigners, rich or poor and regardless of status, gender, ethnicity or political views. Pope John Paul II stated that 'Love of our country unites us and must unite us above all divergences. It has nothing in common with a narrow nationalism or chauvinism, but springs from the law of the human heart.' Indeed, this welcoming and virtuous patriotism is the one that is promoted by the Roman Catholic Church today. Immigration, then, is supported through the principle of an 'open' patriotism.

Key quote

In this context, we need to clarify the essential difference between an unhealthy form of nationalism, which teaches contempt for other nations or cultures, and patriotism, which is a proper love of one's country. True patriotism never seeks to advance the well-being of one's own nation at the expense of others. (Pope John Paul II)

In terms of this welcoming approach of patriotism and the concept of immigration, the term 'migrant' simply describes a person moving from one country to another to live. An immigrant is therefore the term given by the patriot to the incoming migrant. There are a number of reasons for immigration including: to improve a standard of life; study; take up a job opportunity; retirement; escape poverty; escape oppression; escape life-threatening situations. There are probably more reasons, however, the term 'economic migrant' tends to cover the first five reasons. The last two refer to asylum seekers and refugees.

An economic migrant is one who seeks out a better standard of life by making a living in another country where there may be several opportunities, often due to limited opportunities in his or her country. A refugee is an officially recognised, legal migrant who has successfully been accepted by the British government and is entitled to humanitarian protection under paragraph 339C of the Immigration Rules. A refugee may previously have been an asylum seeker. Refugees are protected under international law by the 1951 Refugee Convention and have this status usually due to not being able to return to their own country, having fled civil war, threats of death or natural disasters such as famine. Refugee status entitles

Key quote

The Athenian loved Athens, less because it had been the home of his fathers than because it was the home of his own ideals. (Stewart)

quickfire

2.27 What is meant by the term patriotism?

Key terms

Asylum seeker: one who is seeking refuge from a life-threatening situation

Economic migrant: one who seeks out a better standard of life through migration

Migrant: one who moves from one country to another

Refugee: one who has sought refuge from a life-threatening situation and been granted asylum

Athens was the ideal patriotic community.

Key quotes

A closed country is a dying country. (Ferber)

Pity the nation that knows no other language than its own and no other culture but its own. (Ferlinghetti)

Preference for a single country is both irrational and selfish. (Stewart)

Key quote

The only patriotism which can be accounted objectively a virtue must be the patriotism of him who both allows and encourages the foreigner to be patriotic too. What we believe in for ourselves we must also believe in for our neighbour. (Stewart)

the holder to be given access to social housing and welfare benefits and helped to find a job and integrate into society. Under the 1951 United Nations Convention on the Status of Refugees, a person is able to seek asylum in another country if it can be demonstrated that a return to the country of origin would result in persecution or worse on account of race, religion, nationality, political belief or membership of a particular social group. Asylum seeker is a temporary status; an asylum seeker is one waiting for refugee status to be approved.

The current British immigration system categorises applicants into different tiers based upon the points they achieve from their application and assessment. Points are awarded for skills, education, talents, experience and age. It was established in 2008.

Tier 1: 'High-value migrants' from outside the EEA and covers entry of entrepreneurs, investors and those very few people who come under the 'exceptional talent' category.

Tier 2: 'Skilled workers' from outside the EEA with a job offer in the UK. It includes skilled workers who are transferred to the UK by an international company, skilled workers where there is a proven shortage in the UK, this can include ministers of religion and sportspeople.

Tier 3: Low-skilled workers filling specific temporary labour shortages.

Tiers 4 and 5 are for temporary stays associated with foreign students for universities or professional artists, sporting, charity, and religious workers. This can involve paid or voluntary work.

The implications of this, for applicants from poorer countries, are obvious: those who have no education, hence no real skills, have less chance of being accepted by the system. Generally, the poor and aged are also less likely to score highly. Those who are educated, highly skilled and in general from more affluent backgrounds are more successful. Indeed, a Tier 3 Visa has never been issued and was shut down altogether in 2013 by David Cameron.

In summary:

- Patriotism can be open and inclusive in aiming to promote a better life for its citizens and welcoming when inviting those from without to contribute towards, and participate in, its richness of culture.

- Nationalism is insular and exclusive: it is not supported by the Christian Church.

- Movement between and within countries is a basic human right.

- Permanent residence in a foreign country is not a right.

- Not all migrants are the same.

- In the UK, a points system determines the nature of the acceptable immigrant.

In considering the application of theories to immigration, there are some key questions to focus on in order to see how Finnis' Natural Law and Proportionalism can be applied to each:

- Do they support immigration?

- How could they respond to uncontrolled immigration?

- Do people have a moral obligation to support refugees and asylum seekers?

- Do people have a moral obligation to support 'economic migrants' and if so is a points-based immigration system morally right?

Capital punishment

In approaching **capital punishment**, the issue appears to be less complex than immigration. This is not yet an exercise in evaluation and so the arguments 'for' and 'against' capital punishment that you may have met at GCSE Level are not relevant here (they may be used for an AO2 evaluation if relevant). What we are considering is a straightforward question of whether or not Finnis' Natural Law and Proportionalism, when applied to the issue of capital punishment, would support or reject it. In other words, according to each theory, is capital punishment an acceptable form of punishment?

The Criminal Justice Act of 2003 is clear on the purposes of a judicial sentence:

a. The **punishment** of offenders,

b. The reduction of crime (including its reduction by **deterrence**),

c. The **reform** and rehabilitation of offenders,

d. The **protection** of the public, and

e. The making of **reparation** by offenders to persons affected by their offences.

The last point must not be confused with **retribution**, which is the appropriate punishment inflicted upon a person that commits a crime. Reparation is focused on the victims; retribution is focused on the criminal. It could be argued that capital punishment addresses all of (a) to (e) above. It can also be argued that it addresses none of the above (you may have seen this in the arguments for and against capital punishment at GCSE)! For example, on the one hand, it is claimed that the death penalty punishes the individual, it deters others from killing, that the criminal has opportunity and is more likely to repent before execution, that it protects the public, and, provides reparation for the victim's family. However, on the other hand, it is argued that the death penalty is not an appropriate form of punishment because it is unreliable and irrevocable, leading to injustices, that the evidence for it serving as a deterrent is poor, that it does not provide ample opportunity for reform, that there are other ways of protecting the public, and, not all families of victims want retribution as reparation.

Capital punishment in UK law

Capital punishment has been used in the UK for centuries for certain crimes including treason, murder, robbery, larceny, rape and arson. The usual method was hanging and the Murder Act 1752 stated this was to be done within 48 hours of sentencing. In 1968, the Prisons Act abolished hangings in public view and the Children and Young Persons Act 1933 brought in the law that anyone under 18 was not to be executed for crimes committed. Capital punishment was abolished in 1965 after 17 years of formal debate within Parliament and the House of Lords. Treason, piracy with violence and arson in Royal Dockyards all remained capital crimes. Treason incorporated times of war; however, after several amendments, and in response to the pressures of the Human Rights Act 1998, Protocol 13 of the Second Optional Protocol to the International Covenant on Civil and Political Rights (ICCPR) was accepted and capital punishment was completely abolished in the UK in 2002. Despite this, there are a significant number of the population that would still approve of capital punishment, debates have still been held in Parliament after the abolishment in law, and there are certainly religious groups that would argue its case.

> ## Key terms
>
> **Capital punishment:** the death penalty, execution, as a form of punishment
>
> **Deterrence:** to put someone off a committing a crime
>
> **Protection:** to protect the common good of society as a whole
>
> **Reform:** to change one's character from criminal to law-abiding
>
> **Reparation:** to make amends to the victims of crime
>
> **Retribution:** to 'pay back' the criminal that which they are due

> ## quickfire
>
> **2.28** What is the difference between reparation and retribution?

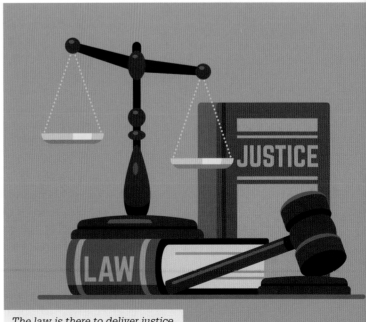

The law is there to deliver justice.

2018 amendment to the Catholic Church Catechism

2267. Recourse to the death penalty on the part of legitimate authority, following a fair trial, was long considered an appropriate response to the gravity of certain crimes and an acceptable, albeit extreme, means of safeguarding the common good. Today, however, there is an increasing awareness that the dignity of the person is not lost even after the commission of very serious crimes. In addition, a new understanding has emerged of the significance of penal sanctions imposed by the state. Lastly, more effective systems of detention have been developed, which ensure the due protection of citizens but, at the same time, do not definitively deprive the guilty of the possibility of redemption. Consequently, the Church teaches, in the light of the Gospel, that the death penalty is inadmissible because it is an attack on the inviolability and dignity of the person, and she works with determination for its abolition worldwide.

Key terms

Commutative justice: justice between individuals

Distributive justice: economic, political, and social frameworks that each society has including its laws, institutions, policies to ensure fairness and equality

Study tip

This section of the textbook also includes some additional background material about Natural Law's ongoing debate over capital punishment and also an explanation of some different proportionalist methodologies for applied ethics. Since these topics are new, and targeted resources have been slender at best, this is an attempt to provide a context of the debates as well as a Specification-specific presentation of their applications.

The theological context: Aquinas and Natural Law

Aquinas' methodology when addressing the issue of capital punishment has been a topic of intense debate in recent years. A traditional understanding of Aquinas has been that capital punishment is permissible. In *Summa Theologica* 2–2, q. 64, a. 2 Aquinas writes, 'Therefore if any man is dangerous to the community and is subverting it by some sin, the treatment to be commended is his execution in order to preserve the common good.' This appeared to be straightforward enough and up until 2018 the official line of the magisterium was that it was licit as 'a last resort'.

Professor Edward Kaczor (2002) traces Aquinas' thinking back to the distinction Aristotle makes between **distributive** and **commutative** justice and thereby indicating that capital punishment is not an intrinsic evil but instead upholds the traditional view that punishments are a necessary good for society; Kaczor, however, agrees that it is never appropriate for today. Eleanor Gardner (2009) supports Kaczor's interpretation and has argued that it is a classic example of the application by Aquinas of practical reasonableness or Aristotle's practical reasoning under Natural Law. However, in 2018 the Roman Catholic Church made an official amendment to the *Catholic Church Catechism* and declared the death penalty 'inadmissible because it is an attack on the inviolability and dignity of the person'.

This has caused another debate to emerge. All involved in the debate are in agreement as to the fact that Aquinas justified the application of capital punishment. Nonetheless, Aquinas' reasoning and justification for this statement is far from clear. There is, by any means, no universal agreement. This is crucial because the issue for Christians is whether or not it can be justified today using the same reasoning, especially since the Roman Catholic Church is now officially opposed to it.

Peter Black, in a paper published in *Theological Studies* (1999), pointed out that 'there is a growing tendency in both church and society to apply it in very limited circumstances or even to abolish it completely'. Black also brought to the forefront of the debate the legitimacy of Aquinas' principle of 'circumstances that change the moral nature of an act' and bringing Aquinas' reasoning the centre of the debate. Richard McCormick and John Finnis had already questioned the validity of this principle and questioned its objectivity. Black concluded that the debate about capital punishment demonstrates an attempt to wrestle with the problems of a purely deontological one-size-fits-all approach to ethics.

Recently there has been more debate between Ed Feser and John Finnis. Feser upheld the licitness of capital punishment in Aquinas and is concerned about the inconsistency of the Roman Catholic magisterium and its implications for papal Infallibility. The debate seems to hinge upon whether or not the recent teaching of the Roman Catholic Church suggests that capital punishment is an intrinsic evil. Finnis, as we will see, is in total agreement with the magisterium and rejects Aquinas' arguments. In saying all this, the full extent of the debate is far too complex to detail here. All this demonstrates that the application of Natural Law to the issue of capital punishment has been problematic.

Key quotes

Therefore if any man is dangerous to the community and is subverting it by some sin, the treatment to be commended is his execution in order to preserve the common good. Therefore to kill a man who retains his natural worthiness is intrinsically evil, although it may be justifiable to kill a sinner just as it is to kill a beast, for, as Aristotle points out, an evil man is worse than a beast and more harmful. (Aquinas, *Summa Theologica* 2-2, q. 64, a. 2)

The nature and extent of the punishment must be carefully evaluated and decided upon and ought not go to the extreme of executing the offender except in cases of absolute necessity; in other words, when it would not be possible otherwise to defend society. Today, however, as a result of steady improvements in the organisation of the penal system, such cases are very rare, if not practically non-existent. (John Paul II, *Evangelium vitae* no. 56)

quickfire

2.29 In what year was the death penalty fully abolished in the UK?

AO1 Activity

Why not take opportunity at this point to note down significant facts and issues about the background to immigration and capital punishment? Look at the summaries for each and see if you have similar content.

Hanging was used in the UK to administer capital punishment.

In summary:

- Death is ontic evil; although the act of killing may include moral evil, killing itself is not an intrinsic evil act. God has the power to take life and God cannot perform intrinsically evil acts. God can allow evil for the greater good.
- Killing of the guilty criminal, where appropriate, is just and part of the good of punishment according to Aquinas.
- In traditional teaching, then, capital punishment is therefore, a legitimate form of punishment.
- Aquinas' theology suggests it is a last resort only and this had always been the view taken by the magisterium up until 2018. In other words, in establishing the legitimacy of capital punishment, this was a legitimacy to be avoided by exhausting all other options rather than being a prescribed absolute.
- The Roman Catholic Church today officially stands against capital punishment since it argues that the 'last resort' argument can no longer be applied.
- Debates are still ongoing within the Roman Catholic Church about capital punishment. Those in support would argue that Aquinas' 'last resort' still applies today and that the Pope's declarations suggest that capital punishment is an attack on a basic good and thereby an intrinsic evil. This latter point is the controversy.

In considering the application of theories to immigration, there are some key questions to focus on in order to see how the Finnis' Natural Law and Proportionalism can be applied to each:

- Does Finnis' Natural Law and Proportionalism support or reject capital punishment?
- Are there any circumstances in which capital punishment may be deemed as licit by Finnis' Natural Law or Proportionalism?

Key quotes

In a certain sense, moral theology is not theology at all. It is moral philosophy, pursued by persons who are believers. (O'Connell)

For a fully objective judgment, the facts are what matter, not our limited, fallible beliefs about the facts. (Hallett)

Study tip

Application is an AO1 exercise. It is good to demonstrate in an answer that you have an understanding that the way Finnis' theory is applied is built into the theory itself and that it is not an understanding of the theory that changes but rather that the results may be different when applying to different ethical problems. Since Proportionalism is not an ethical theory as such, there is more interpretation as to how this ethical norm should be applied.

Specification content

The application of Finnis' Natural Law to immigration and capital punishment.

Application of the theories

Before applying 'theories' to an issue, it is important to consider that ethics and ethical reasoning is a specific discipline within philosophy and needs to be as precise and logical as any philosophical argument. Just as a philosophical argument is subject to scrutiny; likewise, the reasoning of an ethical argument should be subject to the same robust analysis. In terms of the two developments of Natural Law (Finnis and Proportionalism) in Theme 2, what we need to do is look at how each particular theory, composed of its various criteria, is, or can be, applied to resolve a particular question. This involves an understanding of any methodology used.

For John Finnis' development of Natural Law, the basic goods are a complete integrated package; the nine requirements of practical reasonableness are a holistic framework under the guidance of practical reasonableness. The methodology of Finnis' Natural Law is not to consider the 'for' and 'against' of each particular good in a given situation (one is not balanced against another); this not only goes against the grain of the theory but also is a form of consequentialism whereby the 'situation' dictates how we interpret the goods. This will not do, since the goods themselves never change. It is the other way around whereby the goods determine an answer for an ethical question or issue in the sense of how a particular response may affect the integrity of the goods. Finnis' system – although often stated to be 'secular' – clearly demonstrates that a Christian approach to Natural Law is a perfectly sound philosophical ground and framework for ethics.

The challenge of applying Proportionalism is very different and very difficult. Since Proportionalism is not a fully developed ethical theory (more like a statement that provides guidance), in order to apply this statement to an ethical issue there needs to be a clear and distinct ethical methodology. Whilst many have attempted to devise a unified methodology for Proportionalism, this has not been possible. James J. Walter, himself a proportionalist and writing at the same time as Hoose, attempted to identify some form of criteria for guiding and assessing the application of proportionate reason. This was not universally accepted and Walter did admit himself that his six suggested principles were really more like six possible ways to define proportionate reason itself rather than establishing a clear methodology for application. Walter concluded, like Hoose did, that it was the **way** in which Proportionalism was to be applied that should be the task of revisionist theologians. Moving on 35 years from Walter's article and Hoose's book, there have been some different developments in identifying a way in which proportionate reason could be applied. We shall be considering these.

Proportionalism is, like Finnis' system, also firmly entrenched within the Natural Law of Aquinas and takes its guidance from the magisterium. The maxim 'it is **never** right to go against a principle ...' is the foundation for applying proportionate reason and originates from the 'principle of double effect' (PDE). Both ethical theories can also be located within the whole framework of Christian religious ethics, which means that general Christian ethics are also applicable.

Finnis' Natural Law methodology

Natural Law is a holistic approach to ethics based upon the five primary precepts or, in the case of Finnis, the basic goods. Human laws and ethical principles are derived from these and are clarified with precision through the process of practical reasonableness.

1. What we are not doing is selecting specific goods and evaluating these against each other. For example, we are not just taking one of Finnis' basic goods and applying it to an issue, only then to contrast it with, or pit it against, a different good. Each good is of value in itself and there is to be no hierarchy of goods.

2. Neither can we take a specific good and argue how it both supports and rejects a problem depending upon how we understand the good. A good is either in support or against; it cannot be both. The goods do not change, as they are firmly established and understood; however, it is the specific nature of a problem that creates the variable factors and it is these factors that shift according to circumstances.

This does not mean that we cannot consider the range, or balance, of the goods within the theory when applied. Indeed, instead of dissembling a theory into different contrasting parts, what we should be doing when considering the application of Finnis' theory, is understanding how the parts work together as a whole and this will help us to find a solution.

Although Finnis' Natural Law is essentially directed for the purpose of guiding the establishment of legal frameworks, it is essentially a system that applies to humanity and not just a particular legal system. It is intended to be universal and objective, both in terms of the goods and also by way of practical reasonableness through which the goods are participated in by society through law and morality.

In summary, then, the goods are the norm that direct what should be aimed for; the requirements of practical reasonableness provide the methodology by which said goods can be participated in and enable society and the individuals within it to flourish. Both should determine any ethical decision made.

Applying Finnis' Natural Law to immigration

In terms of immigration, in itself, it does nothing to damage the goods of a flourishing society. Indeed, it will be seen that the ideal of migration is a good thing, an ideal, almost a good ethical norm in itself fostering the basic goods that enable a society to flourish even more. The issues arise when the ideal meets particular circumstances that may challenge the basic goods it supports. Natural Law has its basis not only in primary precepts and Finnis' basic goods which are self-evident, but in the **rational fulfilment** of these precepts and goods.

However, uncontrolled immigration may well be different; and then, there are different degrees of uncontrolled immigration. Likewise, the way in which immigration is managed may be different depending upon what criteria are used to establish eligibility of the immigrant. In other words, it is the circumstances that determine what the ethical problem is and these will differ and create variables for immigration, that may or may not, restrict the goods and diminish opportunities for society to flourish. **Never**, however, do the situations have any impact upon what the goods in themselves are, or understood to be. Finnis' system is, of course, in essence, a deontological theory. We now need to address the initial questions highlighted earlier that were related to the issue of immigration?

Does Finnis' Natural Law support immigration?

It is also clear that, in principle, immigration is a practice that fully participates in the goods of Finnis' Natural Law and through practical reasoning allows full participation in all goods so as to enable a flourishing society. As Clare Lloyd, Philosophy Ninja writes, 'Through practical reasonableness Finnis requires us to see the goods holistically rather than separately and a requirement of practical reason is that we do not arbitrarily prioritise one good over another.'

First and foremost the practice of immigration engages both parties with participation in the good of **friendship**. This is using the principle of practical reasonableness that there is **no arbitrary preference amongst persons**. However, it is also a Christian attitude. Pope Francis has urged Christians to open up 'without prejudice to their rich diversity of migrants and refugees, to understand the hopes and potential of the newly arrived as well as their fears and

The **basic goods**, as we have seen, are:

- Life
- Knowledge
- Play
- Aesthetic experience
- Friendship
- Practical reasonableness
- Religion.

quickfire

2.30 Is Finnis' Natural Law a secular theory?

Key quote

Some of the collaboration between one person and another is no more than instrumental to the realisation by each of his or her own individual purposes. But friendship involves acting for the sake of one's friend's purposes, one's friend's well-being … friendship with at least one other person is a fundamental form of good, is it not? (Finnis)

Key quotes

The classical non-philosophical expression of the requirement is, of course, the so-called Golden Rule formulated not only in the Christian gospel but also in the sacred books of the Jews, and not only in didactic formulae but also in the moral appeal of sacred history and parable. **(Finnis)**

The basic good of life covers complete bodily and mental health but also supports people and institutions that work towards this, whether it be at local, government level or international level. **(Barker)**

vulnerabilities'. It is clear that the magisterium support immigration in principle. As Finnis himself alludes to, this is similar to the Christian ideal of the Golden Rule of treating others as one would like to be treated. It is, thereby, using the principle of practical reasonableness in following one's ***conscience***.

From this extended arm of friendship brings a respect for the fullness of ***life***, another basic good which sees collaboration in ensuring preservation as a bedrock of a flourishing society, as Finnis indicates through various means: a 'teamwork of surgeons and the whole network of supporting staff', 'ancillary services', 'road safety laws and programmes', 'farming and rearing and fishing', etc. Immigrant workers can contribute and support self-preservation of both the individual and society.

Through immigration society can flourish in terms of richer participation in the goods of ***knowledge*** (new insights and empathy with different philosophies, scientific progress and the pursuit of truth), through ***play*** and ***aesthetic experience*** with immigrant populations providing opportunity for richer participation through cuisine, clothing, sports, arts and music. The underlying framework of ***religion*** in Finnis' system demonstrates clearly that not only does it enable a flourishing society with a particular world view, but that it can also work with other world views that have an understanding of the 'bigger picture' or 'ultimate purpose' of Natural Law, whether religious or not. It also ensures that resulting goods are enhanced in line with the principles of practical reasonableness in supporting a ***coherent plan of life***, equality (***no arbitrary preference amongst goods or persons***), and a balanced approach (***commitment and detachment***) hence having ***regard for every value*** for the ***common good***. It is clear that Finnis' presentation of Natural Law is fully supportive of the notion of immigration as far as it allows full participation in the goods through the principles of practical reasonableness.

Key quote

There is no Christian joy when doors are closed; there is no Christian joy when others are made to feel unwanted, when there is no room for them in our midst. **(Pope Francis)**

quickfire

2.31 What is meant by the term 'flourish'?

The aim of Natural Law is for individuals and society to flourish.

How could Finnis' Natural Law respond to uncontrolled immigration?

For Finnis, as opposed to other proposed legal frameworks, there is a **direct** link between morality and the law. This makes Finnis' understanding of law unique and has been a long-standing debate between Finnis and his former teacher and mentor Professor Herbert Hart, who has been the most influential figure within jurisprudence over the last century. Hart, who also taught at Oxford as Professor of Jurisprudence for many years, was a firm believer that there was no relationship between the law and morality. Finnis' Natural Law suggests the opposite and it has been this aspect that has raised the most controversial debates in regard to some very sensitive moral issues, but in particular Finnis' remarks about uncontrolled immigration. In an essay on Hart's political philosophy (*The American Journal of Jurisprudence*, Vol.54 2009) Finnis wrote:

'European states in the early twenty-first century move ever more clearly out of the social and political conditions of the 1960s into a trajectory of demographic and cultural decay; circumscription of political, religious and educational speech and associated freedoms; pervasive untruthfulness about equality and diversity; population transfer and replacement by a kind of reverse colonisation; and resultant internal fissiparation foreshadowing, it seems, ethnic and religious inter-communal miseries of hatred, bloodshed and political paralysis reminiscent of late twentieth-century Yugoslavia's or the Levant's. So the time seems ripe for a wider reflection on whether late twentieth-century political philosophies so characteristic, so suasive, so victorious as Hart's correspond or correlate with these evils, or indeed contribute to their onset or progression.'

Finnis goes on to argue that the normative political philosophy advocated by Herbert Hart has been too liberal and has exerted great influence on the formulation and interpretation of laws last century. This has inevitably had an impact on immigration laws. He writes: 'Hart's normative political philosophy has little indeed to say about the inter-relations of common good, justice and liberty' and that the 'law, marks out for them a path towards, first the loss of national self-determination'. Part of this loss of self-determination, according to Finnis, involves a 'replacement' of population that has little consideration for 'the incomers' compatibility of psychology, culture, religion or political ideas and ambitions'. For Finnis this is a great irony since an eradication or replacement of ideals is a 'ruinous loss of most or much that Hart worked for, or took for granted, as precious'. What Finnis seems to mean about this is that excessive 'freedoms' have led to 'untruthfulness about equality and diversity' in the sense that limitations on freedoms have ignored the common good for the sake of individualism.

Much has been made of Finnis' essay. Indeed, his views are often taken out of context and presented as religious and moral propaganda. This is not the case as his essays are perfectly reasoned. It may be useful here to clarify what Finnis is arguing. First of all, he is not opposed to immigration at all as we have seen earlier. Indeed immigration is positive and in line with what Hart's liberal philosophy aimed to achieve. However, just as uncontrolled immigration is irresponsible, Finnis argues that there had been a tendency to allow many things to happen in society without due attention to the underpinning moral scrutiny of the law. Obviously he disagreed with Hart. Secondly, the quotation about immigration covers Europe and beyond; it is by no means just directed at the UK. Former Yugoslavia is given as an example of 'ethnic and religious inter-communal miseries of hatred' and the ethnic cleansing that resulted. In other words, Finnis is talking about extreme cases and his words are more of a warning about the dangers of uncontrolled immigration and unmanaged integration of groups of people as opposed to immigration proper. Finally, the time period is extremely significant; Finnis is pointing out that this was more of a gradual building up and simmering over throughout history as opposed to any immediate problems with immigration in general.

Key quote

Finnis felt that modern society has become so obsessed with individual liberty, or the freedom to pursue any project that we please, that it has taken the existence of our society for granted. (Lloyd)

Key Person

Herbert Lionel Adolphus Hart was an esteemed barrister and Professor of Jurisprudence at Oxford University from 1952 to 1969 and John Finnis' academic mentor, and then later his colleague at Oxford. In stark contrast to Finnis, Hart argued in his seminal work **The Concept of Law** (1961) that there is no necessary connection between law and morality.

Key quotes

So the time seems ripe for a wider reflection on whether late twentieth-century political philosophies so characteristic, so suasive, so victorious as Hart's correspond or correlate with these evils, or indeed contribute to their onset or progression. (Finnis)

It could be argued that the common good may be damaged if it made it impossible for existing indigenous people to participate in all the benefits of the current society as a direct result and it would damage that society's ability to benefit the common good in the rest of the world. (Lloyd)

In everything do to others as you would have them do to you; for this is the law and the prophets. (Matthew 7:12)

The cry of the poor is a kind of a prayer; it opens our hearts and teaches us to be attentive. (Pope Francis)

quicKfire

2.32 Why did Hart and Finnis disagree about the law?

However, the real issue here seems to be at what point is immigration uncontrolled? Concern is often given about the strain on a country's resources. Dr Greg Barker raises a very significant point here when he suggests that it is surely part of a Christian attitude to accept some level of discomfort and compromise for the sake of others, to share and take the burden of their suffering and to eradicate inequalities. But where is the line drawn?

One would think that Finnis' reaction to uncontrolled immigration is based in the fear that 'laws, cultures and traditions' of a country will be changed or eroded. In support of this view, Pope Francis has also called on new arrivals 'to know and respect the laws, the culture and the traditions of the countries that take them in'. However, whether this is a good thing or not in terms of Finnis' overall system is not altogether clear. Some could argue that British values as taught today are of a better quality due to immigration. Finnis would simply reply that this is not necessarily true and that their interpretation of the goods is simply that – an interpretation that bears no resemblance to moral fact as exemplified through his principles of practical reasonableness. This is why scholars such as Brigita White have questioned the underlying agenda of Finnis' Natural Law and the fact that his own presentation of it assumes a 'traditional' Roman Catholic overview of morality. For example, for Finnis, a society that promotes absolute equality in law, but does not differentiate on what he may see as significant issues of morality in applying that law, may be seen to be damaging the basic goods indirectly. His views on issues of marriage, sexuality and related issues are well documented. Nonetheless, it may also be worth bearing in mind that whilst many see Finnis as traditional and conservative, at the same time he has always passionately argued to preserve the legal rights of those with whom he may disagree morally, and indeed, as we shall see, as a practising Christian and influential theologian categorically opposes the idea of capital punishment.

Do people have a moral obligation to support refugees and asylum seekers according to Finnis' Natural Law?

The simple answer here is 'yes'. Finnis' Natural Law demands ultimate respect for life and all that it encompasses. Freedom is essential for this. Asylum seekers are, by the very definition of the term, those who are fleeing from situations wherein their individual rights and freedoms have been removed and life is endangered. In cases where life is endangered, the immediate need for action must be taken. Acceptance of asylum seekers is a priority in terms of immigration law.

Finnis' Natural Law is just and humane but also, in the good of friendship, demands compassion to participate in life and the other associated goods. Eradicating the pain and suffering of asylum seekers and allowing them to temporarily participate in the 'asylum' of goods a society offers is a universally accepted principle and an example of how Finnis' Natural Law can be embraced internationally. Once refugee status is established, a refugee is protected by the 1951 United Nations Convention on the Status of Refugees. It allows them to be given access to social housing, welfare benefits and encouragement to participate in the goods and find self-esteem through employment, integration into society and building up positive relationships. The principle of practical reasonableness that demands no arbitrary preference amongst persons enables access to, and participation in, the goods will help them flourish and benefit society as a whole. Finnis' comparison of this principle to the Golden Rule is significant here: 'Put yourself in your neighbour's shoes. Do not condemn others for what you are willing to do yourself. **_Do not (without special reason) prevent others getting for themselves what you are trying to get for yourself_**. These are requirements of reason, because to ignore them is to be arbitrary as between individuals.' It is an absolute requirement of practical reason, then, to welcome asylum seekers freely and to work towards integration and flourishment of refugees in society for the common good.

Do people have a moral obligation to support 'economic migrants' and if so, is a points-based immigration system morally right according to Finnis' Natural Law?

The aim of Finnis' Natural Law is enabling everyone to participate in the basic goods for the common good. This inevitably means that those who do not have access to the full range of goods, or full participation in them, are obligated to seek out self-improvement. In other words, we have our answer as to the first part of this question. An understanding of Finnis' Natural Law system certainly brings with it an imperative to support those that have a goal of bettering themselves, but also being allowed to contribute towards the flourishing of society. The 'Golden Rule' approach ensures that society benefits. Economic migrants are seeking a better standard of life.

Pope Francis welcomes immigration.

However, individual countries have an imperative to maintain the common good by managing immigration effectively. The problem with a points system is that it prioritises certain things and values certain things much more highly than others. For example, skills, education, wealth and age are all given more weight than specific individual needs that inevitably mean an individual may 'take' more than they contribute. However, such a utilitarian approach is contrary to Finnis' Natural Law system that promotes equality in participation in the goods and not contribution to a stronger economy. An economy may be strong and wealthy but display a poverty in compassion (friendship) and sense of the common good. Denying economic migrants based upon a points system is arbitrarily permitting participation in the goods and arbitrary preference of persons. It therefore skews Finnis' holistic vision of a flourishing society and is certainly contrary to a Gospel that encourages the strong to support the weak.

Overall, the management of an immigration system – that is the **how** it is to be implemented – in relation to Finnis' system is a logistical nightmare and even with the principles of practical reasonableness someone, somewhere is going to lose out unless an open-door policy is implemented. Even then, there would be moral issues surrounding a first-come, first-served system. No system will ever be perfect; however, Finnis' Natural Law does invite a positive and compassionate approach to economic migration in theory. There is an argument that a points system in reverse would better serve the principles of practical reasonableness; however, there will always be those who point out that the prioritising of needs, rather than individuals, however compassionate and Christian-centred, could be too much strain on society as a whole and be adverse for the common good. Then again, is there any ethical system that would provide an airtight solution to this ethical dilemma?

Applying Finnis' Natural Law to capital punishment

In considering the application of theories to capital punishment there are some key questions to focus on in order to see how Finnis' Natural Law can be applied:

- Do Finnis' Natural Law and Proportionalism support or reject capital punishment?
- Are there any circumstances in which capital punishment may be deemed as licit by Finnis' Natural law or Proportionalism?

Key quote

… there is nothing inherently wrong in the project of immigration where it enables a person to participate in these goods where previously they could not and where, according to practical reason, it does not damage the participation in the goods for other people for there must be respect for every basic value in every act. (Lloyd)

Key quotes

First, it is important to remember that traditional Catholic teaching never claimed that the state must impose the death penalty …
St Thomas held that the government has the responsibility to protect the common good by means of just punishments, but he does not specify that one particular crime (e.g. murder) must always and in every case be punished in one particular way (capital punishment). **(Kaczor)**

John Paul, for his part, does not deny that the state has the right to impose the death penalty. The state retains this right, even though he thinks that the state ought not to make use of this right. **(Kaczor)**

Does Finnis' Natural Law support or reject capital punishment?

We have seen already that the position of the Roman Catholic Church has been influenced by the writing of Aquinas' Natural Law. All are in agreement that Thomas Aquinas justified the use of capital punishment as a last resort. However, it must be said that it is not the case that Aquinas is 'for' or 'against' capital punishment but simply that as a last, desperate measure it can be permissible. Again, this is reflected in *Evangelium Vitae 56* Pope John Paul II declared that the state 'ought not go to the extreme of executing the offender ***except in cases of absolute necessity***: in other words, when it would not be possible otherwise to defend society. Today however, as a result of steady improvements in the organisation of the penal system, ***such cases are very rare, if not practically non-existent.***'

In addition to this, we have seen that there is debate about ***how*** Thomas justifies capital punishment. The position of the Roman Catholic Church has now shifted and openly states that capital punishment can never be justified and the reason given that it violates the dignity of the human person (i.e. life) has engendered the debate about intrinsic evil and papal infallibility.

It is clear that Finnis' version of Natural Law could never allow capital punishment. In addition to this, in his book *Moral Absolutes: Tradition, Revision and Truth* (1991) Finnis questions ***how*** Aquinas arrives at the conclusion that capital punishment could be licit. Finnis summarises Aquinas' position as justifying killing in the administration of justice 'can be done with a **different intentionality**, that is, under a different description; restoring the order of justice violated by the one killed who, moreover, by his violation of justice, his fault, had **removed himself from the dignity of the human**.'

Two points are pertinent here:

(1) Aquinas argues that this 'different intentionality' is to punish – a lawful, God-given authority, administered on behalf of the common good – which is seen as a 'good' act, and,

(2) That in violating the order of justice, the guilty party has 'removed' his or her own human dignity.

The first point has been summarised by Peter Black in *Theological Studies* (1999) where he points out that, 'for Aquinas, ***circumstances surrounding an exterior act can at times enter into the principal condition of the object of the act***, that is … the circumstances give to the act its moral species'. Finnis is also concerned about Aquinas' use of logic in justifying it according to the '***circumstances surrounding an exterior act can at times enter into the principal condition of the object of the act'***. The debate is complex, but according to Aquinas' since punishment is distributive and not commutative, the direct act of punishment is the primary aim/intention and death of the individual is the inevitable by-product of administering this punishment and therefore not the direct object of the act. In other words, the intention, or aim, of the act is now to punish (both psychologically and morally) and killing becomes a by-product. For Finnis this is unacceptable as he considers all acts of capital punishment as involving a direct intention to kill. Indeed, McCormick (a proportionalist) questions the whole objectivity of this thinking and argues that it is dangerous because it opens up a whole new range of possibilities in ethical thinking.

Finnis rejects outright the second point. Finnis sees an inconsistency in Aquinas' thinking. Finnis is opposed to the death penalty since it directly attacks a basic good. A basic good can never be removed and he finds the analogy that Aquinas uses (Matthew 5:29–30) of a diseased body part being amputated as inappropriate

quickfire

2.33 How does Aquinas justify capital punishment?

to argue that the diseased part, that is the guilty party, is devoid in person of the dignity of life. The act may reflect an absence of good but this does not make the person totally lacking.

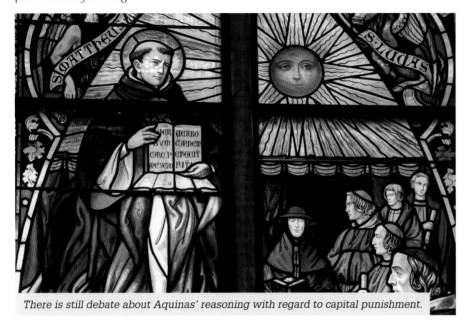

There is still debate about Aquinas' reasoning with regard to capital punishment.

In summary, Finnis is against capital punishment because it violates the basic goods; that is, the good of life and all that is associated with it (knowledge, play, aesthetic experience, friendship and religion) for the individual punished. It also violates practical reasonableness since it is a directly intended evil act. To argue as Aquinas and traditionalists do in favour of this is to violate the principles of practical reasonableness by pitting the goods against each other.

Are there any circumstances in which capital punishment may be deemed as licit by Finnis' Natural Law?

The clear-cut answer to this question is no. Finnis does not deny capital punishment as meeting requirements of retribution but it is still unacceptable and not the right way to administer justice in accordance with the basic goods.

Despite the debates with Ed Feser in 2018 and the works of Professor Elinor Gardner and Professor Kevin E. Miller, no academic has convinced Finnis that Natural Law could ever support the death penalty. Feser and Miller both hold to Aquinas' teaching and see the recent declaration of the Roman Catholic Church as inconsistent and a departure from Aquinas.

Elinor Gardner takes a different line. Gardner attempts to respond to Finnis' own use of practical reasoning. She sees Aquinas' account of capital punishment as an example of determining civil punishments through the exercise of practical reason. Aquinas shows neither absolute acceptance nor an absolute rejection of the death penalty, but that it is justified according to specific historical and cultural circumstances and the needs of a political community, as well as on the severity of the offense. It is only used as a last resort for the good of the community.

Gardner makes a distinction between 'intentionally causing evil' (punishment) and 'intentionally doing evil' (fault); she argues that punishment is an act that belongs to the former category and is, in itself, a good act since the object of punishment is to redress a disorder produced by an offence. She continues: 'while it is always wrong to do evil, it is not always wrong to cause evil. To punish an evil-doer with death is intentionally to cause an evil as a means for the end of a just order.' This distinction, argues Gardner, is not denied by Finnis but he is 'unwilling to apply it to the evil of death because of its final character'.

Key quotes

A life can never be restored, and the killing of the murderer, whilst seemingly in proportion to the crime, will both damage the basic good of life and prevent the pursuance of a life plan. Yet justice or fairness must be done, and this must be in proportion to the crime committed. It is seemingly in the best interest of the common good to remove an unrepentant criminal from society to prevent further crime but capital punishment is not the only way to do this. (Lloyd)

Capital punishment, since it involves the intent to kill as a means, is 'doing evil that good may come', i.e. the pursuit of a good end (the restoration of the order of justice) by inherently immoral means. (Finnis)

Finnis explains this notion of the restoring of order in society, an Aristotelian notion taken up by Aquinas … Restoring the balance requires that offenders undergo something contrary to their will, just as they voluntarily imposed on others what was contrary to their will. (Black)

Despite this argument, Finnis is suspicious of such reasoning that is similar to that used by the 'circumstances entering into the principal condition of the object of the act' argument. For Finnis, whilst capital punishment may be argued not to be direct killing or an act that defends the common good (and this is unconvincing in itself), the reasoning used could **never** justify it as **unintentional** killing. Capital punishment always involves intentional killing, no matter how it is packaged, according to Finnis.

> ### AO1 Activity
>
> Why not take opportunity at this point to note down a list of reasons as to why Finnis rejects capital punishment outright. Look at each point and then try to explain each one to another student to help you practise summarising the material.

Specification content

The application of Proportionalism to immigration and capital punishment.

Key quotes

The criminal is an individual whose good is as good as anyone's, notwithstanding that the criminal ought in fairness to be deprived of some opportunities of realising that good. (Finnis)

I present Aquinas's account of capital punishment as an example of determining civil punishments through the exercise of practical reason … Killing a guilty person is not intrinsically evil, in Aquinas's view, but it is nonetheless a last resort, when nothing else can be done for the good of the community. (Gardner)

When punishment is imposed precisely as retribution, although that which the offender experiences is bad (the restriction, pain, or loss) it is nevertheless chosen by judge and executioner as a good and not as a means to further good, i.e. Finnis' argument that evil is done as a means to an end. (Gardner)

The context of Proportionalism within Roman Catholic theology

The key questions for the application of Proportionalism are:

1. **What** precisely is the proportionate norm?
2. **When** should the norm of proportionate reasoning be used?
3. **How** should proportionate reasoning be used, i.e. is there a methodology?

We have seen from the section about Proportionalism that Hoose's overview was of the debates that were taking place between proportionalists themselves but also the debates that were taking place between the proportionalists and the magisterium. Hoose's study is very complex and in the end admits that whilst his work has 'demonstrated clearly enough the coherence and validity of Proportionalism' he also states: 'If we are satisfied that Proportionalism is **what** must be taught, we must now ask **how** it is to be taught.'

Although Hoose's work did not enter this arena of 'how' Proportionalism was to be taught (i.e. the way in which a methodology must be applied), Hoose absolutely hit the nail on the head when he recognised the cause of all the confusion in the early debates. Roman Catholic theology, and Christian ethics, in general, is not just concerned with 'what we should do?', but also with the deeper questions of how ethical behaviour relates to 'being' a good Christian. Therefore the issues of 'good' and 'right', although separated in philosophy (as G. E. Moore had clarified), could not so easily be separated in Christian theology. Hoose had already identified that the writers on Proportionalism were from diverse theological backgrounds and so it is no surprise that a variety of different understandings of what proportionate reasoning is, but also **when** and **how** to use it, have emerged throughout the debate.

When looking at the history of the Proportionalism debate, it is clear why the term 'revisionist theologian' is more appropriate than 'proportionalist'. Revisionist is a more accurate term because it reflects that the theological 'revisions' are an attempt to work within the Christian tradition of Natural Law as developed by Aquinas in order to refine or develop it. The notion of proportionate reasoning in ethics takes different positions of both emphasis and importance between thinkers depending upon their theological perspectives.

It would not be unfair to say in the times of Aquinas and the following centuries there was a practical need for guiding the pastoral work of the priesthood in absolving sins and penance through confession. In other words, the purpose of Natural Law as an ethical guide was to establish what was sinful and what needed doing when one did fall into sinfulness. As time has developed, these guidelines evolved into hard and fast rules for ethical behaviour. Some of these rules, according to some theologians, uncritically became absolutes in theological terms and beyond question. Garth Hallett in 1989 questioned the whole basis of moral values within Roman Catholic theology and pointed out that such unquestionable 'moral' dictums had in fact been 'smuggled' into theology quite inadvertently. He uses the case of organ transplantation as an example. The Roman Catholic *Dictionary of Moral Theology* (1962), for instance, assumes that the definition of mutilation is synonymous with 'illegitimate removal of organs'. Hallett regards this as a veiled tautology because it does not allow for what could be argued to be legitimate removal or organs; it simply assumes that 'mutilation is always wrong'.

quickfire

2.34 What did Garth Hallett argue about ethical precepts or rules?

Key quote

In traditional precept ethics, the reasoning employed on behalf of various norms was often smuggled in moral values before their time … whether organ transplants are illegitimate and therefore should be termed 'mutilation' must be settled otherwise than by the veiled tautology. (Hallett)

Ethical rules were established by the Roman Catholic Church as a practical means to aid confession.

However, Roman Catholic Natural Law theological ethics during the 20th century and into the 21st century has shifted from a purely deontological focus to a consideration of a more holistic approach to ethics, in particular bringing into more prominence the significance of the moral agent and a focus on virtues. Although the precepts (or goods) do not change, situations and contexts do change and involve wider considerations of what it means to be human, the nature of society, the needs of the individual Christian and the overall collective aim of the Christian community to maintain its relationship with God.

It is this broader understanding of Natural Law theological ethics that appears to have (in the words of John F. Keenan) 'helped resurrect moral theology from the rubble'. Many revisionist theologians would acknowledge their debts to theological anthropology and personalist ethics that both precedes and overshadows the more focused and contextualised debate about proportionate reasoning.

Key theologians in the Proportionalism debates

Louis Janssens coined the phrase 'the human person, adequately considered'. Throughout Janssens' academic career, the human person was a focal point of his interest. For Janssens, the norm of morality is the human person in itself and its relationships (God, others, the world). His interest in pre-moral values and disvalues, and the importance of proportionality in determining the moral rightness of human conduct was only part of this overall theological anthropology, using Aquinas as a source and his own personalism as a frame of reference.

Joseph Selling, another proportionalist (and former student of Janssens), allows just an appendix to the debate about proportionate reasoning and Aquinas'

Key quotes

'… to overcome a one-sided ethic of obedience and to teach a morality of personal resposibility and brotherly love with courageous obedience to one's own sincere but ever searching conscience.' **(Haring)**

Fuchs supports the absolute and universal moral norms found in the Catholic tradition but also recognises the individual call of God based upon personal characteristics of the individual person and the circumstances of one's existence. The emphasis here is on the human person and not human nature. **(Curran)**

By the end of the twentieth century, however, Proportionalism was no longer a major topic in moral theology. … Proportionalism as a theory was quite limited because it dealt with only a comparatively small part of the broad reality of Catholic moral theology. **(Curran)**

'principle of double effect' in his recent work *Reframing Catholic Theological Ethics* published 2016. Selling's work is an interesting interpretation of Proportionalism and so will be referred to later.

Accordingly, **Charles Curran**, another theologian often associated with Proportionalism, has identified the trends of modern moral theology within Roman Catholicism last century in his recent publication in 2018, *Diverse Voices in Modern US Moral Theology* – although the influence is evidently beyond the US. Here he identifies the work of Bernard Haring as 'the most influential Catholic moral theologian of the twentieth century' due to his 'distaste for the manuals of moral theology' and his preference for a 'biblically inspired and Christ-centred moral theology'. In Haring's words, his aims were 'to overcome a one-sided ethic of obedience and to teach a morality of personal responsibility and brotherly love with courageous obedience to one's own sincere but ever-searching conscience'. It is Haring's approach towards a theological anthropology that has influenced many revisionists.

Curran also pinpoints the contributions of **Joseph Fuchs** (another proportionalist) who, like Janssens, addressed the issue of the centrality of the person in ethics and argued that ethical norms had a non-arbitrary absolute as a foundation within the person (Aquinas' 'do good and avoid evil'). However, Fuchs argued that 'right conduct is concerned with the non-absolute realities of the contingent human that would change in history'. Both Fuchs and Janssens held the view that ontic evil was a consistent and ever-present factor in ethical decision making in the fallen world in which we live. Curran's theology of compromise also assumes this.

James Keenan, another theologian sympathetic to the proportionalist debate, agrees with Curran's assessment and writes in his book *A History of Catholic Moral theology in the Twentieth Century* (2010) that 'Catholic theological ethics has been shaped by … Haring on a comprehensive, theologically integrated ethics of responsibility, Fuchs on moral objectivity and the critique of intrinsic evil, and Janssens on personalism.' Both Keenan and Curran also acknowledge probably the most well-known proponent of Proportionalism **Richard McCormick** as a major contributor towards Catholic theological ethics through his book, *Doing Evil to Achieve Good: Moral Choice in Conflict Situations* (1973) and his extensive publications in Notes on Moral Theology from 1965 through to 1984. **Bruno Schuller** (former student of Joseph Fuchs) is also well known for his contributions to the debate, and, despite his arguments with Richard McCormick in *Doing Evil to Achieve Good: Moral Choice in Conflict Situations*, was in general agreement with him. Schuller's significance was evident in clarifying the distinction between goodness and rightness this distinction according to Kaczor 'became standard in the proportionalist literature'.

A final mention needs to be given to **Garth Hallett**, who appears to be the only theologian and philosopher that has developed a specific methodology for proportionate reason in his 2009 book, *Greater Good: The Case for Proportionalism*. As we shall see, Hallett stands apart from others in that he refines and qualifies what a methodology for proportionate reasoning should include.

It goes without saying that all the above were influenced by the paper presented by **Peter Knauer** in the first instance.

Broader context of the debate

What is interesting from a bird's-eye view of the proportionalist debate, is it is clear that it is only one aspect of moral theology for many proportionalists. This is really important to consider, firstly for the role proportionate reasoning has in ethical methodologies overall, and secondly because the focus of the debates tended to be confined to issues of conflict as dictated by Aquinas' PDE.

Due to its relatively small role (although not small in significance), 'revisionists' is often the preferred term (as we noted at the start of T2E) so as not to misunderstand the overall theological perspective from which these theological ethicists operated. In other words, these figures all had broader interests that just the proportionalist debate. Indeed, Curran notes, in *Diverse Voices in Modern US Moral theology* that 'Proportionalism was a transitional phase in Catholic theological ethics trying to establish a method for moral judgement as an alternative to moral manuals ... Its focus was primarily on dilemmas and quandaries ... In time most theological ethicists moved on in search of a context for developing arguments on moral reasoning and moral living in all its dimensions.'

Within this context, Peter Knauer's article, first published in 1952, and the resulting debates on proportionate reasoning, made an important contribution but this was only one aspect of the moral theological debate. Knauer's assertion that proportionate reasoning 'is the fundamental principle of all morality' has been understood in different ways. Hoose's book alludes to this but it is only in the years that followed that this became apparent. For a minority, it meant that proportionate reasoning was an answer to the search for a Christian ethical approach in the modern world. For the majority it was simply indicating that the already established ethical norms were inherently based upon this principle.

quickfire

2.35 Why is a proportionalist 'method' or 'viewpoint' difficult to pin down?

Jesus taught the ethical norm 'treat others as you wish to be treated'.

Identifying suitable 'methodologies' for Proportionalism

To begin with, we must understand what Proportionalism is **not**. It is not, as we have seen, and by any means, an ethical theory or methodology. Garth Hallett has famously made this distinction that is accepted by all revisionist theologians involved in the proportionalist debate. 'Proportionalism' is an ethical norm; that is, it is a simple acceptance that proportionate reason **can** be used in ethics. This was also Hoose's conclusion, the legitimacy of Proportionalism. All so-called proportionalists agree on this.

For example, just as all Christians agree that 'treat others as you wish to be treated' is a useful ethical norm, it is highly doubtful that one could suggest this was an ethical theory. So, to give another example, Fletcher's Situation Ethics is based upon the norm that 'agape' (Christian love) should be the criterion applied to every moral issue. However, his 'methodology' is that of the four working principles and the six fundamental principles. In other words, his expansion on the norm is the guidance on **how** to apply agape by testing its application against certain criteria. Likewise, Max Stirner's Ethical Egoism is very specific in its methodology on **how** self-interest works when it is applied by ensuring that the ego (Einzige)

Key quotes

It is not just any reason, meaningful or important as it may be. Rather a reason is commensurate if the value realisable here and now by measures involving physical evil in a pre-moral sense is not in the long run undermined and contradicted by these measures but supported and maximised. (McCormick)

A criterion is like a weapon. If not carefully and precisely constructed, it can impale its user. (McCormick)

develops a sense of 'ownness' (Eigenheit) in order to realise the purity of its 'uniqueness' (Einzig); in other words, in order to follow the norm that one should follow one's own interests, one should first test one's awareness against his specific understandings outlined in *The Ego and Itself*.

If we are to understand Natural Law, what is clear is that it already has an idea of what 'ought' to be the case in a given situation by way of 'precepts' or 'basic goods'. Such 'rules' are then directed through specific ethical teachings. However, Christian moral duty is not just about following rules. Most revisionists today who advocate Proportionalism would view it as a middle way between deontology and teleology (which is quite different from consequentialism – it may be helpful to look at Hoose's discussion about the deontological and teleological distinction in T4E). Natural Law – and this is very clear in Aquinas – also involves virtues and correct action determined by intention (or as Dr Greg Barker would say 'a good heart distinguished from right action'). For something to be morally right for the majority of proportionalist thinkers, involves an inextricable link to moral goodness. This is not just in terms of an 'act-in-itself', but in terms of the whole context of the moral act and including the moral intention of the individual involved. However, as we shall see, even this is not universally accepted as a methodology.

We have already seen the dangers of understanding proportionate reason as simply 'reasoning' or just a case of 'weighing up' and 'balancing' reasons in a way that is commensurate or proportionate. We are NOT to just think up some arguments as 'in support' or 'against'; this is not only simplistic, but also a serious misunderstanding and misapplication of the principle of proportionate reason and ignores the whole theological framework of Roman Catholic moral theology. Proportionate reason is not a subjective reasoning. It is certainly not a broad, unrestricted and approximate ethical principle to justify desired behaviour any more than Fletcher's agape is simply a case of 'if it can be seen to be loving it is ok'! If it is done this way, then any form of argument can be justified subjectively. Indeed, this is why Hoose clearly states: 'any problems arising from the badness of the agent cannot be cured by a system, a principle or a deontological norm. Love is lacking. **The bad person will do what he wants** ... **he might hypocritically claim to have a proportionate reason for his action** ... who knows how many wars have been "justified" in that way?'

But if this is the case then how do we apply 'Proportionalism' to an ethical issue? The answer becomes much more straightforward, in most instances, when we look at not just the ethical norm of 'what' proportionate reasoning is and that we should apply it, but consider **how proportionalist thinkers themselves** have understood proportionate reason and take note of their different methodologies that direct '**when**' and '**how**' to use it.

Different understandings and methodologies for Proportionalism

For the purpose of application, it may be useful to identify, very tentatively (and with an awareness that this is a brushstroke analysis), some different methodologies that may be used in response to the issues of immigration and capital punishment. As Professor Christopher Kaczor has observed, 'The Proportionalism of Garth Hallett, for example, differs from the Proportionalism of Peter Knauer, and this in turn differs from the Proportionalism of Richard McCormick.' However, what must be considered is that different methodologies do not necessarily mean different positions or viewpoints on the issue. We shall see this more when we apply the specific methodologies.

What is intended here is to guide students and teachers towards some different methodologies of proportionate reasoning or 'types of Proportionalism' associated with particular theologians. In saying this, it must be remembered that all are operating from, and are respectful of, the deontological basis of Natural Law in that they recognise the significance of the precepts or basic goods involved and a duty to maintain them. The types are very 'broad brushstroke' but will help pupils offer different ways of explaining the proportionalist approach to immigration and capital punishment even when there is no significant difference in the outcome.

(1) The Classical proportionalist position – Conflict Situation Proportionalism (CSP)

As we have seen from T2E, the early debate about Proportionalism originated with Peter Knauer's paper on understanding Aquinas' 'principle of double effect' (PDE). When Richard McCormick reviewed this article, it opened up a new debate on **how** Aquinas' PDE should be understood. Knauer together with other early proportionalists found that the first three criteria (good or indifferent act, a good intention, and, evil does not flow directly from the act) of the PDE were adequately summarised and superseded by the fourth condition of 'commensurate' or 'proportionate' reason. Knauer made the statement that although it had merited limited attention in the manuals of theologians, it was in fact the fundamental principle of all morality. However, debates were intense about the precise nature of proportionate reason and notions of direct and indirect acts, the distinction between good and right and also distinctions between psychological and moral intentions. The likes of Janssens, Fuchs, Schuller, Selling, Curran, Keenan and McCormick all debated amongst themselves the details of such issues, often disagreeing on what precisely one aspect or more of proportionate reason meant in relation to Aquinas' PDE.

They all tended to agreement with Knauer's conclusions on the significance of the PDE. As their understanding of moral and pre-moral evil, ontic evil, and values and disvalues developed, Janssens observed that every act brings with it evil due to the fallen nature of our world and of humanity. As such, every moral decision made involved some kind of disvalue. Knauer and Janssens tend to give more weight to the fourth principle of Aquinas' PDE in line with broader anthropological theologies, playing down the significance of psychological intentions and having no impact upon decisions of right and wrong, preferring the weighting of moral intentions. Schuller, Fuchs, McCormick and Curran have all debated the direct/indirect distinction in Aquinas' PDE. For example, the debate between Schuller and McCormick displays different approaches; Selling and Keenan have also developed different methodologies for moral theology. However, all involved in the early debates see themselves as traditionalist Roman Catholic moral theologians who oppose consequentialism and situationism and yet uphold both deontological and teleological aspects of Natural Law as outlined by Hoose (see T4E). Charles Curran in his early writings distinguishes revisionist theologians as 'mixed teleologists' or 'mixed consequentialists', a middle way between absolute deontology and absolute consequentialism. Indeed, Curran was most confused when revisionists were referred to as consequentialists by the magisterium (see T2E). Richard McCormick confirms this position in *Doing Evil to Achieve Good* and refers to them as 'moderate teleologists', seeing this as synonymous with Curran's position.

Key quote

These theologians, in their explanation of materia apta (Janssens), commensurate reason (Knauer), proportionate reason (Schuller), insist that other elements than consequences function in moral rightness and wrongness. I would include myself among those who so insist. (McCormick)

quickfire

2.36 What is meant by 'conflict situation'?

Key term

Materia apta: Latin phrase referring to Janssens' concept of the human person adequately considered (lit. suitable form or matter)

Self-defence is the classic example used by Aquinas for a conflict situation requiring the principle of double effect.

137

Key term

Conflict situation: a situation (dilemma) whereby available options to act ethically include bad actions

Key quotes

Proportionate reason becomes explicit when the pre-moral disvalues that permeate all human activity are on a level that threatens the very pre-moral value that one is striving for in one's act. (Salzman)

What traditional ethics has to teach is allegiance to reason and objective norms. However, it too readily equated objective norms with universal precepts, and rationality with their discovery and application. (Hallett)

What is also interesting from the early debates is the agreement on *when* PR is to be used. What did become clear was that the debates tended to be restricted to what McCormick termed 'conflict situations'; that is, proportionate reason had a specific niche in ethical thinking with regards to when it was appropriate to use and apply. In fact, McCormick's book, *Doing Evil to Achieve Good* had the sub-heading *Moral Choice in Conflict Situations*. Conflict situations are specific ethical dilemmas that, in McCormick's own words, present '*practical conflict-situations where an evil can be avoided or a more or less necessary good achieved only when another evil is reluctantly caused*'. McCormick regards conflict situations as cases where '*there is the situation where the only alternative to causing evil or permitting evil is greater evil*'. McCormick lists areas where proportionate reason has been applied: self-defence, aspects of war, abortion, euthanasia, sterilisation, experimentation and contraception. In other words, McCormick sees it as relevant to debates about ethical dilemmas in which there is a risk to life. Accordingly, the early debates about Proportionalism were confined to such areas and it was the theologian Bernard Haring who coined the phrase 'negative morality' with regard to the areas of debate that involved the PDE and proportionate reason because they focused on death issues.

In saying that, the principles of Proportionalism are such that they are the foundation of every moral act, since every action brings with it the ontic evil associated with humanity's fallen nature and world. However, as stated earlier, this is, in the main, covert and integrated into established ethical norms. As Todd A. Salzman writes: 'Proportionate reason is relevant to every moral judgement that a human being makes, even though in most cases the agent does not consciously reflect on this ambiguity, and merely follows the norm.' Once again, the position of Conflict Situation Proportionalists is that only when a basic good or pre-moral value is threatened does proportionate reason come into play. Despite this reservation, of all the early Conflict Situation Proportionalists Richard McCormick is the one who has engaged, in passing, with the issue of capital punishment. We shall therefore consider his views. In light of his methodology, we could also suggest ways in which Conflict Situation Proportionalists may approach immigration.

(2) Value-maximisation Proportionalism (VMP)

Father Garth Hallett is a well-known and respected American Jesuit priest and philosopher. He served as Professor of Philosophy at St Louis University until 2009. As a philosopher, he has written extensively on Wittgenstein, language and logic.

Hallett in *Christian Moral Reasoning* (published in 1983) criticised the views of Moore on 'good' and also the later school of Emotivism associated with Alfred Ayer and Charles Stevenson. He argued that they failed to address the correct criteria for understanding moral language. For Hallett, like Wittgenstein, ethical discourse has different layers. A definition of good is not impossible because it is a simple word but rather its definition could be found in its more than simple use as an evaluative term. Hallett writes: 'The description of any object or act is decisive for its evaluation, yet we cannot completely characterise its goodness or badness descriptively. Still more clearly, we possess no such definition. We should be slow, however, to infer from this lack ... that goodness is non-descriptive, as Moore did.' In addition, the emotions reveal something beyond approval or persuasiveness that *explains why* we approve or disapprove. Hallett argued that it is this *cognitive primacy of criteria* that matters; that is, the underlying understanding of what merits something as worthy of approval or disapproval according to cognitive deliberations.

This philosophical understanding of the nature of moral terms is Hallett's grounding for Proportionalism and a philosophical approach to Christian ethics. In analysing biblical and historical writings from Ignatius to Aquinas, Hallett argues that the cognitive criteria Christians use when making moral decisions is one of 'value balancing'. This is true of considering moral rules, duty and what appear to be exceptionless precepts. By this, Hallett means truly objective ethical decisions can only be made in avoiding the two extremes of consequentialism and precept ethics (deontology). For Hallett, on the one hand deontology 'slipped moral values into the deliberative process, illegitimately'; on the other hand, 'value ethicists' underestimated the importance of moral rules altogether.

In *Christian Moral Reasoning* Hallett was sympathetic to aspects of the proportionalist debate such as the distinction between what is 'good' and what is 'morally right'. He also challenged the philosophy behind intrinsic evil acts, and this was clearly stated in a later paper in 1989 in which he accused the Church of 'smuggling' in ethical absolutes uncritically. Hallett had already, in *Christian Moral Reasoning*, made the typically proportionalist point that there is a distinction between an act described as bad e.g. 'killing' and one described as morally wrong e.g. 'murder'. Hallett pointed out that the act is first and foremost the act of killing, whereas 'murder is killing with a moral appraisal already attached' and judged prospectively (that is, objectively). Therefore, only when philosophically analysed and evaluated does the act of killing (a bad act) have the potential to be considered murder (a morally wrong act). The problem was that traditional precept ethics had tended to define the bad act as morally bad as well and 'smuggled in moral values before their time'. Nonetheless, what is different about Hallett's Proportionalism is that he disregards the moral/pre-moral distinction in the evaluation process of the whole event. For Hallett, a proportionate evaluation, that is, one that balances values, does so taking into account not just pre-moral or nonmoral values but also balancing and questioning preconceived moral ones. They are seen as forming a complete package!

Accordingly, Hallett then developed this value-balancing process into a system that he called 'value maximisation' that which 'uses reason not only more coherently that preceptive ethics does but also more fully'. In 2009, these conclusions were developed more fully in his book *The Greater Good: A Case for Proportionalism*. Hallett's Proportionalism combines his philosophical approach with that of Peter Knauer's ultimate analysis of the PDE in Aquinas': proportionate reason as the foundation of all morality. Hallett argues that 'value-maximisation' is essentially the application of proportionate reason.

Balancing values need not be complex, according to Hallett.

Key quotes

For a fully objective judgement, the facts are what matter, not our limited, fallible beliefs about the facts. (Hallett)

If the action is right and is done for the reasons that make it right, right motive or intention is assured. (Hallett)

Proportionalist Methodologies

CSP

Conflict-situation Proportionalists. A methodology representing those who were involved in the early debates such as Richard McCormick who saw 'Proportionalism' as applying to the PDE and conflict-situations only.

VMP

Value-maximisation Proportionalists. A later philosophical development of Proportionalism by Garth Hallett that considers balancing values but does not include 'intention' in the ethical deliberations.

RTP

Revisionist theologian 'Proportionalists'. Those theologians that have been influenced by Proportionalism but have developed different ideas as a direct result of the debates about proportionate reasoning. They see an ethical action as an 'event' that has many aspects to consider as opposed to the direct action in itself.

However, there are two key differences between Hallett's Proportionalism and that of the early proportionalists:

(1) Hallett sees no role in ethical decision making for the subjective and so rejects the contribution of intention of the moral agent to the moral event (something that Bruno Schuller had earlier raised). Hallett regards value maximisation as something that is objective and detaches itself from motive or intention. He writes: 'Motive or intention is typically decisive for a judgement of culpability, but typically irrelevant for a judgement of what should be done.' Here he follows the thinking of Moore on the good/right distinction but also the implications of Knauer when he dismisses the first three conditions of Aquinas' PDE in favour of the fourth.

(2) Hallett also denies that the **process** of ethical decision making is as simple as balancing goods and non-goods. Ultimately the end result is **a final evaluative decision** on what is the greater moral good (the ought) and therefore the 'right'; but it is not just non-moral, ontic or pre-moral values and disvalues that need to be balanced but also **secondary moral values** or decisions made **within** this **evaluative process**. Hallett therefore recognises, unlike McCormick and earlier proportionalists, that commensurate or proportionate reasoning is simply entailed in the final decision.

Therefore, in taking the ball, so to speak, from Knauer's observation that proportionate reasoning is the foundation for all morality, and, running with it to develop a purely philosophically objective version of Proportionalism, Hallett's Proportionalism marks a distinctive departure from the early proportionalists. Indeed, he sees it as the **only** version of Proportionalism that is viable for ethical theology – in his own words, '**a species of unrestricted Proportionalism**'.

(3) Revisionist Theology Proportionalism [RTP]

In 2016, Joseph Selling, one of the original proportionalists, published a very significant book for Roman Catholic ethical theology entitled *Reframing Catholic Theological Ethics*. Selling is the classic example of one of the early 'proportionalists' that was involved in revisionist theological ethics in general. He was greatly influenced by Bernard Haring and Louis Janssens and their theological anthropology that put the 'human person adequately considered' at the centre of ethical thinking. Selling writes: 'If the starting point of ethical living is the person and not simply a list of commandments, then it is clear that we need to inquire who this person is, where they are going and what they are trying to accomplish.'

Selling has developed and suggested a new approach to Natural Law in response to the revisionist debates of the last century (of which the Proportionalism debate was just one). His view is that Christian ethics should be person-centred, and ethical actions understood in the light of the complete moral event and the holistic virtuous person. Selling's vision is very much what Hoose indicated in his book on Proportionalism; namely, how to be a good Christian: 'What, precisely, are the goals of ethical living? What kind of persons should we be aspiring to be, and what kind of communities can we build that support such goals and personality types?'

It is interesting that Selling downplays the role of proportionate reasoning and limits it to an appendix that firmly fits it within the debate about the 'principle of double effect'. As with the classic proportionalists he has ascribed a place for proportionate reasoning to conflict situations; however, the questions that the proportionalist debate raised in terms of finding a new methodology for Roman Catholic ethics have firmly influenced his approach. His book is detailed and his style is in a similar vein to Proportionalism in his discussions of intrinsic evil, the moral psychology of Aquinas and ontic evil; however, he frames his whole approach around becoming a good Christian and the idea of developing virtues in ethical behaviour and decision making. Selling acknowledges that there are different ways of ensuring the greater good beyond the proportionate reasoning of the PDE; for example, seeking the greater good and lesser evil, prioritising urgent situations and differentiating between material and moral cooperation in considering the wrongdoing of another. Overall, Selling speaks of the moral 'event' rather than 'act' and acknowledges the complexity of the many aspects to consider, not least of which are the role of God's grace, forgiveness, the Kingdom ideal of which the example of Jesus and what he calls an 'attitudinal approach to morality' as key.

Selling's solution, then, is the attitudinal approach that Jesus presented towards norms combined with the flexibility of the virtues which Selling feels have long been neglected by the Church. His solution is a convergence of traditional with new, in which issuing order, rules and commandments is replaced with a more practical solution of targeting behaviour through 'participating in the construction of a narrative that highlights virtuous living'. He finishes his book by stating: 'Similar to that found in the gospels, it is not a narrative about following rules and fighting against our created humanity. It is a narrative about persons and communities attempting to be attentive to the teaching and life example, the lifeways, of the Lord himself.'

Selling's proposals – although seen by some as a form of Proportionalism – are actually removed from the proportionalist debate and in placing proportionate reasoning in an Appendix with the PDE, he makes a clear statement that his approach to ethics is not dictated by the Proportionalism debate. Instead, his approach to ethics is grounded in the belief that the morality of of action – or as he calls it 'event' – needs to be approached in a different way from traditional deontology. His main priority is a person-centred approach like that of his mentor Louis Janssens who considered ethics in the light of 'the human person adequately considered'. However, what the proportionalist debate did for both Janssens and Selling is made them realise that a more comprehensive system of ethical decision making needed to be developed that considered more than just rules.

Key quotes

At the beginning I stated that the goal of this study was not to reject or replace traditional moral theology but rather to broaden its base and to expand its horizons … Freed from the narrow concern about violating rules and norms, we discovered that new horizons do indeed come into view. (Selling)

A certain humility is called for in the case of a global institution attempting to give advice to hundreds of millions of persons in just about every conceivable interpersonal situation around the globe at any given time. (Selling)

quickfire

2.38 According to Selling, what is the aim of Christian ethics?

The human person adequately considered is at the heart of Selling's ethical theory.

AO1 Activity

Why not take the opportunity at this point to explain in your own words the three possible methodologies to use in applying Proportionalism to moral issues. Try to focus on how they are each different from the other.

Applying the proportionalist norm to immigration

As we now move onto the issues, we are now in a clearer position as to consider what exactly we are applying to an issue. We will, in effect, look at three different styles of reasoning, broadly defined, amongst the wealth of revisionist theology in response to **when** and **how** Proportionalism is to be applied:

- Conflict Situation Proportionalism (CSP)
- Value Maximisation Proportionalism (VMP)
- Revisionist Theology Proportionalism [VP]

However, it must be noted that Proportionalism, as presented by Hoose's overview, in any of its forms, is not strictly speaking directly applicable to immigration or capital punishment in its original form. Abortion, euthanasia, contraception and sterilisation are all relevant and have been debated within Proportionalism. Hoose himself, supported by references to Selling, more or less states this in his book. Proportionalism lends itself more to conflict situations than to general ethical theory. However, Proportionalism does become more relevant when we see how Value Maximisation could be applied directly and this is one way forward.

It is important to remember that when applying Proportionalism to an ethical issue, all three approaches above could be outlined in breadth, or alternatively, one example of an approach could be used in more depth. In applying the theories, it is not just a case of stating what the final outcome would be (as in the information below) but being able to demonstrate how this is reasoned. The information above should help you with explaining why the final decision has been made.

If you look at the tables below you can see the different explanations that could be offered when trying to apply Proportionalism to immigration.

Method	Does Proportionalism support immigration?	How could Proportionalism respond to uncontrolled immigration?
CSP e.g. Richard McCormick	Immigration is not a conflict situation. Pope Francis recently declared, 'There is no Christian joy when doors are closed; there is no Christian joy when others are made to feel unwanted, when there is no room for them in our midst.' Proportionalists would no doubt approve of the Pope's declaration. A criminal record should not deter a welcome, provided the sentence has passed and the person is reformed.	Jesus' ministry teaches care for others in need. He taught 'love your neighbour as you love yourself'. CSP would certainly support welcoming those who wish to share in the benefits of an improved standard of living. Many would agree that free flowing immigrants are a benefit to society; however, even with a strain on public resources, this has to be considered in light of the Christian teaching of fellowship, love and the social praxis of the Gospels. Not a conflict situation.
VMP Garth Hallett	**(A) Value balancing** **Pre-moral values/disvalues**: Justice/fairness; poverty; health; education; compassion. **Moral values**: Sharing and compassion are Christian values and so welcoming the poor virtuous. To be fair to all means access for all to opportunities in society to essential resources. To be indifferent to the needs of others is selfish and irresponsible. Christian teaching suggests that some personal sacrifice for another's sake is good. **(B) Value maximisation** Christian values endorse immigration. (Pre)moral values are maximised.	**(A) Value balancing** **Pre-moral values/disvalues**: Justice/fairness; poverty; health; education; compassion; sacrifice. **Moral values**: Christian values are welcoming to all. To restrict access would be unchristian, selfish and unfair because it denies those who want to join and contribute to society opportunity for essential resources. Christian teaching of personal sacrifice towards others needs balancing against the loss that society could experience; however, helping another in need is good. **(B) Value maximisation** Christian values endorse immigration. (Pre)moral values are maximised.

Method	Does Proportionalism support immigration?	How could Proportionalism respond to uncontrolled immigration?
RTP e.g. Joseph Selling	RTP is a positive and compassionate ethic that emphasises virtue and role models in practice. What better example and following in the footsteps of Jesus could be served? Immigration benefits all and contributes towards any society by enrichment of life experiences and is 'a privileged opportunity to encounter the Lord' (Pope Francis) by serving others.	The issue of moral obligation towards others does not really bring with it a cap; it appears to be incumbent upon all Christians to welcome all who wish to share in the benefits of their society. RTP would see this as promoting the basic goods in accordance with the Christian Gospel and serving as role models to others.

Method	Do Christians have a moral obligation to support refugees and asylum seekers according to Proportionalism?	Do Christians have a moral obligation to support 'economic migrants' and if so, is a points-based immigration system morally right according to Proportionalism?
CSP e.g. Richard McCormick	An asylum seeker/refugee claim is not a conflict situation. However, the basic good of life is threatened. Pope Francis pointed out that refugees are part of the Roman Catholic family of faith. Refusal to acknowledge this was a sin: 'The sin is to refuse to encounter the other, the different, the neighbour, when this is in fact a privileged opportunity to encounter the Lord.' Christians should open up without prejudice to the rich diversity refugees have to offer.	There is no conflict situation here at all. Concerns about strains to the national economy are solved by a 'points system' but the problem is that people are valued according to what they can give. This is unchristian. The Christian Gospel message of love and forgiveness does not differentiate between rich and poor; it values people according to them being human beings and created in the image of God.
VMP Garth Hallett	**(A) Value balancing** **Pre-moral values/disvalues:** Death; suffering; compassion; selfishness. **Moral values:** To allow death or suffering is wrong when it is possible to avoid. Protection of society is right when threatened. To act compassionately is right. To be indifferent is selfish and irresponsible. **(B) Value maximisation** Absolutely yes. The moral 'facts' speak for themselves. It is right to accept refugees and help them get asylum seekers status. The value that is inherent in life and saving those in life-threatening situations is the greater good.	**(A) Value balancing** **Pre-moral values/disvalues:** Justice/fairness; discrimination; poverty; health; education; compassion. **Moral values:** To judge according to wealth and skills is unchristian and discriminative. Not welcoming the poor is unchristian and would also perpetuate poverty. To be fair to all is right so there is a case for a no points system. To be indifferent to specific needs is selfish and so there is a case for the poor to take priority. Christian teaching would suggest a dose of personal sacrifice and loss for the sake of another in need is good. **(B) Value maximisation** A points system is unchristian but Christians should welcome economic migrants. (Pre)moral values are maximised.
RTP e.g. Joseph Selling	The issue of moral obligation towards refugees is not really an issue at all as it appears to be incumbent upon all Christians to welcome asylum seekers and refugees. Proportionalists would see this as promoting the basic goods in accordance with the Christian Gospel and serving as role models to others.	It is a Christian responsibility to be charitable and accepting and helping those who wish to make a better life for themselves and others is a good act. The points system is unfair as it stands because it does discriminate. A fairer system in accordance with Christian teachings would perhaps prefer criteria that looks at what we can offer rather than what the economic immigrant can bring to us.

Key quotes

Other than a tiny proportion of sociopaths, our species is naturally empathetic. It is only when we strip the humanity from people – when we stop imagining them as being quite human like us – that our empathetic nature is eroded. (Jones)

Refugees are human. This simple fact seems to have been forgotten. (Jones)

quickfire

2.39 According to VMP what values need to be balanced and maximised?

Key quotes

Why should abortion and euthanasia be treated differently than warfare and capital punishment? Although all these issues concern defence of human life, the difference is that abortion and euthanasia are intrinsically evil: They are always and in themselves unjust. By contrast, warfare and capital punishment are not intrinsically evil. (Kaczor)

While life is certainly a basic good and killing a basic evil, they assuredly are not to be classified along with moral good and moral evil. (McCormick)

[Capital punishment] serves as an intermittent and ominous response by a society that tolerates the careless and extensive distribution of guns and the deterioration of basic living conditions for the poor, while it declines to invest in improving educational and correctional institutions … It is simply not credible for such a society to present its reliance on capital punishment as a sign of its deep and passionate commitment to justice. (Langan)

Study tip

To point out the Proportionalism lends itself more to conflict situations than to general ethical theory or ethical issues in general is a good way to start an answer on application of the theory. It does not mean we cannot discuss the theory or its application, but it does demonstrate a good understanding of what Proportionalism is all about.

Immigration in the UK has a points system.

Applying the proportionalist norm to capital punishment

In considering the application of theories to immigration there are some key questions to focus on in order to see how the Finnis' Natural Law and Proportionalism can be applied to each:

- Does Proportionalism support or reject capital punishment?
- Are there any circumstances in which capital punishment may be deemed as licit by Proportionalism?

Applying Proportionalism to the issue of capital punishment is very different from applying the theory to immigration. Capital punishment is a direct defiance and rejection of a primary precept or basic good (the right to participate in life); however, it is not a conflict situation because alternative solutions do not damage a primary precept or basic good.

In approaching this we have to remember the following:

- Proportionalism is not a separate ethical theory from Natural Law but **a norm** that operates within Natural Law.
- Proportionalists, known as 'revisionists' within the Roman Catholic theological circles, are practising Roman Catholics and academic theologians.
- For the main part, proportionalists take their starting point from the magisterium.
- The notion of proportionate reason occurs only when it is impossible to avoid making a decision that contravenes a primary precept, that is, a conflict situation.

Does Proportionalism support or reject capital punishment?

(1) The classical proportionalist position – Conflict Situation Proportionalism (CSP)

The issue of capital punishment is not relevant in terms of the PDE and conflict situation. Aquinas' teaching applies different reasoning. The application of capital punishment has been recently condemned in today's world by the Pope. Both Richard McCormick and Bernard Hoose have outlined reasons against capital punishment. Hoose analyses utilitarian arguments in his book *Christian Ethics* (editor) in which he contributes an article on the punishment of criminals and points out the frailty of evidence often presented to justify certain types of punishment. For example, the death penalty is often presented as a deterrent; however, Hoose points out that the facts are different. For example, in Canada an abolition of the death penalty meant that murders actually decreased in numbers. Unlike Aquinas, Hoose argues that punishment is a non-moral (pre-moral) evil because it inflicts suffering on other human beings and refers to punishments that use violence as appealing to the lesser evil argument rather than the 'good' of punishment Aquinas ascribes to it. He supports Langan's view that societies that justify physical punishments often 'tolerate the careless and extensive distribution of guns and the deterioration of basic living conditions for the poor'. Ironically this also at the expense of failing to invest in 'educational and correctional institutions'. Hoose agrees that in such situations it is not credible to justify capital punishment on the grounds it meets the requirements of justice.

In his book *Doing Evil to Achieve Good*, McCormick responds to Baruch Brody on capital punishment and clarifies his position. The key for McCormick is that unless one can clearly establish whether or not the criminal by way of his or her actions gives up the fully-fledged right to life, then one cannot use this as a basis for any argument to justify capital punishment. To simply say they have, through intentional killing of the innocent, been stripped of their right to life is just another way of saying 'we may take their life' – there is no essential reasoned argument there. In contrast, Aquinas' argument was based in different principles in terms of 'duty' to uphold the common good. McCormick, like Finnis, was suspicious of the logic that argues a specific act can take away the right to life as suggested by Aquinas' diseased body part analogy. However, McCormick did argue that the taking of a life was necessarily a moral evil: 'While life is certainly a basic good and killing a basic evil, they assuredly are not to be classified along with moral good and moral evil.'

In this way the traditional teaching of the Roman Catholic Church regarding capital punishment as a last resort may have been justified.

(2) Value Maximisation Proportionalism (VMP)

Garth Hallett writes in *Christian Moral Reasoning*: 'When there has been a question of capital punishment or self-defence or legitimate warfare, traditional moralists have fallen strangely silent about the Creator's rights. They have gone ahead and balanced values, as best they might, on the reasonable assumption that he would too.'

Value Maximisation proportinalists follow the general principle of 'no' but dependent on specific cases and circumstances this could vary. For instance, if there is absolutely no way of safely detaining a threatening and dangerous murderer. However, this may well be an extreme that, in practice, is unrealistic given the modern penal systems available.

Study tip

When answering application questions for AO1 concerning Proportionalism, a good structure would be as follows:

(1) Define Proportionalism and clarify that Proportionalism is not really a full-blown ethical theory but an ethical norm.

(2) Illustrate that there are different understandings of how Proportionalism is to be applied (CSP, VMP, RTP).

(3) Examine, outline or explain each one with reference to a particular issue or issues.

Obviously you will not be assessed on this structure but on the quality of knowledge and understanding that your answer displays in selecting, presenting and exemplifying information.

Key quote

The PDE was never clearly defined or made official, with the result that different authors had different interpretations about how to use it. (Selling)

Study tip

Remember that application is NOT AO2 but AO1. When evaluating Proportionalism you will be assessed on your skills of critical analysis and evaluation; that is, how you USE the information you select in your discussion/argument. However, a similar structure as that to AO1 may help create a suitable framework:

(1) Identify the debate about what Proportionalism 'is'.

(2) Identifying different arguments as to how Proportionalism is applicable.

(3) Remember to comment on / weigh up the different lines of reasoning and evidence that you present in order to reach an appropriate conclusion.

(3) Revisionist Theology Proportionalism [RTP]

As we have seen, the position of the magisterium has changed significantly in recent years towards a total and outright rejection of capital punishment. Oddly enough, proportionate reasoning (Hoose p102) is seen by Selling as 'not applied to cases of capital punishment' and supported by Hoose as an example of proportionate reasoning that would be applied to something that is 'beyond its range'. Proportionate reason is never justified when the situation is simply difficult, awkward or impractical. To argue for breaking a precept on account of awkwardness or human deficiency would be a classic case of reasoning wrongly and seeking an apparent good. This is crucial because whilst intention may undoubtedly be good, the reasoning also needs to be correct.

In Bernard Hoose's *Christian Ethics* Selling contributes a paper that makes the argument that to quote biblical norms in justification for 'ethical' actions can be misleading. He instead, as he does in *Reframing Catholic Theological Ethics* points to the example of Jesus:

'Jesus exercised authority, recognised even by his opponents and sceptics, not by formulating propositions or issuing statements. More often than not, his verbal communication was in the form of parables and exhortations that puzzled and challenged rather than explained. His most profound impact was made by what he did and how he lived.'

In the same book, in an article on 'The human person', Selling sees ethics as having a grounding in the subjective reference of the individual's freedom and intention as 'indispensable elements of moral decisions' and argues that 'the human person, adequately considered, stands in relation to everything, to the whole of reality'.

Are there any circumstances in which capital punishment may be deemed as licit by Proportionalism? (Those who claim Aquinas was right but not relevant today)

Aquinas' use of Natural Law traditionally balanced the protection of society with a duty to preserve life. The issue appears to be not whether or not we should take the life of a criminal, as this is already illicit; however, is there ever a scenario whereby to protect society and, as a last resort, through proportionate reasoning allow the execution of a criminal.

(1) The classical proportionalist position – Conflict Situation Proportionalism (CSP)

First of all, all CSP would agree that this could never be a conflict situation since self-defence of an individual is spontaneous and entirely different from the premeditated act of protecting society through execution of a criminal.

Richard McCormick, in indicating the principles behind Aquinas' thinking, simultaneously acknowledged that this type of reasoning, whether proportionate or not, had been used by Aquinas. However, this does not mean he supported the argument but simply, like Finnis, questioned its objectivity. Indeed, to argue that it is proportionate reason to execute a criminal based upon the fact that society is still endangered by their continued imprisonment, for example a murderer who reoffends or a killer that kills another human being in prison, is simply confused reasoning and certainly not proportionate reasoning. The examples here are related to the inadequacy of a system of protection (social reasons) wherein it fails and *not* in a position whereby it is **impossible** to avoid breaking a primary precept. In such instances the correct reasoning, according to Natural Law would be to persevere and improve a system of protection that has failed. It is also against the reasoning used by

Aquinas since his focus was on the 'good' of punishment and not the consequential or situationist circumstances in any given case. McCormick re-iterates the fact that it can never be morally right to do an injustice; since capital punishment attacks a basic good and sees it as using social circumstances to justify capital punishment. McCormick also disagreed with the idea Aquinas used that some circumstances 'become the principal condition of the object of an act' because he saw it as dangerous reasoning that has no objective criteria as to when this could be extended and therefore be open up to all kinds of unsound arguments.

(2) Value-Maximisation Proportionalism (VMP)

Would apply VM and would follow the general principle of 'no' but dependent on specific cases and circumstances this could vary **in theory**. However, given the intensity of value associated with that which is violated (human life) it is difficult to see how the theory of VM could support a law supporting capital punishment. At the same time Hallett's VM may be presented as a case that rejects exceptionless norms but simultaneously acknowledges the probability that CP is practically redundant!

(3) Revisionist Theology Proportionalism [RTP]

Given such a focus of Selling's theology, it is very difficult to see how RTP could ever justify capital punishment and would be in agreement with the magisterium. Indeed, in his book *Reframing Catholic Theological Ethics*, Selling points out that the 'virtual exclusion' of capital punishment as an option by the magisterium is a sign of progress in Catholic social teaching.

It would appear, then, that unless circumstances dictate an impossible situation in which breaking the first precept is unavoidable, both the magisterium and revisionist theologians who subscribe to a proportionalist view, are indeed united in their unanimous rejection of capital punishment in today's world. Indeed, it may be ironic that it is from within mainstream, traditional Roman Catholicism that any strong voice in support of the death penalty is apparent, and not from the revisionists.

quickfire

2.40 According to Selling, what is the focus of Christian ethics?

Protection of society is not a proportionate reason for capital punishment.

Study tip

Don't get lost in examples. You will want to choose a specific example or two to serve as the backdrop to your discussion. However, do not spend much time describing the example or proving how much you know about this area in current affairs, news, media or history.

Study tip

Your response needs to be devoted to showing how this ethical theory could be applied to this issue – so most of your time will be spent considering ways in which the theory, or proponents of that theory, might approach this area. There may well be different conclusions possible from the same theory.

Key skills Theme 2

The second Theme has tasks that
concentrate on a particular aspect of
AO1 in terms of using quotations from
sources of authority and in the use of
references.

Key skills

Knowledge involves:

*Selection of a range of (thorough)
accurate and relevant information
that is directly related to the specific
demands of the question.*

This means:

- Selecting relevant material for the
question set

- Being focused in explaining and
examining the material selected.

Understanding involves:

*Explanation that is extensive,
demonstrating depth and/or breadth
with excellent use of evidence and
examples including (where appropriate)
thorough and accurate supporting use
of sacred texts, sources of wisdom and
specialist language.*

This means:

- Effective use of examples and
supporting evidence to establish the
quality of your understanding

- Ownership of your explanation
that expresses personal knowledge
and understanding and NOT just
reproducing a chunk of text from a
book that you have rehearsed and
memorised.

AO1 Developing skills

It is now important to consider the information that has been covered in this
section; however, the information in its raw form is too extensive and so has
to be processed in order to meet the requirements of the examination. This
can be achieved by practising more advanced skills associated with AO1. For
assessment objective 1 (AO1), which involves demonstrating 'knowledge' and
'understanding' skills, we are going to focus on different ways in which the
skills can be demonstrated effectively, and also, refer to how the performance
of these skills is measured (see generic band descriptors for A2 [WJEC] AO1 or
A Level [Eduqas] AO1).

▶ **Your final task for this Theme is:** Below is a summary of **Finnis' Natural
Law and the issue of immigration**. You want to use this in an essay but
as it stands it is undeveloped and has no quotations or references in it at all.
This time you have to find your own quotations (about 3) and use your own
references (about 3) to develop the answer. Sometimes a quotation can follow
from a reference but they can also be used individually as separate points.

It is also clear that, in principle, immigration is a practice that fully participates
in the goods of Finnis' Natural Law and through practical reasoning allows
full participation in all goods so as to enable a flourishing society. First and
foremost the practice of immigration engages both parties with participation in
the good of **friendship**. This is using the principle of practical reasonableness
that there is **no arbitrary preference amongst persons**. It is clear that
the magisterium support immigration in principle. As Finnis himself alludes
to, this is similar to the Christian ideal of the Golden Rule of treating others
as one would like to be treated. It is, thereby, using the principle of practical
reasonableness in following one's **conscience**. From this extended arm of
friendship brings a respect for the fulness of **life**, another basic good which
sees collaboration in ensuring preservation as a bedrock of a flourishing society.
Immigrant workers can contribute and support self-preservation of both the
individual and society.

The result will be a fairly lengthy answer and so you could then check it against the
band descriptors for A2 (WJEC) or A Level (Eduqas) and in particular have a look at
the demands described in the higher band descriptors towards which you should
be aspiring. Ask yourself:

- Does my work demonstrate thorough, accurate and relevant knowledge and
understanding of religion and belief?

- Is my work coherent (consistent or make logical sense), clear and well
organised?

- Will my work, when developed, be an extensive and relevant response which is
specific to the focus of the task?

- Does my work have extensive depth and/or suitable breadth and have excellent
use of evidence and examples?

Issues for analysis and evaluation

Whether Finnis provides a basis for moral decision making for believers

This section covers AO2 content and skills

Specification content
Whether Finnis provides a basis for moral decision making for believers.

It is well known that Finnis is a practising Roman Catholic and has been called upon many times to contribute work as a theologian by the Vatican. It is also clear, from his basic good of religion, that his version of Natural Law, although intended to be impartial and universal in its application at the level of law, is also a sound and competent exposition of Natural Law that demonstrates clearly the credibility of religion as an underlying framework. Therefore, it would appear that Finnis' system is a basis for moral decision making for believers. In this sense it could be argued that it is very practical because it covers not just religious norms, but religious norms in the context of a legal framework.

It could be asked what exactly is meant by the phrase, 'a basis for moral decision making' – does this mean it is a general platform for morality? Or, alternatively, are we asking for something that defines moral decision making with more precision and clarity, assisting us with concrete examples, for instance, in relation to the issues raised by the Specification?

First of all, then, as a foundation for ethics it would seem to be a basis for moral decision making for believers since it outlines clearly what basic 'goods' are to be participated in and promoted. Finnis himself points out that the ideal of friendship, respect for life and the rejection of arbitrary preferences amongst persons is similar to the Christian principle of the Golden Rule: 'The classical non-philosophical expression of the requirement is, of course, the so-called Golden Rule.' The basic good of religion also demands answers to key question of an ultimate nature and the benefit of this is that it gives an overall purpose to life: 'But is it reasonable to deny that it is, at any rate, peculiarly important to have thought reasonably and (where possible) correctly about these questions of the origins of cosmic order and of human freedom and reason—whatever the answer to those questions turns out to be, and even if the answers have to be agnostic or negative?'

Another consideration could be that Finnis' Natural Law is attractive for believers only in so far as Finnis' application of practicable reasonableness in relation to the goods is accepted; however, it has been pointed out by Brigita White that Finnis has a definite idea of what ethical principles drive this application that is assumed are universal. She writes, 'Although, Finnis indeed posits a place for morality in the law, the type of morality Finnis has in mind is questionable.' Therefore, the judgement as to whether or not Finnis provides a basis for moral decision making for religious believers rests upon whether or not Finnis' implied ethical principles are accepted by all religious believers; if this is so, then it works. However, as White indicates, his understanding of the application of the principles of practical reasonableness is in line with traditional Roman Catholic morality (if there is indeed such a thing) and any other interpretation Finnis would question. For example, if the ethical principles are affected or misunderstood then so is Natural Law, according to Finnis. Finnis' approach amounts to 'this is how it is and how it works and any other way is defective'. Obviously, this is why scholars such as White are suspicious.

Nonetheless, Finnis distinguishes clearly between the moral elements of law and the moral elements of personal choice: ethical issues that are located within the parameters of law are dealt with by the law; the ethical issues that do not, are debated, resolved and decided upon by individual citizens in a more private realm and without the need for common public approval. It could be argued, therefore, that his presentation is perfectly reasonable. For instance, there has been much made of an academic paper entitled *Law, Morality and Sexual Orientation* Finnis states: 'The commitment of a man and a woman to each other in the sexual

AO2 Activity

As you read through this section try to do the following:

1. Pick out the different lines of argument that are presented in the text and identify any evidence given in support.

2. For each line of argument try to evaluate whether or not you think this is strong or weak.

3. Think of any questions you may wish to raise in response to the arguments.

This Activity will help you to start thinking critically about what you read and help you to evaluate the effectiveness of different arguments and from this develop your own observations, opinions and points of view that will help with any conclusions that you make in your answers to the AO2 questions that arise.

Key questions

What exactly is meant by the phrase, 'a basis for moral decision making'?

Does it matter than Finnis' system is presented with an underlying Roman Catholic view of morality?

Is it a practical and effective way of applying ethics to everyday situations?

Key quotes

A self-evident principle is only self-evident to the subject, in this case Finnis, and then only to the extent that it has become self-evident and not challenged by that subject's experience. It is quite conceivable that different people would come up with entirely different formulations of goods to be attained. Self-evidence provides no real explanation of how each agent generates their own list of basic values corresponding to Finnis's seven. (White)

So, though it certainly has other meanings, 'law' can be used to refer to any criteria of right judgment in matters of practice (conduct, action), any standards for assessing options for human conduct as good or bad, right or wrong, desirable or undesirable, decent or unworthy. (Finnis)

AO2 Activity

List some conclusions that could be drawn from the AO2 reasoning from the above text; try to aim for at least three different possible conclusions. Consider each of the conclusions and collect brief evidence to support each conclusion from the AO1 and AO2 material for this topic. Select the conclusion that you think is most convincing and explain why it is so. Try to contrast this with the weakest conclusion in the list, justifying your argument with clear reasoning and evidence.

union of marriage is intrinsically good and reasonable and is incompatible with sexual relations outside marriage.' Therefore, Finnis rejects homosexual acts as intrinsically unreasonable and non-marital', a view that does not sit well with many people today. However, Finnis is adamant that there should be no discrimination, nor should laws encroach upon personal freedom of consenting adults, he does argue that homosexual activity is always a moral evil. In addition, the word 'evil' is often brandished about by Roman Catholic theologians in a variety of contexts; for Finnis, here it refers to not being in line with Natural Law in terms of not expressing a 'fundamental human good' – but to be fair he says the same of any form of non-unitive, non-marital sexual activity! Finnis, then, presents the traditional notion of marital union between man and woman as the ideal and only notion of family.

Despite this, it could be suggested that perfectly reasoned personal views do not always mean that they are right, and many would argue that his views are out of date and out of touch with society and are to be rejected as an interpretation. However, this does not mean that his theory is to be rejected because it could also be argued that more liberal theological views that reflect up-to-date views of acceptable moral behaviour can also be applied with his system without conflict.

In a different line of argument, Finnis Natural Law is useful as a guide to law and to see how it relates to morality and religion; however, surely for the religious believer a direct access to religious texts would be more appropriate as a means of moral decision making? Church teachings and the inspirational writings of other believers are also considered effective sources for religious believers in guiding their moral behaviour. In this sense, we have to put the statement in context and argue that Finnis' Natural Law is not the only basis or is not the religious basis, but more of a practical elaboration in a social context.

It could be argued that whilst it is useful for ethical debate, it does require support from religious sources for religious believers. For instance, the issues of capital punishment and immigration can be responded to simply from Finnis' Natural Law, but religious believers would need more assurance from appeal to authority such as sacred texts. In addition, it could also be argued that whilst it may appear to be clear on capital punishment, the argument presented does reject Aquinas' reasoning and traditional Natural Law interpretations. This may be uncomfortable for some and Finnis' justification for his own view does need appeal beyond his own system to answer such reservations as, for example, in the debate between himself and Ed Feser. It could also be argued that whilst a response to the issue of capital punishment is clear, a response to the complicated issues surrounding immigration are less so. However, one need ask whether or not a response can ever be clear on this issue.

In conclusion, it seems to be that it all depends on what we are looking for in response to the statement in terms of 'a basis for moral decision making for believers'. Yes, Finnis' Natural Law appears coherent; yes, it gives essential guidance; yes, it distinguishes between personal Christian morality and the law and morality. In addition, its principles can be applied universally accounting for differences in world communities. The only question that seems to remain is 'does a religious believer require something more directly religious and more specific?'

Study tip

It is vital for AO2 that you actually discuss arguments and not just explain what someone may have stated. Try to ask yourself, 'was this a fair point to make?', 'is the evidence sound enough?', 'is there anything to challenge this argument?', 'is this a strong or weak argument?' Such critical analysis will help you develop your evaluation skills.

The effectiveness of Proportionalism in dealing with ethical issues

Specification content
The effectiveness of Proportionalism in dealing with ethical issues.

There was an interesting case of stealing brought before an Italian court a couple of years ago. A homeless man, a vagrant, had stolen bread and sausage from a local store. He was convicted of stealing and sentenced to imprisonment. However, the High Court over-ruled the decision based upon the principles that it was a duty for society to ensure the basic means for survival (e.g. food) and that the vagrant's actions were of a desperate man whose life was in danger. In this sense, the crime of stealing was superseded by the neglect of the common good. Thomas Aquinas also discussed the evils of stealing. However, he also came to the same conclusion with a similar example that 'this was not stealing proper'. Nonetheless, it must be noted that whilst this is an ethical dilemma, for Aquinas it was a matter of the extent of 'sinfulness'. So, although stealing is sinful, there are circumstances that proportion the nature of the act to the extent of sin afforded. Therefore, it could be argued that whilst this is not proportionate reasoning (in its strictest interpretation, i.e. it does not qualify for the PDE or McCormick's conflict situation) some would argue that it is a typical case where the circumstances of the act become the object of the act, or, alternatively a version of the greater good argument, or, a simple example of practical reasoning in ethics. Whatever the case may be, it does indicate the effectiveness of seeing ethical norms as not being exceptionless. If this is accepted then the debates about Proportionalism have served to impact a far-reaching influence on ethics and the law in general and have therefore been proven to be effective in dealing with ethical issues. So, the first line of argument understands Proportionalism in its widest sense, and possibly in line with Selling's development of a broader appreciation of Roman Catholic ethical thinking.

This then adds force to the statement and demonstrates that a flexibility in dealing with religious ethical precepts that is reflective of Christian virtue, has in fact been the most important contribution, if not of Proportionalism itself, but of the debates about ethics that occurred within revisionist Roman Catholic theological ethics.

However, taking a different line of reasoning and from a classical perspective, and from an understanding of Richard McCormick (who sees Proportionalism as 'a way of examining received moral norms according to a conflict model of reality'), Proportionalism can be argued to be very effective in dealing with certain moral issues, for example, abortion. Indeed, this has been well-illustrated by the real-life cases of ectopic pregnancies.

Alternatively, Garth Hallett's version of Proportionalism, that is 'Value maximisation' would argue, like Knauer, that proportionate reasoning is the basis of all moral decision making through balancing values, both pre-moral and moral, and maximising the greater good.

Therefore, all three understandings of Proportionalism do indeed serve to support the statement that Proportionalism is very effective in dealing with ethical issues. One of its major strengths is its willingness to engage in the process of evaluating whether an action brings more or less ontic evil and moral evil into the world to help religious believers to understand both the context and the implications of our actions. Although a deontological approach has often been favoured, Proportionalism could be argued to be more effective because a one-size-fits-all approach is neither a compassionate Christian approach nor a practically useful one in real-life situations. In addition, Garth Hallett's critique of Emotivism means that his system of Proportionalism, 'Value maximisation', prevents any accusations of a purely emotive, superficial or insubstantial response to ethical issues.

AO2 Activity

As you read through this section try to do the following:

1. Pick out the different lines of argument that are presented in the text and identify any evidence given in support.

2. For each line of argument try to evaluate whether or not you think this is strong or weak.

3. Think of any questions you may wish to raise in response to the arguments.

This Activity will help you to start thinking critically about what you read and help you to evaluate the effectiveness of different arguments and from this develop your own observations, opinions and points of view that will help with any conclusions that you make in your answers to the AO2 questions that arise.

Key questions

Is there a single methodology for Proportionalism?

Is there a preferred methodology for Proportionalism?

Is Proportionalism effective for all moral issues?

Should Proportionalism be left to the PDE alone?

Key quotes

The criteria, however, for weighing values and disvalues remain sketchy, often appear to be ad hoc to particular issues, and have not been detailed in any systematic explanation. (Porter)

A single valid criterion may define right and wrong, but the clues that correlate with the criterion, and the corresponding methods… may vary widely. Thus, Value maximisation leaves room for head and heart, custom and explicit thought, reasoning and imagination, calculation and intuition, Scripture and tradition, authority and private judgement, rule-following and case-by-case assessment, discernment of spirits and value-tables, imitation of Christ and personal directives from God. (Hallett)

The major objection that would question the effectiveness of Proportionalism in dealing with ethical issues is that there is no universal agreement on precisely **what** proportionate reasoning actually entails, **when** it should be applied and **how**; that is by which methodology it should be applied. Indeed, for any ethical theory – if Proportionalism is a theory – a sense of uniformity, coherence and agreement in understanding how it works are essential. Hence, in light of the many problems Proportionalism faces, theologians such as Finnis and Grisez together with traditionalists and the magisterium have rejected it outright. Their views are of 'absolutes' and there is a case for the argument that as a practical guideline for moral living societies and individuals demand clear and precise rules. The great danger of not providing such, it could be argued, is that it would just plunge into a chaotic subjectivity that would be of no use at all.

In conclusion, it could be argued that an alternative approach such as that of Selling, that shifts proportionate reasoning to the 'appendix' of an ethical system whilst maintaining the spirit of balancing virtues with rules, and by following the attitude demonstrated in the ministry of Jesus, is possibly the best way of moving forward for theological ethics.

Key quote

The name 'Proportionalism' was coined by those who opposed this approach; the 'ism' term conveys the deceptive impression of an ideologically unified movement. In fact, it is not a method but a way of examining received moral norms according to a conflict model of reality. (McCormick)

Study tip

It is vital for AO2 that you actually discuss arguments and not just explain what someone may have stated. Try to ask yourself, 'was this a fair point to make?', 'is the evidence sound enough?', 'is there anything to challenge this argument?', 'is this a strong or weak argument?' Such critical analysis will help you develop your evaluation skills.

AO2 Activity

List some conclusions that could be drawn from the AO2 reasoning from the above text; try to aim for at least three different possible conclusions. Consider each of the conclusions and collect brief evidence to support each conclusion from the AO1 and AO2 material for this topic. Select the conclusion that you think is most convincing and explain why it is so. Try to contrast this with the weakest conclusion in the list, justifying your argument with clear reasoning and evidence.

AO2 Developing skills

It is now important to consider the information that has been covered in this section; however, the information in its raw form is too extensive and so has to be processed in order to meet the requirements of the examination. This can be achieved by practising more advanced skills associated with AO2. For assessment objective 2 (AO2), which involves 'critical analysis' and 'evaluation' skills, we are going to focus on different ways in which the skills can be demonstrated effectively, and also, refer to how the performance of these skills is measured (see generic band descriptors for A2 [WJEC] AO2 or A Level [Eduqas] AO2).

▶ **Your final task for this Theme is:** Below is an evaluation of **the effectiveness of Proportionalism when dealing with ethical issues**. You want to use this in an essay but as it stands it is a weak argument because it has no quotations or references in it at all as support. This time you have to find your own quotations (about 3) and use your own references (about 3) to strengthen the evaluation. Remember, sometimes a quotation can follow from a reference but they can also be used individually as separate points.

> Proportionalism respects Natural Law which would be attractive to believers who desire a traditional approach. Proportionalism also gives some autonomy to the moral agent by allowing them to weigh up the value or disvalue of an act rather than being ruled mindlessly by laws. However, for classic proportionalists this was only in conflict situations and in accordance with Aquinas' 'principle of double effect'. However, you could argue that Garth Hallett's version of value maximisation would be attractive to a believer in the modern world. It also takes into account a range of influencing factors which might be attractive to believers because it appears to be more logical than simple obedience. Proportionalism is also effective because it recognises that no answer will ever be perfect (there is always ontic evil) but tries to create a solution where ontic evil is lessened.

The result will be a fairly lengthy answer and so you could then check it against the band descriptors for A2 (WJEC) or A Level (Eduqas) and in particular have a look at the demands described in the higher band descriptors towards which you should be aspiring. Ask yourself:

- Is my answer a confident critical analysis and perceptive evaluation of the issue?
- Is my answer a response that successfully identifies and thoroughly addresses the issues raised by the question set?
- Does my work show an excellent standard of coherence, clarity and organisation?
- Will my work, when developed, contain thorough, sustained and clear views that are supported by extensive, detailed reasoning and/or evidence?
- Are the views of scholars/schools of thought used extensively, appropriately and in context?
- Does my answer convey a confident and perceptive analysis of the nature of any possible connections with other elements of my course?
- When used, is specialist language and vocabulary both thorough and accurate?

Key skills Theme 2

The second Theme has tasks that concentrate on a particular aspect of AO2 in terms of using quotations from sources of authority and in the use of references in supporting arguments and evaluations.

Key skills

Analysis involves:

Identifying issues raised by the materials in the AO1, together with those identified in the AO2 section, and presents sustained and clear views, either of scholars or from a personal perspective ready for evaluation.

This means:

- That your answers are able to identify key areas of debate in relation to a particular issue
- That you can identify, and comment upon, the different lines of argument presented by others
- That your response comments on the overall effectiveness of each of these areas or arguments.

Evaluation involves:

Considering the various implications of the issues raised based upon the evidence gleaned from analysis and provides an extensive detailed argument with a clear conclusion.

This means:

- That your answer weighs up the consequences of accepting or rejecting the various and different lines of argument analysed
- That your answer arrives at a conclusion through a clear process of reasoning.

T4 Determinism and free will – Determinism

This section covers AO1 content and skills

Specification content

Religious concepts of predestination: St Augustine.

quickfire

4.1 What two traditions was Augustine instrumental in merging together?

Key quote

For Thyself Thou hast made us, And restless our hearts until in Thee they find their ease. (*Augustine, Confessions*)

quickfire

4.2 What is Augustine's probably best-known writing?

Key terms

Manicheans: those following a dualistic religious system who had a basic doctrine of a conflict between light and dark, matter being regarded as dark and evil

Platonists: those asserting, with Plato, that the phenomena of the world are an imperfect and transitory reflection of the eternal reality of the ideal forms

Predestination: for some it refers to the determining of individual human destiny by God. It does not necessarily deny free will. Others see predestination as a predetermination by God of all actions and events removing free will of any kind

A: Religious concepts of predestination

St Augustine

Aurelius Augustinus was born in 354CE and lived most of his life in Roman North Africa. Raised as a Christian by his mother, he rejected Christianity, regarding it as a religion unworthy of a philosopher. Intellectually, he could not see how the existence of evil could be reconciled with the good God proclaimed by the Church and the Scriptures. For a time, Augustine embraced the dualistic teaching of the Manichees and became a member of the sect of **Manicheans**. In 384CE he moved to Rome and Milan where he became professor of rhetoric. It was during this period that Augustine came across the writings of the **Platonists** which had been translated into Latin. These writings and the preaching of Ambrose eventually led to the conversion of Augustine to Christianity. He was baptised by Ambrose at Easter in 387CE.

From 396CE until his death in 430CE, Augustine was bishop of a busy seaport, Hippo, now named Annaba, in Algeria. He was instrumental in merging the Greek philosophical tradition with the Judeo-Christian religious and scriptural traditions. His writings were numerous and reflect his thinking on various theological controversies of the time. Over the course of his lifetime, Augustine rethought old positions in the light of new situations and demands. In a number of instances, he changed his mind and admitted in his various letters that he had been in error (e.g. he came to see that even faith depends on God's grace). His developing views often require a piecing together from a variety of his writings. It is therefore often quite difficult to package neatly his views; for instance, whether he believed in single or double **predestination**. However, what cannot be doubted is the influence he had on later philosophers such as Aquinas, Descartes and Wittgenstein. Probably his most well-known writing is *Confessions* (397–401CE) which is a spiritual autobiography containing an account of his conversion.

Influences on Augustine

To understand Augustine, it is helpful to be aware of the various influences on his thinking. The Manichean sect claimed there were two ultimate principles – one responsible for good and the soul, one the source of evil, including matter and the body. From his writings in *Confessions*, it seems that Augustine was dominated by sexual and other passions and the Manicheans offered an attractive explanation by arguing that he was not responsible for his sin but something else in him.

By the time he had moved to

St Augustine

Rome and Milan, he had begun to be dissatisfied with Manichaeism and it was then that he came across the writings of the Platonists. These provided him with intellectual satisfaction and convinced him that there was a spiritual reality, and that the existence of evil could be reconciled with the doctrine of creation. Augustine came to believe that evil was not a created thing. It was a privation or lack of good, and moral evil resulting from the absence of the right in the human will. Therefore, the existence of evil was compatible with belief in a good Creator.

When Augustine examined the Church and its scriptural tradition, he was persuaded to turn to Christianity. He saw authority represented by Christ, and reason represented by Plato. Certainly, Augustine's view of Christianity was influenced by Platonic ideas (such as the soul) but where he saw those ideas in opposition to Christianity then he rejected them. For instance, he rejected the Platonic ideas of pre-existence and transmigration. Thomas Aquinas observed that 'Augustine, who was steeped in the doctrines of the Platonists, whenever he found anything in their statements consistent with the Faith he accepted it, but amended what he found hostile'.

Augustine was ordained priest in 391CE and became a bishop a few years later. As time went by, he was confronted by various controversies within the Church. For example, there was a dispute amongst the churches in North Africa, as to whether the validity of the sacraments depended on the worthiness of the clergy administering it. This was known as the **Donatist** controversy. The Donatist group separated themselves from what they saw as the corrupt church.

However, the controversy that occupied most of Augustine's energies was the **Pelagian controversy** and it reshaped his views on human freedom and predestination. The Pelagian debate engaged him from about 411 until his death in 430.

Confessions
ST AUGUSTINE

A fresh translation by Benignus O'Rourke OSA

Foreword by Martin Laird

Cover of St Augustine's book **Confessions**

St Augustine's baptism

quickfire

4.3 Identify three main influences on Augustine's thinking.

Key terms

Heresy: a belief that is contrary to orthodox Christian theology/dogma

Omnipotent being: a being with unlimited power

Original Sin: the sin committed by Adam in the Garden of Eden. More particularly, it refers to the doctrine that sin is inherent to human nature as a result of the Original Sin by Adam

The Fall: the descent from perfection to sin recounted in Genesis 3

quickfire

4.4 Why did Augustine reject Pelagius' free will theory?

Specification content

Doctrine of Original Sin: role of concupiscence, humanity as 'a lump of sin' (massa peccati).

The Pelagian controversy

Pelagius (354–420CE) was a monk from Britain who taught in Rome from about 380CE. However, he was incensed by the lax moral attitude of the Roman Christians and blamed the teaching of grace, especially that taught by Augustine. In *Confessions*, Augustine wrote 'Give me the grace to do as you command, and command me to do what you will'. Pelagius saw that this teaching as putting the responsibility on to God – not ourselves. Therefore, he thought Christians used this as an excuse for any moral failings. This idea of God's grace as the sole necessity for obeying God's commands was rejected by Pelagius. He was not opposed to grace, only to the idea that grace was the only thing necessary for obeying God's commands. However, Augustine saw this rejection of the absolute nature of God's grace as a **heresy**. It seemed to diminish the power of God and make God something less than an **omnipotent being**. The claim that a person could freely decide to be morally good implied that the person would then be able to claim that salvation from God was on their own merit, so denying the grace of God. Furthermore, it made the sacrificial death of Jesus redundant. To Augustine this was an affront to God.

The debate soon focused on the nature of Adam's fall, the extent of corruption in our humanity, and the doctrine of baptism. In response to Pelagius' free will theology and on behalf of the Church, Augustine developed the Doctrine of **Original Sin** and included in this the theory of predestination. Pelagianism was repudiated by the Council of Carthage (418CE), mainly through the influence and arguments of Augustine.

Doctrine of Original Sin: role of concupiscence

In his book *City of God*, Augustine portrays an idyllic picture of the Garden of Eden before the Fall. 'In Paradise, then, man ... lived in the enjoyment of God, and was good by God's goodness ... no sadness of any kind was there.'

Genesis 3 recounts the story of **the Fall**. The story of Adam and Eve expresses the idea that human nature has fallen from its original pristine state. Augustine believed that Adam and Eve had an original righteousness and were entirely able to avoid sinning. Although they were mortal by natural constitution, they were immortal by a divine gift that would not have been withdrawn had they not sinned. Therefore, the present state of human nature is not what God intended it to be. The created order has been spoiled – but not irredeemably, since salvation is possible. Augustine argued that creation now exists at a lower level than that intended for it by God.

The question arises as to why Adam sinned? Augustine argued that Adam had already in his heart turned away from God and that is why the Devil successfully tempted him. He saw that pride was at the heart of Adam's sin – the desire to live by the rule of self.

This was at sharp variance to the views of Pelagius. Pelagius argued that sin only comes about through moral choice, it cannot be passed down from one's ancestors. Individual human beings have the capacity to save themselves since human beings are not tainted with sin from birth in their being. Each person is born as a new, free agent with the same powers of choice and responsibilities as Adam. Pelagius believed that the power of sin, too, was enormous, but did believe we could strive for holiness through effort and God's grace and forgiveness.

Adam and Eve committed the Original Sin.

In Augustine's replies to the Pelagian heresy, he developed the doctrine of Original Sin. He drew a distinction between Adam's sin that Adam willed, and the sin that new-borns contract without any will of their own (Original Sin). Adam's sin was so great that it brought a change not only in Adam's nature but the nature of the entire human race. Human beings were now born with weakened faculties and subject to death.

What then is this inherited sin? Augustine states that it is 'the guilt from our origin which was contracted by birth'. The guilt remains in us as a stain unless it is forgiven in baptism. In some way, Augustine thinks we actually participated in Adam's sin and so are judged and penalised for what Adam did. However, as a result of Adam's sin, our human nature is weakened. We have a corrupted orientation, away from God and towards lesser goods, which Augustine calls carnal concupiscence. The Catechism of the Catholic Church (405) states '... human nature has not been totally corrupted: it is wounded in the natural powers proper to it, subject to ignorance, suffering and the dominion of death, and inclined to sin – an inclination to evil that is called concupiscence'.

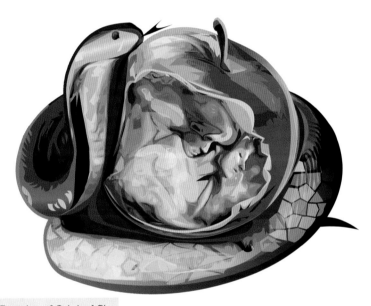

The Doctrine of Original Sin

The word 'concupiscence' can refer to any intense form of human desire. In Catholic theology, it refers to the inclination of human beings to commit sins. This inclination is the effect of Adam's sin that has been transmitted to us through birth. Although it comes from sin and induces to sin, yet it is not itself sin. It makes us vulnerable to sin but susceptibility to temptation is not sin. It just wants to pull us a certain way. It is a deficiency in a person's ability to choose good and resist earthly desires when they are in conflict with God's laws. Augustine refers to carnal concupiscence which is desire or disordering of the whole person, body and soul, for things forbidden – 'disobedience coming from ourselves and against ourselves'. It would be mistaken to think that Augustine thought of carnal concupiscence in terms only of sexual desire. However, he used sexual pleasure as an example of concupiscence since those desires are neither under direction of the conscious will nor often orientated toward higher goods. The Catholic Catechism (1264) states that 'since concupiscence is left for us to wrestle with, it cannot harm those who do not consent but wilfully resist it by the grace of Jesus Christ'.

Key quote

It was the position of Pelagius that Adam's sin affected Adam and only Adam. That is to say, as a result of Adam's transgression there was no change wrought in the constituent nature of the human race. (Sproul)

Key term

Concupiscence: strong desire for earthly pleasures. It stems from the disobedience of the first sin by Adam and, without itself being a sin, inclines human beings to commit sins

Key quotes

When the woman saw that the fruit of the tree was good for food and pleasing to the eye, and also desirable for gaining wisdom, she took some and ate it. (Genesis 3:6)

Augustine's doctrine means that all humans are born moving away from God. (Rowan Greer)

quickfire

4.5 According to Augustine, what two changes in human nature did Adam's sin bring about?

Two further issues arising from this doctrine of Original Sin

(i) How did human nature become tainted by the sin of Adam?

Augustine argued that each person inherits the effects of Adam's sin through the sexual act of procreation. Hence, Jesus remained sinless, since he was conceived without the sexual act (born of a virgin).

(ii) Why is Baptism important?

Original Sin carries condemnation to all human beings. It is baptism that removes Original Sin and is therefore necessary for salvation. It imparts the life of Christ's grace, makes them a new creature, members of the Body of Christ, adopted sons and daughters of God and turns a person back towards God, but it does not remove concupiscence (the inclination to sin). As the creed stated – baptism is for the forgiveness of sins.

Infant deaths were very common in Augustine's day. Augustine contended that whilst infants have no sins of their own, they inherit Original Sin (this stain of guilt) and therefore they needed baptism. In *Confessions* he quotes from Psalm 51:6 'Surely I was sinful at birth, sinful from the time my mother conceived me.' Augustine believed that this sin must refer to Original Sin, since it would not be possible for the infant at this age to be guilty of choosing to sin. The Catholic catechism (1283) states that 'With respect to children who have died without baptism, the liturgy of the Church invites us to trust in God's mercy and to pray for their salvation.' Augustine believed that unbaptised infants went to the underworld (later called limbo) as a consequence of Original Sin.

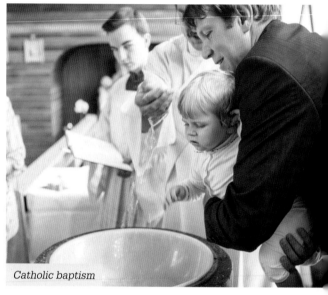

Catholic baptism

quickfire

4.6 According to Augustine, how did Jesus avoid inheriting Original Sin?

Key quotes

… sin entered the world through one man, and death through sin, and, in this way death came to all men, because all sinned.
(Romans 5:12)

For just as through the disobedience of the one man the many were made sinners, so also through the obedience of the one man the many will be made righteous.
(Romans 5:19)

For as in Adam all die, so in Christ all will be made alive.
(1 Corinthians 15:22)

Augustine's explanation of concupiscence

In *Marriage and Concupiscence*, Augustine explained concupiscence:

'Concupiscence, which is atoned for [expiatur] only by the Sacrament of regeneration [Baptism], does most certainly, by generation, pass on the bond of sin to the progeny, if they are not loosed from it by the same regeneration. For concupiscence itself is certainly no longer a sin in the regenerate, when they do not consent to illicit deeds and when their members are not applied by the ruling mind to the performance of such deeds....But because the guilt of concupiscence is prevalent in man who was born, that is called sin, in a certain manner of speaking, which was made by sin and which, if it conquers, produces sin. This guilt, however, through the remission of all sins, is not allowed to prevail in the man who is reborn, if he does not obey it when in some way it commands him to perform evil works....This concupiscence of the flesh is the daughter of sin, as it were, and, as often as it consents to shameful deeds, it is the mother of more sins. Whatever offspring is born of this concupiscence of the flesh is BOUND BY ORIGINAL SIN [originali est obligata peccato], unless it be REBORN in Him whom the Virgin conceived without that concupiscence; for which reason, when He designed to be born in the flesh, He ALONE WAS BORN WITHOUT SIN...'

quickfire

4.7 According to Augustine, why is infant baptism important?

Doctrine of Original Sin: humanity as 'a lump of sin' (massa peccati)

As a result of the Fall, all humanity is born 'massa peccati'. Massa peccati is a Latin term meaning a 'lump of sin' or 'mass of sin'. The entire human race was lumped together with Adam when he sinned; as a result, the whole of mankind is a 'condemned lump'. Therefore, for Augustine, humanity's ability to choose freely is infected by sin and incapable of raising itself from spiritual death.

Doctrine of Original Sin: liberium abitrium and libertas

According to Augustine, fallen humanity still has free will (*liberium arbitrium*) in that they can make choices, but they have lost their moral liberty (*libertas*).

Sproul (*The Pelagian Controversy* 2005) explains Augustine's view: 'The state of Original Sin leaves us in the condition of being unable to refrain from sinning. We still are able to choose what we desire, but our desires are dominated by our evil impulses. Therefore, the freedom that remains in the will always leads to sin.'

It is freedom without liberty, a moral bondage. Although still able to choose what we desire, our desires are affected by sin. Baptism was seen to address Original Sin, but it left untouched concupiscence, the inclination toward sin that Original Sin had introduced. True liberty can only come from the work of God on the soul. Therefore, we are totally dependent upon grace to liberate the soul from the bondage of sin. Only after the initial divine work of liberation do we cooperate with this grace.

Key quote

[Human beings are] so hopelessly corrupted that we are absolutely incapable of doing anything good by our own forces; free choice, if it means a choice between good and evil, has been utterly wasted by sin; our will, insofar as it is ours, and not God's, can merely do evil and desire evil. (Augustine)

God's grace and atonement for the elect/saints

St Augustine at prayer

As we have seen, Augustine saw the will as enslaved to sin. In *Confessions* he wrote 'Without exception we all long for happiness ... All agree that we want to be happy, just as, if they were asked, they would all agree that they desired joy.' But Augustine was aware that true happiness is found only in God, and our wills, though free, are not directed to desiring the things of God. Because of this, the role of God's grace in his doctrine is crucial.

Key quote

All humans were seminally present in the loins of Adam. (Augustine)

Specification content

Doctrine of Original Sin: an essentially 'free' human nature (liberium abitrium), the loss of human liberty (libertas) to our sinful nature.

quickfire

4.8 Why do people lose their free will?

Specification content

Doctrine of Original Sin: God's grace and atonement for the elect/saints.

Key terms

God's grace: the love and mercy given to humanity by God because God desires humanity to have it, not because of anything humanity has done to deserve it

Liberium arbitrium: Latin phrase meaning a person has the power of making choices that are free from predestination

Libertas: Latin phrase meaning liberty

Massa peccati: Latin term meaning lump or mass of sin

Christ's crucifixion

Grace involves God changing our heart's desires so that we can freely obey him and find happiness. This makes sense of Augustine's prayer after his conversion – 'Give me the grace to do as you command, and command me to do what you will'. It was that very prayer that had so enraged Pelagius as he saw it causing a lax moral attitude amongst the Christians. Augustine argues that it is by the law we discover what ought to be done, and by grace we are enabled to do what the law commands.

Augustine also argued that God's grace would keep people secure in God until the final day. This teaching is known as the Perseverance of the Saints.

Chosen before the creation of the world

In Ephesians 1:4 Paul wrote to the Christians at Ephesus 'For he chose us in him before the creation of the world to be holy and blameless in his sight.' Pelagius saw no problem with this verse and interpreted it as meaning that God elected them before the creation of the world, because God, in his foreknowledge, knew that they would live holy lives. Augustine regarded such an interpretation as heresy as it appealed to a person's merit (choosing to live a holy life) to gain salvation rather than because of God's grace. Original Sin and concupiscence, according to Augustine, made living a holy life impossible without baptism and God's grace. For Augustine, God predestined them before the creation of the world in order that they might become holy (through God's grace) – not that they could live holy lives in their own strength. It is about God's will not our will.

Augustine also draws attention to John 15:16 'You did not choose me, but I chose you…'. He argues that this makes clear that we are not chosen because we believe but that we may believe.

Key quote

Our wills are ours and it is our will that affects all that we do by willing and which could not have happened if we had not willed … the fact that God foreknew that a man would sin does not make a man sin; on the contrary, it cannot be doubted that it is the man himself who sins … a man does not sin unless he wills to sin …' **(Augustine)**

Predestination

Those chosen for salvation are also called '**the elect**' and those receiving God's wrath are called by Augustine '**the reprobates**'. Two of Augustine's key Bible passages about predestination are Romans 8:29–30 'And those he predestined, he also called: those he called, he also justified; those he justified, he also glorified …' and Ephesians 1:5, 11 '…he predestined us to be adopted as his sons …, In him we were also chosen, having been predestined according to the plan of him who works out everything …'

John Lennox (*Determined to Believe*, 2017) comments that 'the phrase "the doctrine of predestination" is usually taken as shorthand for the view that some are predestined to salvation'. However, he also argues that the use of the term in the Bible is wider than that as it also applied to the death of Christ and his resurrection.

Single or double predestination?

There is some disagreement as to whether Augustine believed in single predestination (predestined to salvation) or double predestination (predestined also to condemnation). It is not clear whether Augustine taught that God creates some with the express intention of damming them and others with the opposite intention of saving them, or whether, as Hick (*Evil and the God of Love*) concludes, 'that people fall freely and culpably and that out of the fallen race God saves some, leaving others to perish; although God knows from the beginning which he intends to save and which to abandon'.

McGrath (*Christian Theology: An Introduction*, 1994) takes a similar view arguing, 'that the remainder were not, according to Augustine, actively condemned to damnation; they were merely not elected to salvation'. He goes on to say that Augustine treated predestination as something that was active and positive, by which McGrath means that predestination was a deliberate decision to redeem on God's part rather than a deliberate decision to condemn.

However, it has to be acknowledged that there are texts by Augustine which seem to state clearly of double predestination. For example, 'As the Supreme Good, he made good use of evil deeds, for the damnation of those whom he had justly predestined to punishment and for the salvation of those whom he had mercifully predestined to grace.' As John Lennox states 'It is hard to see how one can maintain so-called single predestination without logically affirming double predestination'.

Key quotes

'… God leads some in mercy and repentance and others in just judgement does not lead'. (Augustine)

It is unthinkable that He [Jesus] should deliberately have shed his blood for hell-dwellers-to-be. (Augustine)

For not only has God given us our ability and helps it, but He even works [brings about] willing and acting in us; not that we do not will or that we do not act, but that without His help we neither will anything good nor do it. (Augustine)

The Last Judgement by Michaelangelo (1536–1541)

Why are not all predestined to salvation?

Augustine was only too aware of the problematic nature of his doctrine but saw the resolution in divine knowledge. He thought that the fallen human intellect was incapable of understanding the workings of divine salvation. Grace itself only leads to partial restoration of the intellect. At one point Augustine concludes:

'… I confess that I can find no answer to make … even as His anger is righteous and as His mercy is great, so His judgments are unsearchable.'

The problem is that Augustine seems to offer two contradictory explanations as to why some people are not saved to eternal life. Firstly, because it shows God's mercy in that he saves some although all should be judged (yet this seems to contradict

quickpire

4.9 Give three Biblical references that support predestination.

Specification content

Religious concepts of predestination: John Calvin.

Key quote

Far from being a central premise of Calvin's thought, predestination is an ancillary doctrine … (McGrath)

Key terms

Calvinism: a branch of Protestantism based on the theological beliefs promoted by John Calvin. It is also referred to as Reformed Protestantism or the Reformed tradition

Systematically arranged theology: theology arranged primarily for teaching purposes

Systematically derived theology: theology derived from first principles

The Protestant Reformation: a sixteenth-century European movement aimed initially at reforming the beliefs and practices of the Roman Catholic Church

the view of a God who would not want any to be lost – he is God of love). Secondly, God foresees that they will resist his grace and so block his will (this seems to suggest that judgement is based on a person's free choice to block his will yet they could not do otherwise).

This whole issue of predestination resurfaced with John Calvin who featured the doctrine as part of his theological system.

John Calvin

John Calvin was born in France in 1509 and was a prominent figure during **the Protestant Reformation**. Having left Roman Catholicism, he joined the Protestant movement and became one of its leaders in Paris. In 1536 he journeyed to Basel. On the way he passed through Geneva where he was persuaded to stay there to help with the reforming of the church. He stayed in Geneva (apart from a short move to Strasbourg 1538–1541) until his death in 1564.

During his life he wrote many books on theology, especially commentaries on the books in the Bible. However, his most famous book was the *Institutes of the Christian Religion*, first published in 1536. What began as a short six-chapter work, by its final form (1559) had grown to a hefty four volumes and comprised a thorough systematic theology.

John Calvin

Although John Calvin (and **Calvinism**) are often associated with the doctrine of predestination, this particular doctrine is by no means the major pivot around which Calvin formulated his other doctrines. Neither was the doctrine an innovation of Calvin's. As we have seen, Augustine and others, had expounded the doctrine of predestination. Indeed, in the *Institutes*, doctrines such as justification by faith, the work of the Holy Spirit and union with Christ are more central. Perhaps the two most central themes for Calvin are (i) the sovereignty of God and (ii) the Bible as the revealed Word of God.

McGrath (*Christian Theology: An Introduction*) traces the highlighting of the doctrine of predestination in Calvinism to the new development in distinguishing between **systematically arranged theology** and **systematically derived theology**. Calvin presented systematically arranged theology whereas many Calvinists, having to defend their ideas, were forced to start from first principles and show how their doctrines were derived from these principles. In so doing, the doctrine of predestination became a major plank in the debate.

Some modern scholarship has challenged the extent to which later Calvinism accurately represented Calvin's own views. This has become known as the 'Calvin against the Calvinists' school of thought. For instance, R.T. Kendall (*Calvin and English Calvinism*) argues that Calvin was not himself a Calvinist on the point of limited atonement (see page 166).

quickpire

4.10 What is regarded as Calvin's most famous book?

John Calvin's Doctrine of Election: the corrupted nature of human beings, the absolute power of God

Specification content
John Calvin: Doctrine of Election: the elect and the reprobates, unconditional election.

Calvin follows Augustine in his understanding of the fall of humanity. He states in his *Institutes* that Man was created as an immortal soul in a state of original righteousness. Adam's choice of good and evil was free, but Genesis 3 recounts the fall. The consequences of the fall were that 'the heavenly image was obliterated in him' and of everyone since. So humanity has lost its original freedom and is now enslaved to sin.

Calvin believed totally in the **sovereignty of God** – the all-pervasive and over-ruling providence of God, and scripture as the source of knowledge of and about God. Nothing happens by chance. In *Institutes* he wrote 'The will of God is the supreme and first cause of all things, because nothing happens but by his command or permission.' The sovereignty of God was an essential feature of the doctrine of predestination. As we shall see, Calvin insisted that the pure sovereignty of God's good pleasure is the origin and explanation of reprobation no less than of election.

Calvin's book Institutes of the Christian Religion

In Calvin's *Institutes* he stated that scripture functions as a set of 'spectacles' that bring **general revelation** back into proper focus. Calvin thus dismisses all efforts at going beyond the scriptures as pure speculation, both wrong and sinful. This central driving force of scripture rather than philosophy is Calvin's reasoning in his doctrine of election.

The need for the doctrine of election

Calvin's beliefs about predestination were derived not from just his ideas about divine omnipotence, but also from reflection about human experience, interpreted in the light of scripture. He was aware that some people responded to God's grace whilst others did not. According to Calvin, scripture makes clear that some people respond to the gospel whilst others do not; for example, the parable of the Sower in Mark 4:1–20. He was also convinced that sin had corrupted both the will and the intellect. He regarded humanity as totally depraved (morally corrupt) owing to the fall of Adam and Eve. Totally depraved here does not mean completely depraved or as depraved as you could possibly be. It means tainted or depraved in all areas of the heart, mind and will. Humanity was unable to respond in faithful obedience to the invitation of God through Jesus. In other words, people cannot choose for themselves to repent and believe.

Parable of the Sower

Key quotes

… all of us, who have descended from impure seed, are born infected with the contagion of sin. (Calvin, *Institutes*)

For we unjustly defraud God of his right, unless each of us lives and dies in dependence on his sovereign pleasure. (Calvin)

Events are often fortuitous to us because their order, reason, end, and necessity are hid in the counsel of God and are not apprehended by the mind of man. But they are not fortuitous for God – they proceed from his will. (John Murray commenting on Calvin's beliefs)

Belief in predestination is not an article of faith in its own right but is the final outcome of scripturally informed reflection on the effects of grace upon individuals in the light of the enigmas of experience. (McGrath)

For it is by grace you are saved, through faith, and this is not of yourselves, it is the gift of God. (Ephesians 2:8)

Key terms

General revelation: knowledge about God discovered through natural means such as reasoning or observation of the physical universe

Sovereignty of God: the teaching that all things are under God's rule and control. He is sovereign both in principle and practice

quickfire

4.11 What ideas/beliefs led Calvin to the belief in predestination?

Key quote

God preordained, for his own glory and the display of His attributes of mercy and justice, a part of the human race, without any merit of their own, to eternal salvation, and another part, in just punishment of their sin, to eternal damnation. (Calvin)

A potter working on some clay.

Unconditional election

Coupled with the doctrine of unconditional election was Calvin's insistence on the sovereignty of God. God is active and sovereign in his actions. It follows, therefore, that God must actively choose to redeem or to damn. Hence, the doctrine of predestination. In *Institutes* Calvin defined predestination as the 'eternal decree of God, by which he determined what he wished to make of every individual. For he does not create all in the same condition, but ordains eternal life for some and eternal damnation for others.'

Like Augustine, Calvin was clear that there is nothing in humanity to merit any favour or mercy. Each person is worthy of God's wrath and incapable of saving themselves.

Election and grace

Calvin believed that God chose to elect people regardless of their merit. In this action, he saw God's graciousness demonstrated, since God redeems individuals irrespective of their merits. For Calvin,

the elect receive a twofold grace of **justification** and **sanctification**. He wrote in *Institutes*:

'... we principally receive a double grace: namely, that being reconciled to God through Christ's blamelessness, we may have in heaven instead of a Judge a gracious Father; and secondly, that sanctified by Christ's spirit we may cultivate blamelessness and purity of life.'

Larry Sharp in an article *The Doctrines of Grace in Calvin and Augustine* comments that 'justification is God's gift of the imputed righteousness of Jesus Christ. Through this gift of credited or reckoned righteousness we have a new standing before God, namely the same standing or position as that of Christ.' Sanctification is the process of growth in holiness and piety through life. Justification is therefore a one-time event whereas sanctification is the continual process of being made more holy.

Though justification and sanctification are distinct they are not separable. Calvin argued that there cannot be justification without sanctification; and there cannot be sanctification without justification. In *Institutes* he wrote, 'Therefore Christ justifies no one whom he does not at the same time sanctify.'

Key quotes

For he chose us in him before the creation of the world to be holy and blameless in his sight. (Ephesians 1:4)

But who are you, a human being, to talk back to God? Shall what is formed say to the one who formed it, 'Why did you make me like this?' Does not the potter have the right to make out of the same lump of clay some pottery for special purposes and some for common use? What if God, although choosing to show his wrath and make his power known, bore with great patience the objects of his wrath – prepared for destruction? (Romans 9:20–22)

AO1 Activity

Work in groups of four. Think of an imaginative way to present the Doctrine of Election to the other three that does not involve just reading it out. Each person does a presentation to the other three.

Calvin further developed his theory by stating that God made among people two predestined groups: the elect and the reprobates. This view on predestination was later referred to as double predestination. This is because God has actively chosen people into two predestined groups; either for damnation (reprobates) or for salvation and eternal life (the elect). This act of predestination took place before creation, clearly demonstrating that the election had nothing to do with meritorious works. God actively chooses to redeem or to damn since he is active and sovereign in his actions. Eternal life is based solely on God's grace.

The elect

If a person belongs to the elect then they have been chosen by God to have their sins forgiven, through the atonement for sins achieved by the death of Jesus Christ.

Calvin believed that whilst no one can be certain whether they are one of the elect, the elect will persevere to the end. They will persevere because Christ will care for the elect so that they will not fall away. Therefore, if apparent believers fall away, then Calvin concludes they were not part of the elect. 1 John 1:19 says, 'They went out from us, but they did not really belong to us. For if they had belonged to us, they would have remained with us: but their going showed that none of them belonged to us.'

Calvin believed that a person can have the assurance that they are among the elect. Indeed, he believed they could and should. In *Institutes* Calvin wrote 'Predestination, rightly understood, brings no shaking of faith but rather its best confirmation'. One indicator of election is what Calvin referred to as 'the calling of God' – a subjective inward certainty. He also expected the elect to show traits of their godly status even though at times, they might be sinful. There was assurance because 'if we are in communion with Christ, we have proof sufficiently clear and strong that we are written in the Book of Life' (*Institutes*).

The reprobates

Calvin was very clear that whilst God elected some for salvation and eternal life, he also barred others from access to salvation and so sentenced them to eternal death. This election took place before creation, making clear that merit is not an explanation for why some are saved, and others are not. However, the reprobate sins of their own free choice rather than by divine coercion. They resist grace because they are not chosen. Therefore, in one sense, God did not make them sinners. It was more the case that God left them to their sin.

Calvin appealed to Romans 11:11–13 for scriptural support that all are not created on equal terms: 'Yet, before the twins were born or had done anything good or bad – in order that God's purpose in election might stand: not by works but by him who calls – she was told, ... Jacob I loved, but Esau I hated.'

Key quotes

The secret of the Kingdom of God has been given to you. But to those on the outside everything is said in parables. **(Jesus in Mark 4:11)**

… a man will be justified by faith when, excluded from righteousness of works, he by faith lays hold of the righteousness of Christ, and clothed in it, appears in the sight of God not as a sinner, but as righteous … **(Calvin)**

You see how every thing is denied to free will, for the very purpose of leaving no room for merit. And yet, as the beneficence and liberality of God are manifold and inexhaustible, the grace which he bestows upon us, inasmuch as he makes it our own, he recompenses as if the virtuous acts were our own. **(Calvin)**

Christ is indeed presented to all, but God opens the eyes of the elect alone, and enables them by faith to seek after him. **(Calvin)**

quickfire

4.12 State two differences between justification and sanctification.

Key quote

I am the good shepherd; I know my sheep and my sheep know me. **(John 10:14)**

The elect are those who have been chosen by God have their sins forgiven.

Key term

Atonement: Christian doctrine concerning the reconciliation of God and humankind, accomplished through the life, suffering and death of Christ

Key quote

I am sure He chose me before I was born, or else He never would have chosen me afterwards; and He must have elected me for reasons unknown to me, for I never could find any reason in myself why He should have looked upon me with special love. **(Spurgeon)**

Specification content

John Calvin: Doctrine of Election: limited atonement, irresistible grace and perseverance of the elect.

Key quotes

First and last for Calvin, God is not a celestial tyrant but a loving parent who cannot forget her nursing child, and a father who gives good things to his children. (Lindberg)

This inheritance is kept in heaven for you, who through faith are shielded by God's power until the coming of the salvation … (1 Peter 1:4–5)

They went out from us, but they did not really belong to us. For if they had belonged to us, they would have remained with us; but their going showed that none of them belonged to us. (1 John 2:19)

Key term

Limited atonement: the view that Christ died for the sins of the elect only and no atonement was provided for the reprobate

quickfire

4.13 How does John 10:15 support the view for limited atonement?

Limited atonement

According to Calvin, God made a predestined choice for all peoples, before they were even born. Certain people progress to eternal life (the elect) and some to eternal damnation (the reprobates). That number, according to Calvin, is fixed by God from eternity and no one can do anything during their lifetime to change it.

Calvin saw the main purpose of predestination as the means for God to be glorified. Hence, McGrath argues that for Calvin, predestination was never a central premise but more an ancillary doctrine. However, for later followers of Calvin, this doctrine became more developed and more central. One consequence that resulted was the doctrine of **limited atonement**. By 'limited atonement' is meant that Christ died for the sins of the elect and no atonement was provided for the reprobate. Calvin himself never used this phrase and some scholars, such as R.T Kendall (*Calvin and English Calvinism*) argued that Calvin limited the extent of the *intercession* of Christ rather than his work of atonement. In response, others such as Paul Helm point out that in Calvin's own commentary on 1 Timothy 2:5, Calvin argues that 'the universal term "all" must always be referred to classes of men and not to persons' (*Calvin's Commentaries Volume XXI*), i.e. it is limited and does not mean 'all without exception'.

Further argument appeals to John 10:15 where Jesus laid his life down for the sheep. The next verse comments that Jesus said that people did not believe because they were not his sheep. This implies that if Jesus lays his life down for the sheep and there are people who were not his sheep, then he did not lay his life down for those who are not his sheep. Hence Christ's redeeming work was intended to save the elect only and therefore limited in its extent.

This view of the scope of the atonement is also called 'definite' by some because they believe it certainly secures the salvation of those for whom Christ died. 'Particular redemption' is another phrase used since the intention of God is to save particular persons through the atonement as opposed to human beings in general.

Greek Orthodox icon of Jesus the good shepherd

Irresistible grace and perseverance of the elect

Calvin also argued that since God has drawn the elect to faith in Christ by regenerating their hearts and convincing them of their sins, then it follows that they will be kept by the same power to the end and so enter heaven. They are eternally saved and kept in faith by the power of God and so persevere to the end. But what of those who profess to be believers but then later fall away? The doctrine maintains that it only applies to those who have a genuine faith in Christ. Those who appear to profess and then fall away are deemed not to have had genuine faith and are therefore not part of the elect.

The change of heart that the Holy Spirit makes in regeneration, as well as the indwelling presence of the Spirit in the believer, ensures that the believer will continue to love Christ. It does not suggest they will be perfect in this life. However, it teaches that believers do not strive to keep God's commands to gain salvation or maintain salvation but rather out of love and gratitude to God.

The Synod of Dort

After the death of Arminius in 1609, forty-six of his followers in the Netherlands issued their protest against Calvinist teaching. They summarised their creed under five points concerning predestination, the atonement, faith, grace and perseverance. Unable to reach any agreement with the Calvinists, a synod was convened. The Synod of Dort (1618–19CE) was an international meeting organised by the Dutch Reformed Church to settle the divisive controversy between Calvinism and Arminianism.

The rejection of Arminianism was a foregone conclusion since Arminian delegates were not permitted to vote although they were allowed to speak and their views were given full hearing.

It is important to note that the famous 'Five Points of Calvinism' were a direct response to the 'Five Points of Arminianism' and so in no way represent the sum of Calvinism.

The five points of Calvinism are sometimes summed up with the acronym T.U.L.I.P.

Total depravity

As a result of Adam and Eve's disobedience to God, sin has extended to every part of a person's being: their thinking, their emotions and their will. Therefore, it is impossible for the ordinary 'natural' human being to understand or respond to God. They are spiritually helpless.

1 Corinthians 2:14 'The man without the Spirit does not accept the things that come from the Spirit of God, for they are foolishness to him, and he cannot understand them because they are spiritually discerned.'

Unconditional election

God has divided humanity into two groups. One group is 'the elected'. This includes all those whom God has chosen for salvation and eternal life. The rest, 'the reprobates', remain in sin and eternal condemnation. God alone chooses the elect. Election is not on the basis of any foreseen merit, quality, or achievement. God chooses the elect based solely upon his will and he did this before creation.

Romans 9:21 'Does not the potter have the right to make out of the same lump of clay some pottery for noble purposes and some for common use?'

Limited atonement

Christ's death and atonement for the sins of human beings was for the elect only. Calvinists believe that the Bible teaches that Christ died for those whom God gave him to save, the elect. Therefore, Christ died for many people (the elect), but not all (the reprobates).

Matthew 26:28 'This is my blood of the covenant which is poured out for many for the forgiveness of sins.'

Irresistible grace

The result of God's irresistible grace is the certain response by the elect to the inward call of the gospel. Calvinists believe that the elect cannot resist the call which will result in them being redeemed.

Acts 13:48 '...and all who were appointed for eternal life believed.'

Perseverance of the elect

The elect will be kept by God through their earthly life until they are finally glorified in heaven. God will begin and continue a process of sanctification which will continue until they reach heaven. None are lost. It is impossible for them to lose their salvation. The elect will therefore be unable to commit apostasy by giving up their faith.

Philippians 1:6 '...being confident of this, that he who began a good work in you will carry it on to completion until the day of Christ Jesus.'

Key terms

Arminianism: the doctrinal teachings of Jacobus Arminius and his followers who argued for free will and that Christ died for everyone rather than just the elect

Synod: an assembly of church clergy of a particular church

Key quote

Although men are not totally corrupt in the sense that they are incapable of doing any good at all – it would be absurd to say that – the truth is that the best of men and their best accomplishments are tainted or poisoned at the core by their pride or egotism or self-centredness, however far they may look from outside. **(Vidler)**

quickfire

4.14 Explain why it is a mistake to assume that the 'Five points of Calvinism' provide the sum total of teaching about Calvinism.

quickfire

4.15 Explain what the acronym T.U.L.I.P. stands for.

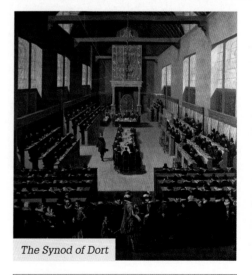

The Synod of Dort

Total Depravity
Unconditional Election
Limited Atonement
Irrisistible Grace
Perseverance of the Saints

TULIP

Similarities and differences between Augustine and Calvin on predestination

On first reading of Augustine and Calvin, they appear to be saying the same things. Indeed, Calvin quotes Augustine in various places in his *Institutes*. Some of the apparent differences on predestination may be because of the way they expressed their views. In substance there were lots of similarities.

However, Larry Sharp (*The Doctrines of Grace in Calvin and Augustine*) argues that unlike Calvin, Augustine never made a clear distinction between the grace of God and the Holy Spirit. For Calvin, grace is not some sort of healing power infused in believers, it is primarily about the character of God. – benevolent and merciful.

As we have seen earlier, some scholars conclude that Calvin taught double predestination and Augustine did not. It is argued that Augustine believed that God chose some for eternal life but did not in any direct sense deliberately reject others. Rather he leaves them for rightful judgement. However, as was noted earlier, many feel that this is not as clear a doctrine as is claimed. There are some passages in Augustine's writing that do suggest a doctrine of double predestination. Others point out that if God can choose some to be given mercy and receive forgiveness, then by implication God is deliberate leaving others to suffer judgement without forgiveness. Whatever Augustine's actual views, it is clear that Calvin taught the doctrine of double predestination. In *Institutes* Calvin writes 'all are not created in equal condition; rather, eternal life is foreordained for some, eternal damnation for others. Therefore, as any man has been created to one or the other of these ends, we speak of him as predestined to life or to death.'

Calvin's approach to predestination also moves away from Augustine's view. Augustine viewed that all are created in an equal condition of being justly condemned but God mercifully decides to save some. In contrast, Calvin does not regard all being created in equal condition. Human beings have been created to either eternal life or eternal damnation.

Augustine and Calvin

Another area where there appears to be a difference concerns justification. Both Augustine and Calvin see justification as a gift from God. For Augustine, justification is something done in us. It is an infused righteousness whereby we are enabled to live a life pleasing to God and so be saved. However, for Calvin, justification is about the imputed righteousness of Jesus Christ. By this he meant that righteousness was credited to us or reckoned to us, such that we had a new standing before God. That standing is the same standing as Christ has before God. As can be seen, this is not about a person's ability to live righteously.

AO1 Activity

Divide into two groups. Each group looks at the following list of biblical verses that illustrate the five points of Calvinism. Each group identifies which ones relate to which of the five points. Then the two groups compare their groupings, discussing where there are any differences between the groupings.

John's Gospel: 6:37; 6:39; 6:44; 10:28–29; 17:9

Romans 5:12; 8:14; 8:30; 9:15

Ephesians 4:18

2 Thessalonians 2:13

Titus 1:15

1 Peter 1:2

AO1 Developing skills

It is now important to consider the information that has been covered in this section; however, the information in its raw form is too extensive and so has to be processed in order to meet the requirements of the examination. This can be done by practising more advanced skills associated with AO1. The exercises that run throughout this book will help you to do this and prepare you for the examination. For assessment objective 1 (AO1), which involves demonstrating 'knowledge' and 'understanding' skills, we are going to focus on different ways in which the skills can be demonstrated effectively, and also refer to how the performance of these skills is measured (see generic band descriptors for A2 [WJEC] AO1 or A Level [Eduqas] AO1).

▶ **Your task is this:** Look back at page 167 to the list off the **five points in which Calvinists expressed Calvin's Doctrine of Election at the Synod of Dort in 1619**. It is 300 words long. Discuss what you think are the two main points from the **each** of the five doctrines, explaining why you have selected those points.

Now write the five points into your own summary (as in Theme 1 Developing skills) trying to make the summary more personal to your style of writing.

1. ....

2. ....

3. ....

4. ....

5. ....

Key skills Theme 4

This theme has tasks that deal with the basics of AO1 in terms of prioritising and selecting the key relevant information, presenting this in a personalised way (as in Theme 1) and then using evidence and examples to support and expand upon this (as in Theme 2).

Key skills

Knowledge involves:

Selection of a range of (thorough) accurate and relevant information that is directly related to the specific demands of the question.

This means:

- Selecting relevant material for the question set

- Being focused in explaining and examining the material selected.

Understanding involves:

Explanation that is extensive, demonstrating depth and/or breadth with excellent use of evidence and examples including (where appropriate) thorough and accurate supporting use of sacred texts, sources of wisdom and specialist language.

This means:

- Effective use of examples and supporting evidence to establish the quality of your understanding

- Ownership of your explanation that expresses personal knowledge and understanding and NOT just reproducing a chunk of text from a book that you have rehearsed and memorised.

Specification content

A consideration of whether
religious believers should accept
predestination.

> ### Key term
>
> **Council of Carthage:** Catholic
> Church meetings or synods held
> between the 3rd and 5th centuries in
> the city of Carthage, in Africa

Council of Carthage

AO2 Activity

As you read through this section try to
do the following:

1. Pick out the different lines of
   argument that are presented in
   the text and identify any evidence
   given in support.

2. For each line of argument try to
   evaluate whether or not you think
   this is strong or weak.

3. Think of any questions you may
   wish to raise in response to the
   arguments.

This Activity will help you to start
thinking critically about what you
read and help you to evaluate the
effectiveness of different arguments
and from this develop your own
observations, opinions and points
of view that will help with any
conclusions that you make in your
answers to the AO2 questions that
arise.

Issues for analysis and evaluation

A consideration of whether religious believers should accept predestination

Both Augustine and Calvin argued for predestination from their understanding
of the Bible. They appealed to various texts in the Bible because they accepted
the authority of the religious text. If a
religious believer accepts the authority
of a religious text that refers to
predestination then it will be persuasive
to them.

The two main Christian texts quoted are
usually Romans 8:29–30 which says, 'For
those God foreknew he also predestined
to be conformed to the image of his Son,
that he might be the firstborn among
many brothers and sisters. And those
he predestined, he also called; those he

A religious text

called, he also justified; those justified, he also glorified.' And Ephesians 1:4–5, 'For
he chose us in him before the creation of the world to be holy and blameless in his
sight. In love he predestined us to be adopted as his sons through Jesus Christ, in
accordance with his pleasure and will.'

However, even if a religious believer accepts the religious texts as authoritative,
they may interpret their meaning differently. For instance, some religious
believers argue that predestination refers to the plan and goal of salvation itself,
not to specific individuals. Eternal life is the proper destination of every human
being but only those who cooperate with God will reach that destination. Hence,
predestination, according to these religious believers, should be interpreted in
terms of a corporate sense rather than that each individual was predestined to
either eternal life or eternal condemnation.

Other religious believers may reject the authority of the religious texts and argue
that the texts have gone through a period of transmission and change. Therefore,
they must decide on other criteria as to what to believe.

One criterion to help understand religious texts and doctrines would be to consider
Church history and to examine how such doctrines have come about. Both Calvin
and Luther drew heavily from the views of Augustine. It might be argued that the
concepts of predestination and election were dominated by Augustine's attack
against Pelagius. Many may feel that in his desire to oppose free will, Augustine
veered too far the other way.

In a similar way, Church Councils through the ages have formulated doctrine
including that of the doctrine of predestination and election. For instance, the
Council of Carthage of 418CE fully approved Augustine's predestination Doctrine
of Original Sin and denounced the contrary view as presented by Pelagius.

A further example that could be used is the Synod of Dort in 1619CE. The Synod of
Dort sought to settle a divisive controversy between the predestination arguments
of Calvinism and the free will arguments of Arminianism. The Synod concluded
with a rejection of the Arminian view and the acceptance of all five of the Calvinist
points. As a result, the doctrine became the teaching of the Church. Unless one
argued that God infallibly guided the decision of the various Church Councils,
one would need to assess the different arguments that were presented at those
Councils.

Another line of argument focuses on religious texts that are actually contrary to the doctrine of predestation. If the religious believer accepts the authority of the religious text then they could conclude that predestation is a wrong belief. There are texts that state that a person freely chooses to follow God or not to follow God. For instance, Joshua 24:15 says 'But if serving the Lord seems undesirable to you, then choose for yourselves this day whom you will serve' and Matthew 23:37 'O Jerusalem, Jerusalem, you who kill the prophets and stone those sent to you, how often I have longed to gather your children together, as a hen gathers her chicks under her wings, but you were not willing'.

A different line of argument that supports the view that religious believers should accept predestation is that it is consistent with the traditional understanding of God, in terms of God's attributes. **Monotheistic religions**, like Islam, Judaism and Christianity, generally attribute the quality of omnipotence to their deity. The concept of predestation seems to support the concept of God's omnipotent nature. This is because only an omnipotent deity could have had an eternal predestation plan for all of humanity that he was able to execute. However, some religious believers may question predestation since if God is omnipotent, then surely he could create beings that always chose to do good. Others point out that it is logically impossible to be both free and controlled at the same time. It is not that God is not powerful enough, it is that the task is a logical contradiction and God cannot actualise contradictions. Therefore, predestation does not challenge classical theism.

In contrast, free will seems to diminish the omnipotent nature of God, since a person would could thwart the plans of God by enacting a free will choice contrary to God's plan. However, it could be argued that God has limited his omnipotence.

Some religious believers see no conflict between the doctrine of predestation and the belief in free will. They may claim that the religious texts are authoritative, and they teach both beliefs. Therefore, both beliefs must be compatible. For example, free will is limited in that it cannot ultimately thwart the plans and purposes of God. God giving up the exercising of his sovereignty is not the same as God giving up his sovereignty.

Monotheistic religions also attribute the quality of **omnibenevolence** to their deity. Omnibenevolence is the quality of being all-loving, sometimes stated as being all-good. However, the concept of free will, not predestation, seems to support God's omnibenevolent nature. The free will theory opens up the possibility that all people can achieve salvation by freely following God's eternal moral laws. This seems a better illustration of God's omnibenevolence than the doctrine of predestation. The doctrine of predestation implies that only some are forgiven and inherit eternal life. This limited atonement (that Christ died for some not all) might cause some religious believers to reject the doctrine of predestation. It seems contrary to a loving God as well as some religious texts that state that Christ died for all rather than just the elect, e.g. 'He is the atoning sacrifice for our sins, and not only for ours but also for the sins of the whole world' (1 John 2:2). Isaiah 53:6 says: 'We all, like sheep, have gone astray, each of us has turned to his own way; and the LORD has laid on him the iniquity of us all' (Isa. 53:6). This verse doesn't seem to make sense unless it is read to say that the same 'all' that went astray is the 'all' for whom Christ died.

Other religious believers cite texts to support a limited atonement and so see no contradiction with the doctrine of predestation, e.g. 'The good shepherd lays down his life for the sheep' (John 10:11). They argue this just refers to specific people – his sheep (the elect). Other texts appealed to include Matthew 20:28 '... the Son of Man did not come to be served, but to serve, and to give his life as a ransom for many'. And Matthew 26:28: 'This is my blood of the covenant, which is poured out for many for the forgiveness of sins.'

Key terms

Monotheistic religions: Monotheism literally means the belief in only one God. The major monotheistic religions are Judaism, Christianity and Islam

Omnibenevolence: the quality of being all-loving, sometimes stated as being all-good

Key quotes

… everyone whose name has not been written from the foundation of the world in the book of life of the Lamb who was slain. (Revelation 13:8)

God has saved us and called us with a holy calling, not according to our works, but according to his own purpose and grace which was granted us in Christ Jesus from all eternity. (2 Timothy 1:9)

Study tip

It is vital for AO2 that you actually discuss arguments and not just explain what someone may have stated. Try to ask yourself, 'was this a fair point to make?', 'is the evidence sound enough?', 'is there anything to challenge this argument?', 'is this a strong or weak argument?' Such critical analysis will help you develop your evaluation skills.

AO2 Activity

List some conclusions that could be drawn from the AO2 reasoning from the above text; try to aim for at least three different possible conclusions. Consider each of the conclusions and collect brief evidence to support each conclusion from the AO1 and AO2 material for this topic. Select the conclusion that you think is most convincing and explain why it is so. Try to contrast this with the weakest conclusion in the list, justifying your argument with clear reasoning and evidence.

Key terms

Methodism: religious movement founded primarily through the work of John Wesley, whose preaching centred upon the theology that God's grace was given to all

Omniscience: the state of knowing everything

Key quotes

Feinberg believes that all acts must be causally determined by God, yet he holds that God does not coerce us. But is this possible? … how can God decisively guarantee the result without forcing or coercing the individual? (Norman Geisler)

Seek the Lord while he may be found; call on him while he is near (Isaiah 55:6)

Specification content

The extent to which God predestines humanity.

AO2 Activity

As you read through this section try to do the following:

1. Pick out the different lines of argument that are presented in the text and identify any evidence given in support.

2. For each line of argument try to evaluate whether or not you think this is strong or weak.

3. Think of any questions you may wish to raise in response to the arguments.

This Activity will help you to start thinking critically about what you read and help you to evaluate the effectiveness of different arguments and from this develop your own observations, opinions and points of view that will help with any conclusions that you make in your answers to the AO2 questions that arise.

A religious believer who believes God is omniscient may well support the doctrine of predestination since it is consistent with God knowing the future. They would argue that if God doesn't know the future, then he is not omniscient. **Omniscience** also raises the question of whether God is in time or is timeless. Some religious believers might argue that predestination implies God is outside of time since he knows all things. All of time is present to God's mind from all eternity. Clark Pinnock (*Predestination and Free Will*) rejects this view and argues that the idea of a God outside of time is not consistent with the biblical description of God. A timeless God cannot deliberate or anticipate or remember. He cannot do anything or respond to anything. There cannot be any before or after. However, it is questionable whether the God who creates time can himself be time-bound. The problems posed by predestination and time may lead a religious believer to reject the doctrine of predestination.

Clearly religious believers are divided over the doctrine of predestination. Religious denominations have developed, with some supporting the doctrine of predestination and limited atonement (e.g. the Calvinists); whilst others have argued for free will and atonement offered to all (e.g. the Methodists). The Methodist Church's doctrine on salvation is almost entirely based on Arminian principles. For example, one of the founders of **Methodism**, John Wesley, taught that a person is free not only to accept salvation but also to reject it.

The extent to which God predestines humanity

The supporters of the doctrine of predestination can be divided into two main groups. Those who argue that there is no free will and God predestines every aspect of a person's life; and those who accept that it refers to the determining of individual human destiny by God, but it does not necessarily deny free will.

Religious texts can be appealed to on either side. For example, Ephesians 1:11 states that 'In him we were also chosen, having been predestined according to the plan of him who works out everything in conformity with the purpose of his will …' and 2 Thessalonians 2:13 says '… because from the beginning God chose you to be saved through the sanctifying work of the Spirit …'. Both these religious texts imply that God predestined from the beginning of time and therefore it implies God predestines all events and actions.

John Feinberg (*Predestination and Free Will*) argues that 'God has chosen at once the whole interconnected sequence of events and actions that have and will occur in our world. Such choices were not absolutely necessary (I reject fatalism) but necessary as a consequence of other choices God made.' God deliberates, chooses and accomplishes all things on the basis of his purposes.

Others appeal to biblical prophecy such as the death of Jesus, implying that God is absolutely sovereign and possesses absolute self-determination. Certainly, religious texts such as Romans 9:20–21 imply total predestination – 'Shall what is formed say to him who formed it, "Why did you make me like this?" Does not the potter have the right to make out of the same lump of clay some pottery for noble purposes and some for common use?'

Others maintain that human beings have real choices in life and so the outcome of every event or action is not predetermined, e.g. a person is held morally responsible for an action. The only thing predetermined is the final destiny of the elect. This is supported by the idea that it is God who forgives and gives eternal life and it is nothing to do with anything a human being does by their operating a free choice. In this view the result is the same as total predestination. They have free will, unlike total predestination but in terms of final destiny it is God who brings it about (just as it is in total predestination). For example, Ephesians 2:4–5 says, 'God, who is rich in mercy, made us alive with Christ even when we were dead in transgressions – it is by grace you have been saved'.

However, there are also religious texts that imply that our free actions can reject God's salvation. Clark Pinnock (*Predestination and Free Will*) says, '... God energetically pursues his will for the world in all areas ... but that does not mean God's will is actually done in every case. Quite the contrary, Jesus made it plain that the Pharisees "rejected the purpose of God for themselves"'.

As always when considering religious texts, the force of the argument will depend on whether the religious texts are taken as authoritative and whether the particular texts can be interpreted in an alternative way.

Another line of argument might focus on whether Jesus' death and atonement was for all human beings or just the elect. This has implications regarding the extent that God predestines humanity. If the atonement was for all human beings then that would imply that we freely choose or reject God's offer of forgiveness and eternal life. Again, religious texts are used by both sides of the argument to support their view. Those advocating that it was limited atonement appeal to religious texts that refer to Christ dying for the many rather than for all. E.g. '... the Son of Man did not come to be served, but to serve, and give his life as a ransom for many' (Matthew 20:28) and 'This is my blood of the covenant, which is poured out for many for the forgiveness of sins' (Matthew 26:28).

However, there are other religious texts that refer to 'all' rather than 'many' and so support **unlimited atonement**. E.g. 'He is the atoning sacrifice for our sins, and not only for ours but also for the sins of the whole world' (1 John 2:2); and 'This is good and pleases God our Saviour, who wants all men to be saved and to come to a knowledge of the truth ... who gave himself a ransom for all men' (2 Timothy 2:3–4). If unlimited atonement is correct then this implies that God is not omnipotent, since not all receive eternal life even though God wants all to be saved. It also raises questions about the whole doctrine of predestination since it does not seem in the control of God as to who is saved or not saved.

Another area of debate about the extent to which God predestines humanity revolves around whether God predestines those who are not the elect. Scholars seem divided about Augustine's view. Some statements by Augustine suggest he only thought God predestined the elect. McGrath (*Christian Theology: An Introduction*, 1994) argues 'that the remainder were not, according to Augustine, actively condemned to damnation; they were merely not elected to salvation'. However, John Lennox (*Determined to Believe?*) points out that 'It is hard to see how one can maintain so-called single predestination without logically affirming double predestination'.

Key quote

He is patient with you, not wanting anyone to perish, but everyone to come to repentance. (2 Peter 3:9)

Study tip

It is vital for AO2 that you actually discuss arguments and not just explain what someone may have stated. Try to ask yourself, 'was this a fair point to make?', 'is the evidence sound enough?', 'is there anything to challenge this argument?', 'is this a strong or weak argument?' Such critical analysis will help you develop your evaluation skills

Key term

Unlimited atonement: Christ's atoning death was for all humanity

AO2 Activity

List some conclusions that could be drawn from the AO2 reasoning from the above text; try to aim for at least three different possible conclusions. Consider each of the conclusions and collect brief evidence to support each conclusion from the AO1 and AO2 material for this topic. Select the conclusion that you think is most convincing and explain why it is so. Try to contrast this with the weakest conclusion in the list, justifying your argument with clear reasoning and evidence.

Key skills Theme 4

This theme has tasks that deal with specific aspects of AO2 in terms of identifying key elements of an evaluative style piece of writing, specifically counter-arguments and conclusions (both intermediate and final).

Key skills

Analysis involves:

Identifying issues raised by the materials in the AO1, together with those identified in the AO2 section, and presents sustained and clear views, either of scholars or from a personal perspective ready for evaluation.

This means:

- That your answers are able to identify key areas of debate in relation to a particular issue

- That you can identify, and comment upon, the different lines of argument presented by others

- That your response comments on the overall effectiveness of each of these areas or arguments.

Evaluation involves:

Considering the various implications of the issues raised based upon the evidence gleaned from analysis and provides an extensive detailed argument with a clear conclusion.

This means:

- That your answer weighs up the consequences of accepting or rejecting the various and different lines of argument analysed

- That your answer arrives at a conclusion through a clear process of reasoning.

AO2 Developing skills

It is now important to consider the information that has been covered in this section; however, the information in its raw form is too extensive and so has to be processed in order to meet the requirements of the examination. This can be achieved by practising more advanced skills associated with AO2. The exercises that run throughout this book will help you to do this and prepare you for the examination. For assessment objective 2 (AO2), which involves 'critical analysis' and 'evaluation' skills, we are going to focus on different ways in which the skills can be demonstrated effectively, and also refer to how the performance of these skills is measured (see generic band descriptors for A2 [WJEC] AO2 or A Level [Eduqas] AO2).

▶ **Your task is this:** Below is a one-sided view concerning **the extent to which God predestines humanity**. It is 120 words long. You need to include this view for an evaluation; however, to just present one side of an argument or one line of reasoning is not really evaluation. Using the paragraph below, add a counter-argument or alternative line of reasoning to make the evaluation more balanced. Allow about 200 words for your counter-argument or alternative line of reasoning.

Another line of argument about the extent to which God predestines humanity is to consider theological arguments for predestination such as the ones presented by Augustine. It could be argued that theological arguments for predestination mean that the extent of God's predestination for humanity is complete. For example, one potential support for Augustine's Doctrine of Original Sin is to look at the outcome of the Council of Carthage in 418. In the 3rd, 4th and 5th centuries 'Councils of Carthage' were assembled by the Catholic Church to discuss theological matters of great importance. In 418 one such Council of Carthage fully approved Augustine's predestination Doctrine of Original Sin and denounced the contrary view of Pelagius. Therefore, the Council of Carthage was in many ways agreeing and confirming that this was authoritative Christian teaching.

Next, think of another line of argument or reasoning that may support either argument or it may even be completely different and add this to your answer.

Then ask yourself:

- Will my work, when developed, contain thorough, sustained and clear views that are supported by extensive, detailed reasoning and/or evidence?

B: Concepts of determinism

This section covers AO1 content and skills

Specification content

Hard determinism: philosophical (John Locke – free will is an illusion, man in bedroom illustration).

Hard determinism

The idea of **determinism** is firmly grounded in the principle of causality. The world around us appears to be a 'closed' phenomenon. We can observe causality and the interaction of phenomena, and it appears that every event is necessitated by antecedent events and conditions together with the laws of nature. We therefore look for an explanation for everything, including the way in which we choose to act. Any decision made has a cause. If this is the case then **hard determinism**, a term coined by William James in 1884, takes the no-nonsense line that everything that occurs in the universe has a sufficient explanation through causes and conditions. This is what we call the law of cause and effect. Our actions, the ones we actually do, are the only ones that we can do. Therefore, human beings are not free to act; free will is no more than an illusion. It is illogical to speak of 'free' choice or 'free' will because it is clear from observing the interaction of phenomena that everything is determined by causality.

Human beings have preconditioned, programmed choices over which they have no control. One implication of this thinking is that it would make no sense to praise good deeds, for example, because the person who did them had no alternative. Neither can a person be blamed for a bad deed. Our behaviour could not have occurred other than it did.

The idea of determinism is very different from fatalism. Fatalism is the theory that all events are destined to occur no matter what we choose. Whereas determinism looks to Natural Laws and cause-effect relations, fatalism looks to the wills of gods, divine foreknowledge or mystic forces to guarantee those events will happen. Determinism is also very different from the idea of predestination. Predestination is the doctrine that God has foreordained souls to either salvation or damnation. Whereas determinism has no concept of some final goal, predestination is all about final goals foreordained by God.

Various forms of predestination also accept the notion of limited free will. It is limited free will in that God is in ultimate control and his final purposes cannot be thwarted. However, it is argued that God also holds us responsible for our actions so allows us some free choices.

> **Key terms**
>
> **Determinism:** the doctrine that the past determines a unique future. Every event, including human action is determined by previously existing causes
>
> **Hard determinism:** the doctrine that determinism is true and hence no human actions are free

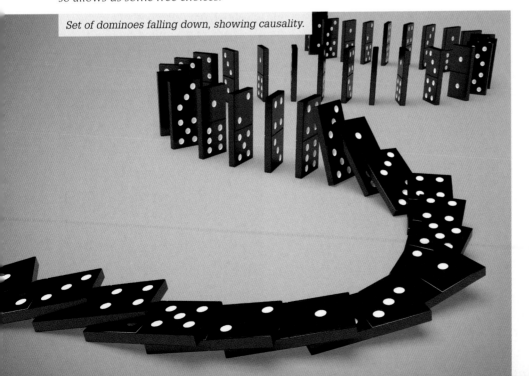

Set of dominoes falling down, showing causality.

Study tip

If you are asked about determinism on an exam, do not speak about theological concepts of predestination. Determinism is a philosophical concept which involves empirical notions of cause and effect and philosophers covered in this section.

Philosophical determinism (John Locke – free will is an illusion)

John Locke (1632–1704) was an English philosopher who is usually considered the first of the British Empiricists and a leading Enlightenment thinker. He argued that all our ideas are ultimately derived from experience and so our knowledge is limited in both scope and certainty.

In his book *An Essay Concerning Human Understanding* (Book 2, Chapter 21), Locke developed views on the nature of freedom of action and freedom of will. There were several editions of the book and his ideas developed in some areas in the later editions.

First, he distinguished between voluntary and involuntary actions. For action A to be voluntary, it must be caused by a volition to do A (e.g. raising your arm to show you want to say something or ask a question). For an action to be involuntary, it must be an action performed without a volition. This includes actions preceded by the right kind of volition but not caused by the volition. An example might be of someone pushing my arm up or a convulsive leg motion caused by an illness. Locke noted that voluntary actions often feel free and we seem to have the power to choose certain thoughts and actions. He called this power the will, which he then went on to consider. In particular, he considered whether the will is itself free.

In the first edition of his book he argued that the will was determined. However, in the later editions he qualified this slightly, arguing that although the most pressing desires for the most part determine the will, there are occasions when the will weighs them against other desires which may change their preference. Some regard this later view as moving towards a form of soft determinism (see page 182).

Locke regarded the idea of freedom as the idea of a power in a person to do any particular action, according to the determination or thought of the mind. Therefore, freedom is not an idea belonging to volition or preference, but to the person having the power of action according to whatever their mind chooses. On this understanding, Locke regarded the question of free will (whether the will is free) as 'altogether improper'. Both the will and freedom are powers, and it is absurd, he argued, to suppose that powers are capable of having powers. As Locke writes 'A person in respect of willing any action in their power once proposed to their thoughts cannot be free.' In other words, free will was an unintelligible concept since the concept of freedom cannot be put alongside the concept of the will.

Key quotes

Hard determinists say that our actions are caused in a way that makes us not as free as we might have thought, so that responsibility, if it implies free will, is an illusion. (Lacey)

It follows ... about states of the brain as effects, as correlates and as causes, that on every occasion when we decide or choose, we can only decide or choose as in fact we do. (Honderich)

Any other future set of outcomes than the one fixed from eternity is impossible. (James)

There is no absolute or free will, the mind is determined to wish this or that by a cause. (Baruch Spinoza)

quickfire

4.16 Explain the difference between determinism and predestination.

quickfire

4.17 Why did John Locke think that the idea of free will was an unintelligible concept?

John Locke

John Locke – man in bedroom illustration

In the light of Locke's conclusion about the phrase free will, he commented, 'I think the question is not proper, whether the will be free, but whether a man be free.' In other words, freedom and liberty are about whether a person is free to enact their will and not about whether our wills are somehow free. In Book 2 Chapter 21 of *An Essay Concerning Human Understanding*, Locke illustrates his understanding of freedom in his example of the man in the bedroom:

'Again: suppose a man be carried, whilst fast asleep, into a room where is a person he longs to see and speak with; and be there locked fast in, beyond his power to get out: he awakes, and is glad to find himself in so desirable company, which he stays willingly in, i.e. prefers his stay to going away. I ask, is not this stay voluntary? I think nobody will doubt it: and yet, being locked fast in, it is evident he is not at liberty not to stay, he has not freedom to be gone. So that liberty is not an idea belonging to volition or preferring; but to the person having the power of doing, or forbearing to do, according as the mind shall choose or direct. Our idea of liberty reaches as far as that power, and no farther. For wherever restraint comes to check that power, or compulsion takes away that indifferency of ability to bear acting, their liberty, and our notion of it, presently ceases.'

In the illustration, Locke concludes that the man is not free, and it is his ignorance of the fact that the door is locked, that gives him this illusion of freedom. Locke considers freedom with respect to actions. The illustration shows that though the man wills to stay in the room and it is therefore a voluntary action, this is not sufficient for freedom. If the man wills to leave the room, he cannot. He does not have the power to as the room is locked. Therefore, in this respect, he is not free. The man can only stay in the room though he has the illusion that he chose voluntarily.

Locke also considers freedom with respect to avoiding willing an action. He argues that human beings are not free to do this. Determinism, which Locke believed in, implies that what a person does is what they willed, and it could not be otherwise. Therefore, a person having willed an action cannot but do it. In other words, he is not free to avoid willing the action.

Finally, Locke considers whether a person is free with respect of willing a particular action. Because of determinism, only the willed action is enacted. No alternative action is possible since it is not willed. Therefore, the person is not free with respect to willing a particular action, other than the one they have willed.

In all these ways, Locke shows that no human actions are free. Therefore, he is often seen as a classic example of a hard determinist.

Key quotes

For how can we think anyone freer, than to have the power to do what he will? (Locke)

… freedom consists in the dependence of the existence, or not existence of any *action*, upon our *volition* of it; and not in the dependence of any action, or its contrary, on our preference. (Locke)

Key quotes

… liberty being as little applicable to the will, as swiftness of motion is to sleep, or squareness to virtue. (Locke)

… Liberty, which is but a power belongs only to agents, and cannot be an attribute or modification of the will, which is also but a power. (Locke)

quickfire

4.18 How did Locke illustrate his view that a person is not free?

Specification content

Hard determinism: scientific
(biological determinism – human
behaviour is controlled by an
individual's genes).

Genetic fixity

Human Genome Project

Key terms

DNA: deoxyribonucleic acid, or DNA,
is the hereditary material in humans.
Nearly every cell in a person's body has
the same DNA and it carries genetic
instructions

Genes: a unit of heredity and is
a region of DNA that influences
a particular characteristic of an
organism

Genome: the genetic material of an
organism. A person's complete genetic
code

Human Genome Project: an
international scientific research
project with the goal of determining
the sequences that make up human
DNA, and of identifying and mapping
all of the genes of the human genome
from both a physical and a functional
standpoint

Scientific determinism (biological determinism – human behaviour is controlled by an individual's genes)

In 1814, in an introduction to his book *A Philosophical Essay on Probabilities 1814*, Pierre-Simon Laplace postulated a super-intelligence that could know the positions, velocities, and forces on all the particles in the universe at one time, and thus know the universe for all times. This view marked the beginnings of scientific determinism. It claimed that given the initial state of a system, we can determine any future state by applying the laws of nature and the information about the initial state. In other words, the future occurrence of an event is predictable.

Key quotes

We may regard the present state of the universe as the effect of its past and the cause of its future. (Laplace)

The law of causation, according to which later events can theoretically be predicted by means of earlier events, has often been held to be *a priori*, a *necessity* of thought, a category without which science would not be possible. (Russell)

The loss of particles and information down black holes meant that the particles that came out were random. One could calculate probabilities, but one could not make any definite predictions. Thus, the future of the universe is not completely determined by the laws of science and its present state, as Laplace thought. God still has a few tricks up his sleeve. (Hawking)

In more recent times, biological determinism has gained support furthered by the claim that the development of a person is determined by their genetic inheritance and human behaviour is determined by **genes** and other biological attributes. This denies free will since it implies that human beings have no internal control over their behaviour and so are devoid of responsibility for their actions.

This view was developed considerably by the discovery of **DNA** (deoxyribonucleic acid). The discovery of DNA was a gradual process and had several important contributors including Nikolai Koltsov (1872–1940) and Frederick Griffith (1879–1941) but it wasn't until James Watson (b1928) and Francis Crick (1916–2004) developed the double-helix model of DNA structure in 1953, that this theory was universally accepted in the scientific community.

The theory of genetic fixity states that the genes of parents inevitably determine the characteristics of their children. Therefore, some claim that a child's characteristics, health and even future behaviour, is determined at the moment of conception. The **Human Genome Project** (1990–2003) attempted to map the genes of the human genome. Although the project was not able to sequence all the DNA found in human cells, it did sequence 92%. The work on interpretation and analysis of **genome** data is still ongoing but some of the findings of the project were seen to support genetic fixity. For example:

(i) Criminality and violent behaviour

In a survey of the prison population from 131 countries, it was found that 96% were male. This seems overwhelming evidence that there is a correlation between the Y chromosome (with its unique set of genes) and criminality. In 2014 a study was published in the journal *Molecular Psychiatry* based on a genetic analysis of almost 900 offenders in Finland. Amongst those who had a history of repeated violent behaviour, they identified two genes they had in common that appeared thirteen times more likely in that group than the rest of the sample. It was also found that the association between genes and previous behaviour was strongest for the 78 who fitted the 'extremely violent offender' profile.

(ii) Psychiatric illnesses

In 2013, the *Lancet* reviewed the findings of a study that analysed genetic data from more than 30,000 people with autism, ADHD, depression, bipolar disorder or schizophrenia and compared it with genetic sequences of more than 27,000 people who did not have these conditions. They concluded that common genetic variations were associated with all five disorders. These included variations in two genes that code for the cellular machinery that helps regulate the flow of calcium into neurons.

(iii) Addiction

Research has shown that addiction is influenced by genes, although no single gene has ever been isolated for people who get addicted to drugs, gambling or smoking. Studies have been carried out based on large families or identical twins, when they have a history of addiction. They compare DNA sequences of family members who are affected by addiction with those who are not, and they look for pieces of DNA that are shared among affected individuals and less common in the unaffected. Because of the complexities of human life, researchers often use mice to learn about genetics of addiction.

A number of genetic clusters have been identified that affect behaviour and mood and so could be connected with addiction. Genes on eight chromosomes have been linked to chemical dependence. However, one difficulty is separating between genes and environmental factors as influences on addiction.

(iv) Sexual orientation

In December 2017 *New Scientist* reported that a study comparing DNA from 1077 homosexual men and 1231 heterosexual men had pinpointed two genes whose variants seem to be linked to sexual orientation. One gene is on chromosome 13 which is in the brain region containing the hypothalamus. Interestingly, the neuroscientist Simon LeVay had, as early as 1991, already discovered that the hypothalamus differed in size between homosexual and heterosexual men. The other gene identified is found on chromosome 14 and mainly active in the thyroid.

However, many factors play a role including the environment. Many people would see this as explaining why sexual orientation might be considered more a spectrum and would include bisexuals. Little research has been carried on homosexuality in women (lesbianism) or on people who are asexual.

Overall, the latest research adds evidence that sexual orientation is not a 'lifestyle choice'.

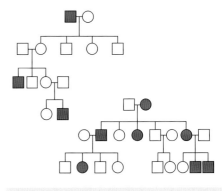

Can addiction be inherited?

Key quotes

The latest findings open the prospect to identifying the whole pathway of genes involved in both homosexual and heterosexual orientation. (Dr Dean Hamer, *New Scientist* 7 December 2017)

In the fertilised egg, the genetic program is complete. (Christiane Nusslein-Volhard)

quickfire

4.19 State four areas that could be referred to that might illustrate possible genetic fixity.

Gay Pride has long advocated scientific support for genetic links to sexual orientation, demonstrating that individuals are 'born this way'.

Biological determinism appears to support the view that a person's destiny is written into their genome. This can lead to genetic fatalism that subverts the idea of personal responsibility. If this is the case, then by extension we should not be held criminally responsible for our actions. Certainly, such a defence has been argued for in some criminal trials. For example, in Italy in 2009 Stefania Albertani pleaded guilty to the murder of her sister and an attempt to murder her parents. Her sentence was reduced from life in prison to 20 years based on neuroscience and behavioural genetics evidence. However, where genetics evidence has been presented, to date most have been unsuccessful.

Scientists are careful not to give the impression that there is any such entity as a 'gene for' some human trait. Nevertheless, research also makes it clear that genes make a significant contribution to our personality differences.

Psychological determinism (Ivan Pavlov – classical conditioning)

Whilst biological determinism sees the sources of determinism as being internal, e.g. genes, psychological determinism sees the sources as external, e.g. conditioning or reinforcement. One particular form of psychological determinism is behaviourism. One branch of behaviourism is classical conditioning, which is learning by association or reflex learning. A Russian psychologist named Ivan Pavlov (1849–1936) discovered this by accident whilst he was conducting experiments on digestion in dogs. He began to study what triggers dogs to salivate. They should produce saliva when presented with food as the saliva helps break down food. However, he noticed that they started drooling when they saw lab coats, even though no food was in sight. He realised that the dogs made an association between lab coats (the people who fed Pavlov's dogs wore lab coats) and food appearing. So he ran a study in which he rang a bell every time he fed the dogs. Before long, just ringing the bell made the dogs salivate. This was an example of classical conditioning that is learned. The dogs had been conditioned to produce the unconditioned reflex of saliva to the neutral stimulus of the bell.

Specification content

Hard determinism: psychological (Ivan Pavlov – classical conditioning).

Pavlov

Key terms

Behaviourism: also known as behavioural psychology, is a theory of learning based on the idea that all behaviours can be explained without the need to consider internal mental states or consciousness

Conditioning: a theory that the reaction to an object or event by a person can be determined by stimuli

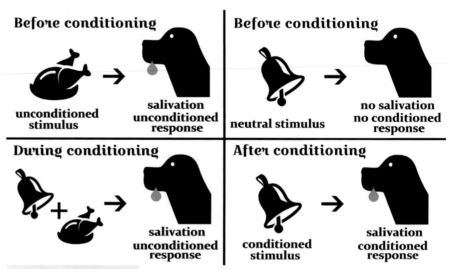

Pavlov's dog experiment

An American psychologist John Watson (1878–1958) and Rosalie Rayner (1898–1935), who later became his wife, furthered Pavlov's work by attempting to show the same conditioning also happens in human beings. He took a baby of nine months, popularly known today as Little Albert and exposed the child to a series of stimuli including a white rat, a rabbit and burning newspapers and each observed the child's reaction. The child showed no fear of any of the objects he was shown.

The next time Albert was shown the rat, Watson made a loud noise by hitting a metal pipe with a hammer. As expected, the child began to cry. After repeatedly pairing the white rat with the loud noise, Albert began to cry simply at seeing the rat. This demonstrated that emotional responses could be conditioned in human beings.

Watson and Rayner also found that Albert had generalised his fear to other furry objects including Raynor's fur coat and Watson wearing a Santa Claus beard.

Following Pavlov and Watson, some of the behaviourist school of thought in psychology started to argue that the concept of free will was simply an illusion. They believed that all human action was the direct result of conditioning. One such supporter was an American psychologist named B.F. Skinner, who referred to this view as 'radical behaviourism'.

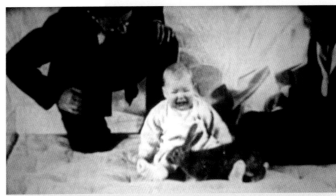

A study of Little Albert has suggested that free will may well be an illusion if we can be conditioned.

Skinner proposed a further development of classical conditioning, called operant conditioning. Here a person is conditioned to always repeat behaviour that is rewarded, but not repeat behaviour that is punished. Through operant conditioning, an individual makes an association between a particular behaviour and a consequence. Reinforcement comes in two forms:

Positive reinforcers – favourable events or outcomes given to the individual after the desired result (e.g. rewards).

Negative reinforcers – removal of an undesired or unpleasant outcome after the desired behaviour.

The behaviourists argued that the mind is not directly observable and so cannot be fully understood, so behaviourism focuses on observable physical reactions of people to stimuli.

However, some neuroscientists argue that we are all just a bundle of electrical impulses and our behaviour is 100% predictable. In the 1980s, a neuroscientist named Benjamin Libet (1916–2007) conducted a series of experiments which famously claimed to have proven that free will was simply a trick of the mind. The Libet experiments were able to show that activity occurs in the brain a fraction of time before we act on it. According to Libet, our brain decided for us and we acted on impulse, only later coming to believe we had chosen the action. This outcome, while widely regarded for a time as evidence, has now been regarded as just a theory. Many neuro-philosophists are unconvinced that this detectable activity in our brains can actually prove that no level of consciousness was involved in the decision. Perhaps, they surmise, the formula is more like subconscious activity – the brain is activated, action is taken, and finally post-action reflection, or conscious thought takes place.

AO1 Activity

Work in groups of three. Firstly, divide the three types of hard determinism argument (philosophical, scientific and psychological) between the three of you – one each. Each person summarises their type of determinism in no more than 80–100 words. Each person then presents their summary to the other two people in their group.

The other two members of the group discuss whether anything should be added or deleted from the summary, giving their reasons.

The three summaries are then exchanged with another group to read and they discuss whether they think they are good summaries.

The strengths and weaknesses of some of the summaries are then shared in a plenary session.

Key quotes

Give me a dozen healthy infants, well-formed, and my own specified world to bring them up in and I'll guarantee to take any one at random and train him to become any type of specialist I might select – doctor, lawyer, artist, merchant-chief and, yes, even beggar-man and thief, regardless of his talents, penchants, tendencies, abilities, vocations and the race of his ancestors. (John Watson)

Men believe themselves to be free, simply because they are conscious of their actions and unconscious of the causes. (Spinoza)

Man has no will, intention, self-determinism or personal responsibility. (Skinner)

Responses that produce a satisfying effect in a particular situation become more likely to occur again in that situation, and responses that produce a discomforting effect become less likely to occur again in that situation. (Edward Thorndike)

quickfire

4.20 Explain the difference between classical conditioning and operant conditioning.

Specification content
Soft determinism: Thomas Hobbes
(internal and external causes).

Key terms

Classical soft determinism: a theory that believes that a human action can be called free when the beings have an element of freedom despite their moral choices being completely determined by outside factors

Compatibilism: a theory that believes that freedom and determinism are mutually compatible in the case of some human actions. There is no logical inconsistency in believing in both

Origination: the bringing-about of decisions and actions in such a way that these are not effects from a chain of cause and effect, they are in control of the person

Key quotes

If determinism is true, as the theory of soft determinism holds it to be, all those inner states which cause my body to behave in whatever ways it behaves must arise from circumstances that existed before I was born; for the chain of causes and effects is infinite, and none could have been the least different, given those that preceded. (Taylor)

Man is free when he chooses what he wants, but he cannot will what he wants. (Schopenhauer)

Life is like a game of cards. The hand that is dealt you represents determinism; the way you play it is free will. (J. Nehru)

quickfire

4.21 Explain the difference between hard determinism and soft determinism.

Soft determinism

William James coined the terms 'hard determinism' and 'soft determinism' in an address to Harvard Divinity School in 1884 that was published later that year. Soft determinism is an attempt to combine the opposing theories of hard determinism and libertarianism (the idea that we can be totally free in our moral decision making). The theory argues that people are determined but nonetheless still free. This is because of the understanding of 'free'. To a soft determinist, being free is about being able to do what one wants to do, without external coercion or interference from anyone else. It accepts that human actions have causes (background, genetics, education, etc.) but they are free if actions are caused by our choices rather than external forces. Soft determinism is sometimes called **compatibilism.** This is not a proposition that determinism is consistent with free will or **origination**. It is not claimed that we can both originate choices and also be subject to causal necessity. Rather, it sees freedom (which is not the same as free will) and determinism working together. There is a causal story for my action.

Study tip

Remember that soft determinism is not a combination of fatalism and free will. It accepts determinism and redefines free will in terms of a freedom to act.

Indeed, freedom requires determinism in order to make sense of things, otherwise everything would be random with no explanation. Freedom involves the empowerment to act and thus control the desired effect. A. J. Ayer stated this clearly when he wrote: 'If I suffered from a compulsion neurosis, so that I got up and walked across the room, whether I wanted to or not ... then I should not be acting freely. But if I do it now, I shall be acting freely. ... For it is not when my action has any cause at all, but only when it has a special sort of cause, that it is reckoned not to be free.'

This view of our actions allows for moral responsibility, whilst hard determinism does not. The soft determinist theories of Thomas Hobbes and A. J. Ayer are known as **classical soft determinism**. Classical soft determinism is the claim that determinism is true and that we act freely when we are not constrained or coerced.

Modern forms of soft determinism

Some more recent variations of soft determinism have challenged this limited view of freedom meaning no constraints, and argued that some of the determining factors can be overcome. Peter Vardy (b1945) argues that our intellect is capable of understanding the effects of conditioning and genetics. Being aware of such forces and influences can lead to more freedom and towards a path of self-determination. Vardy admits that true freedom may never be achieved because of the complexity of genetic and environmental influences on us; however, this does not mean that freedom is not possible at all.

Robert Kane (b1938) takes a similar view in which he refers to a 'torn decision', in which a person has equally powerful reasons for choosing either way between two alternatives. Whatever way they choose, the person is making a rational decision and Kane claims that the person is therefore in control of the decision. The decision was caused by the person's efforts. Kane is an example of a philosopher that sees no problems with free will in the face of indeterminism and causal relationships (see pp.254–255).

Daniel Dennett (b1942) sees intelligence as the key feature. He argues for a concept of freedom that is a highly developed ability, refined in the course of evolution, enabling us to envisage future possibilities and to avoid those we don't like. Dennett sees this as compatible with determinism and is all that is required for us to be regarded as free. In essence, this modern approach is proposing that we can 'step outside' of ourselves to reflect on what we have become and decide whether we want to remain that way. This self-awareness allows us to be free to make new decisions.

Thomas Hobbes

Thomas Hobbes (1588–1679) is probably most well-known for his book *Leviathan* (1651), written during the English Civil War. In the book, Hobbes compares the state to the mythical biblical monster 'Leviathan', which is mentioned six times in the Bible, e.g. Psalm 104:26. A supporter of the Royalists, the book discusses civil government and Hobbes sets out the social contract theory (an implicit agreement to give up some rights by those being governed for protection by those governing).

Thomas Hobbes

A few years earlier in 1645, the Marquess of Newcastle had invited the philosopher Thomas Hobbes and the then Bishop of Derry John Bramhall to his house in Paris to have a philosophical discussion about human freedom. All three men were supporters of the Royalists during the English Civil War and all three had been forced to flee and live abroad. Resulting from that debate, Hobbes wrote a treatise *Of Liberty and Necessity*. Although this was written as a private exchange with Bramhall, it was later published in 1654 without permission. This drew a response from Bramhall to which Hobbes responded with *The Question concerning Liberty, Necessity and Chance* (1656).

Internal and external causes

Hobbes was a determinist who believed that everything that happens, including every human action, was the necessary effect of antecedent causes. However, he also argued that there are free actions, but he conceived freedom in such a way that it is consistent with necessity. Hobbes was also a materialist and rejected the idea of a will as a distinct part of the mind. He saw desire as the thing that motivates a person to act.

He therefore denied that choosing or willing are about some special kinds of rational power uniquely possessed by human beings. For Hobbes, there was no such power as 'the will'. He also rejected the idea that a being could determine itself. In his treatise, Hobbes states 'nothing takes beginning from itself, but from the action of some other immediate agent without itself'.

So what is Hobbes' conception of freedom or liberty?

He defined it as the absence of external impediments (i.e. those that are not contained in the nature of intrinsic quality of the agent). In this sense a person is as free as an unimpeded river. A river that flows down a hill necessarily follows a channel. However, it is also at liberty to flow within the channel. He claimed that the voluntary actions of people are similar. To be at liberty is not to be restrained, which is not the same as to be uncaused. People are free because their actions follow from their will (desires). The actions, however, are necessary in the sense that they originate from a chain of causes and effects. Freedom is all about acting as we will and not being coerced in any way.

Therefore, an **internal cause** refers to the willing to do an act and actually doing it or the forbearing to do an act and the will to forbear. In such cases the action is voluntary. This includes actions that are compelled since it works upon the desires of the person and causes the action. As an example of compulsion Hobbes stated, 'A man is said to be compelled when fear makes him willing to do something, as when a man willingly throws his goods into the sea to save himself.'

In contrast, an **external cause** refers to coercion or force and makes the act involuntary since it is against the agent's will (desire). Hobbes used the example of 'when a man by force, seizing on another man's limbs, moves them as himself, not as the other man pleases … the action so done is not the action of him that suffers, but of him that uses the force.'

Key quote

When first a man has an appetite or will to something, to which immediately before he had no appetite nor will, the cause of his will is not the will itself, but something else not in his own disposing. So that whereas it is out of controversy that of voluntary actions the will is the necessary cause, and by this which is said the will is also caused by other things whereof it disposes not, it follows that voluntary actions have all of them necessary causes and therefore are necessitated. **(Hobbes)**

Key terms

External cause: when a person's will is stopped from carrying out its predetermined choice

Internal cause: internalised moral choice (or the person's will to do something) that is completely determined

quickfire

4.22 Explain the difference between an internal and external cause, according to Hobbes.

An unimpeded river

Specification content

Soft determinism: A. J. Ayer
(caused acts vs forced acts).

Key quotes

We began with the assumption that freedom is contrasted with causality, so that a man cannot be said to be acting freely if his action is causally determined. But this assumption has led us into difficulties and I now wish to suggest that it is mistaken. For it is not, I think, causality that freedom is to be contrasted with, but constraint. (Ayer)

But now we must ask how it is that I come to make my choice. Either it is an accident that I choose to act as I do, or it is not. If it is an accident, then it is merely a matter of chance that I did not choose otherwise; and if it is merely a matter of chance that I did not choose otherwise, it is surely irrational to hold me morally responsible for choosing as I did. But if it is not an accident that I choose to do one thing rather than another, then presumably there is some causal explanation of my choice: and in that case we are led back to determinism. (Ayer)

A. J. Ayer

Key term

Logical Positivism: school of Western philosophy that sought to legitimise philosophical discussion by arguing philosophical language should be based on scientific language

A. J. Ayer (caused acts vs forced acts)

A. J. Ayer (1910–1989) was a British philosopher, particularly known for the development of **Logical Positivism**. Like Hobbes before him, Ayer supported classical soft determinism. He argued that a person who did action A could be considered to have acted freely if that person could have refrained from doing action A. The fact that an action A can be explained by a cause did not mean that it was not therefore a free action. For Ayer, the key factor involved is constraint. Indeed, his empirical studies of language showed him that people make a language distinction between hard determinism and soft determinism. He stated that if he walked across a room because someone compelled him to, observers would conclude he was not acting freely and that this 'forced' movement was completely determined. However, if he walked across a room without being compelled by another, observers would still assume it had a cause because all actions must be willed by the person, even if our will is determined. In this case, however, they would not say he was 'forced'. Therefore, for Ayer, it all centred on what is considered as a 'constraint'.

He put forward three conditions that identified a person's action as constrained such that they could not have acted differently:

(i) Coercion – when a person is compelled by another to do the action (e.g. forced by gunpoint).

(ii) Habitual ascendancy – when a person does not engage in the deliberative process (e.g. a soldier under orders).

(iii) Internal constraint – when a person's deliberative process is irrelevant (e.g. kleptomania).

All actions have causes but it is a special cause that makes the action not free. Therefore, for a person to act freely, it means that they could have acted otherwise; and for this to happen Ayer argued three conditions had to be fulfilled:

(i) The person could have acted otherwise had they so chosen.

(ii) The person was not compelled by another person.

(iii) The person's action was voluntary and free from internal constraints.

In this way Ayer argued for soft determinism, since it is possible to explain the cause of the action and that the person could have acted otherwise. However, many might argue that it is difficult to identify an internal constraint. In particular, in Ayer's example of kleptomania, it is not clear whether the person could have chosen to stop stealing in a similar way that some alcoholics could stop drinking alcohol. Indeed, it is impossible to show that the person could have chosen to act differently in any given situation, since only one action resulted (i.e. the action they actually took).

Key quote

It may be said of the agent that he would have acted otherwise if the causes of his action had been different, but they being what they were seems to follow that he was bound to act as he did. (Ayer)

AO1 Activity

Draw up a table with three columns. Use one for Hobbes, one for Ayer and then one for similarities and differences. Write some key bullet points about their respective arguments for soft determinism and then in the final column identify key similarities and differences using + bullet for similarities and – bullet for differences.

AO1 Developing skills

It is now important to consider the information that has been covered in this section; however, the information in its raw form is too extensive and so has to be processed in order to meet the requirements of the examination. This can be done by practising more advanced skills associated with AO1. The exercises that run throughout this book will help you to do this and prepare you for the examination. For assessment objective 1 (AO1), which involves demonstrating 'knowledge' and 'understanding' skills, we are going to focus on different ways in which the skills can be demonstrated effectively, and also refer to how the performance of these skills is measured (see generic band descriptors for A2 [WJEC] AO1 or A Level [Eduqas] AO1).

▶ **Your task is this:** Below is a summary of **John Locke's hard determinist theory**. It is about 200 words long. This time there are no highlighted points to indicate the key points to learn from this extract. Discuss which five points you think are the most important to highlight and write them down in a list.

John Locke developed a philosophical determinism theory based on universal causation. This is the belief that all human actions and choices have a past cause and therefore all events that happen are determined by an unbreakable chain of past causes. The future must logically be as fixed and unchangeable as the past. William James later summed up this theory as 'the iron block universe'. From this theory Locke coined the phrase: 'free will is just an illusion'. People who believe they have free will think they do because they can pause and reflect before making a choice; Locke believed that all such thoughts were just the person's ignorance of universal causation. Indeed, Locke argued, most people do not have the intelligence to see that there are no choices at all to be made.

Locke developed the idea of universal causation by creating an analogy to illustrate the theory. His analogy starts with a man who wakes up in a room that, unknown to him, is locked from the outside. He chooses to stay in the room believing he has chosen freely to stay there. In reality, however, he has no option but to stay in the room, it is only his ignorance that the door is locked, that gives him an illusion of freedom.

Now make the five points into your own summary (as in Theme 1 Developing skills) trying to make the summary more personal to your style of writing. This may also involve re-ordering the points if you wish to do so.

1. ....

2. ....

3. ....

4. ....

5. ....

Key skills

Knowledge involves:

Selection of a range of (thorough) accurate and relevant information that is directly related to the specific demands of the question.

This means:

- Selecting relevant material for the question set

- Being focused in explaining and examining the material selected.

Understanding involves:

Explanation that is extensive, demonstrating depth and/or breadth with excellent use of evidence and examples including (where appropriate) thorough and accurate supporting use of sacred texts, sources of wisdom and specialist language.

This means:

- Effective use of examples and supporting evidence to establish the quality of your understanding

- Ownership of your explanation that expresses personal knowledge and understanding and NOT just reproducing a chunk of text from a book that you have rehearsed and memorised.

Specification content

The extent to which philosophical, scientific and/or psychological determinism illustrate that humanity has no free will.

Key terms

Nature: inborn or hereditary characteristics as an influence on or determinant of personality

Nurture: upbringing, education, and environment as an influence on or determinant of personality

Nature vs. nurture

AO2 Activity

As you read through this section try to do the following:

1. Pick out the different lines of argument that are presented in the text and identify any evidence given in support.

2. For each line of argument try to evaluate whether or not you think this is strong or weak.

3. Think of any questions you may wish to raise in response to the arguments.

This Activity will help you to start thinking critically about what you read and help you to evaluate the effectiveness of different arguments and from this develop your own observations, opinions and points of view that will help with any conclusions that you make in your answers to the AO2 questions that arise.

Issues for analysis and evaluation

The extent to which philosophical, scientific and/or psychological determinism illustrate that humanity has no free will

Philosophical determinism, such as that advocated by John Locke, views free will as an illusion. For Locke, free will was an unintelligible concept since the concept of freedom cannot be put alongside the concept of the will. Freedom and liberty are about whether a person is free to enact their will and not about whether our wills are somehow free. Hence, philosophical determinism rejects the idea of free will.

However, this view does not demonstrate that hard determinism is therefore correct. To deny one thing is not proof of another. Indeed, determinism is seen by some as self-refuting. If free will is an illusion and everything is predetermined, then the ultimate cause why a person believes that free will is an illusion must also be predetermined. Therefore, there can be no way of knowing whether free will is true or false.

Another line of argument would be to consider the case for free will (see section 4E). The twentieth-century philosopher, Jean-Paul Sartre argued that people create a self-deception of determinism, called 'bad faith'.

Another difficulty with determinism is that it cannot account for the commencement of activity, since the fundamental premise of determinism is that all activity is the effect of prior activity. So it is not clear what can be said to be prior to the commencement of activity.

Jean-Paul Sartre

Key quote

A person in respect of willing any action in their power once proposed to their thoughts cannot be free. **(Locke)**

One of the strengths of the case for determinism is that in everyday life we observe causality, and the idea of determinism is grounded in the principle of causality. We therefore look for an explanation for everything, including the way in which we choose to act and the decisions we make. Scientific determinism and psychological determinism claim to explain what those causes are acting on us that make us behave in a certain way. The debate between scientific determinism and psychological determinism is essentially a debate between **nature** and **nurture**. However, many would argue that it is limiting to describe behaviour solely in terms of either nature or nurture. Human behaviour is much more complex and at the very least is likely to be an interaction between both genes and conditioning. Indeed, there may be other factors that influence or determine how we act. Moreover, what is true and appropriate for the physical sciences is not necessarily true for the social and behavioural sciences.

One line of argument might be to challenge the claimed deterministic influence of our genes. Certainly, the flourishing of genomics in the twenty-first century has led people to believe that their destiny is written in their genome. Reports of the addiction gene and the violence gene have figured in the popular press. However, there is no gene for any complex human trait. Denis Alexander, in his Gifford lectures, made clear that thousands of genes collaborate together during human development in interaction with the environment to generate each individual's character. Even identical twins are not really genetically identical since they develop different profiles of **epigenetic** modification as they go through life. So having a Y chromosome with its unique set of genes, does not determine human criminality. Therefore, genes may contribute to our personality but they do not determine it.

Another approach might be to appeal to modern quantum mechanics and Heisenberg's uncertainty principle to argue that modern science is no longer so confident about causation. However, randomness is hardly what is envisaged when referring to free will. Though scientific study has not demonstrated that humanity is determined, it hasn't explained free will either.

Certainly, behaviourism does give evidence that implies human beings have no free will. Pavlov argued that all our actions are just conditioned reactions to our environment. This argument was supported by several eminent psychologists including John Watson and B. F. Skinner. For example, Skinner argued that people can be conditioned from a young age by a system of rewards and punishments for certain behaviours. However, such views have not gone unchallenged.

One of the main criticisms has been that it has derived its evidence from experiments on animals and their behaviour. It has then been assumed that any findings apply equally to human behaviour. However, it does not take into account the possibility of both voluntary and involuntary human behaviour. It assumed determinism was a true and full account of human behaviour. Boulding (*Behavioural and Brain Sciences 7*) comments that Skinner is making the big assumption that general laws relating to the behaviour of animals can be applied to describe the complex relations in the human world. If this assumption proves false, then the entire foundation upon which behaviourism rests will come crashing down.

Other criticisms of behaviourism have been voiced including by Seligman (*Psychological Review*) who argued that although behaviourism may explain phobias and neuroses, it was unable to explain the development of human language and memory. Others, such as Wyrwicka, see behaviourism as a contradiction of Darwin's ideas. He argued that the natural selection drive is dependent on what is necessary for the survival of the species, but behaviourism is more about sensory gratification. What is pleasurable to the senses is not always what is best for survival.

Others have appealed to the experience of emotion. If determinism is true then it is difficult to see why the human brain experiences emotion. It seems that the human brain cannot be fully measured and quantified to the point of predicting behaviour.

It could be argued that everyone who deliberates must believe in free will, for it is impossible to deliberate without acting on the conviction that the decision is up to you to resolve. However, the perception of more than one option during the deliberative process does not preclude determinism. The ultimate outcome of a decision-making process can be determined, meaning only one outcome is possible, but the individual may still consider multiple options, weighing pros and cons against each other while deciding. Even the decision-making process is determined, the extent of deliberation, the options considered, and the potential influences (both biological and psychological) that might affect such a decision.

Key quote

If actions were determined solely by external rewards and punishments, people would behave like weather vanes, constantly shifting in radically different directions to conform to the whims of others **(Bandura)**

Key quotes

Free actions, if there are any, are not deterministically caused nor are they caused by random processes of the sort countenanced by quantum physicists or complexity theorists. Free actions need to be caused by me, in a non-determined and non-random manner. **(Flanagan)**

To some extent we're all products of genetics and the environment but I don't think that robs us of free will or understanding right and wrong. **(Ferguson)**

AO2 Activity

List some conclusions that could be drawn from the AO2 reasoning from the above text; try to aim for at least three different possible conclusions. Consider each of the conclusions and collect brief evidence to support each conclusion from the AO1 and AO2 material for this topic. Select the conclusion that you think is most convincing and explain why it is so. Try to contrast this with the weakest conclusion in the list, justifying your argument with clear reasoning and evidence.

Specification content
Strengths and weaknesses of hard
and/or soft determinism.

Strengths and weaknesses of hard and/or soft determinism

One of the strengths of determinism is the clear evidence of causality. Evidence from biology and psychology can identify causal chains that explain why we act in certain ways. In contrast, free will lacks any explanation as to how it functions. Indeed, philosophical determinism as exemplified by people like John Locke, argues that the concept of free will is meaningless and contradictory.

An added strength of the case for determinism is its **cumulative argument**. Explanations in a variety of social sciences can account for our apparent choices. Various analogies have been used to illustrate this approach. For instance, if you have a leaky bucket (a weak argument) and insert other leaky buckets inside it (more arguments) then the leaks are sealed (i.e. the arguments gain strength). Others have been quick to point out that 0 + 0 = 0 (i.e. a failed argument added to another failed argument results in both failing).

Just because some events are clearly determined does not justify the widespread belief in an absolute universal determinism. Indeed, modern science casts some doubt about such confidence in causation and predictability. The development of quantum mechanics and indeterminism has challenged the traditional understanding of Newtonian views about cause and effect and predictability. This weakens the argument from causation, which is one of the determinists' main arguments. Those who argue for free will point out that to argue that there are no causes or to suggest actions are random or chaotic is not what is meant by free will.

Some may argue that the unpredictability is only at quantum levels and so does not affect actions of human beings. But the issue of the initial commencement of the chain of cause and effect remains a problem for the determinist. If the fundamental premise of determinism is that all activity is the effect of prior activity, it is not clear what can be said to be prior to the commencement of activity. If it is God then the debate moves into considerations of predestination and God's omnipotence.

Philosophy has also identified major weaknesses with the determinist position. One of the main problems involves moral responsibility. It is argued that a person is usually only considered to be morally responsible for what they have done if they could have done otherwise. When we say that someone did something because they were unable to do otherwise, we excuse them any moral responsibility since moral responsibility demands there is a real choice. If determinism is true then it implies that a person could not have done otherwise.

Other philosophers have challenged this view that moral responsibility requires alternative possibilities. Instead, they associate moral responsibility with control and reason. A person is morally responsible because the action resulted from the person's own reasons-responsive mechanism. This seems to allow for moral responsibility whilst accepting hard determinism.

Another approach that may mitigate the weakness of the determinist position is the counter-argument that states that in some sense, human beings do choose and deliberate, but only in a way that obeys Natural Laws. Indeed, the chain of events behind a particular cause may go back to uncaused creative events in our mind during deliberations. Also, a person's behaviour may be modified through punishment since it can be a deterrent and become a part of the causal chain.

In the case of soft determinism, the understanding of a free choice supports the view that a person is morally responsible or can be given credit for something. An action is considered free even if causally determined so long as the causes are non-constraining. The fact that a person not only performed the act, but wanted to perform the act, even when influenced by past events, makes the person morally

Key quote

A random event does not fit the concept of free will any more than a lawful one does, and could not serve as the long-sought locus of moral responsibility. (Pinker)

Key term

Cumulative argument: a series of arguments that gain collective force and are seen to corroborate the effectiveness of each single argument in the series

AO2 Activity

As you read through this section try to do the following:

1. Pick out the different lines of argument that are presented in the text and identify any evidence given in support.

2. For each line of argument try to evaluate whether or not you think this is strong or weak.

3. Think of any questions you may wish to raise in response to the arguments.

This Activity will help you to start thinking critically about what you read and help you to evaluate the effectiveness of different arguments and from this develop your own observations, opinions and points of view that will help with any conclusions that you make in your answers to the AO2 questions that arise.

responsible. Indeed, it could be argued that if free will has no causal chain then it implies it is random and so the person is not morally responsible.

One line of argument to highlight the weakness of determinism is the problem of self-refuting. If free will is an illusion and everything is predetermined, then the ultimate cause why a person believes that free will is an illusion must also be predetermined. Therefore, there can be no way of knowing whether free will is true or false.

Another issue that is raised against determinism is the experience a person has that they do in fact choose freely. It is impossible to deliberate without acting on the conviction that the decision is up to the person to resolve. I am free to deliberate. The philosopher Charles Pierce argued that a belief that cannot be consistently acted on cannot be true. People act as though they are in control and exercising a power of self-determination. However, there has been development of successful modern therapies for people who have mental disorders. These successes have occurred because of the predictive power and the control of human behaviour, i.e. a deterministic view of human behaviour.

Determinism assumes that people are theoretically 100% predictable since all their actions are caused. Many challenge such a view and point to actions that did not seem to be at all predictable. However, determinists will always claim that causes exist to account for behaviour even if all those causes cannot be identified. The difficulty is that determinism is unfalsifiable, since it is impossible to test. How is it possible to show that an action was not the result of some cause? Determinists might appeal to the difference between foresight predictability and hindsight predictability. Even though someone acts in a way that was not predictable, they would claim that with hindsight, it is clear why they acted as they did. Alternatively, determinists may claim that the

Determinism

more we know about patterns of human behaviour, the better our ability to predict actions will be.

Another line of argument could be to make the case for soft determinism. It is asserted that people are determined by internal causes but are free when they can act free from external causes. Ayer argued that people distinguished between the idea of hard determinism and soft determinism by the language they used. If hard determinism they spoke of being 'forced', whilst if soft determinism they used the term 'caused'. Freedom is when a person's actions are caused but not constrained. In response many would not agree that this is what is meant by freedom or free will.

Key quote

Either determinism is true or it's not. If determinism is true, then my choices are ultimately caused by events and conditions outside my control, so I am not their first cause and therefore … I am neither free nor responsible. If determinism is false, then something that happens inside me (something that I call 'my choice' or 'my decision') might be the first event in a causal chain leading to a sequence of body movements that I call 'my action'. But since this event is not causally determined, whether or not it happens is a matter of chance or luck. Whether or not it happens has nothing to do with me; it is not under my control any more than an involuntary knee jerk is under my control. Therefore, if determinism is false, I am not the first cause or ultimate source of my choices and … I am neither free nor responsible. (*Stanford Encyclopedia of Philosophy*)

AO2 Activity

List some conclusions that could be drawn from the AO2 reasoning from the above text; try to aim for at least three different possible conclusions. Consider each of the conclusions and collect brief evidence to support each conclusion from the AO1 and AO2 material for this topic. Select the conclusion that you think is most convincing and explain why it is so. Try to contrast this with the weakest conclusion in the list, justifying your argument with clear reasoning and evidence.

AO2 Developing skills

It is now important to consider the information that has been covered in this section; however, the information in its raw form is too extensive and so has to be processed in order to meet the requirements of the examination. This can be achieved by practising more advanced skills associated with AO2. For assessment objective 2 (AO2), which involves 'critical analysis' and 'evaluation' skills, we are going to focus on different ways in which the skills can be demonstrated effectively, and also refer to how the performance of these skills is measured (see generic band descriptors for A2 [WJEC] AO2 or A Level [Eduqas] AO2).

▶ **Your next task is this:** Below is an evaluation concerning **soft determinism**. It is about 200 words long. After the paragraph, there is an intermediate conclusion highlighted for you in yellow. As a group try to identify where you could add more intermediate conclusions to the rest of the passage. Have a go at doing this.

Another line of argument could be that soft determinism has strengths. Soft determinism can be seen as a strong argument because Hobbes assertion, that people are determined by internal causes but are free from external causes, is supported by the language used by people. Ayer, who argued this point, empirically studied that when a moral situation is soft determinist the person will use the phrase 'caused'. For example, suppose a person got into their car and drove to an ATM machine to take some cash out on their debit card because they needed some money to put in a birthday card to send to someone. Then, it could be argued that the person was 'caused' by an internal cause, a desire to send a gift. However, suppose a person is threatened and told to drive in their car to an ATM machine to withdraw cash and to hand the cash over. Then, in this case, the person is determined by an external cause and is an example of a hard determinist situation. The person will use the phrase 'forced' rather than 'caused'. Therefore, Ayer is clearly illustrating that soft determinism is a valid theory because it is illustrated by people in everyday language.

When you have done this, you will see clearly that in AO2 it is helpful to include a brief summary of the arguments presented as you go through an answer and not just leave it until the end to draw a final conclusion. This way you are demonstrating that you are sustaining evaluation throughout an answer and not just repeating information learned.

Key skills

Analysis involves:

Identifying issues raised by the materials in the AO1, together with those identified in the AO2 section, and presents sustained and clear views, either of scholars or from a personal perspective ready for evaluation.

This means:

- That your answers are able to identify key areas of debate in relation to a particular issue

- That you can identify, and comment upon, the different lines of argument presented by others

- That your response comments on the overall effectiveness of each of these areas or arguments.

Evaluation involves:

Considering the various implications of the issues raised based upon the evidence gleaned from analysis and provides an extensive detailed argument with a clear conclusion.

This means:

- That your answer weighs up the consequences of accepting or rejecting the various and different lines of argument analysed

- That your answer arrives at a conclusion through a clear process of reasoning.

C: The implications of determinism and predestination

The implications of hard determinism for moral responsibility: the worth of human ideas of rightness, wrongness and moral value

To hold someone morally responsible involves an attitude or feeling. It is an attitude of disapproval or approval with respect to an action. We measure actions against our standards of morality. We blame or praise people accordingly provided they had a real choice of action. If they could not have pursued any other course of action, then praise or blame seems inappropriate. It would seem that if hard determinism is true then none of us can be held morally responsible since people are unable to act differently from how they in fact acted.

Certainly, some philosophers have acknowledged the inconsistency between belief in determinism and moral responsibility. John Hospers (1918–2011) argued that moral choice 'is all a matter of luck'.

He argued that moral values are worthless because there is always some cause that compels a person to act in the way that they do.

Such a view has been used as a defence in a court of law. One of the most famous is that of two teenagers, Leopold and Loeb, who in 1924 admitted to killing a 14-year-old boy. Clarence Darrow was their lawyer at the trial and he claimed that the two teenagers 'were decidedly deficient in emotion' since they did not feel revolted by their act. The defence

The Leopold and Loeb trial 1924

was that they did not make a conscious choice between right and wrong since it was psychological, physical and environmental influences that controlled their behaviour. The result was that the judge sentenced them to life imprisonment rather than to death. How much that particular argument swayed the judge is not clear since Darrow also argued that no person under 21 who had pleaded guilty had ever been sentenced to death.

A different approach is to focus on the idea that morality is about something a person 'ought' to do. But if they ought to do an action then it assumes they are able to do it. However, hard determinism claims that they could not have acted differently. Therefore, there is no moral responsibility. Such a view about moral responsibility has implications for the way we view ourselves as moral beings. To what extent can we consider ourselves as being morally responsible?

It is important to understand that the argument that moral responsibility cannot exist does not mean that morality itself cannot exist. There is a difference between morality and moral responsibility.

This section covers AO1 content and skills

Specification content

The implications of determinism (hard and soft) on moral responsibility: the worth of human ideas of rightness, wrongness and moral value.

Key quotes

Why did they kill little Bobby Franks? Not for money, not for spite; not for hate. They killed him as they might kill a spider or a fly, for the experience. They killed him because they were *made* that way. Because somewhere in the infinite processes that go to the making up of the boy or the man something slipped, and those unfortunate lads sit here hated, despised, outcasts, with the community shouting for their blood. (Clarence Darrow at the trial of Leopold and Loeb)

Life calls the tune, we dance. (Galsworthy)

Any other future set of outcomes than the one fixed from eternity is impossible. (William James)

Man has no will, intention, self-determinism or personal responsibility (B. F. Skinner)

Punishment as punishment is not admissible unless the offender has the free will to select this course. (Darrow)

quickfire

4.23 Explain why a person is not responsible for their moral actions if hard determinism is true.

The implications of soft determinism for moral responsibility: the worth of human ideas of rightness, wrongness and moral value

Soft determinism argues that a free choice or action is one that is voluntary and accords with the person's desires and true nature. This understanding of a free choice supports the view that a person is morally responsible or can be given credit for something. The fact that a person not only performed the act, but wanted to perform the act, even when influenced by past events, makes the person morally responsible.

Another argument is that if a person had chosen differently, they would have acted differently. Therefore, they are morally responsible. In other words, choice creates moral responsibility.

However, many would argue that this is not enough for moral responsibility. Free and voluntary actions demand genuine choice where the chooser is free from mental conditioning caused by either previous behaviour or external influences. Therefore, the idea is often rejected that if soft determinism is true, a person can be held morally responsible.

As with hard determinism, it does not mean we always act immorally. Neither does it mean that morality does not exist. The process of causal determination does not affect whether an act is moral or immoral, but it does affect whether we can be held responsible. Neither hard nor soft determinism invalidate the concept of moral value – of rightness and wrongness. Determinism of any kind merely addresses the issue of moral accountability rather than the existence of morality itself.

The implications of hard determinism for moral responsibility: the value of blaming moral agents for immoral acts

Holding someone morally responsible may involve the desire for retribution and justice – a concern for those negatively affected by the immoral act and a desire that the person who did the immoral act is aware that others disapprove. If hard determinism is true, then how can these attitudes and feelings be addressed? As has been argued, hard determinism seems to imply that a person is not morally responsible.

However, hard determinism accepts that a person can be changed in the future and some form of blame and punishment could bring this about. Rewards and punishments have causal effects on people's behaviour. Punishment can be a means of reinforcing moral acts and discouraging immoral acts. The difficulty arises as to what would be the most appropriate punishment to bring about a correction of a tendency towards immoral acts. Ted Honderich in his book *How free are you?*, argues against retributive punishment – 'It cannot be that we should satisfy grievance by imposing great distress on other people. The means of great distress is not justified by the end of satisfaction.'

If there is no blame allocated to immoral acts, then the action results in being a possible contributing cause to future actions which lead to more undesirable outcomes.

The implications of soft determinism for moral responsibility: the value in blaming moral agents for immoral acts

The fact that we blame people implies they are responsible agents. We regard people as very different from, for example, an earthquake, in terms of 'blame'. In soft determinism, a person not only performs the act but they wanted to perform

Key quote

Without free will, we seem diminished, merely the playthings of external forces. How, then, can we maintain an exalted view of ourselves? Determinism seems to undercut human dignity, it seems to undermine our value. (Nozick)

Specification content

The implications of determinism (hard and soft) on moral responsibility: the value in blaming people for immoral acts.

quickfire

4.24 Name a legal case that has used hard determinism as a defence.

the act. They were not forced to against their desires. Acts are willed actions, however inevitably they might have followed from past events.

As with hard determinism, blame and punishment become part of the causal chain and so can influence future events and actions. The value in blaming is that disapproval is shown and so discourages immoral acts whilst encouraging moral acts.

The implications of hard determinism for moral responsibility: the usefulness of normative ethics

Normative ethics examine the sources of, and standards for, moral judgements. They act as a moral guide explaining what people should do and why, and whether their current moral behaviour is reasonable given whatever moral standards are being used in that context. An example of a normative ethic is the Divine Command Theory. This states that an action's status as moral or immoral is based on what God wills and commands. In Christianity, God's commands are claimed to be in the Bible. The Decalogue found in Exodus 20 is an example. Therefore, if this is the normative ethic being followed, then it is morally wrong to murder since a moral command in the Decalogue is 'You shall not murder'.

As with the issue of blame, the statement of the ethic can form part of the causal chain and so influence future actions. Though hard determinists would not agree that a person can freely choose to follow a particular ethic, they do accept that the normative ethic can influence actions.

The implications of soft determinism for moral responsibility: the usefulness of normative ethics

Classical soft determinism accepts that freedom to act depends on freedom to make a choice, regardless of the causal chain behind that choice. With soft determinism as well as hard determinism, normative ethics can influence later actions by being part of the causal chain and encouraging moral actions and discouraging immoral actions.

Specification content

The implications of determinism (hard and soft) on moral responsibility: the usefulness of normative ethics.

Key quote

Nature has placed humankind under the governance of two sovereign masters, pain and pleasure. (Bentham)

Moses receiving the Tablets of Law by Raphael (1518–1519).

AO1 Activity

Use three types of different coloured paper or flashcards to create some bullet points to use in answers that differentiate between:

1. The worth of human ideas of rightness, wrongness and moral value.
2. The value in blaming people for immoral acts.
3. The usefulness of normative ethics.

Key terms

Decalogue: a term for the Ten Commandments

Normative ethics: the study of how people ought to act morally

Specification content

The implications of predestination for religious belief: the implications for God's omnipotence and omnibenevolence, the use of prayer, the existence of miracles and the link between God and evil.

Implications of predestination for religious belief

Predestination

Whereas determinism is a philosophical concept which involves empirical notions of cause and effect, predestination implies that events are specifically directed by God rather than some neutral causal chain. For some, predestination is more about final goals, foreordained by God. It does not necessarily deny free will as such, though at no point can human free will thwart the plans and purposes of God. Others see predestination as a predetermination of all actions and events removing free will of any kind. Neither hard determinism nor soft determinism have any concept of some final goal since it sees the world as a 'closed' phenomenon of universal causation which is neutral regards final outcomes.

The implications of predestination for God's omnipotence

Although omnipotence is usually defined as unlimited power, many theologians and philosophers would want to qualify that definition. C. S. Lewis in his book *Problem of Pain*, argued that God's omnipotence means the 'power to do all that is intrinsically possible, not to do the intrinsically impossible … not because his power meets an obstacle but because nonsense remains nonsense even when we talk it about God.' Another qualification often cited is that God is able to do anything that is in accord with his own nature.

Clearly, predestination implies God's omnipotence since he orchestrates the final destiny of each human being. Both Jewish and Christian teachings make clear God's omnipotence. For instance, 'I know that you can do all things; no purpose of yours can be thwarted' (Job 42:2). Similarly, in the Qur'an it states in 76:30 'But you cannot will, unless Allah wills'. A person can do nothing without God, a human being is totally reliant upon God's omnipotent will.

Yet God also creates us as moral beings that are held responsible for our actions. Augustine opposed the teachings of the Celtic monk Pelagius because his free will theology, according to Augustine, seemed to diminish the omnipotent nature of God.

Aquinas reconciled freedom with predestination by arguing that not only is everything done that God wills to be done, but it is also done in the way God wants it to be done. The way omnipotence wants human acts done is freely. It is because God is all-powerful that human beings are free. God is all loving therefore God cannot use that power lovelessly.

Others argue that by choosing to create human beings with free will, God has chosen to limit his omnipotence. However, the free will is limited in that it cannot ultimately thwart the plans and purposes of God.

If God is all powerful, then could he not have created a species of human beings who always chose good and so would not fall and rebel against God? In such a case, none would fall from grace and all would be united with God.

The implications of predestination for God's omnibenevolence

The earliest record for the use of the word omnibenevolence is 1679 and it literally means 'willing all good'. This is usually equated with God being described as 'all-good' or 'infinitely good'. In a number of texts, the Bible presents God as always good. For example, Psalm 18:30 says 'As for God, his way is perfect; the word of the Lord is flawless'. Similarly, Psalm 100:5 'For the Lord is good and his love endures forever'.

Key quotes

But you cannot will, unless Allah wills. (Qur'an 76:30)

And if Allah had known any good in them He would have made them hear, and if He makes them hear they would turn back while they withdraw. (Qur'an 8:23)

quickfire

4.25 Briefly explain why predestination enhances the idea that God is omnipotent.

Many would argue that because humanity had fallen and inherited Adam's sin, then all deserve judgement from God. However, because God is omnibenevolent, he predestines some to be saved even though they do not deserve to be saved. The difficulty is that both Augustine and Calvin argue that God only predestines some people to be forgiven of their sins. It might be argued that if God is omnibenevolent then he would surely predestine everybody to salvation and forgiveness of their sins. Bertrand Russell (1872–1970) stated that God must be 'a monster', because 'a God that punishes or rewards on the basis of God's own eternal decisions in unfair and immoral'.

Some take predestination further and argue that all actions and events are predetermined by God and there is no free will. However, many reject this idea of predestination as it seems to imply God is the author of all sin.

Bertrand Russell

Key quotes

A God that punishes or rewards on the basis of God's own eternal decisions in unfair and immoral. **(Russell)**

If we are faithless, he [God] remains faithful, for he cannot disown himself. **(2 Timothy 2:13)**

The implications of predestination for the use of prayer

If God has predestined all actions and events, it is difficult to see how prayer could have any influence. If the purpose of prayer is to change an outcome then this seems to contradict the view that all things are preordained by God and so cannot change.

It might be argued that prayers that are in line with God's plans are the prayers that are answered. However, this would seem to make the purpose of praying redundant since the events would have happened regardless as they were part of God's plan.

quickfire

4.26 Briefly explain two reasons why predestination may suggest God is *not* omnibenevolent.

quickfire

4.27 Briefly explain why prayer maybe a pointless activity if God predestines all events.

Muslims at prayer

The Calvinist theory of unconditional election, (i.e. that it is God alone who chose the elect, based solely upon his own will, before the Earth was even created) also seems to question the value of prayer. Any attempt to pray to the divine to earnestly ask to become an elect would appear to be a complete waste of effort. However, perhaps prayer does have a use but only for the predestined elect. This is because prayer can be used to build a rapport with a God, including seeking forgiveness for sin. Calvin supports this when he stated that the 'elect' could still be sinful but God predestines them to have faith in the saving atonement of Jesus Christ. Therefore, when the predestinated elect sin they cannot resist the calling on their lives to seek forgiveness, which could be through prayer.

If God has determined all outcomes, then God has also determined the means by which those outcomes will take place (e.g. prayer). For instance, Elijah prayed for drought and then rain (1 Kings 18–19). If God had already determined that Elijah would pray for those events, such that the events would not have taken place if Elijah had not prayed for them.

Those who believe that predestination is about final outcomes and feel there is a place for free will within normal everyday events, have no problem in seeing prayer as an agent of change.

The implications of predestination for the existence of miracles

Aquinas defined a miracle is an event beyond the natural power of any created being. It has a 'divine cause' and so is not a normal part of the nature of things. He identified three kinds of miracles:

(i) Events in which God does something which nature could never do. For example, the sun going back on its course across the sky.

(ii) Events in which God does something which nature can do but not in this order. For example, someone living after death.

(iii) Events in which God does something that the working of nature usually does, but without the operation of the principles of nature. For example, someone being cured of an illness that usually takes much longer to cure.

Moses parting the Red Sea

In all three events God is active and this activity could have been pre-planned by a predestining omnipotent and omniscient God. Such a God knows the timing of all events past, present and future and therefore knows the timing of all miracles that he chooses to do. Predestination therefore, cannot be an issue here since God alone is involved in the decision about whether to perform a miracle, whether we have any free will or not.

Those who support the view of predestination that accepts free will in everyday actions and events, accept that God cannot control all earthly affairs, but argue that God can still achieve his goals by judicious intervention. They maintain that God can and frequently does override human freedom or intervene in the natural order (i.e. performs miracles) when he deems it necessary.

The implications of predestination for the link between God and evil

If God is omnipotent and omnibenevolent then the problem arises as to why there is evil. Both natural and moral evil can cause suffering and it would seem that God has both the power and the motivation to intervene. Predestination implies God is directing individuals to a final outcome. Therefore, one explanation is that the evil experienced is a necessary part of that route to the final outcome. Certainly, the Irenaean type theodicies argue that God is justified in allowing evil since it is part of his plan for soul-making. Equally it could be argued that God is not predestining a person to be evil but predestining them to seek forgiveness. The 'elect' are not without sin but rather they are predestined to have faith in Jesus Christ and ask for forgiveness and so be forgiven. They may sin but they cannot resist the calling on their lives to seek forgiveness. Predestination sees evil as humanity's fault. God predestines what a person does about their rebellion and sin.

Those who believe in the form of predestination that accepts free will in everyday actions and events might argue that free will allows for human beings to choose either good or evil. They would argue that God wanted human beings to be free and responsible agents and not to be automatons.

Key quote

God might not be considered the author of all sin. (Arminius)

AO1 Activity

For each of the following implications:

1. The implications of predestination on God's omnipotence.
2. The implications of predestination on God's omnibenevolence.
3. The implications of predestination on the use of prayer.
4. The implications of predestination on the existence of miracles.
5. The implications of predestination on evil.

Outline in 50 words:

(a) What possible problems there may be for a religious believer.

(b) How a religious believer could respond.

AO1 Developing skills

It is now important to consider the information that has been covered in this section; however, the information in its raw form is too extensive and so has to be processed in order to meet the requirements of the examination. This can be done by practising more advanced skills associated with AO1. The exercises that run throughout this book will help you to do this and prepare you for the examination. For assessment objective 1 (AO1), which involves demonstrating 'knowledge' and 'understanding' skills, we are going to focus on different ways in which the skills can be demonstrated effectively, and also refer to how the performance of these skills is measured (see generic band descriptors for A2 [WJEC] AO1 or A Level [Eduqas] AO1).

▶ **Your final task for this theme is:** Below is a summary of **how Darrow used the ethical theory of hard determinism**. It is 150 words long. This time there are no highlighted points to indicate the key points to learn from this extract. Discuss which five points you think are the most important to highlight and write them down in a list.

The Leopold and Loeb murder case of 1924 is an example of hard determinism being used by the defending counsel in a court of law in America. The defending lawyer was Clarence Darrow. Leopold and Loeb, two intelligent university students from affluent backgrounds, had been charged with the murder of a fourteen-year-old boy from a much less affluent background. It quickly became apparent that the two boys had murdered the other boy; however, Darrow used the theory of hard determinism in his defence argument in order to try and save Leopold and Loeb from capital punishment. Darrow argued that the boys had diminished responsibility because they were merely products of their affluent upbringing. Therefore, they had been predetermined to have a superiority complex over poorer individuals. Thus, they could not possibly be blamed for something they were always going to be and ultimately for what they were always going to do. As Darrow stated in the trial: 'Punishment as punishment is not admissible unless the offender has the free will to select this course'. Darrow's line of deterministic argument was successful because the boys' sentences were reduced to life imprisonment as opposed to the death penalty.

Now make the five points into your own summary (as in Theme 1 Developing skills) trying to make the summary more personal to your style of writing. This may also involve re-ordering the points if you wish to do so. In addition to this, try to add some quotations and references to develop your summary (as in Theme 2 Developing skills).

The result will be a fairly lengthy answer and so you could then check it against the band descriptors for A2 (WJEC) or A Level (Eduqas) and in particular have a look at the demands described in the higher band descriptors towards which you should be aspiring. Ask yourself:

- Does my work demonstrate thorough, accurate and relevant knowledge and understanding of religion and belief?
- Is my work coherent (consistent or make logical sense), clear and well organised?
- Will my work, when developed, be an extensive and relevant response which is specific to the focus of the task?
- Does my work have extensive depth and/or suitable breadth and have excellent use of evidence and examples? etc.

Key skills

Knowledge involves:

Selection of a range of (thorough) accurate and relevant information that is directly related to the specific demands of the question.

This means:

- Selecting relevant material for the question set
- Being focused in explaining and examining the material selected.

Understanding involves:

Explanation that is extensive, demonstrating depth and/or breadth with excellent use of evidence and examples including (where appropriate) thorough and accurate supporting use of sacred texts, sources of wisdom and specialist language.

This means:

- Effective use of examples and supporting evidence to establish the quality of your understanding
- Ownership of your explanation that expresses personal knowledge and understanding and NOT just reproducing a chunk of text from a book that you have rehearsed and memorised.

Issues for analysis and evaluation

Whether moral responsibility is an illusion

When considering this issue, it is important to identify what has to be the case for someone to be judged morally responsible. It is something a court of law does on many cases and influences the final sentencing. Age (very young) and mental state (psychologically/morally abnormal or underdeveloped) of a person are two criteria that challenge the degree of moral responsibility a person has. For instance, the plea that in the Darrow murder case the two accused teenagers did not make a conscious choice between right and wrong, may well have influenced the judge who imposed imprisonment rather than a death sentence. The defence lawyer at the murder of case of James Bulger, in 1993, used a similar line of defence. He argued that the two defendants had been predetermined to carry out the murder because they had been allowed to play violent video games and watch violent films from a young age; therefore, they were just repeating what they had seen. Therefore, it can be argued that moral responsibility is just an illusion because people just repeat behaviour they are taught from a young age.

It is in with the theories of determinism and free will that the issue becomes debatable. The compatibilists arguing that the truth of determinism would not undermine the underlying judgements of holding people morally responsible; whilst incompatibilists judge that someone is morally responsible could never be true if the world were deterministic.

The incompatibilists argue that if hard determinism is true then moral responsibility is indeed an illusion. The reason is that a person is usually only considered to be morally responsible for what they have done if they could have done otherwise. When we say that someone did something because they were unable to do otherwise, we excuse them any moral responsibility since we understand it to mean that when they did what they did, it was not because that was what they really wanted to do. John Hospers makes this point when he said that moral choice 'is all a matter of luck'. By this, he meant that because there are always causes that compel a person to act in the way that they do, they have no real choice, and moral responsibility demands there is a real choice. This requirement of a real choice is called the criteria of possible alternatives.

However, is this criterion about possible alternatives really the key? Harry Frankfurt (*The Importance of What We Care About*) has argued that although it is true that causal chains made it impossible for a person to avoid doing something, these circumstances actually played a role in bringing about what the person did. Therefore, they did it because that it was what they really wanted to do. The fact that they could not have done otherwise becomes irrelevant.

Fischer and Ravizza (*Responsibility and Control: A Theory of Moral Responsibility:1998*) have also argued that moral responsibility is possible with hard determinism. Their criterion for moral responsibility is similar to the plea in the Darrow murder case – a person must be able to recognise reasons why they are doing a particular action and so would react to at least one sufficient reason to do otherwise in a different situation. In other words, although they do not believe that moral responsibility requires alternative possibilities, they do associate moral responsibility with control and reason. A person is morally responsible because the action resulted from the person's own reasons-responsive mechanism. This allows for moral responsibility whilst accepting hard determinism.

Many might argue that the criteria should focus more on what we mean by morality. Morality is about something a person 'ought' to do. If they ought to do an action then it assumes they are able to do it. However, this implies that hard determinism and moral responsibility are incompatible, since hard determinism claims that they could not have acted differently.

This section covers AO2 content and skills

Specification content
Whether moral responsibility is an illusion.

Key quote
Among physically possible actions, only those which we actually think of are to be regarded as possible. When several alternative actions present themselves, it is certain that we can both do which we choose and choose which we will. In this sense all the alternatives are possible. What determinism maintains is that our will to choose this or that alternative is the effect of antecedents; but this does not prevent our will from being itself a cause of other effects. And the sense in which different decisions are possible seems sufficient to distinguish some actions as right and some as wrong, some as moral and some as immoral. (Russell)

Key quotes

Man has no will, intention, self-determinism or personal responsibility. (Skinner)

Our most excellent creator (God) wished us to be able to do either (be good or bad) ... this very capacity to do evil is also good – good, I say, because it makes the good part better by making it voluntary and independent. (Pelagius)

Man is not free not to be free. (Sartre)

.... man must rely upon his own fallible will and moral insight. He cannot escape choosing. (Sartre)

AO2 Activity

As you read through this section try to do the following:

1. Pick out the different lines of argument that are presented in the text and identify any evidence given in support.

2. For each line of argument try to evaluate whether or not you think this is strong or weak.

3. Think of any questions you may wish to raise in response to the arguments.

This Activity will help you to start thinking critically about what you read and help you to evaluate the effectiveness of different arguments and from this develop your own observations, opinions and points of view that will help with any conclusions that you make in your answers to the AO2 questions that arise.

The philosopher P.F Strawson made a major contribution to this debate in his essay *Freedom and Resentment* (1962). He rejected the theoretical judgement approach (i.e. whether the person has control or used reason or could have enacted other alternatives). He saw the key in the attitudes expressed in holding persons responsible – namely attitudes that derive from our participation in personal relationships, e.g. resentment, indignation anger, hurt feelings, gratitude. Strawson comments that the function of these attitudes is to express 'how much we actually mind, how much it matters to us, whether the actions of other people – and particularly some other people – reflect attitudes towards us of good will, affection, or esteem ... or contempt, indifference ...' He refers to these attitudes as participant reactive attitudes. So for Strawson the key to moral responsibility rests on interpersonal relationships and our reaction to others who are participants in such relationships. We can excuse people and we can argue that people may be justified and on such decisions, we regard them as outside the boundaries of the moral community. However, our holding the rest of people morally responsible is embedded in our way of life and our reaction to their attitude and actions in the relationship. In other words, our responsibility practices are inherently social. Hence, determinism is compatible with moral responsibility and is not an illusion.

How convincing Strawson is, is debateable. For instance, it is not clear how existing practices, that receive positive or negative reactions, can ever be modified. In fact, we do change our views about moral responsibility based on whether the person's actions were deterministic.

In 2005, in Hall County, Georgia, Stephen Mobley tried to avoid execution by claiming that his murder of a Domino's Pizza store manager was the result of a mutation in a specific gene, i.e. the Monoamine Oxidase A gene (MAOA). In the end, the judge turned down the appeal, saying that the law was not ready to accept such evidence. However, the basic idea that the MAOA gene is a determining cause of violence has now become widely accepted, and it is now commonly called the 'warrior gene'.

In the case of soft determinism, the understanding of a free choice supports the view that a person is morally responsible or can be given credit for something. The fact that a person not only performed the act, but wanted to perform the act, even when influenced by past events, makes the person morally responsible. In addition, the arguments that supported compatibilism with hard determinism would equally apply to soft determinism. However, if it is argued that choice creates moral responsibility, then it is also argued that genuine choice demands that that the chooser is free from mental conditioning caused by either previous behaviour or external influences. Therefore, the idea is often rejected that if soft determinism is true, a person can be held morally responsible.

If free will is true and we are free of deterministic factors, then it would seem difficult to see how it could be argued that moral responsibility is an illusion. Certainly, Pelagius argued that we were moral responsible beings.

Free will ticks all the boxes regards criteria necessary for moral responsibility. However, recent research by scientists from the Max Planck Institute for Human Cognitive and Brain Sciences has shown that some moments before we are aware of what we will do next – a time in which we subjectively appear to have complete freedom to behave however we please – our brain has already determined what we will do. We then become conscious of this decision and believe that we are in the process of making it. This suggests that free will is an illusion and therefore moral responsibility is an illusion. A counter-argument might be that although decisions are unconsciously prepared, we do not yet know where the final decision is made. Perhaps it should be noted that what is true and appropriate for the physical sciences is not necessarily true for the social and behavioural sciences.

Does the argument change when God is seen as in control of the universe? Belief in the Fall and the moral corruption of human beings may suggest that moral responsibility is an illusion. Augustine argued that we are 'so hopelessly corrupted that we are absolutely incapable of doing anything good by our own forces; free choice, if it means a choice between good and evil, has been utterly wasted by sin; our will, insofar as it is ours, and not God's, can merely do evil and desire evil'.

Yet God is portrayed as a moral God and we are made in his image – which implies that we are moral beings. Indeed, God holds us morally accountable. Throughout the Bible God calls on people to exercise a choice. For instance, Joshua charged Israel 'Choose for yourselves this day whom you will serve' (Joshua 24:15) and Jesus held people responsible, crying, 'O Jerusalem, Jerusalem … how often I have longed to gather your children together … but you were not willing' (Matthew 23:37). The issue that God predestines some to forgiveness and salvation does not necessarily change the view that we are still morally responsible for our actions.

Others, like Jacobus Arminius, argue that God has limited control since he does not force his will, via the Holy Spirit, onto people. However, it could be argued that Arminius' argument is watering down the worth of human moral responsibility because the Holy Spirit acts as the person's moral guide, it does not come from their own 'will'.

As was stated earlier, the idea that people have free will, and therefore that people have moral responsibility, is enshrined in the UK legal system. The criminal courts accept what is known as 'rational choice theory', unless there is a very specific reason not to, for example certified mental illness. Rational choice theory is the belief that people are reasoning agents who freely weigh up means and ends, costs and benefits, and therefore make freely willed rational choices when committing an illegal act. Therefore, a court is right to punish such people when found guilty of an illegal act. A good example occurred after the 2011 riots in several British cities. In response to the death of Mark Duggan, 1566 people were punished by the British justice system. It was accepted by the courts that each of these individuals acted rationally through their own free will. This can be seen from the comments made by Lord Judge, the Lord Chief Justice of England and Wales, when he was considering appeals against the lengthy jail sentences for some of the people involved in the riots: 'Those who deliberately participate in disturbances of this magnitude … are committing aggravated crimes', i.e. the people were committing crimes that they were fully aware were wrong. Lord Judge dismissed all the appeals. Therefore, whatever may be the philosophical or theological arguments, the law clearly supports the idea that moral responsibility is not an illusion.

2011 British riots

Key term

Rational choice theory: the legal theory that people are reasoning agents who freely weigh up means and ends, costs and benefits, and therefore make freely willed rational choices when committing an illegal act

AO2 Activity

List some conclusions that could be drawn from the AO2 reasoning from the above text; try to aim for at least three different possible conclusions. Consider each of the conclusions and collect brief evidence to support each conclusion from the AO1 and AO2 material for this topic. Select the conclusion that you think is most convincing and explain why it is so. Try to contrast this with the weakest conclusion in the list, justifying your argument with clear reasoning and evidence.

Specification content

The extent to which predestination
influences our understanding of God.

Key quotes

[God's omnipotence means] the power to do all that is intrinsically possible, not to do the intrinsically impossible ... not because his power meets an obstacle but because nonsense remains nonsense even when we talk it about God (C. S. Lewis)

But you cannot will, unless Allah wills. (Quran 76:30)

A God that punishes or rewards on the basis of God's own eternal decisions in unfair and immoral. (Russell)

AO2 Activity

As you read through this section try to do the following:

1. Pick out the different lines of argument that are presented in the text and identify any evidence given in support.

2. For each line of argument try to evaluate whether or not you think this is strong or weak.

3. Think of any questions you may wish to raise in response to the arguments.

This Activity will help you to start thinking critically about what you read and help you to evaluate the effectiveness of different arguments and from this develop your own observations, opinions and points of view that will help with any conclusions that you make in your answers to the AO2 questions that arise.

The extent to which predestination influences our understanding of God

Various philosophers have attempted to list the possible attributes of the nature of the God of classical theism. Such a list has been derived from philosophers such as Aquinas, Anselm and Descartes who sought to define God. For instance, Anselm defined God as 'that than which nothing greater can be conceived'. By this he meant that God was the greatest possible being, the one who maximised all possible qualities. Descartes defined God as a 'supremely perfect being'. This incorporates the idea of God as an object worthy of worship.

If one takes the doctrine of predestination as true then this doctrine may reveal insights into God's nature. One of the most obvious attributes is God's omnipotence. Certainly, predestation implies God's omnipotence since, according to this doctrine, God orchestrates the final destiny of each human being but allows for limited free will. Another understanding of the doctrine is that God determines each action and event with no free will enacted by human beings. It is this issue of limited free will that raises questions about the extent of God's omnipotence. It suggests that God has limited his omnipotence. In response, it is argued that the free will is limited in that it cannot ultimately thwart the plans and purposes of God. God giving up the exercising of his sovereignty is not the same as God giving up his sovereignty. Nevertheless, this limitation sheds light on the idea of God's omnipotence. In one sense it is not unlimited power.

This understanding may also support the view that God's omnipotence means that God is able to do anything that is in accord with his own nature. God is love and Aquinas saw this as the explanation of God being omnipotent and human beings acting freely. Because God is all loving, he cannot use that power lovelessly. Everything is done that God wills to be done, but it is done in the way that God wants it to be done. However, the idea of free will is seen by some (e.g. Augustine) as contradicting the attribute of omnipotence and therefore they would deny free will. Maybe it is not the concept of predestination that influences our understanding of God's omnipotence, it is free will.

Another approach would be to question the idea of God's omnipotence since God seems unable to create a species of human beings who always chose good. If God did that then there would be no need for any to fall from grace as all would be united with God. This could be countered by arguing that it is logically impossible to be both free and controlled at the same time. It is not that God is not powerful enough, it is that the task is a logical contradiction and God cannot actualise contradictions.

The doctrine of predestination does make it clear that human beings can do nothing themselves to be forgiven and receive righteousness. It is only by means of God's grace and only an omnipotent deity could execute an eternal predestination plan for all of humanity.

Another key attribute of God is his omnibenevolence. Certainly, the doctrine of predestination supports this view. Given that humanity fell and inherited Adam's sin, then all deserve judgement from God. However, God shows his loving nature, for humanity, by saving some people; these people Augustine called the elect. God did this by sending his son Jesus to die on the cross, so that the elect can receive atonement for their sins and be united with God.

Others have challenged such a conclusion since both Augustine and Calvin argue that God only predestines some people to be forgiven of their sins. It might be argued that if God is omnibenevolent then he would surely predestine everybody to salvation and forgiveness of their sins. Indeed, it suggests that God decreed something for a particular individual which neither is nor can be good. Namely, he has predestined some people to eternal separation from himself. It is particularly contrary to omnibenevolence since God seems to decide eternal destinies without regard to how people live and in which they have no choice.

In reply, some draw attention to verses in the Bible that suggest people do have some choice. For instance, Joshua 24:15 says, 'But if serving the Lord seems undesirable to you, then choose for yourselves this day whom you will serve.' Similarly in the New Testament in Luke 7:30: 'But the Pharisees and the experts in the law rejected God's purposes for themselves.'

Yet, other verses suggest we can do nothing to save ourselves or earn God's forgiveness. It is God who decides whom he will forgive. Romans 9:15–16 reads 'Is God unjust? Not at all! For he says to Moses "I will have mercy on whom I have mercy, and I will have compassion on whom I have compassion." It does not, therefore, depend on human desire or effort, but on God's mercy.'

Some take predestination further and argue that all actions and events are predetermined by God and there is no free will. However, many reject this idea of predestination as it seems to imply God is the author of all sin. If God has predetermined everything that is going to come to pass, then it implies that when Adam sinned in the Garden of Eden, God had willed that he sin. This would be true of all the sins that people commit. Understanding why evil exists if there is an omnipotent, omnibenevolent God who has both the means and the motivation to remove evil, has remained a lasting philosophical problem. The doctrine of predestination in some of its forms only reinforces this problem.

Perhaps the very idea of omnibenevolence is in fact a meaningless concept. If omnibenevolence is defined as a state of 'all-loving', then some philosophers have argued that love has no limits. They express it in terms of 'love has no intrinsic maximums'. If this is true, then the term is indeed meaningless.

The doctrine of predestination that allows for free will also raises the problem of God's omniscience. How can God know the future, since it has not yet been decided? If God does know the future, some would argue it implies there are no acts of free will, since God knows what will happen. In response to this view, Bruce Reichenbach (*Predestination and Free Will*) comments '... one cannot make the event depend on God's knowledge of the event, as the objector does when he says that God's foreknowledge determines, for the foreknowledge depends on the event, and not vice versa'. In other words, God's knowledge does not cause the action.

Alternatively, if God doesn't know the future, then it could be argued that God is not omniscient. It might be that even if God does know the future, this does not necessitate God over-riding a person's free will. God merely knows what free choice I make. Though I am in time, God is outside of time. However, many might argue that the idea of a God outside of time is not consistent with the biblical description of God. A timeless God cannot deliberate or anticipate or remember. He cannot do anything or respond to anything. There cannot be any before or after. It would seem that if God is timeless then there is no free will. But can the God who creates time be himself time-bound? It seems unlikely that the Creator must partake of the nature of his creation.

However, perhaps God does know all at once and has always known and foreordains all things simultaneously. This may not demand that there is no logical order in what he foreordains. For instance, God knew that Christ's birth must precede Christ's death.

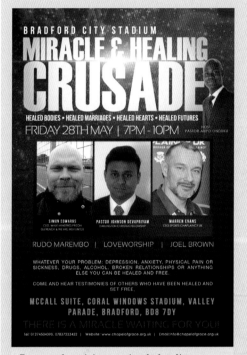

Poster advertising a miracle healing crusade meeting

Perhaps it is the case that God knows everything that can be known, but he does not know what is unknowable. Future choices made freely are not knowable since there is nothing yet to be known. Therefore, it could be argued that this is not a deficiency in God's omniscience. The God of the Bible is a loving God who interacts with his creatures. However, the question may then arise as to whether God's plans can be thwarted by our free choices.

Key quotes

Forgive us our sins…and lead us not into temptation. (Luke 11:4)

But when the time had fully come, God sent his Son … to redeem those under law. (Galatians 4:4)

If God is outside of time, then it may influence our understanding of the place of prayer. It may suggest that prayer has little or no influence and God is not responding to the prayer since he is timeless. If the purpose of prayer is to change an outcome and bring God into the situation, then it is not clear how that is possible with a God who is outside of time. Equally, if God has predestined all actions and events, it is difficult to see how prayer could have any influence since all things are preordained by God and so cannot change.

If predestination is true, then any attempt to pray to the divine to earnestly ask to become an elect would appear to be a complete waste of effort. However, perhaps when the predestinated elect sin they cannot resist the calling on their lives to seek forgiveness, which could be through prayer. If predestination is about final outcomes and there is free will, then there would appear to be no problem in seeing prayer as an agent of change.

1 John 4:16 states that 'God is love' and Romans 2:11 says that 'God does not show favouritism'. But if God is all-loving, then how can he love only some so as to give them and only them the desire to be forgiven and saved? Those who believe in the form of predestination that accepts free will in everyday actions and events might argue that free will allows for human beings to choose either good or evil. They would argue that God wanted human beings to be free and responsible agents and not to be automatons. This could be seen as consistent with the view that God can still achieve his goals by judicious intervention. God could override human freedom or intervene in the natural order (i.e. performs miracles) when he deemed it necessary.

The doctrine of predestination certainly raises problems over God's sovereignty and God's omniscience and moral responsibility!

AO2 Activity

List some conclusions that could be drawn from the AO2 reasoning from the above text; try to aim for at least three different possible conclusions. Consider each of the conclusions and collect brief evidence to support each conclusion from the AO1 and AO2 material for this topic. Select the conclusion that you think is most convincing and explain why it is so. Try to contrast this with the weakest conclusion in the list, justifying your argument with clear reasoning and evidence.

AO2 Developing skills

It is now important to consider the information that has been covered in this section; however, the information in its raw form is too extensive and so has to be processed in order to meet the requirements of the examination. This can be achieved by practising more advanced skills associated with AO2. For assessment objective 2 (AO2), which involves 'critical analysis' and 'evaluation' skills, we are going to focus on different ways in which the skills can be demonstrated effectively, and also refer to how the performance of these skills is measured (see generic band descriptors for A2 [WJEC] AO2 or A Level [Eduqas] AO2).

▶ **Your final task for this theme is:** Below are listed three basic conclusions drawn from an evaluation of **whether moral responsibility is an illusion**. Your task is to develop each of these conclusions by identifying briefly the strengths (referring briefly to some reasons underlying it) but also an awareness of challenges made to it (these may be weaknesses depending upon your view).

1. The only conclusion that can be drawn is that people have no control over their moral attitudes because a person cannot freely choose the moral path they take. Therefore, all human ideas of moral responsibility are just an illusion.

2. Augustine argued that we are absolutely incapable of doing anything good by our own forces; therefore, human ideas of rightness and wrongness are pointless concepts because humanity cannot choose between good and evil and so moral responsibility is clearly an illusion.

3. William James concluded that 'any other future set of outcomes than the one fixed from eternity is impossible'. If this is the case and the person was completely overridden by determining forces then moral responsibility is clearly an illusion.

The result should be three very competent paragraphs that could form a final conclusion of any evaluation.

When you have completed the task, refer to the band descriptors for A2 (WJEC) or A Level (Eduqas) and in particular have a look at the demands described in the higher band descriptors towards which you should be aspiring. Ask yourself:

- Is my answer a confident critical analysis and perceptive evaluation of the issue?
- Is my answer a response that successfully identifies and thoroughly addresses the issues raised by the question set?

Key skills
Analysis involves:

Identifying issues raised by the materials in the AO1, together with those identified in the AO2 section, and presents sustained and clear views, either of scholars or from a personal perspective ready for evaluation.

This means:

- That your answers are able to identify key areas of debate in relation to a particular issue

- That you can identify, and comment upon, the different lines of argument presented by others

- That your response comments on the overall effectiveness of each of these areas or arguments.

Evaluation involves:

Considering the various implications of the issues raised based upon the evidence gleaned from analysis and provides an extensive detailed argument with a clear conclusion.

This means:

- That your answer weighs up the consequences of accepting or rejecting the various and different lines of argument analysed

- That your answer arrives at a conclusion through a clear process of reasoning.

T4 Determinism and free will – Free will

Specification content
Religious concepts of free will.

D: Religious concepts of free will

Introduction

The Philosophy of Religion involves various aspects of both philosophy and theology as the title suggests. The debate about free will is said to be the most debated issue in the history of philosophy from the Ancient Greek philosophers to modern-day philosophy, neuroscience and psychology. In this sense the Specification may appear both artificial and superficial since the idea of determinism is just one possible response to the free will debate.

In addition to this, since philosophers and theologians take different approaches then this can sometimes be confusing. For example, in Theme 4A–E *Determinism and free will* there are also components on religious ideas about free will and religious views on predestination. Whilst the philosophical, scientific and psychological debates are 'open ended', the religious debates are grounded in the traditional understanding of God as omnipotent, omniscient and omnibenevolent. Therefore, these are all very different debates. Here are a few points to bear in mind:

1. The term determinism is a philosophical concept; predestination is theological. They are very different in scope. The philosophical, scientific and psychological debates answer to no higher power or assume there is such a thing. Therefore, we must keep this important distinction in mind when writing about them.

2. Determinism covers all human actions; predestination can refer to just human 'destination' (i.e. salvation or not) and not necessarily every individual action.

3. With religious ideas about predestination, we sometimes do see raised the issue of the extent to which a human being's behaviour is 'determined by God'. Here, the word 'determined' is used in a very different way in theology from that of the random indeterminism of modern physics, or the various types of causal determinism that philosophy explores. In theology, 'determined' really equates to whether or not behaviour can be explained by the 'control' or intervention of an omnipotent, omniscient and omnibenevolent God.

4. In theology, the issue of free will is one of 'to what extent can free will be compatible with a God that is omnipotent, omniscient and omnibenevolent?' In philosophy, the same constraints do not necessarily apply to free will issues per se.

5. In addition to this, there is also a rich tradition of debate within philosophy and theology that involves a **compatibilist** approach; that is, those philosophers and theologians who feel that the debate between libertarianism and determinism / free will and predestination is not as clear-cut as the Specification breakdown may suggest.

6. Compatibilist arguments see merit in exploring the idea that there may actually be some middle ground. Obviously there are many examples and variants in exploring this and some of these ideas and arguments have been included (especially in sections C and F) to assist with evaluation of the issues (AO2).

Key term

Compatibilist: the view that one theory does not contradict another (i.e. a person can both have free will and be determined)

7. The *Philosophy of Religion* in Theme 4 also considers the issues of determinism and libertarianism, and the religious notions of predestination and free will from an ethical perspective. This is explored most fully in sections C and F, which look at the implications of the debate for non-religious ethics and for religious ethics.

8. Finally, the philosophical and psychological issues of free will have moved on significantly since the time of Sartre and Rogers, and in particular, contemporary research into neuroscience has thrown up some interesting dialogue between philosophy, psychology, theology and science. Note that this is referred to as dialogue rather than debate, since the term 'debate' may well give the misleading impression that the three areas each own a particular unified view or overall consensus. As we shall see, this is not the case and we will look at this 'dialogue' in Section 4F.

Pelagius was a British Celtic monk who lived during the 4th century CE and promoted the ascetic lifestyle and a life of good works.

Key terms

Abstinence: the option taken not to participate in something

Ascetic: the disciplined lifestyle of a monk

The teachings of Pelagius

Key quote

Pelagius is one of the most maligned figures in the history of Christianity. It has been the common sport of the theologian and the historian of theology to set him up as a symbolic bad man and to heap upon him accusations which often tell us more about the theological perspective of the accuser than about Pelagius. **(Evans)**

Pelagius (354–420) was a Christian monk from the British Isles and an **ascetic**, more associated with Celtic Christianity (closely linked to the Eastern rather than Western church tradition). Pelagius had chosen **abstinence** from materialism and pleasures so that he could set his sights without distraction on religious matters and spiritual goals. The church historian Robert F. Evans points out that many have seen Pelagius as more of a moralist than a theologian concerned with the 'concrete problems of the Christian life'; however, his theological ideas did direct his ethical views. There is a key paragraph from the writing of Pelagius that provides some indication about his views about free will. He writes:

You will realise that doctrines are the invention of the human minds, as it tries to penetrate the mystery of God. You will realise that scripture itself is the work of human recording the example and teaching of Jesus. Thus it is not what you believe (in your head) that matters; it is how you respond with your heart and your actions. It is not believing in Christ that matters, but becoming like him.

Specification content

The teachings of Pelagius.

What Pelagius is expressing here is the ancient debate within Christianity about soteriology. The term soteriology, from the Greek word 'soter' (σωτήρ) meaning salvation, refers to theories about salvation and how a human being can achieve or receive this from God.

In the New Testament this debate is central to Paul's theology of sola fide (faith alone) when he writes in Romans 3:23–24: 'all have sinned and fall short of the glory of God; they are now **justified by his grace as a gift**, through the redemption that is in Christ Jesus'.

An alternative perspective on the debate can be found in the letter of James chapter 2: verse 14 onwards:

> 'What good is it, my brothers and sisters, if you say you have faith but do not have works? Can faith save you? If a brother or sister is naked and lacks daily food, and one of you says to them, "Go in peace; keep warm and eat your fill," and yet you do not supply their bodily needs, what is the good of that? So faith by itself, if it has no works, is dead. But someone will say, "You have faith and I have works." Show me your faith apart from your works, and I by my works will show you my faith.' (James 2:14–19)

This reference in the letter of James is often misunderstood as advocating that salvation can only be achieved through doing good deeds due to the phrase 'You see that a person is justified by works and not by faith alone' that occurs later in verse 24. Just as with the letter of James in the New Testament, some would argue that Pelagius has been open to over-interpretation and that Pelagius is often associated with such an unqualified view.

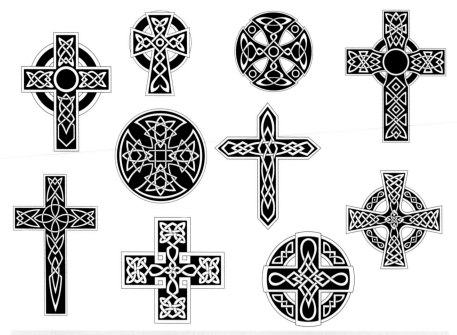

Celtic Christianity is often associated with ornate images of the cross.

For Pelagius, God's image is found in every person and his was a practical Christianity. For example, whilst in Rome, he drew the criticism of orthodox leaders for teaching women to read scripture and for spending too much time talking indiscriminately to the public in town. In terms of orthodox Christian theology, Pelagius is the 'bad boy', the 'villain' of Christian theology.

Study tip

The key to the debate about Pelagius is understanding three key points:

(1) Pelagius' unique teaching was to reject the notion of Original Sin.

(2) It is important, in studying Pelagius, to be aware that there may be a significant difference between
(a) what he actually wrote;
(b) how he is understood by others (both opponents and followers).

(3) His 'holiness' teachings do not exclude God's grace in human free will, but the specific role Pelagius gives to God's grace has been the subject of great debate and disagreement.

As regards Pelagius, there are two main accusations made against him:

(1) Augustine saw Pelagius as the enemy of the grace of God because he rejected Original Sin; accordingly, for Augustine, Pelagius made the sacrificial death of Christ redundant by suggesting human beings were responsible for their own salvation. Karl Barth continued this accusation in the 20th century, insisting that Pelagius sets out a doctrine of man's own self-determination in the place of a proper doctrine of man's being determined by God. The real issue here was that God's role in salvation, as an omnipotent, omniscient and omnibenevolent deity was not recognised. It is God who saves, through God's grace and by faith alone and not through good works.

(2) For Jerome, Pelagius is the promoter of the perfectionism of Origen and his doctrine of sinlessness, who, according to church historian Harnack, represented no more than a 'rationalistic moralism'. This was the outcome of Pelagius' insistence on the autonomy of free will within the context of salvation. Pelagius insisted that it was possible to achieve a sinless life (although whether he meant everyone in practice is debatable).

Adam and Eve were expelled from the Garden of Eden because of their sin against God.

Despite this 'bad boy' image, the theology of Pelagius on free will and salvation has constantly been the underlying irritant for the doctrine of Original Sin, Augustine's theology and the theologies within traditional Christianity. Despite its rejection as heresy, Pelagius' theology does still attract curiosity and have a sense of earthy honesty to it for some Christians today. Indeed, the delicate conflict between faith and works is not a new dilemma, as we have already seen from the quotations found in the New Testament in the letters from Paul and James. Even early Christians did ask, if salvation was through faith alone then what do we make of good works which is why James goes on to write in verse 24 of chapter 2:

> 'You see that a person is **_justified by works and not by faith alone_**.'

Indeed, for some Christians the idea of heresy is not as bad as it may sound; it does not necessarily mean that one is a bad person. After all, Pelagius advocated an open-to-all approach to the gospel and the inclusion of women in reading scripture. In addition, considering Pelagius' opening quotation, theology is the human mind attempting to make sense of the divine and thus is not infallible.

As church historian Evans explains, 'Pelagius and the heresy called by his name continue to provide occasion for careless slogans and confident postures' within Christianity. In an article in *The Aisling*, a Celtic magazine devoted to Celtic Christianity and spirituality, Bishop Bennett J. Sims (an Anglican of the Episcopal Church in the USA) argues that the origin of this scorn is a direct result of the writings of Augustine. In particular, Augustine's influence of the Church throughout history can be seen in the teachings of Original Sin and predestination. Sims argues that Augustine's obsession with Original Sin has been adopted by the Church and used to overemphasise humanity's guilt, confession and general depravity so as to make humanity's potential disappear beneath the smokescreen generated by church authority. In other words, Sims is arguing that the villainous nature of the heretic Pelagius is over-exaggerated.

Key quotes

The doctrine that holds an unbaptised child as going straight to hell is the invention of human minds at work to secure the ecclesiastical establishment as a system of control. (Bishop Sims)

All Christians are free to choose for themselves what, for them, is orthodox or heretical; what seems to them the straightest kind of searching into the enduring mysteries of God and the world. (Bishop Sims)

Key term

Rationalistic moralism: the theory that morality is purely accessible through reason and has no need for God

There are two possible approaches to the study of Pelagius; namely, a theological approach and a historical approach. Evans chooses a historical approach to understanding Pelagius over against the theological approach. A theological approach, for Evans, may well ignore the hostilities and distortions of historical context; however, abstraction inevitably brings with it its own measure of distortion. For example, a theological analysis does not differentiate between what Pelagius actually said and what people say he said. It also does not differentiate between Pelagius' statements and that doctrine which later became known as Pelagianism. For example, Sicilian Pelagianism does not always sit neatly with what Pelagius actually taught.

For philosophers, free will may be seen as the opposite of determinism. However, free will in a religious context is not necessarily the opposite of the doctrine of predestination. That is because theology is operating within the context of an omnipotent deity; whilst in philosophy, all events are the result of the will of the human being per se. For theology, free will means that God

Confession is a key aspect of Roman Catholic religious tradition.

has **given** human beings freedom, particularly when making moral decisions on whether to do good works based on the word of God or to rebel by rejecting the word of God. The outcome of free will for theology is that human beings are responsible for their own actions but not necessarily for their eternal life with God, i.e. to gain salvation or to be separated from God. In contrast, philosophy is only focused on human beings being ultimately responsible for their actions. A religious concept of free will, therefore, can be considered a form of religious libertarianism, that is, a theologically refined form of philosophical libertarianism or philosophical soft determinism – free but within certain constraints.

Pelagius' perspective on life was a sharp reaction to the hypocrisy and immorality of what he encountered in Rome, the centre of the Western church tradition. Pelagius blamed the debauchery he found in Rome on an absolutist understanding of divine predestination and the doctrine of Original Sin whereby human beings appeared condemned to a life of sinfulness. This notion later became prevalent in the Roman Catholic Church with Augustine's doctrine of Original Sin. According to Pelagius, predestination suggested that human beings were unable to control their moral conduct. As a result, Original Sin was seen as an excuse for their immoral behaviour and so encouraged people not to even try to control their urge to sin. Sins could be confessed and be forgiven.

Pelagius insisted that people were responsible for their own action through freedom to choose good or evil. He wrote some important documents on free will: 'On Nature' and 'Defence of the Freedom of the Will' in which his arguments evidence the influence of early Christian writers like Saint Justin (100–165CE) who argued that it was not possible for anyone to do good or bad wilfully because they 'had not the power of turning either away'. Pelagius' views were not welcomed by the Church and he was officially declared a heretic in 418 at the Council of Carthage. This was mainly due to the writings of Augustine against Pelagius; Augustine was petrified of the implications that a teaching of unfettered free will would bring for the doctrine of salvation.

Pelagius and the role of Original Sin

For Pelagius, the force of sin does not result from degraded human nature (as for Augustine), but from a corruption and ignorance of righteousness that results from the long-term habit of sin. As Evans writes, 'Pelagius' theology finds its centre of gravity in the problem of man – his nature, his relation to God, and his moral obligation.'

Pelagius argued that human beings were created as rational creatures and had the ability to distinguish between good and evil; this ability, however, is God-given. Natural goodness in human beings is voluntary goodness, goodness that is spontaneously willed. This autonomy, albeit given by the grace of God, is the only way to make virtue meaningful. However, the crucial thing here for Pelagius was the fact that human beings cannot take credit for their freedom to choose, this is not willed by humanity but the creative activity of God. In other words, a human being may be able to do good, but they can only do this good because God has allowed them to in the first place, and, as we shall later see, enables them to do this.

In the biblical book of Genesis, the story of Adam and Eve involves their disobedience against the explicit instructions of God in eating from the tree of the knowledge of good and evil. Pelagius' free will is grounded in a specific interpretation of this fall from grace. Pelagius saw this as the Original Sin but not an Original Sin inherent in humanity. It belonged to Adam and Eve and was their sin alone. Pelagius was convinced that an omnibenevolent God would never punish someone for another's sin, quoting Deuteronomy 24:16 'Parents are not to be put to death for their children, nor children put to death for their parents; each will die for their own sins.' Pelagius thus rejects the doctrine of Original Sin and along with it the notions of sin that not only permeates the whole of humanity with a fallen tendency to sin, but also that sinfulness is there present in a human being from the moment of birth as part of human nature. In Pelagius, the nature of humanity as pre-stained with sin is removed.

This is the crucial point at which Augustine and Pelagius depart. Both thinkers accept free will; however, Augustine is wary that God's sovereign nature is upheld. For Augustine, free will is a kind of 'restricted' free will that is demonstrably within the control of the Almighty God, otherwise:

(1) it would imply human beings have achieved their own salvation; (2) also that human beings could become perfect like God; and, (3) that God's omnipotence would be affected.

We can see from Augustine's theodicy in the face of the problems of evil and suffering that the idea of God's omnipotence could in no way ever be compromised.

Pelagius proposed that it is **participation** in the fallen world that leads to sin and not an inherited tendency. Pelagius argued that to see sin as inherited from Adam and Eve, that is, as human beings we have an inherent element of sin within us, is to fall foul of the doctrine of Manichaeism, which incorporated determinism and dualism. For Pelagius, sin was the ownership of the individual soul; to argue that it was inherited means that it becomes a necessary element of human existence and implies that we are essentially dualistic by nature. As Evans writes, 'To make sin necessary would be to deny the nature of will, whose only necessity lies in its capacity both to sin and not to sin'.

Specification content

The role of Original Sin.

Key quotes

Will is irreducibly characterised by its own freedom of choice as it is related both to the will of God and to the non-human creation. (Stanglin and McCall)

Looking into the face of a newborn child is not to see a soul already corrupted but alight with the beauty of God's goodness. Each child is corruptible to be sure, and quickly, since evil is real, and humanity bears the burden of free moral choice. But everything newborn is a gift already cherished by God. This is Pelagian doctrine. (Bishop Bennett Sims)

Pelagius is indeed perfectly clear that Adam was in fact the first sinner … that sin entered the world through the one man Adam. By this he means simply that men allowed themselves to follow the example set by Adam in disobeying the will of God. (Evans)

Key term

Manichaeism: a belief in two equally forceful powers of light and darkness in constant battle against each other

Manichaeism taught that people had a dualistic nature battling within, reflecting an elaborate dualistic cosmological struggle between a spiritual world of light and a material world of darkness.

Specification content

Humanity maturing in God's image
and accepting the responsibility of
free will.

Key term

Autonomous: self-governing

Key quote

If God had simply instructed Adam
and Eve to eat from the tree, and
they had obeyed, they would have
been acting like children. So he
forbade them from eating the fruit;
this meant that they themselves
had to make a free will decision,
whether to eat or not to eat. Just as
a young person needs to defy his
parents in order to grow to maturity,
so Adam and Eve needed to defy
God in order to grow to maturity in
his image. (Pelagius)

Pelagius: humanity maturing in God's image and accepting the responsibility of free will

This idea of participation in the world enabled human beings to engage with their **autonomous** will and choose their actions carefully. Pelagius then went further by arguing that 'the fall' can actually be seen as a good thing for human beings. The gift of free will enabled Adam and Eve to choose whether or not to eat the forbidden fruit; but also, in eating the fruit, allowed the process of maturity to begin. Pelagius' reasoning was that humans go through a learning process, and, as they do, they grow and mature in wisdom, learning from their mistakes. Part of this process is defiance – just like Adam and Eve – in order to discover for oneself how things are. Therefore, in exercising their free will and making their own decisions, the long-term benefits outweigh the short-term pitfalls.

This free will meant that Adam and Eve, and thus all their descendants, became responsible to God for their own actions. Therefore, human beings had gained free will to choose and independently determine either to do good or turn to sin.

Pelagius developed this further in relation to the Old Testament where he identified two clear periods of development and maturity in following God's laws.

The first period is from Adam to Moses. This offers examples of men who did live according to the laws and did in fact lead sinless lives. Such men as Abel, Noah, Melchizedek, Abraham and Job, Pelagius saw as men who were equipped with and in touch with their own nature, recognising God's law and enabling them to freely choose to act without sin.

The laws of Moses were introduced as a reminder for human beings, as a remedy for ignorance to their own nature that had the capacity to choose between good and evil. By constant application of the laws, ignorance to this is gradually removed, revealing in the words of Evans 'man's newly polished nature' that would 'stand out again in its pristine brilliance'.

The laws of Moses were there to make human beings aware of their capacity to do good.

Pelagius: free will as used to follow God's laws and the role of grace in salvation

Pelagius wrote: 'No one knows better the true measure of our strength than He who has given it to us ... this very capacity of ours to be able ...' and unashamedly advocated an absolute case for free will. In doing so, Pelagius' notion of moral responsibility led to the logical conclusion that there was human autonomy to freely follow and also have the capacity to fulfil God's commandments. His argument continued that God would not create commandments that were impossible to follow.

However, this brings us once again to the heart of the debate between Augustine and Pelagius. For Augustine, Original Sin ensured that human beings could never be worthy of their own salvation. This was very clear. Paul also stated this in his biblical writings and according to Church teaching it is only through the grace of God as demonstrated in the atonement of Christ that salvation could be received. It is salvation freely given by God. According to Evans, therefore, Pelagius was condemned for 'teaching a correlative doctrine of the possibilities of human achievement which appeared to deny the necessity of grace'.

Nonetheless, Pelagius did have something to say about the role of grace in salvation. According to Pelagius there was a role for grace in salvation. Even though many have considered it to be a 'deficient' role in comparison to Augustine's role, it is still there.

So what was the role of grace in salvation for Pelagius?

Although Pelagius argued that human beings had the freedom, potential and opportunity to fulfil the moral commandments of God, his ultimate view was God's grace that initiates and stimulates but does not forcibly determine.

This is a kind of balancing of the responsibilities between God and humanity to create the best possible way to achieving the life God intends for humans. As Pelagius states: 'Free will is in all good works always assisted by divine help.' It is almost as if Pelagius envisages God's grace as the gentle helping hand of a parent teaching a child to become independent.

Therefore, God is not just acting as a guide to do good works, God is the agent of empowerment that allows us the freedom, potential and opportunity to do good works in the first place. This opportunity, provided by God's grace, is significant for Pelagius, and like Irenaeus, he saw the notion of the freedom, potential and opportunity to choose good over evil as the optimum condition conducive to creating a better quality of 'good' because it is voluntary: 'this very capacity to do evil is also good – good, I say. Because it makes the good part better by making it voluntary and independent'.

Nonetheless, with this framework in place there is also the freedom, potential and opportunity to do evil and sin. Grace is not irresistible for Pelagius. Once again, the option of evil freely chosen makes the good freely chosen even more meaningful. It is this particular aspect that causes most difficulty for Augustine because, although Pelagius believed that salvation is only by way of atonement through the sacrifice and death of Jesus Christ, for all those who freely have faith in Christ, Pelagius also felt that forgiveness for sins needed to be matched by a will to not sin and shored up with demonstrable acts that are good. This was an essential criterion for the road to the holy life and ultimate salvation. For Pelagius, true repentance was not just asking to be forgiven but demonstrating an attitude and aptitude for good.

Specification content

Free will as used to follow God's laws and the role of grace in salvation.

Key quote

No one knows better the true measure of our strength than He who has given it to us nor does anyone understand better how much we are able to do than He who has given us this very capacity of ours to be able ... (Pelagius)

The cross of Christ was the ultimate source of grace.

According to Evans, this aspect of Pelagius has also been one of the main contributors to misunderstandings of his view. To get an accurate picture of Pelagius, it is important to distinguish between this historical, undeveloped view and those views of Pelagius associated with later Pelagianism or the restricted view of Pelagius as seen through the eyes of Augustine.

Indeed, the initial dialogue between Augustine and Pelagius is always seen through the eyes of Augustine – Original Sin is necessary to ensure that salvation is by the grace of God and through faith alone. There is no in-between ground for Augustine. This then becomes the main question and focus: is grace necessary for salvation? The answer can only be if we all have sinned.

However, what we should be asking, according to Pelagius – and to avoid any accusation of Manichaeism – is, 'what is the **role** and **nature** of that grace that is required for salvation?' For Pelagius, justification by faith alone can take place without respect to human merits but at the same time he also speaks of the 'merit' of faith and deserving the grace of God. As Evans writes, 'Faith "merits" grace in the sense that it is the indispensable and freely chosen condition of the effectual working of grace.' It seems that rather than disposing of the role of grace in salvation as is often understood of Pelagius, instead Pelagius appears to give the role of grace a 'light touch' as it were, rather than the fully-fledged and absolute dependence of Augustine's theology. It is this 'correlative doctrine' between good works and God's grace that opens up Pelagius to the accusation, whether justified or not, that he preaches a gospel of salvation through good works.

In summary, it appears that we are back where we started. Free will allows good works but challenges the nature of salvation; Original Sin raises the question of the possibility of such depraved creatures achieving good. Augustine was terrified of Pelagius' theology because it suggested that humans have some decisive role in their own salvation; Pelagius was horrified that the idea of Original Sin was closely linked with the Manichaean teaching of dual nature as well as being a general excuse not to strive for the moral life.

Maybe both Augustine and Pelagius were not poles apart and that their concerns reflect the possible extremes of challenge to Christian theology; the two sides of the Christian theological coin, so to speak. Just as *sola fide* leads to James' concerns about 'good work', then maybe Pelagius' insistence on morality as a means to salvation naturally throws up concerns about the role of God's grace for Augustine?

It is clear from the history of Christianity that Augustine won the battle. It could be argued that it is a shame there is no 'middle ground'. However, maybe that is where Arminius enters the debate?

quickfire

4.29 Briefly explain why the fall of Adam and Eve was a good thing for human beings.

Key quotes

It is also true that Pelagius' understanding of the term 'grace' is a very deficient one when regarded from the point of view of Augustinian theology. (Evans)

Our most excellent creator wished us to be able to do either (be good or bad) but actually to do only one, that is, good. (Pelagius)

Pelagius' insistence that men can be without sin is an emphatic assertion of the doctrine of creation by a just God; it is nothing more, and it is nothing less. (Evans)

AO1 Activity

(1) Working together in groups of 4 try to arrive at a collective summary of each aspect of Pelagius' ideas about about free will: the role of Original Sin; maturing into God's image; responsibility of free will; following God's laws; grace and salvation, etc.

(2) Try to make the summary of each one around 50 words.

(3) Jointly present this to the rest of the class.

Religious concept of free will: Arminius' rejection of Calvin's theory of predestination

Jacobus Arminius (1559–1609) was taught by Theodore Beza, the son-in-law and successor of predestination proponent John Calvin. In his early life Arminius identified as a Calvinist and was a supporter of Beza who continued to promote Calvin's teachings of predestination. However, Arminius became dissatisfied with Calvinism and rejected Calvin's predestination for a version of predestination that he developed himself. Arminius' predestination was grounded in the theological concept of God's providence and was compatible with the notion of free will.

Jacob Arminius (1559–1609)

Specification content

Religious concepts of free will, with reference to the teachings of: Arminius. Denial of the Calvinist view of predestination.

Key quote

It is important to note that Arminius does not abandon predestination. He is careful, however, to define it with specific reference to Scripture. (Studebaker)

Arminius did not reject or deny predestination. In his very own words:

'The Dogma of predestination and its opposite, reprobation, is taught and emphasised in the Scriptures, for which reason it is also necessary. But it must be seen which and what kind of predestination it is that is treated in the Scriptures as necessary, and which is called the foundation of our salvation.'

In the same way, Arminius was not a teacher of the priority of free will. He instead wrestled directly with the problem that we stated initially, that is, the delicate relationship between human free will and the sovereignty of God. In doing so, Arminius came up with a revised form of **conditional predestination** or **middle knowledge** predestination.

Conditional predestination is foreknowledge without determinism. This type of predestination is linked closely with the idea of **providence**. Providence is the idea that God is closely involved in monitoring and guiding the created world. Arminius writes in his seminal work *Declaration of Sentiments*:

'Providence is a solicitous, continued, and universally present supervision of God over the whole world in general, and all creatures in particular, without any exception, in order to preserve and to direct them in their own essence, qualities, actions and passions, such as befits him and is suitable to them, to the praise of his name and the salvation of believers.'

The notion of providence for Arminius involves both preservation of the world but crucially governance of it. God sustains the universe by being involved in it. Without God's preservation the world would cease to be; without God's governance there would be chaos within it. Rustin Brian observes that 'Arminius agrees that predestination should not be founded upon anything other than God's pure goodness'.

quickfire

4.30 How was Arminius associated with Calvinism?

Key Person

Jacob Arminius was born in 1559 in Oudewater, Utrecht, only five years before the death of John Calvin. His father and mother died whilst Jacob was still a child, leaving a priest, Theodorus Aemilius, to adopt Jacob. After completing his education at Leiden, Arminius travelled to study at Calvin's academy in Geneva. Theodore Beza, a successor to Calvin, was the Chair of theology at the university, and he and Arminius became close friends. Later, Arminius challenged Beza's 'high Calvinism' and argued for conditional election and hence a different understanding of predestination. Arminius died in 1609.

Key terms

Conditional predestination: the complex theological notion based upon the idea that free will and predestination are compatible (see later)

Middle knowledge: a theory developed by Luis de Molina, a Spanish Jesuit priest, that argues God is aware of every computation of possible choices (see below)

Providence: the theological idea that God is closely involved in monitoring and guiding the created world

Providence means God preserves and governs the world throughout time.

Key quote

Nothing in life occurs fortuitously or by chance. Both the will and the actions of rational beings are subject to divine providence, so that nothing can be done outside God's control. There is, however, a distinction between the good which God both wills and performs and the evil which he only permits. (Skevington-Wood)

The key to the governance of the world is the theological idea of **divine concurrence**. Divine concurrence, in the words of scholars Stanglin and McCall, 'is meant to give an account of divine activity in relation to the contingent agency of finite creatures'. God 'concurs' human activity through being part of it and providing the powers and abilities to act. Free will then, nor the actions of any creature, cannot be outside the parameter of God's providence. However, this does not mean that creatures are merely vehicles through which God acts. Arminius writes:

'The concurrence of God is not his immediate influx into a second or inferior cause, but it is an action of God immediately flowing into the effect of the creature, so that the same effect in one and the same entire action may be produced simultaneously by God and the creature.'

God is the enabler, or one that empowers, but this is not the same as actually performing or doing the action for the creature. This is crucially important for Arminius' idea of free will and his overall theology of how this is compatible with predestination.

Key quote

No creature acts in complete independence of God; without God's preserving activity they would pass from existence, and without God's concurrence they would be unable to do anything at all. At the same time that he preserves, God also gives creatures the ability to perform actions and concurs with their effects. (Stanglin and McCall)

Arminius: Original Sin and God's 'prevenient' grace (the Holy Spirit) in allowing humans to exercise free will

In regard to sin, Arminius rejected any idea that it is an illusion; however, he was also definitely and resolutely opposed to any suggestion that the origin of sin can be found in God. In line with concurrence, God permits sins and allows sinful acts to occur, rather than making them impossible, but this does not at all mean that God approves of sinful behaviour.

Stanglin and McCall state, 'some things happen because God *does* them, but others because he *allows* them to be done'. Arminius' argument is very much in line with Augustine here: that because God is omnipotent and omnibenevolent, part of God's omnipotent goodness is to be able to produce goods from evils and that this is a far superior solution than to not allow evils at all.

Key quote

Sin is the result of the abuse of creaturely freedom of choice. Sin was not inevitable for creation. It was not forced upon human creatures by some independent evil force … it was not forced upon humans by God. … Sin is the result of the abuse of the precious gift of freedom that God graciously bestowed upon humanity. (Stanglin and McCall)

Unlike the earlier free will theology by Pelagius, Arminius believed that Original Sin, when Adam and Eve ate the forbidden fruit, was bad for humankind. For Arminius, Original Sin is a lack of original righteousness, but it is also a punishment. The physical punishments are pain and death, but the spiritual punishments are less clear to him.

Arminius considers whether spiritually Original Sin meant deprivation or depravation. Deprivation is to be deprived of the original spiritual likeness to God, created in his image that existed prior to Original Sin but has somehow been lost due to the fall of humanity. Depravation is the idea that a certain state was generated, or in Arminius' words 'infused' into humanity because of Original Sin. Arminius tends towards the idea that the consequence of Original Sin was to be deprived of, or lacking, what he calls 'original righteousness and of primeval holiness, with an inclination to sinning, which likewise formerly existed in humanity, although it was not as vehement nor so disordered as it is now'. Despite all this, the two meanings of deprivation and depravation have often been conflated and seen as two sides of the same Original Sin coin.

Therefore, in the fallen state, human beings are deprived of that original righteousness that could so easily seek out good. Despite this, God's providence does give the grace to choose freely the righteous path in life through faith.

Key quotes

Arminius believed that the culpability of that first sin affected, and continues to affect all people, both biologically and socially. (Brian)

In this [fallen] state, the free will of man towards the true good is wounded, infirm, bent, and weakened. (Arminius)

Arminius also believes that God is providentially active in a world marred by sin. Because God is good, he exercises his omnipotence to bring good from evil. (Stanglin and McCall)

Study tip

The key to understanding the difference between deprivation and depravation as a result of Original Sin is to remember 'loss' and 'gain'. For Arminius, the consequences of Original Sin had two elements: (1) 'gaining' a state that had an inclination to sin and (2) 'losing' the original righteous nature God had intended for them before Original Sin.

God's providence provides the grace to choose freely a righteous path in life.

Arminius' understanding of Original Sin means that human beings are not necessarily predestined to continually sin. This is because of God's loving grace. God's grace, for Arminius, is associated with the Holy Spirit. This association of God's grace with God's Holy Spirit is called 'prevenient grace' because God's grace precedes each human moral decision.

Arminius believed that within all human beings God has placed his Holy Spirit. God's subsequent grace works through God's Holy Spirit. The Holy Spirit encourages all human beings to do good works. As Arminius stated, the Holy Spirit will: 'fight against Satan, sin, the world and their own flesh'. Furthermore, the Holy Spirit will be ever present to aid and assist believers through various temptations.

Accordingly, salvation is freely chosen by the righteous but it is not awarded on grounds of merit, as Rustin Brian comments:

'That God might save an infant that has committed no sin is definitely within the realm of possibility for a loving, gracious and all-powerful God. It must also be pointed out that if God elects to do so, it is surely not because salvation is owed, in any way, to any human, let alone an infant. Rather, salvation is the result of God's grace. It is God's hope for humanity, sinful as it is, and it is the hope of God that all might be saved.'

Therefore, despite the encasement of divine providence and the notion of concurrence, Arminius held very strongly that free will was possible within the divine plan. By free will Arminius meant a clear and obvious choice not based upon determinism of causality or context, but a real choice between authentic and actual unconstrained alternatives.

The way this was made possible was through the notion of conditional predestination based upon middle knowledge.

In summary, the notion of divine providence as outlined above, combined with the doctrine of middle knowledge, provided Arminius with the underpinning basis of his theology of conditional predestination. Stanglin and McCall summarise it thus:

'Working from the doctrine of middle knowledge, with its divine knowledge of all possible choices and actions of creatures prior to the divine decision, Arminius is thus able to insist upon a robust doctrine of divine providence. It is one in which the particulars of life are within the overall divine plan – but without divine determinism and its implications for God's involvement with (or "authorship" of) sin.'

God knows all possible outcomes of any possible choices to be made.

Arminius' summarises it as, 'A thing does not happen because it has been foreknown or predicted, but it is foreknown or predicted because it is about to be'. This idea of middle knowledge was developed just before Arminius in the 16th century by Luis de Molina, a Spanish Jesuit priest. Like Arminius, Molina held that middle knowledge did not mean that predestination had to be rejected as God has full knowledge of future contingent events.

Middle knowledge (MK) has certain characteristics:

- MK is prior to any creative act of God (prevolitional)
- MK is independent of God's will
- MK is contingent
- God has full awareness of the various possible outcomes of MK
- MK informs God of what humans would do if a certain scenario beset them.

This aspect of God's providence is the key to understanding the compatibility between free will and predestination according to Arminius. Molinism was made popular again last century through the works of William Lane Craig and Alvin Plantinga.

In order to clarify his position on predestination and salvation, Arminius presented his *Declaration of Sentiments*, a written exposition of his theology, delivered before the states of Holland, at the Hague, on the 13 October 1608. Arminius' theological ideas, and in particular his ideas on free will and predestination, were never meant to spearhead his thinking. His notions were firmly set within the 'bigger picture', or overall decree, of God's providence. As Stanglin and McCall attest:

> 'God's decree is one, yet manifold, dealing with all sorts of matters. The general decree about anything concerning the created order is called God's providence; the special decree about election and salvation in particular is God's predestination.'

This overall framework of providence holds that God does nothing without purpose or plan. Although God's providence is eternal, this is a logical rather than temporal, and this means that it can be 'enacted in time by various means leading to *salvation* or *condemnation*' according to Stanglin and McCall.

Key quote

The decrees of election and reprobation are founded in God's will alone, but salvation and condemnation in time are based on Christ's work and human sin, respectively … Arminius brings Christ back as the foundation of election (not just salvation) and impenitent unbelief as the cause of reprobation. (Stanglin and McCall)

The *Declaration of Sentiments*

Rustin Brian writes:

> 'The issues of predestination and election were so important to Arminius that he risked everything ... to defend his fundamental impulse, namely, that all are elect in Christ, and thus have the real possibility of salvation. God does not will that anyone should perish or be damned.'

This is a crucial point to understand about Arminius. His belief was that despite God's providence and middle knowledge, the fundamental principle was that salvation was available to all. All do not choose salvation, but in principle and within the workings of his theology, they could do. However, God's middle knowledge foresees the conditional predestination of humanity. The fact still remains, God's grace and the possibility of salvation are prior to this predestination.

In order to clarify his views, Arminius was asked to present them. He did so in what is called his *Declaration of Sentiments*. The *Declaration of Sentiments* has four sections (decrees).

The first decree is Christological: Christ fulfills roles as 'Mediator, Redeemer, Saviour, Priest and King'. It is through Christ that people receive salvation. This is the foundation upon which the rest of the decrees rest.

The second decree reads:

> 'To receive into favour those who repent and believe, and, in Christ, for HIS sake and through HIM, to effect the salvation of such penitents and believers as persevered to the end; but to leave in sin and under wrath all impenitent persons and unbelievers, and to damn them as aliens from Christ.' (Arminius)

It is this decree that deals with election and reprobation but according to scholars it is meant to be generic and not about individuals. Stanglin and McCall write, 'It is a decree of corporate salvation and condemnation with reference to the

Key quotes

Arminius affirms foreknowledge without determinism. In his omniscience, God knows all that exists and he also knows all that will be. Middle knowledge means that God knows the result of any contingent event under any hypothetical set of circumstances without necessarily determining that outcome. (Skevington-Wood)

Arminius wrestled with divine sovereignty and human freedom without sacrificing either on the altar of the other. (Stanglin and McCall)

Specification content

Arminius: The Elect and the possibility of rejecting God's grace and the election of believers being conditional on faith.

Key quote

It is, moreover, markedly and deliberately Christ-centred and Christ-controlled. Instead of starting off with God's predestination of individuals, Arminius puts first the decree by which God appointed his Son Jesus Christ for a 'Mediator, Redeemer, Saviour, Priest and King'. (Skevington-Wood)

Key quotes

Arminius is careful to differentiate his understanding of man's free will and ability to do good from that of Pelagius … since it always remains dependent upon the work of God's grace in and through man. (Strudebaker)

God's grace is a 'gratuitous affection' … It is also an 'infusion' of all the gifts of the Holy Spirit which pertains to the regeneration and renewing of man. It is not, however, irresistible, since Arminius sees many scriptural examples of those who do, indeed, 'resist the Holy Spirit and reject the grace that is offered'. (Strudebaker)

God's love is communicated not as an irresistible coercion, but as a tender persuasion that will not finally override the human will. (Stanglin and McCall)

The stress on prevenient, redeeming, and preserving grace makes it abundantly clear that it is on the basis of God's work in them and not their own that believers are elected. (Skevington-Wood)

God has limited his control in correspondence with man's freedom. (Arminius)

… provided they (believers) stand prepared for the battle, implore his help, and be not wanting to themselves, the Spirit preserves them from falling. (Arminius)

properties of belief and unbelief in general.' Arminius states, 'election to salvation and reprobation to condemnation are conditional. God chooses those who are foreknown to be penitent believers, and he condemns those he knows to be impenitent unbelievers'.

Skevington-Wood writes, 'What distinguishes Arminius and Calvinism, in other words, is not that

Jesus Christ is Mediator, Redeemer, Saviour, Priest and King.

the latter has a doctrine of election or predestination while the former does not. Rather, what distinguishes them is the ground of election or predestination. For Calvinists, election is unconditional. For Arminius, it is conditional, based on God's foreknowledge – middle knowledge, to be precise – of a person's faith.'

This conditional predestination is enacted in the third decree in which God manages, directs and orchestrates the divine plan together through God's wisdom and justice, and, by grace in accordance with what is necessary for repentance and faith.

The final decree is the climax of Arminius' theology in that he identifies the means to salvation through God's prevenient grace; he states, 'grace must still precede the human will to enable any turn toward God'. This is the sharp distinction from Pelagius' thinking. Whilst Pelagius, as we have seen, did have some idea of grace and its role, unfortunately he did not establish how exactly this worked and where it belonged in relation to free will. Arminius does this.

Arminius writes that this final decree is, 'in the foreknowledge of God, by which he knew from eternity which persons … through his prevenient grace would believe and through subsequent grace would persevere, and also who would not believe and persevere'. Through middle knowledge God knows who will have faith and who will reject his prevenient grace and then persevere in God's subsequent grace to salvation through Christ's redeeming grace.

However, the security provided by the Spirit was conditional on the believers' own will to follow through on the guidance of the Holy Spirit. As Arminius stated: 'provided they (believers) stand prepared for the battle, implore his help, and be not wanting to themselves, the Spirit preserves them from falling'. Therefore, a human being's impulse to sin, because of their inherited Original Sin, is balanced by the work of the God's Holy Spirit. However, Arminius was clear that the Holy Spirit balances the impulse to sin, rather than overrides it, because the Holy Spirit does not force itself on to a human being; it acts only as a God given moral guide. As Arminius states: 'God has limited his control in correspondence with man's freedom.'

Rustin Brian summarises this fact well:

'Arminius maintained that God's divine foreknowledge does not result in determinism and, therefore, that, while God's eternal foreknowledge includes knowledge of all those that will be saved as well as those that will be damned, it does not guide, force, or fate any person into either salvation or damnation.'

AO1 Activity

(1) Working together in groups of 4 try to arrive at a collective summary of each aspect of Arminius' ideas about free will: rejection of Calvin's predestination theory; Original Sin and free will; 'prevenient' grace of God; the Elect; salvation as conditional upon faith, etc.

(2) Try to make the summary of each one around 50 words.

(3) Jointly present this to the rest of the class.

Arminius free will theory – Synod of Dort

Arminius died in 1609 and a year later his followers put forward their objections to Calvinism in what was called a 'Remonstrance' to the States-General (The Senate and the House of Representatives) of the Netherlands. The document, compiled from Arminius' writings and a development on the latter's *Declaration of Sentiments* (1608), was heavily critical of the Belgic Confession and the teachings of John Calvin, Theodore Beza and Calvinist doctrine; such was the force of the protest that these protestors became known as the Remonstrants.

In 1618–19 a synod was held in the Dutch town of Dordrecht (Dort) consisting of international representatives of the Reformed Protestant Churches from Germany, Switzerland, England and the Netherlands. The meetings had the main aim of uniting the disparate Reformed Churches under the Belgic Confession of 1566, which set out systematically the declaration of faith of Calvinism. One of the other purposes of the synod was to sort out the debate over Arminianism which had risen within the Dutch Reformed Church. Nonetheless, in inviting the Remonstrants to present it appears that this was a mere formality as it is widely held that the teachings of Arminius had already been rejected as reflected in the Counter-Remonstrance of 1611 written by Festus Hommius. The Synod at Dort were to consider both remonstrances and rule on their authenticity. The Arminian teachings were not the only item on the agenda but certainly proved to be a major landmark in establishing the line of the official Dutch Reformed Church.

The Remonstrants presented their objections by way of five articles, extracts from which are detailed below with a summary of their meaning:

Article 1

That God... hath determined, out of the fallen, sinful race of men, to save in Christ ... **those who, through the grace of the Holy Ghost, shall believe on this his son Jesus** ... and, on the other hand, to leave the incorrigible and unbelieving in sin and under wrath, and to condemn them as alienate from Christ ...

Meaning: Salvation is for those who accept God's grace through the Holy Spirit and ascent to faith in Christ.

Article 2

That agreeably thereunto, Jesus Christ the Saviour of the world, **died for all men** and for every man, so that he has obtained for them all, by his death on the cross, redemption and the forgiveness of sins; **yet that no one actually enjoys this forgiveness of sins except the believer** ...

Key terms

Belgic Confession: a Latin document consisting of 37 articles which dealt with the doctrines of God, Scripture, humanity, sin, Christ, salvation, the Church, and the end times from the Dutch Reformed Protestant perspective.

Remonstrance: a word specifically used of the forceful protest of the Arminians of the Dutch Reformed Church in 1610 to the Staten-Generaal in the Netherlands

The Synod of Dordrecht was held between 1618 and 1619.

Meaning: Although freely available to all, this salvation is only available to those who have this faith through the grace of the Holy Spirit.

Article 3

That man has not saving grace of himself ... but that it is needful that he be born again of God in Christ, through his Holy Spirit, and renewed in understanding, inclination, or will, and all his powers, in order that he may rightly understand, think, will, and effect what is truly good, according to the Word of Christ, John 15:5, 'Without me ye can do nothing'.

Meaning: It is only possible to believe and do good through the grace of God since the will of the human being is incapable of resisting sin; the Holy Spirit renews the will to believe and do good.

Article 4

That this grace of God is the beginning, continuance, and accomplishment of all good ... so that all good deeds or movements, that can be conceived, must be ascribed to the grace of God in Christ, but respects the mode of the operation of this grace, it is not irresistible; inasmuch as it is written concerning many, that they have resisted the Holy Ghost.

Meaning: God's grace is not irresistible and human beings can reject the Holy Spirit.

Article 5

That those who are incorporated into Christ by true faith, and have thereby become partakers of his life-giving Spirit, have thereby full power to strive against Satan, sin, the world, and their own flesh, and to win the victory; it being well understood that it is ever through the assisting grace of the Holy Ghost; and that Jesus Christ assists them through his Spirit in all temptations ...

Meaning: Through the assisting grace of the Holy Spirit a believer is enabled to partake the life-giving power of the Spirit.

Although rejected by the synod as contrary to the Bible, the Remonstrants refused to accept the ruling and were expelled from the Dutch Reformed Church. This then prompted the Dutch Reformed Church to respond by adding to the Belgic Confession by way of the canons of Dort, which were an official written response to the five points of the original Arminian remonstrance. These are the basis of the Dutch Reform Church today and the teachings of Arminius found home with the Methodist Protestant Church under the leadership of John Wesley, the founder of Methodism.

quickfire

4.31 Do the 'Five Articles of Remonstrance' accurately sum up Arminius' free will argument?

AO1 Developing skills

It is now important to consider the information that has been covered in this section; however, the information in its raw form is too extensive and so has to be processed in order to meet the requirements of the examination. This can be achieved by practising more advanced skills associated with AO1. The exercises that run throughout this book will help you to do this and prepare you for the examination. For assessment objective 1 (AO1), which involves demonstrating 'knowledge' and 'understanding' skills, we are going to focus on different ways in which the skills can be demonstrated effectively, and also refer to how the performance of these skills is measured (see generic band descriptors for A2 [WJEC] AO1 or A Level [Eduqas] AO1).

▶ **Your new task is this:** you will have to write a response under timed conditions to a question requiring an examination or explanation of **the implications of free will on God's omnipotent nature**. This exercise is best done as a small group at first.

1. Begin with a list of indicative content, as you may have done in the previous textbook in the series. It does not need to be in any particular order at first, although as you practise this you will see more order in your lists that reflects your understanding.

2. Develop the list by using one or two relevant quotations. Now add some references to scholars and/or religious writings.

3. Then write out your plan, under timed conditions, remembering the principles of explaining with evidence and/or examples.

When you have completed the task, refer to the band descriptors for A2 (WJEC) or A Level (Eduqas) and in particular have a look at the demands described in the higher band descriptors towards which you should be aspiring. Ask yourself:

- Does my work demonstrate thorough, accurate and relevant knowledge and understanding of religion and belief?
- Is my work coherent (consistent or make logical sense), clear and well organised?
- Will my work, when developed, be an extensive and relevant response which is specific to the focus of the task?
- Does my work have extensive depth and/or suitable breadth and have excellent use of evidence and examples?
- If appropriate to the task, does my response have thorough and accurate reference to sacred texts and sources of wisdom?
- Are there any insightful connections to be made with other elements of my course?
- Will my answer, when developed and extended to match what is expected in an examination answer, have an extensive range of views of scholars/schools of thought?
- When used, is specialist language and vocabulary both thorough and accurate?

Key skills Theme 4

The final sections of theme four have tasks that consolidate your AO1 skills and focus these skills for examination preparation.

Key skills

Knowledge involves:

Selection of a range of (thorough) accurate and relevant information that is directly related to the specific demands of the question.

This means:

- Selecting relevant material for the question set
- Being focused in explaining and examining the material selected.

Understanding involves:

Explanation that is extensive, demonstrating depth and/or breadth with excellent use of evidence and examples including (where appropriate) thorough and accurate supporting use of sacred texts, sources of wisdom and specialist language.

This means:

- Effective use of examples and supporting evidence to establish the quality of your understanding
- Ownership of your explanation that expresses personal knowledge and understanding and NOT just reproducing a chunk of text from a book that you have rehearsed and memorised.

Specification content

How convincing are religious views
on free will?

Key quote

God has limited his control in
correspondence with man's freedom.
(Arminius)

AO2 Activity

As you read through this section try to
do the following:

1. Pick out the different lines of
argument that are presented in
the text and identify any evidence
given in support.

2. For each line of argument try to
evaluate whether or not you think
this is strong or weak.

3. Think of any questions you may
wish to raise in response to the
arguments.

This Activity will help you to start
thinking critically about what you
read and help you to evaluate the
effectiveness of different arguments
and from this develop your own
observations, opinions and points
of view that will help with any
conclusions that you make in your
answers to the AO2 questions that
arise.

Issues for analysis and evaluation

How convincing are religious views on free will?

The initial point of departure for this critical analysis and evaluation is the omnipotence of God. Ideas of free will have been reflected in the philosophy section of this Specification in response to the problem of evil and suffering. In response to the idea that God is 'all-powerful', a theodicy of free will, in various forms, has been presented, not least by Augustine. In terms of 'free will' as a defence, as a notion to pacify the existence of evil and suffering, the other side of the coin so to speak is to then justify the nature of free will in itself in relation to the omnipotence of God. Indeed, it could be argued that Augustine wrestled with both these problems in different ways.

It could be argued that with the problem of evil, Augustine laid emphasis on the fall of humanity and the inadequacy of the human condition, whereas with the nature of free will in itself he stressed the omnipotence of God. Augustine appears to have bridged the gap thus absolving God of any responsibility for evil and allowing free will with an emphasis on God's grace. The thrust of Augustine's argument seems to be that an omnipotent God can retain these characteristics since God has an overall plan through his omnibenevolence; namely, the felix culpa and the opportunity for God's grace.

Some may argue that Augustine is inconsistent, since the notion of free will in the fall emphasises humanity's freedom to disobey, and this seems at odds with the idea of an omnipotent God. The Australian philosopher John Mackie clearly identified the nub of the issue when he raised his concerns about what he called the paradox of omnipotence. The essence of this is that if God is omnipotent, then to suggest there is something that God is not able to control or do then we are admitting that God cannot be omnipotent. In other words, if we allow free will for humanity then how can God be omnipotent? Mackie pointed out that the solution of free will, or any theodicy, is to compromise God's omnipotence.

However, some could argue that Mackie's assumption was that he failed to distinguish between having something and using it. In a sense Mackie's definition of God's characteristic of omnipotence is absolute power, authority and strength but something that is a constant not just in what it is but what it does. Therefore, Mackie's own understanding of omnipotence is skewed.

Religious believers can argue that omnipotence has a definitive absolute of being but also by logic an infinite range of action. In other words to say God is omnipotent does not mean God can only do omnipotent things; God must be allowed to exercise the full range of possible actions. Similar to Hick's epistemic distance, the calculated step backwards is not that God 'gives up' control or 'allows' freedom but that God exercises omnipotence within the full range of possibilities that omnipotence allows.

In support of this line of argument, Augustine clearly identifies the omnipotence of God as a God who is within its power to permit freedom whilst simultaneously having an overall plan that demonstrates God's omnipotent nature. For Augustine, the end of salvation maintains the integrity of God's omnipotence.

To return to Mackie's paradox, some could argue that Mackie had this the wrong way around: it should be 'Can God create something that God *chooses* not to exercise/use control over?' The answer 'yes' is not denying omnipotence at all, as God is *not losing* power but *using power*. For religious believers, then, God, in allowing free will, does give up 'control' but the mistake would be to equate this with giving up omnipotence. Therefore God does not lose omnipotence nor do we need to redefine it, simply God chooses as and when to exercise omnipotence, to what extent and how far.

The key issue here could be that it is possible to argue that it is unconvincing to argue that omnipotence can be maintained when abdicating some authority, and whether or not Mackie's whole point of re-defining omnipotence is valid.

It is this same principle that is at the heart of the debate between predestination and free will from a religious perspective. Augustine, Calvin, Pelagius and Arminius are all seeking an answer to the problematic relationship between predestination and free will. This may seem to challenge traditional notions of how the Christian God could be omnipotent, omniscient and omnibenevolent; but it is not the same way as it is for philosophy.

Following on from this, it could be argued that through Arminius' doctrine of divine concurrence, Arminius ensures God's control in that God 'concurs' human activity by being part of it, providing the powers and abilities to act. The notion of divine providence for Arminius involves both preservation of the world but crucially governance of it whilst simultaneously allowing for human freedom. God sustains the universe by being involved in it. Free will, then, or the actions of any creature, cannot be outside the parameter of God's providence.

Indeed, there are many other examples of how the idea of free will is explained by religious believers. There are examples from other religions. The notion of free will is central to some Holocaust theologies in Judaism; in Islam, the debate between the Mu'tazilites and the Asharites tries to make sense of free will and the omnipotence of Allah; in Buddhism, the notion of anatta (not self) has raised the issue for many of moral responsibility; there have been developments in the free will debate by such philosophers as Alvin Plantinga and the possible worlds argument; and, contemporary works in theology and neuroscience by such writers as Nancey Murphy and Neil Messer are examples of explaining free will and moral responsibility.

It could be argued that all the above are coherent attempts to explain the notion of free will in light of an omnipotent deity (or, in the case of Buddhism the absence of a self) and for many, the notion of free will is essential to religious belief. There could be said to be a strength in relation to the statement. Indeed, it does appear that the evidence seems to suggest that religious views on free will are convincing; and yet, the crucial question is 'for whom?'

This raises an important distinction between persuasiveness – that is, being convincing – and that of coherency. It is clear they are 'coherent' arguments and merit some debate, but whether they are convincing is another question altogether.

Key quotes

The concurrence of God is not his immediate influx into a second or inferior cause, but it is an action of God immediately flowing into the effect of the creature, so that the same effect in one and the same entire action may be produced simultaneously by God and the creature. (Arminius)

A thing does not happen because it has been foreknown or predicted, but it is foreknown or predicted because it is about to be. (Arminius)

AO2 Activity

List some conclusions that could be drawn from the AO2 reasoning from the above text; try to aim for at least three different possible conclusions. Consider each of the conclusions and collect brief evidence to support each conclusion from the AO1 and AO2 material for this topic. Select the conclusion that you think is most convincing and explain why it is so. Try to contrast this with the weakest conclusion in the list, justifying your argument with clear reasoning and evidence.

Specification content
The degree to which beliefs about
free will can be reconciled with beliefs
about predestination

Key quotes

Give me the grace to do as you
command, and command me to do
what you will. (Augustine)

… people fall freely and culpably
and that out of the fallen race God
saves some, leaving others to perish;
although God knows from the
beginning which he intends to save
and which to abandon. (Hick)

We (humanity) may not seem to be
forced to do evil through a fault in
our nature. (Pelagius)

AO2 Activity

As you read through this section try to
do the following:

1. Pick out the different lines of
   argument that are presented in
   the text and identify any evidence
   given in support.

2. For each line of argument try to
   evaluate whether or not you think
   this is strong or weak.

3. Think of any questions you may
   wish to raise in response to the
   arguments.

This Activity will help you to start
thinking critically about what you
read and help you to evaluate the
effectiveness of different arguments
and from this develop your own
observations, opinions and points
of view that will help with any
conclusions that you make in your
answers to the AO2 questions
that arise.

The degree to which beliefs about free will can be reconciled with beliefs about predestination

This critical analysis and evaluation are concerned not with free will, in general, but with whether or not the idea that we are free during life can be reconciled with a belief that God has already determined how the religious and non-religious will respond to God's grace, that is, an offer of salvation. Predestination is to do with 'final destination' and surely must be part of God's omnipotent character, which also incorporates omniscience? If we are responsible for freely choosing or rejecting God, then how can God be omnipotent?

If one accepts the arguments put forward by Pelagius then free will is exercised beyond God's control if one rejects the idea of predestination. However, we need to be careful since some argue that Pelagius does allow for a role of God's grace in salvation in that the Holy Spirit assists the believer in leading the good life that will lead to salvation.

Augustine argued the case that our wills, though free, are not directed to desiring the things of God due to Original Sin. Therefore God's grace is crucial because it is this that redirects desires so that human beings can freely obey him and find happiness.

Alister McGrath in his book *Christian Theology: An Introduction* argues that the idea of predestination is often viewed in a very direct and very deterministic way. Indeed, it could be argued that it is very different from the idea of causal determination. McGrath points out that Augustine sees those who reject God as not actively condemned to damnation but that 'they were merely not elected to salvation'. For McGrath, predestination is a positive concept and when seen in this light it is much more meaningful; that is, predestination is a deliberate decision to redeem on God's part rather than a deliberate decision to condemn. This is often called the notion of single predestination. The 'election' is part of God reaching out and enabling people to freely accept salvation. Viewed from this perspective one could defend the coherency of a free will and predestination partnership in conceptual terms.

Key quote

Working from the doctrine of middle knowledge, with its divine knowledge of all possible choices and actions … the particulars of life are within the overall divine plan – but without divine determinism and its implications for God's involvement with (or 'authorship' of) sin. (Stranglin and McCall)

However, it has been demonstrated by some scholars that there are texts by Augustine which seem to present an idea of double predestination. Indeed, John Lennox argues that it is illogical to argue that it is just a matter of God's choice to redeem because this also implies a rejection of some. Lennox supports his argument with a quote from Augustine: 'As the Supreme God, he made good use of evil deeds, for the damnation of those whom he had justly predestined to punishment and for the salvation of those whom he had mercifully predestined to grace.'

The main objection to the reconciliation of free will with predestination appears to be the problem of God controlling and knowing everything as suggesting that if some were to be damned then this was the plan all along. However, this is where one could use the arguments of Arminius, who distinguished between an immanent knowledge and a plan that will be executed. Arminius was influenced by molinism, an idea presented by a 16th-century Spanish Jesuit priest called Luis de Molina. It is called 'middle knowledge' and attempts to maintain God's omnipotent character in terms of predestination but also acknowledge that God is both benevolent and allows for free will. Arminius argued, 'A thing does not happen because it has been foreknown or predicted, but it is foreknown or predicted because it is about to be'. In other words, God has full knowledge of future contingent events, that is full awareness of the various possible outcomes and informs God of what humans would do if a certain scenario beset them; however, it is prior to any creative act of God (pre-volitional) and independent of God's will. This aspect of God's providence is the key to understanding the compatibility between free will and predestination according to Arminius. Indeed, in support of this understanding of the reconciliation of free will and predestination, molinism was made popular again last century through the works of William Lane Craig and Alvin Plantinga.

It could be argued that the key issue from a religious perspective is to offer a solution to understanding the nature of the terms 'predestination' and 'free will' in the light of God's absolute omnipotence. Theologians focus much more on how our choices affect our salvation. Their concern is about whether our salvation is achieved through our own free ethical actions or whether our salvation can only be achieved through God's actions, and our choices have no ultimate effect on our salvation. Although it may not make sense to some philosophers, theologians tend to ask different questions such as 'how much free will?' and 'how much does God choose to control and determine?' rather than see the problem as clear cut, either it does reconcile or it doesn't.

In the history of the problem of free will, philosophers are more concerned about such questions as 'do we have free will?' or 'are human beings determined?' per se; they are different because questions from a religious perspective are already encased within the belief in an almighty, omnipotent deity who has ultimate power and control. However, it is interesting to see that in the last 60 years the idea of 'absolute free will' has often been seen to be illogical for philosophers.

In practice, it could be argued that this involves positions that are not poles apart as the Specification may suggest, between free will and predestination or free will and determinism. The issue for any religious concepts or theologies is not therefore, are free will and predestination compatible? The answer to this is clearly 'yes'. The issue seems to be to what extent is this compatibility balanced or distributed between the two parameters of free will and God's omnipotent nature. Therefore, it could be concluded that we may find that thinkers such as Pelagius, Augustine and Arminius share much more common ground than at first is thought.

Key quotes

Arminius maintained that God's divine foreknowledge does not result in determinism and, therefore, that, while God's eternal foreknowledge includes knowledge of all those that will be saved as well as those that will be damned, it does not guide, force, or fate any person into either salvation or damnation. (Rustin Brian)

… people fall freely and culpably and that out of the fallen race God saves some, leaving others to perish; although God knows from the beginning which he intends to save and which to abandon. (Hick)

AO2 Activity

List some conclusions that could be drawn from the AO2 reasoning from the above text; try to aim for at least three different possible conclusions. Consider each of the conclusions and collect brief evidence to support each conclusion from the AO1 and AO2 material for this topic. Select the conclusion that you think is most convincing and explain why it is so. Try to contrast this with the weakest conclusion in the list, justifying your argument with clear reasoning and evidence.

Key skills Theme 4

The fourth theme has tasks that consolidate your AO2 skills and focus these skills for examination preparation.

Key skills

Analysis involves:

Identifying issues raised by the materials in the AO1, together with those identified in the AO2 section, and presents sustained and clear views, either of scholars or from a personal perspective ready for evaluation.

This means:

- That your answers are able to identify key areas of debate in relation to a particular issue
- That you can identify, and comment upon, the different lines of argument presented by others
- That your response comments on the overall effectiveness of each of these areas or arguments.

Evaluation involves:

Considering the various implications of the issues raised based upon the evidence gleaned from analysis and provides an extensive detailed argument with a clear conclusion.

This means:

- That your answer weighs up the consequences of accepting or rejecting the various and different lines of argument analysed
- That your answer arrives at a conclusion through a clear process of reasoning.

AO2 Developing skills

It is now important to consider the information that has been covered in this section; however, the information in its raw form is too extensive and so has to be processed in order to meet the requirements of the examination. This can be achieved by practising more advanced skills associated with AO2. The exercises that run throughout this book will help you to do this and prepare you for the examination. For assessment objective 2 (AO2), which involves 'critical analysis' and 'evaluation' skills, we are going to focus on different ways in which the skills can be demonstrated effectively, and also refer to how the performance of these skills is measured (see generic band descriptors for A2 [WJEC] AO2 or A Level [Eduqas] AO2).

▶ **Your new task is this:** you will have to write a response under timed conditions to a question requiring an evaluation of **the effectiveness of religious views on free will**. This exercise is best done as a small group at first.

1. Begin with a list of indicative arguments or lines of reasoning, as you may have done in the previous textbook in the series. It does not need to be in any particular order at first, although as you practise this you will see more order in your lists, in particular by way of links and connections between arguments.

2. Develop the list by using one or two relevant quotations. Now add some references to scholars and/or religious writings.

3. Then write out your plan, under timed conditions, remembering the principles of evaluating with support from extensive, detailed reasoning and/or evidence.

When you have completed the task, refer to the band descriptors for A2 (WJEC) or A Level (Eduqas) and in particular have a look at the demands described in the higher band descriptors towards which you should be aspiring. Ask yourself:

- Is my answer a confident critical analysis and perceptive evaluation of the issue?
- Is my answer a response that successfully identifies and thoroughly addresses the issues raised by the question set?
- Does my work show an excellent standard of coherence, clarity and organisation?
- Will my work, when developed, contain thorough, sustained and clear views that are supported by extensive, detailed reasoning and/or evidence?
- Are the views of scholars/schools of thought used extensively, appropriately and in context?
- Does my answer convey a confident and perceptive analysis of the nature of any possible connections with other elements of my course?
- When used, is specialist language and vocabulary both thorough and accurate?

E: Concepts of libertarianism

This section covers AO1 content and skills

Specification content
Philosophical (Jean-Paul Sartre: man is not free not to be free, waiter illustration).

Libertarianism

The strict interpretation of philosophical libertarianism is of a will that is totally free, usually referred to as causa sui (meaning self-caused). In other words, a will that is free because it is independent of causes or conditions.

Traditionally, such libertarianism has been associated with the dualism of body-mind (soul) with its typical expressions found in Descartes and Kant. This dualist position proposed that the will is a process initiated by a controlling metaphysical entity (mind or soul). Descartes presented his philosophical justification for dualism in the form of thought-awareness or consciousness, but he could not link the mind with the brain. Kant, through transcendental idealism, argued that 'pure reason' was the link between the material and the metaphysical.

However, the idea of dualism for understanding how the will is free is not a popular position that is taken today. As such, most neuroscientists and philosophers tend to reject the role of a metaphysical entity as determining a person's decisions. Therefore, the idea that a 'free' and independent central 'control room' that can now be explained in purely materialistic terms – as a similar notion to the 'soul' or 'mind – is the focus for debate today. This does not necessarily mean, however, that the term 'soul' or 'self' is no longer relevant, but simply that many have re-defined what this could refer to.

Over the last 100 years or so – and particularly with the advancements in neuroscience and technology – different and significant understandings of free will have emerged. For French philosopher Jean-Paul Sartre free will is undeniable, but his views have steadily lacked support and are in decline. In recent times there has been a surge in the popularity of different materialist explanations for the body and mind (consciousness), e.g. Daniel Dennett's 'simulated self', or Robert Kane's 'self-forming actions'. Therefore, it is clear that different answers given to what is actually meant by the term 'free will' mean that there are different explanations of libertarianism today. In addition, Galen Strawson's claim that *a priori* the notion of an absolute and radical free will is impossible has meant a shift to a more empirical basis for the debate. Hence the Specification states '**concepts** of libertarianism'.

In this section we will look at three different versions for free will (libertarian concepts) from Jean-Paul Sartre's existential thought, Sirigu's scientific evidence and Rogers' psychological theory of self-development; however, directly linked is T4F, which deals with the implications of libertarianism, or free will, for ethics. For some, the notion of free will cannot be separated from ethics. In addition, as we have seen, there is no small debate about exactly what is meant by the term 'free will'. Indeed, this affects views on moral responsibility (see T4F) and so this debate will be explored briefly there. In a similar way in T4C (though less complicated), there are debates about what is meant by determinism.

In order to address this, T4E will be shorter than T4F and at the start of T4F there is a little tour through the history of the different understandings of free will that may be beneficial to contextualise the whole debate about free will and serve as background but it will also provide some breadth to any critical analysis and evaluation (AO2) pertinent to the whole of T4, including this section.

Key term
Causa sui: something that is independent of cause

Philosophical Libertarianism – Jean Paul Sartre (1905–1980)

Being and nothingness: consciousness

Descartes is famed for his famous declaration: cogito ergo sum, meaning 'I think, therefore I am'. To help understand Sartre, it may be useful to consider the reverse: sum ergo cogito, which would mean 'I am therefore I think'. Sartre begins with Descartes' observation that consciousness implies existence, but the nature or essence of existence is not located in the 'I am' but rather, in the 'I think'. For Sartre, an **existentialist** philosopher, his famous declaration was the 'existence precedes essence'; that is, our life experience is one of a constant wrestling of the ego to become self-conscious and define our authentic identities. As O'Donohoe writes, 'consciousness is necessarily embodied: it comes into being only with our advent in the world at birth and goes out of being with our exit from the world in death'.

The philosopher Jean-Paul Sartre

Sartre's philosophy is, therefore, completely atheistic; indeed, the absence or negation of any controlling factor outside humanity is key to his definition of existence. He writes, 'Atheistic existentialism, of which I am a representative, declares with greater consistency that if God does not exist there is at least one being whose existence comes before its essence, a being which exists before it can be defined by any conception of it. That being is man or, as Heidegger has it, the human reality. What do we mean by saying that existence precedes essence? We mean that man first of all exists, encounters himself, surges up in the world – and defines himself afterwards.'

Our existence in the world is down to our constituent parts, our bodies, and yet our experience of the world is being self-conscious and that in some way we are part of the world and yet simultaneously not part of it. In *Being and Nothingness* Sartre states, 'a human is that which is not what it is, and, is what it is not'.

This means that for Sartre our self-consciousness is a result of the process of interaction of our consciousness with existence; in 'essence' consciousness is nothing in itself other than being conscious of something; that is, the something, that which is experience, is integral to consciousness. Consciousness is not the object. Consciousness is no-thing, or, nothingness (**neant**); not having being, it is supported by being. A human being's very essence is nothingness, that is 'what it is not'.

Key quote

… there has never been any possibility of not choosing oneself. It is absurd in this sense – that the choice is that by which all foundation and all reasons come into being, that by which the very notion of the absurd receives its meaning. **(Sartre)**

Key quotes

Man is nothing else but that which he makes of himself. That is the first principle of existentialism … Before that projection of the self, nothing exists … Man is responsible for what he is. **(Sartre)**

The existence precedes essence. This means that man first exists, occurs, arises in the world, and he then defines himself. **(Sartre)**

quickfire

4.32 Why are Kant and Descartes significant for libertarianism?

Key terms

Existentialism: a philosophical theory that understands the existence of the individual person as free and responsible for determining their own development through acts of the will

Neant: Sartre's understanding of human essence as empty of being-in-itself or 'nothingness', not having being, it is supported by being

Freedom is existence

Sartre explains human existence, this interaction of 'surging' upwards into the world, as 'being-for-itself' (etre-pour-soi). The being-for-itself brings its nothingness into the world and therefore can stand out from being-in-itself by seeing what it is not. By this, Sartre meant that self-consciousness defines itself as awareness of objectivity through an annihilation of being-in-itself. This was in contrast to 'being-in-itself' (etre-en-soi) which has no say in its destiny because it lacks consciousness. Being-in-itself, for Sartre, is what he calls facticity. Through the process of reflection (reflexion) self-consciousness defines itself as reflection (reflet), that is, the form in which the being-for-itself founds its own nothingness.

For Sartre, a human being is 'condemned to be free' because (s)he is 'thrown into the world'. The great irony is that human beings are determined to be free in the sense that they have no choice! The concept of freedom is inherent to the nature of self-consciousness. He writes: Freedom 'is a choice of its being but not the foundation of its being ... This choice is absurd, not because it is without reason but because there has never been any possibility of not choosing oneself ... It is absurd in this sense – that the choice is that by which all foundation and all reasons come into being, that by which the very notion of the absurd receives its meaning.' Therefore, the very being of the for-itself is condemned to be free. It must forever choose for itself and thereby define itself.

When Sartre spoke about freedom he was not referring to particular cases but rather the distinction between the character of human existence and other forms of existence. He claimed that human beings are unconditionally free regardless of their circumstances. Just as the 'being-in-itself' is conditioned physically, the idea that the 'being-for-itself' is anything other than free is an absurdity; the condemnation of human existence is that it defines itself by its freedom.

The ego and authenticity

For Sartre, the struggle and anxieties of self-consciousness (ego) is the essential discriminating freedom to see the 'self', from outside itself, as an object within the world and this brings with it the insight that we can make things as other than they had been, are or will be. For Sartre it was this 'gap' of self-consciousness that is the very defining feature of our freedom. Freedom scares and brings with it anxiety and insecurity; and yet, it is this very gap that allows self-consciousness to define itself without being restricted by the nauseous and inanimate nature of being-in-itself.

However, this does not mean that in defining oneself in one's freedom creates an empirical or metaphysical 'self' but an existential, authentic conscious self that supersedes facticity. He writes: 'For the for-itself, to be is to nihilate the in-itself which it is. Under these conditions, freedom can be nothing other than this nihilation. It is through this that the for-itself escapes its being as its essence; it is through this that the for-itself is always something other than what can be said of it.'

In other words, this act of nihilation of the in-itself forms part of, and contributes towards, our authentic identity. The authenticity of self-consciousness was, for Sartre, the ultimate goal for an existentialist – he writes: '[I am] condemned to exist forever beyond my essence, beyond the causes and motives of my act. I am condemned to be free.' Authenticity means taking full responsibility for our life through freedom, choices and actions.

Key quotes

Freedom has no essence. It is not subject to any logical necessity. (Sartre)

Everything has been figured out, except how to live. (Sartre)

We are our choices. (Sartre)

Every man must invent his own path. (Sartre)

Actually, we are a freedom which chooses, but we do not choose to be free: we are condemned to freedom. (Sartre)

I build the universal in choosing me, I build it by understanding the project from any other man, whatever time it is. (Sartre)

Key terms

Etre-en-soi: Sartre's phrase for inanimate matter and being without consciousness, a 'being-in-itself'

Etre-pour-soi: Sartre's innovative distinction of the authentic self in the process of becoming, a being-in-itself

Facticity: the reality of 'being-in-itself'

Gap: Sartre's notion of distance between a person's consciousness and the physical world that necessitates people to have free will

Reflet: Sartre's subtle distinction of the reflecting process that is a 'mirror' of the self-conscious but yet in itself has no essence; in his own words, 'that precise obligation to be a revealing intuition of something'

Anxiety is the dizziness of freedom. (Sartre)

Not choosing is a choice. (Sartre)

Choice and consciousness are one and the same thing. (Sartre)

Key term

Mauvaise foi: bad faith, but better understood as self-deception

quickfire

4.33 Why did Sartre think the waiter in the café was acting in bad faith?

Is this waiter a little too waiter-esque for Sartre?

'Bad faith' as self-deception: the waiter as an illustration of bad faith

For Sartre, the establishment of authentic and free existence could only be achieved through eradication of what he called 'mauvaise foi', which literally translates as 'bad faith' but is better understood as self-deception.

Self-deception is an attitude of fear in which one remains being-in-itself because it is safe from the anxiety of freedom. Why does an individual do this? It is because the individual would know exactly what was expected, what is allowed and what is not allowed. Such an attitude seeks the safety of being-in-itself by hiding beneath the expectations of etiquette and social constraints. In short, although this is in itself a free choice, it is also an act of self-negation because it avoids the reality of their own freedom. Sartre used the illustration of a waiter in a café to demonstrate mauvaise foi.

His movement is quick and forward, a little too precise, a little too rapid. He comes toward the patrons with a step a little too quick. He bends forward a little too eagerly; his voice, his eyes express an interest a little too solicitous for the order of the customer. Finally there he returns, trying to imitate in his walk the inflexible stiffness of some kind of automaton while carrying his tray with the recklessness of a tight-rope walker by putting it in a perpetually unstable, perpetually broken equilibrium which he perpetually re-establishes by a light movement of the arm and hand. All his behaviour seems to us a game. He applies himself to chaining his movements as if they were mechanisms, the one regulating the other, his gestures and even his voice seem to be mechanisms, he gives himself the quickness and pitiless rapidity of things … He is playing, he is amusing himself. But what is he playing? We need not watch long before we can explain it; he is playing at being a waiter in a café.

There is no doubt that as a matter of facticity (being-in-itself) the man is being a waiter. There is no deception in the nature of waiting upon tables; however, the self-deception arises in the identification of self with 'waiter' since being a waiter offers no form of ultimate security. There is no deception in earning a living as a waiter; however the self-deception arises when that is considered the sum of his identity. As Professor Vincent Spade writes:

'But of course being a waiter is not the end of the story about this man. It doesn't give him any kind of definition once and for all, as if he were a waiter and nothing else. On the contrary, he is a waiter who is free. Every morning he freely gets up early and sweeps out the café, he freely starts the coffee. At any time, he could stop doing that. He could just decide to stay in bed some morning. He might get fired, of course, but he is free to get fired. He could quit, he could burn the café to the ground. He could run off and join the Foreign Legion.'

In other words, a person's essence cannot be defined by a role; the role simply provides the springboard for the pursuit of being-for-itself and the context from which one exercises free will. A person is more than being defined by a label, more than being 'just' a waiter. Sartre's point is that in trying too hard to be a waiter one cannot transcend beyond facticity. It is this 'attitude' of 'self-negation', where consciousness 'turns it toward itself', toward the being-in-itself instead of directing its negation outward.

Sartre, free will and moral responsibility

Sartre sees human beings as moving from an initial state of being at birth that is fixed (being-in-itself) towards a state of freedom from such constraints that physical life brings through becoming self-consciousness, i.e. a being-for-itself. However, the journey of free will is challenging and full of anxieties, constantly being restrained by the nausea of being-in-itself. To be truly free means to be fully responsible. To live life amongst facticity with the self-deception of being-in-itself is a free choice to make but such an attitude means one is not truly free. It is an act of mauvaise foi, 'bad faith' that is the defining feature of self-deception.

Max Stirner spoke of uniqueness; Sartre speaks of 'authenticity'. Stirner speaks of 'spooks', of being subconsciously slave to norms or ideals; Sartre speaks of 'self-deception' or 'bad faith'. However, Sartre's freedom has very different implications to Stirner's self-interest when it comes to ethics. Sartre is an interesting case in the debate about free will.

Betty Stoneman (PhD Emory University) sees Sartre as an ethical egoist; however, Sartre identified himself as a Marxist. This problem of reconciling an existentialist philosophy that lends itself to Ethical Egoism with Marxist principles was a problem for Sartre but one that he worked through by his explanation of 'being-for-others' (etre-pour-autrui). In a similar way that Ethical Egoism is not necessarily 'individualistic' but through long-term goals and co-operation with others, Sartre extends this to the Marxist ideal. For Sartre, there was a moral duty to oneself to be ethical in one's dealings with others. Even more so if one truly appreciated the authenticity of being-for-itself. Sartre's understanding of freedom and free will inevitably means that one is fully responsible for one's behaviour and actions.

> **Key term**
>
> Etre-pour-autrui: Sartre's new dimension in which the self exists as an object for others, a 'being-for-others'

Key quotes

Man is condemned to be free; because once thrown into the world, he is responsible for everything he does. It is up to you to give [life] a meaning. (Sartre)

Life has no meaning a priori … It is up to you to give it a meaning, and value is nothing but the meaning that you choose. (Sartre)

> **AO1 Activity**
>
> Sartre is extremely complex and challenging because of the way he expressed himself, even for professional academics and philosophers today. Try to focus on key notions and create some flash cards with the notion on the front and an explanation of this *in your own words* on the back.

Study tip

The key for understanding Sartre is the analogy he uses of the waiter – the main idea to understand is the idea of self-deception. Try to see if you can find other analogies Sartre used to explain this. It may reinforce your learning.

Specification content

Scientific (Angela Sirigu's research evidence that the brain allows for free will).

Key terms

Cognitive neuroscience: scientific study of the biological processes and neural connections in the brain

Parietal cortex: one of the four major lobes of the cerebral cortex in the brain containing grey matter that transforms visual information into motor commands

Premotor cortex: one of the four major lobes of the cerebral cortex in the brain that initiates movement

Scientific libertarianism – Dr Angela Sirigu

We now move on to consider the evidence of cognitive neuroscience. This particular focus is on how the brain communicates messages from one area to another in order to create decisions for action. The researchers involved have experimented in manipulating the key areas for initiating choice and for initiating movement to see whether or not our intentions to act and our actions themselves based upon such volitions can be explained.

In 2009, a team of scientists led by Dr Michel Desmurget and Dr Angela Sirigu, based at the *Centre for Cognitive Neuroscience* in Lyon, France, published an article in the international journal *Science*. It claimed that by electrically stimulating the posterior parietal cortex of the brain (containing grey matter that transforms visual information into motor commands) it was possible to produce intentions to act. Subjects reported a 'desire' for movement; however, no subjects actually carried out the movement to which they referred.

This is the published abstract, summarising their findings:

> Parietal and premotor cortex regions are serious contenders for bringing motor intentions and motor responses into awareness. We used electrical stimulation in seven patients undergoing awake brain surgery. Stimulating the right inferior parietal regions triggered a strong intention and desire to move the contralateral hand, arm, or foot, whereas stimulating the left inferior parietal region provoked the intention to move the lips and to talk. When stimulation intensity was increased in parietal areas, participants believed they had really performed these movements, although no electromyographic activity was detected. Stimulation of the premotor region triggered overt mouth and contralateral limb movements. Yet, patients firmly denied that they had moved. Conscious intention and motor awareness thus arise from increased parietal activity before movement execution.
>
> ***Desmurget, Michel & Reilly, Karen & Richard, Nathalie & Szathmari, Alexandru & Mottolese, Carmine & Sirigu, Angela. (2009). Movement Intention After Parietal Cortex Stimulation in Humans.* Science (New York, N.Y.)**

This experiment involved specific cortical circuits that, when triggered, are associated with sensations that arise in the course of wanting to initiate and then carry out a voluntary action.

(1) It was found that when specific junctions of nerve cell communication were identified and these circuits were given fixed boundaries and limits, it created the neuronal correlates of consciousness for intention and agency. When such correlates in the parietal cortex were manipulated by increasing stimulation, patients believed that they had actually moved or talked, but no muscle activity was detected.

(2) When, however, the premotor cortex region of the frontal lobes was stimulated, movements were induced. However, patients did not experience these movements as produced by a conscious internal act of will. Indeed, they were not even aware that they had moved. Increasing stimulation intensity increased the amplitude or complexity of the movement but never made it reach consciousness.

Neuroscientists at work

quickfire

4.34 What experiment did Sirigu complete in 2009?

The same team have been working over the last 10 years. Their most recent research in 2018 looked at how volitions could be prevented and it concluded: 'These results provide direct evidence that a specific area in the dorsoposterior parietal cortex can inhibit volitional upper-limb responses with high selectivity.' In other words, this once again demonstrated that the parietal cortex appears to be the area where decisions are initiated. 'During motor inhibition, all patients were fully aware of their inability to move. Typical verbatim were as follows: "I cannot do it; it's hard" or "I cannot move anymore". When prompted to describe how they felt after the stimulation, the patients reported that they felt the blockage and that they could not move, no matter how hard they tried.'

Desmurget concluded that: 'Our results indicate that electrical stimulation at focal sites within a restricted area of the dorsoposterior parietal cortex inhibits volitional upper-limb motor responses with high selectivity. Identification of this inhibitory process is of primary importance to understand how intended actions are suppressed either at the preparation stage or following movement completion.'

Conclusions: How does the work that Desmurget and Sirigu were involved with fit in with the wider philosophical debate about free will?

For Professor Koch, the studies demonstrate 'true progress, beyond the eternal metaphysical question of free will that will never be answered'; however, as Koch correctly points out, knowing how something works does not necessarily answer the question of voluntary agent control, or free will.

Indeed, this is another leap in reasoning sometimes illogically made. An article in *National Geographic* written by science writer Ed Yong in 2009 concluded: 'they show that our feelings of free will originate (at least partially) in the parietal cortex. It's the activity of these neurons that creates a sense that we initiate actions of our own accord.' However, Yong quotes another neuroscientist, Professor Patrick Haggard, who describes all such experiments as 'unsatisfactory, even paradoxical'. In Haggard's view this is no different to instructing people to 'have free will now!'

It is clear that such experiments do create a sense of ownership over our own movements; however, the mystery of ownership in terms of 'who' or 'what' still seems to be the key question. Indeed, Yong concludes, that traditional notions of dualism and an operating agent have been challenged by neuroscientific studies like these because they demonstrate that the conscious intention to move emerges from electrical activity in neurons, tangible objects that are all too real.

AO1 Activity

If you have some time, try doing an Internet search on free will and neuroscience in order to gather some more evidence and quotes to use in your explanations.

Study tip

You are not being examined on your ability to express a scientific argument here; what is expected is that you are aware of developments in neuroscience and the evidence it presents us with in relation to how the will works and what conclusions we can draw from this.

Key quotes

How can this ghost, made out of some kind of metaphysical ectoplasm, influence brain matter without being detected? What sort of laws does Casper follow? Science has abandoned strong dualistic explanations in favour of natural accounts that assign causes and responsibility to specific actors and mechanisms that can be further studied. And so it is with the notion of the will. (Koch)

In the debate concerning the meaning of personal freedom, these discoveries represent true progress, beyond the eternal metaphysical question of free will that will never be answered. (Koch)

When stimulation intensity was increased in parietal areas, participants believed they had really performed these movements, although no electromyographic activity was detected. Stimulation of the premotor region triggered overt mouth and contralateral limb movements. Yet, patients firmly denied that they had moved. (Desmurget)

quickfire

4.35 Why is the work of Sirigu inconclusive about free will?

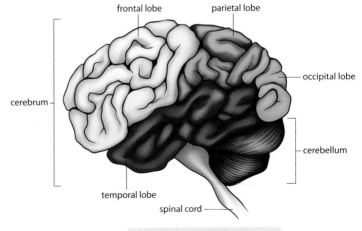

Anatomy of the human brain

Specification content
Psychological (Carl Rogers: humanist approach, self-actualisation).

Key quotes

The only means of healing that psychotherapy has learned to use is itself a human being, the therapist, whose own psychology also must have a decided influence upon the treatment and its outcome. (Rank)

Psychology does not deal primarily with facts as science does but only with the individual's attitude towards facts. (Rank)

Psychological Libertarianism – Carl Rogers (1902–1987)

Carl Ransom Rogers was an American psychologist and is often seen as the founder of the humanistic approach to client therapy. His approach is known as Rogers Client-Centred Therapy (RCCT) and throughout his lifetime Rogers was given numerous awards for applied psychology.

Rogers advocated humanistic psychology, which is not to be confused with psychological humanism or humanism itself. The RCCT approach is a stark contrast to Sartre's existentialism; for Rogers' RCCT the assumption was that 'essence precedes existence'; that is, human beings were born with innate goodness. Rogers was a professional practitioner and this is the context from which his ideas of free will must be understood.

Rogers rejected two trends in psychotherapy:

- Freud's stand-off objectivity of the therapist and a view of the client as an object to be analysed as opposed to a subject to be engaged with.
- The idea that our behaviour is determined solely by external social conditioning and that the purpose of psychotherapy is to deal with any negativity of the past and develop behaviours to cope with the future.

In Carl Rogers we see another understanding of the free will of the individual to 'grow' themselves through change. The ability of the will to induce change was essential for Rogers. Carl Rogers is seen as the official founder of a humanistic psychology; however, Rogers was inspired at an early age by the teachings of Otto Rank (himself influenced by Eastern ideas of spirituality). It was Otto Rank who proposed a departure from the Freudian tradition and suggested a client-centred approach. It was also Otto Rank who first argued that the psychiatrist or psychologist advocates only the authority to become the 'assistant I' (that is, an extension of the patient's self and not an onlooker from outside) and deliver 'a Philosophy of Helping'.

Although the professional term is RCCT, the approach of Rogers was to focus on the 'person' as a whole. Rogers published his first book *Client-Centered Therapy* in 1951. In this first work he highlighted his ideas about understanding the relationships human beings have with each other and the ability humans have to help each other emerge from this interaction as self-empowered individuals. His later book in 1961 was duly titled *Becoming a Person* and is a selection of papers that outline aspects of his theories and practical approaches to understanding self-growth or self-development towards a congruent, creative and fully functioning person.

Rogers held that any therapist should have three essential characteristics. Therapists must:

- Be congruent individuals, which means a fully balanced personality and fully functioning person.
- Accept that the client is a separate individual with their own perspectives and interpretations of life.
- Have genuine empathy with the client and sensitive to their needs.

Underlying Rogers' approach were the following principles:

- All people are inherently good and are born with 'essence' of good character.
- A holistic approach to human existence was required to become fully functioning.
- Special attention should be afforded to creativity, free will, and the positive human potential.
- We need to view ourselves as a 'whole person' greater than the sum of our parts, that is, something beyond mere physicality.

- Self-exploration is the key to becoming a stronger individual rather than trying to study and learn from the behaviour found in others.
- Humanistic psychology acknowledges spiritual aspiration as an integral part of the psyche, that is, the desire to be fulfilled.

Key quotes

This approach lays stress upon the therapeutic relationship itself as a growth experience. (Rogers)

Real therapy has to be centred around the client, his difficulties, his needs, his activities … My technique puts the patient himself as chief actor in the centre of the situation set up by the analysis. (Rank)

Rogers' theory of free self-development

Rogers' actual theory of self-development assumed that with innate goodness, human beings were also born with an inherent and underlying 'actualising tendency', which 'aims to develop all capacities in ways that maintain or enhance the organism and move it toward autonomy'. This tendency requires the belief in free will and is directional, constructive and present in all living things. It is a directional tendency in each of us to grow, to seek new and varied experiences. Rogers argued that 'the organism has one basic tendency and striving – to actualise, maintain, and enhance the experiencing organism'.

Rogers argued that although there was a possibility that throughout the ups and downs of childhood and adulthood the actualising tendency could be suppressed, it could never be destroyed without destruction of the person. It is almost as if we are born with a positive attitude to succeed. Rogers then used this idea to develop a psychological therapy based on self-actualisation that involved a person's own psyche, in particular, their perspective and understanding of themselves in the 'here and now'. Two terms that were significant were the 'actual self' or 'real self' and the 'ideal self'.

The real or actual self describes the ideas of self-worth that have been formed in childhood and through early relationships with parent(s). It also incorporates the perceptions of self-image, both outward (body image) and inward (personality). In contrast, the ideal self is one of aspirations and a reflection of the innate actualising tendency. This is the person who we would like to be. It includes the goals and ambitions that we have in life. The ideal self is a fluid notion, creative, dynamic and ever-changing.

Congruence

Congruence is a word Rogers introduced to measure the self-actualising process. Congruence, in geometrical terms, means that things are identical in form, or, when superimposed they overlap exactly. In general usage, congruence means that things are in agreement or in harmony. Rogers' theory begins with the therapist and their status in the relationship. This must be one of congruency. He writes:

> 'It is found that personal change is facilitated when the psychotherapist is what he *is*, when in the relationship with his client he is genuine and without "front" or façade, openly being the feelings and attitudes that are flowing *in* him. We have coined the term "congruence" to try to describe this condition.'

The idea is that consistency between a person's ideal self and what they actually experience in life (real/actual self) is not always apparent. The less apparent it is, the more incongruent they are and prone to psychological problems. The greater level of consistency between the two concepts, the better the congruency

quickfire

4.36 Why was the approach of Carl Rogers to psychotherapy considered innovative?

The correct client–therapist relationship was key for Rogers.

Key terms

Actual self: the view that we have of our self as a result of life experience

Actualising tendency: an innate directional tendency in each of us to grow, to seek new and varied experiences

Congruence: that a person has harmony between real and ideal selves

Ideal self: our aspiration of who we want to be

of a person. That is, where a person's ideal self and real/actual self-experiences are consistent or very similar, a state of congruence exists. It is very rare for the geometrical alignment to exist as a total state of congruence; it is in the very nature of human experience to encounter a certain amount of incongruence.

Rogers' theory of congruence is often represented by two intersecting circles:

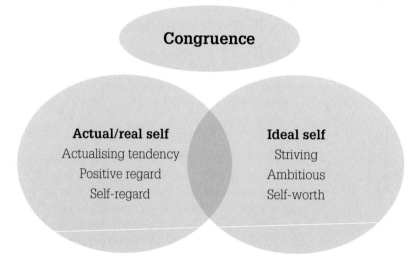

The idea is that the greater the overlap (shaded area), the more fulfilled a person will be. Incongruent individuals have less overlap. As stated above, complete geometrical overlap is extremely unlikely; however, the aim is to bring them as close together as possible through self-actualisation for congruency. The congruent individual – generally that is, and not precisely vis a vis mathematically – is what he called a **fully functioning person**. The ideal is not one of 'achievement' of a final state, or journey's end, but rather a process of becoming through balanced participation in, and open response to, the constant changes one experiences.

Key quotes

I have since become keenly aware that the point of view I developed in therapy is the sort of help I myself would like. (Rogers)

If I can provide a certain type of relationship, the other person will discover within himself the capacity to use that relationship for growth and change, and personal development will occur. (Rogers)

The fully functioning person

Rogers' therapy is unashamedly optimistic because everyone is free to achieve their goal of fulfilment in life. Indeed, Rogers argued that fully functioning individuals are balanced, adjusted and interesting and this meant quite naturally that they are often what we may call 'high achievers' in society. To be a fully functioning person (FFP) involves fluidity of experience, being in touch with – and understanding – the 'here and now' so that subjective feelings in response to the flow of experience lead to growth and change. According to Rogers, there are four areas to be developed to become a fully functioning person:

1. Openness

An FFP is increasingly open to all experiences, including those that are threatening. Such 'negative' experiences are opportunities to work through the problems rather than fight against them. Rogers called this 'the polar opposite of defensiveness'. He writes: 'A large part of the process of therapy is the continuing discovery by the client that he is experiencing feelings and attitudes which heretofore he has not been able to be aware of, which he has not been able to "own" as being part of himself.'

Key term

Fully functioning person: a congruent person that participates in the fulness of life experience

---

Key quote

One aspect of this process which I am naming the 'good life' appears to be a movement away from the role of defensiveness toward the pole of openness to experience. (Rogers)

2. Existential living

For the FFP, the ability for existential living means an ability to move forward by living 'fully in each moment'. Rogers did not want this idea to be confused with 'living **for** each moment'. Existential living means the acceptance of fluidity of experience, avoiding rigidity, being adaptable and being 'a flowing, changing organisation of self and personality'. In other words, it is the experience of participation rather than one of control through preconceived ideas. Rogers concludes: 'It means that one becomes a participant and an observer of the ongoing process of organismic experience, rather than being in control of it.'

3. Increasing trust

This is like a sort of self-confidence that one's feeling, instincts and gut-reactions are reliable, or, as Rogers states, 'an increasing trust in his organism as a means of arriving at the most satisfying behaviour in each existential situation'. In other words, we trust ourselves to make the right choices. Rogers makes an analogy with an 'electronic computing machine' whereby the FFP can evaluate effectively and make competent decisions based upon data available. Rogers' recognises that this process is not infallible but the beauty of this 'trust' is balanced with the openness to the 'process of being corrected, because they would be continually checked in behaviour'.

4. Functioning more fully

For the FFP, life experience was 'fuller' in its entirety according to Rogers. This last feature is really where, in the words of Rogers, 'I should like to draw together these threads describing the process of the good life into a more coherent picture.' This fourth aspect is where Rogers' creates a sum of all parts of the previous three: openness to feelings, being able to make use of one's 'organic equipment to sense, as accurately as possible, the existential situation within and without', and, trusting one's judgement 'in all its complexity in selecting from the multitude of possibilities, that behaviour which in this moment of time will be generally and genuinely satisfying'.

Key quotes

It appears that the person who is psychologically free moves in the direction of becoming a more fully functioning person. He is more able to live fully in and with each and all of his feelings and reactions.

The paradox is that when I accept myself just as I am, then I can change for the better. (Rogers)

The organism has one basic tendency and striving – to actualise, maintain and enhance the experiencing organism. (Rogers)

How does Roger's psychology fit in with the wider philosophical debate about free will?

Rogers was a psychologist and not a philosopher. His view of free will was completely ingrained within the idea of his theory of personal change and development. But, as a psychologist, he was also a scientist and appreciated that there was growing evidence that in terms of the human person 'we are, like any scientist, committed to a complete determinism'. Rogers adds, 'From this point of view every thought, feeling and action of the client is determined by what preceded it. There can be no such thing as freedom.'

However, it is interesting that in his book *On Becoming a Person* published in 1961, Rogers openly faced the challenges of the free will and determinism debate in the light of the implications of his FFP theory. He argued that he now saw the 'age-old issue … in a new light'. For Rogers, the dilemma disappears in light of his theory.

Key quotes

One way of expressing the fluidity which is present in such existential living is to say that the self and personality emerge from experience, rather than experience being translated or twisted to fit pre-conceived self-structure. (Rogers)

Yet as I observe the clients whose experience in living have taught me so much, I find that increasingly such individuals are able to trust their organismic reaction to a new situation because they discover an ever-increasing degree that if they are open to their experience, doing what 'feels right' proves to be a competent and trustworthy guide to behaviour which is truly satisfying. (Rogers)

quickfire

4.37 Why is openness a key concept for Rogers?

For Rogers an FFP was a measure of strong and positive personal development.

Key quote

I am impelled to believe that I, like many others, have underestimated the importance of this mystical, spiritual dimension. (Rogers)

He argued that 'in the optimum of therapy the person rightfully experiences the most complete and absolute freedom'. This is because Rogers saw the course of action of an FFP as 'the most economical vector in relationship to all the internal and external stimuli ... But this is the same course of action which from another vantage point may be said to be determined by all the factors in the existential situation.' In contrast, the incongruent person who is 'defensively organised' is determined by denial and distortion and is not free to make an effective choice. Rogers concluded that it is the FFP that 'not only experiences, but utilises, the most absolute freedom when he spontaneously, freely and voluntarily chooses and wills that which is absolutely determined'.

It would appear, then, that Rogers was a compatibilist. That is, he accepts the nature of deterministic features whilst simultaneously acknowledging the freedom that we experience. His logic was that there had to be some form of freedom for 'direction' and change to be made in our lives. There also needs to be room for creativity in the FFP and that this is typical of the type of behaviour 'that adapt and survive under changing environmental conditions'; in short, such a person would be 'a fit vanguard of human evolution'.

It is interesting to note that nine years before his death Rogers, writing in his 1978 book *Is this the only reality?*, stated that despite not having any spiritual experience or 'glimpse of a world different from our secure "real" world', the evidence seemed 'more impressive' to him. He continued:

'Perhaps in the coming generations of younger psychologists ... there will be a few who will dare to investigate the possibility that there is a lawful reality that is not open to our five senses; a reality in which present, past and future are intermingled, in which space is not a barrier, and time has disappeared; a reality that can be perceived and known only when we are passively receptive, rather than actively bent on knowing. This is one of the most exciting challenges posed to psychology.'

Indeed, this is characteristic of his later interest in the relationships between the scientific foundation of psychology and expressions of eastern mysticism, different forms of spiritual experience and Taoism.

Quick overview comparing Sartre and Rogers on free will

Theme	Sartre	Rogers
Self	Existence precedes essence – thrown into freedom	Essence precedes existence – innate goodness
Life experience	Future gives the present meaning	The 'here and now' is the focus
Aims of using free will	Awareness and acceptance of the human condition as self-consciousness	Awareness and acceptance of innate goodness and the potential of the human self
Means of achieving aim	Through the process of reflection (reflexion) self-consciousness defines itself	Self-actualisation
Outcome	State of being-in-itself	Congruence: a fully functioning person (FFP)
Good life =	Use free will to achieve a life lived without bad faith that is authentic	A use of free will to ensure creative, fulfilled life trusting feelings and experience

Study tip

Always make sure that you assign the correct concepts to the correct thinker. Devising mnemonics is an effective way of doing this.

AO1 Activity

Using the table comparing Sartre and Rogers on free will, try to write a paragraph for each theme that would explain their differences and similarities.

AO1 Developing skills

It is now important to consider the information that has been covered in this section; however, the information in its raw form is too extensive and so has to be processed in order to meet the requirements of the examination. This can be achieved by practising more advanced skills associated with AO1. For assessment objective 1 (AO1), which involves demonstrating 'knowledge' and 'understanding' skills, we are going to focus on different ways in which the skills can be demonstrated effectively, and also refer to how the performance of these skills is measured (see generic band descriptors for A2 [WJEC] AO1 or A Level [Eduqas] AO1).

▶ **Your new task is this:** you will have to write a response under timed conditions to a question requiring **an explanation of Sartre's views on free will**. This exercise can either be done as a group or independently.

1. Begin with a list of indicative content, as you may have done in the previous textbook in the series. This may be discussed as a group or done independently. It does not need to be in any particular order at first, although as you practise this you will see more order in your lists that reflects your understanding.

2. Develop the list by using one or two relevant quotations. Now add some references to scholars and/or religious writings.

3. Then write out your plan, under timed conditions, remembering the principles of explaining with evidence and/or examples. Then ask someone else to read your answer and see if they can then help you improve it in any way.

4. Collaborative marking helps a learner appreciate alternative perspectives and possibly things that may have been missed. It also helps highlight the strengths of another that one can learn from. With this in mind, it is good to swap and compare answers in order to improve your own.

When you have completed the task, refer to the band descriptors for A2 (WJEC) or A Level (Eduqas) and in particular have a look at the demands described in the higher band descriptors towards which you should be aspiring. Ask yourself:

- Does my work demonstrate thorough, accurate and relevant knowledge and understanding of religion and belief?

- Is my work coherent (consistent or make logical sense), clear and well organised?

- Will my work, when developed, be an extensive and relevant response which is specific to the focus of the task?

- Does my work have extensive depth and/or suitable breadth and have excellent use of evidence and examples?

- If appropriate to the task, does my response have thorough and accurate reference to sacred texts and sources of wisdom?

- Are there any insightful connections to be made with other elements of my course?

- Will my answer, when developed and extended to match what is expected in an examination answer, have an extensive range of views of scholars/schools of thought?

- When used, is specialist language and vocabulary both thorough and accurate?

Key skills

Knowledge involves:

Selection of a range of (thorough) accurate and relevant information that is directly related to the specific demands of the question.

This means:

- Selecting relevant material for the question set

- Being focused in explaining and examining the material selected.

Understanding involves:

Explanation that is extensive, demonstrating depth and/or breadth with excellent use of evidence and examples including (where appropriate) thorough and accurate supporting use of sacred texts, sources of wisdom and specialist language.

This means:

- Effective use of examples and supporting evidence to establish the quality of your understanding

- Ownership of your explanation that expresses personal knowledge and understanding and NOT just reproducing a chunk of text from a book that you have rehearsed and memorised.

Specification content

The extent to which philosophical, scientific and/or psychological views on libertarianism inevitably lead people to accept libertarianism.

Key quotes

Man can will nothing unless he has first understood that he must count on no one but himself; that he is alone, abandoned on earth in the midst of his infinite responsibilities, without help, with no other aim than the one he sets himself, with no other destiny than the one he forges for himself on this earth. (Sartre)

One has to help them to get beyond the deadlock in their personality and in the process find their own self. (Rogers)

AO2 Activity

As you read through this section try to do the following:

1. Pick out the different lines of argument that are presented in the text and identify any evidence given in support.

2. For each line of argument try to evaluate whether or not you think this is strong or weak.

3. Think of any questions you may wish to raise in response to the arguments.

This Activity will help you to start thinking critically about what you read and help you to evaluate the effectiveness of different arguments and from this develop your own observations, opinions and points of view that will help with any conclusions that you make in your answers to the AO2 questions that arise.

Issues for analysis and evaluation

The extent to which philosophical, scientific and/or psychological views on libertarianism inevitably lead people to accept libertarianism

One could argue that in terms of philosophy, Sartre's argument that we cannot not be free inevitably leads people to accept libertarianism. Sartre sees human beings as moving from an initial state of being at birth that is fixed (being-in-itself) towards a state of freedom from such constraints that physical life brings through becoming self-consciousness, i.e. a being-for-itself. However, there is a subtle paradox with Sartre in that the 'state' of being-for-itself is the nihilation of being-in-itself. This being-in-itself he refers to as facticity. Nonetheless, through the process of reflection (reflexion) self-consciousness defines itself as reflection (reflet), that is, the form in which the being-for-itself founds its own nothingness. Therefore, one is left with the question 'what' exercises the free will? It appears to be that Sartre is arguing that there is an inherent misconception in asking 'do we have free will?' since the very nature of true freedom means that there is no substantial agent to perform it.

A different line of argument is taken by Professor Galen Strawson, who is renowned for establishing an *a priori* proof through a philosophical argument of logic that rejects the notion of free will. It is referred to as the basic argument and involves the term causa sui, a Latin term meaning 'cause of itself'. For Strawson, unless it could be demonstrated that human beings are 'free to choose what to do in such a way that they can be truly, genuinely responsible for their actions in the strongest possible sense', then we cannot accept the notion of free will.

Despite this, it also needs to be pointed out that Strawson argues that the way in which we have a sense of freedom is of interest, what he calls the 'general cognitive phenomenology of freedom'. He writes that it is still of interest since, 'this experience is something real, complex, and important, even if free will itself is not real'. He concludes that we must accept free will as an illusion. In other words, we accept the illusion of libertarianism despite rejecting its truth! Nonetheless, for Strawson we can never be fully responsible for our actions and so this is certainly not accepting of libertarianism.

Key quote

Dualist philosophers like Descartes believed that the mind and consciousness exist outside the physical world, producing our actions by interacting with the physical meat of our brains. The idea has become commonplace, but it's challenged by neuroscientific studies like this one, which show that the conscious intention to move emerges from electrical activity in neurons, tangible objects that are all too real. (Yong)

In terms of psychology, Carl Rogers, in his book *On Becoming a Person* openly faced the challenges of the free will and determinism debate in the light of the implications of his 'fully functioning person' ideal. He argued that he now saw the 'age-old issue ... in a new light'. For Rogers the dilemma disappears in light of his theory. He argued that 'in the optimum of therapy the person rightfully experiences the most complete and absolute freedom' because it is the most economical response to all surrounding conditions. In other words, Rogers argues that in being determined by conditions in line with the fully functioning person, an individual is actually exercising free will. For Rogers, an individual under such conditions 'freely and voluntarily chooses and wills that which is absolutely determined'. However, it could be argued that Rogers was a more of a compatibilist than a fully blown libertarian even though he still insisted that there had to be some form of freedom for 'direction' and change to be made in our lives. His views on creativity contain a similar argument that a creative response to stimuli is typical of the type of behaviour 'that adapt and survive under changing environmental conditions' and therefore 'a fit vanguard of human evolution'. In this way one could say that Rogers' understanding of free will is not at all libertarian. Therefore, it would be difficult to say that a 'libertarian' view of free will in terms of Rogers' psychological theories inevitably leads to an acceptance of libertarianism.

Another psychologist is Susan Blackmore. Blackmore presents a very different argument about free will and so it could be argued that alternative views in psychology – just as in philosophy above – mean that people do not inevitably accept the theory of libertarianism. Blackmore rejects the Cartesian Theatre since she is a practising Buddhist and so adheres to the notion of anatta (not-self). She argues that because we do not look back and reflect momentarily or continually on what we were previously conscious of raises a serious question about the credibility of a 'continuous consciousness'. For Blackmore, the notion of a self being conscious of its own consciousness loses its power because the same self would, if it existed, be free and independent and have such oversight. In reality there was no-one to be conscious. It appears that the argument from Buddhist psychology would be that when we try to find a point of existence that would verify this free and independent self it just slips though our fingers. Many Buddhists would also reject the notion of libertarianism since it would argue that the self that it seeks is not the same empirical self of reality.

Finally, it is almost a universal acceptance that when evidence is indeterminate it would be an error to argue it is convincing. So, if I had a 50:50 chance of winning the lottery, I could not say that it was an inevitable conclusion that I would win the lottery – that would be absurd. The evidence from science for libertarianism is at best indeterminate. Most scientists would say it is simply unconvincing. However, if we do not take a strict, absolutist definition of libertarianism, it could be accepted that some kind of will executing decisions from various computations, is in a sense 'free' in that it chooses or selects the optimum from the options available. Many modern agent-causal theories do this and indeed, Daniel Dennett would see himself as a compatibilist.

Therefore, the evidence from Sirigu's research is indeterminate. Even fellow scientists are sceptical of making too much of this. Professor Koch argues that whilst progress is made, the eternal metaphysical question of free will can never be answered.

The free will **taxonomy** demonstrates that there are too many different and attractive alternatives to absolute libertarianism and this in itself challenges the assertion of the statement. However, we may speak of new forms of 'libertarianism' other than one absolute version, which now seems redundant. In conclusion, the 'inevitable' aspect suggested by the initial statement seems to be too far; at best libertarianism as presented by philosophy, psychology and science is not even convincing.

Key term

Taxonomy: the overall scheme of classification of ideas

AO2 Activity

List some conclusions that could be drawn from the AO2 reasoning from the above text; try to aim for at least three different possible conclusions. Consider each of the conclusions and collect brief evidence to support each conclusion from the AO1 and AO2 material for this topic. Select the conclusion that you think is most convincing and explain why it is so. Try to contrast this with the weakest conclusion in the list, justifying your argument with clear reasoning and evidence.

AO2 Developing skills

It is now important to consider the information that has been covered in this section; however, the information in its raw form is too extensive and so has to be processed in order to meet the requirements of the examination. This can be achieved by practising more advanced skills associated with AO2. For assessment objective 2 (AO2), which involves 'critical analysis' and 'evaluation' skills, we are going to focus on different ways in which the skills can be demonstrated effectively, and also refer to how the performance of these skills is measured (see generic band descriptors for A2 [WJEC] AO2 or A Level [Eduqas] AO2).

▶ **Your new task is this:** you will have to write a response under timed conditions to a question requiring an evaluation of **the extent to which an individual has free will.** This exercise can either be done as a group or independently.

1. Begin with a list of indicative arguments or lines of reasoning, as you may have done in the previous textbook in the series. It does not need to be in any particular order at first, although as you practise this you will see more order in your lists, in particular by way of links and connections between arguments.

2. Develop the list by using one or two relevant quotations. Now add some references to scholars and/or religious writings.

3. Then write out your plan, under timed conditions, remembering the principles of explaining with evidence and/or examples. Then ask someone else to read your answer and see if they can then help you improve it in any way.

4. Collaborative marking helps a learner appreciate alternative perspectives and possibly things that may have been missed. It also helps highlight the strengths of another that one can learn from. With this in mind, it is good to swap and compare answers in order to improve your own.

When you have completed the task, refer to the band descriptors for A2 (WJEC) or A Level (Eduqas) and in particular have a look at the demands described in the higher band descriptors towards which you should be aspiring. Ask yourself:

- Is my answer a confident critical analysis and perceptive evaluation of the issue?

- Is my answer a response that successfully identifies and thoroughly addresses the issues raised by the question set?

- Does my work show an excellent standard of coherence, clarity and organisation?

- Will my work, when developed, contain thorough, sustained and clear views that are supported by extensive, detailed reasoning and/or evidence?

- Are the views of scholars/schools of thought used extensively, appropriately and in context?

- Does my answer convey a confident and perceptive analysis of the nature of any possible connections with other elements of my course?

- When used, is specialist language and vocabulary both thorough and accurate?

Key skills

Analysis involves:

Identifying issues raised by the materials in the AO1, together with those identified in the AO2 section, and presents sustained and clear views, either of scholars or from a personal perspective ready for evaluation.

This means:

- That your answers are able to identify key areas of debate in relation to a particular issue

- That you can identify, and comment upon, the different lines of argument presented by others

- That your response comments on the overall effectiveness of each of these areas or arguments.

Evaluation involves:

Considering the various implications of the issues raised based upon the evidence gleaned from analysis and provides an extensive detailed argument with a clear conclusion.

This means:

- That your answer weighs up the consequences of accepting or rejecting the various and different lines of argument analysed

- That your answer arrives at a conclusion through a clear process of reasoning.

F: The implications of libertarianism and free will

This section covers AO1 content and skills

Specification content
The implications of libertarianism on moral responsibility.

Implications of libertarianism on moral responsibility (the general debate)

As we have seen from Theme 4E, the debate about libertarianism has taken several turns, most pertinently around trying to define what precisely is meant by 'free'. The notion of volition (will) is central to much philosophical and neuroscientific study. Therefore, this section of the Specification is very open-ended. It attempts to deliver a broad survey of the debate about free will and indicate the implications that this debate has for morality.

As explained earlier in T4E, this section is intended to be a tour through the history of the different understandings of free will (notions of libertarian thought) that may be beneficial to contextualise the whole debate about free will and serve as background. It is also hoped that it will provide some more breadth to any critical analysis and evaluation (AO2) pertinent to the whole of T4, including this section. Therefore, as such, it is offered in the spirit of presenting teachers and students with an authentic AO1 assessment skill experience whereby they can **select**, **organise** and **present** from the range of evidence and examples presented here to 'demonstrate knowledge and understanding of religion and belief' (AO1). Obviously not everything here can be downloaded into an examination answer and so it is important to be selective. However, the material is also there to be **used** (not presented), that is, 'analyse', as evidence and examples and 'evaluate aspects of, and approaches to, religion and belief, including their significance, influence and study' (AO2).

> **Key term**
> Volition: the 'will' or mind process that initiates action

Study tip

Remember that this section contains many different examples of how free will has been understood in relation to morality. Obviously not everything here can be selected for an examination answer and so it is important to plan your answers with this in mind depending upon the focus of the question set.

Hard determinism is a relatively straightforward concept. Everything is beyond 'our' control in the sense that we cannot freely control the decisions we make; however, we may think we choose freely but the fact is everything is determined for us, biologically, neurologically and chemically. This is distinct from a fatalistic view (as observed in T4B). For determinists, then, it seems we do not need to worry about whether we are free or not. If we think we have free will, then we are just deluded by an illusion.

It certainly may appear amusing that determinists, then, take a conscious decision and choose to write about why they are not free! That, however, is only a very basic perspective; however, it seems reasonable because it is the experience that human beings are presented with. Dr Susan Blackmore, a hard-line determinist, once asked the philosopher John Searle whether he believed in free will or not and he replied, 'Well, I don't have a choice about that!' The ironic paradox is that if he had deliberated and answered that there was no free will, that is itself only intelligible as an exercise of free will! In the words of Sartre, 'Not choosing is a choice'. But this is all part of what some call the 'illusion' of free will and the reason John Searle believes we are, after thousands of years of debate, no closer to solving the problem.

Study tip

Whilst students are expected to know the scholars on the specification in depth, with no need to bring in added scholars, this section introduces a host of scholars not on the specification which can enhance comprehension. It may be useful for a more general question for AO1 and can be freely brought in, where appropriate, and used as evidence for AO2 questions.

Key term

Dualism: the idea that there is both
a physical reality and a metaphysical
reality; a body and soul or a mind
and body

Key quotes

All theory is against the freedom
of the will; all experience is for it.
(Johnson)

Human brains are just the most
complicated thing that's yet evolved,
and we're trying to understand them
using our brains. (Dennett)

quickfire

4.38 Why did John Searle think he has no
choice about believing in free will?

The debate about free will is also inextricably connected to the debate about personal identity, that is, the nature of freedom. Many philosophers may have rejected traditional dualism and embraced a deterministic platform for the debate, but to say we have only an illusion of free will does not answer the question as to **why** we have that experience – albeit an illusion – of free will. We would certainly choose to dodge an incoming brick aimed at our head, or we would certainly select and order our preference of food on a menu. In either case we would decide to act. As John Searle argues, we would not see an oncoming brick and say, 'Well it is going to hit my head and so whatever will be, will be'; neither, do we reply to a waiter who asks us what we would like to eat by saying, 'I'll have whatever arrives because I am a determinist'.

It is therefore this **experience of free will** – and not just establishing the philosophical validity of free will – that has been explored quite intensely in philosophy over the last 100 years. In addition, this has been considered in an **inter-disciplinary** way in light of the advances in science, psychology and neuroscience. It is a logical necessity that how we understand free will determines the level of culpability that we have for our actions. This will be the focus of this section.

The definition of a 'radical libertarianism' is 'one's actions are not determined by anything prior to a decision, including one's character and values, and one's feelings and desires' but even contemporary radical libertarians such as Robert Kane argues that accounts of true libertarianism are unintelligible because they cannot account coherently for indeterminism and chance. Therefore, to begin with, there is an important

When it is time to eat is it our free will that chooses for us or are our choices determined?

distinction to be made between some different understandings of freedom in the process of decision making for a human being:

1. That the physical body that presents the will is controlled by some form of independent conscious entity (mind) or metaphysical entity (soul) – also known as traditional dualism.

2. A free (independent) decision is exercised by some form of personal consciousness (that is, an understanding of an independent process within the consciousness) that initiates the will.

3. There is freedom in the sense there is some form of 'calculation' that occurs within and by a whole organism (that is, an understanding that freedom is not an independent notion but one that is contained within physical/materialistic processes) and is a direct cause for the will.

The second and third perspectives open us up to versions of contemporary libertarian thinking that incorporate the 'determined' physical nature, including biological and neuroscientific processes. Indeed, there has been a shift in the last sixty years or so from dualism as two separate modes of existence (i.e. physical and metaphysical) to one that considers the viability of a dualistic process of decision making within a physicalist or materialist explanation and the implications of this. The traditional dualist base for reflection has been replaced to incorporate up to date neuroscientific and psychological understandings and the goal posts, so to speak, have been shifted. Philosophical responses have reflected this shift in understanding.

However, this is not just true of libertarianism but also of determinism. For example, Galen Strawson's solution as a determinist is to say we have no alternative but to embrace the illusion of free will even though it is untrue. Rather than answering why, however, he explores **the different ways** this may be so; ultimately, nonetheless, according to Strawson we cannot therefore be fully responsible for our actions. As Natasha Gilbert stated in *Philosophy Now* (2016): 'A revolution is occurring in the debate on free will that requires the renouncement of instinctively held ideals and beliefs ... Giving up libertarianism, however, isn't a step to be taken lightly, since it encapsulates the kind of freedom we normatively think we have and need. The greatest obstacle, therefore, is going to be whether people can live with the truth concerning free will.' The philosopher Saul Smilansky has suggested that we need to 'start from the collapse that results from the realisation of the absence of libertarian free will and its implications, and then reconstruct the free will related conceptual world on the basis of the shallower compatibilist resources'.

This reaction is not solely from philosophical perspectives. Theologically there has also been a shift. We shall see that the likes of Professor Nancey Murphy and Professor Neil Messer have proposed ways to make sense of the classical views of dualism in light of the contemporary debate. Buddhist psychology has also contributed to the debate through intellectuals like Dr Susan Blackmore.

What we understand by the term 'free will' is the very heart of the problem but also what we mean by the '**agent**' of free will. This question has been asked for thousands of years and has been said to be the most difficult topic in philosophy. For some, the notion of free will cannot be separated from ethics since it raises issues of ultimate responsibility for actions. Therefore, before this can be meaningfully teased out, there needs to be some notion of what the debate about free will has been about. In order to do this, a little tour through the history of philosophy may be beneficial to contextualise the debate about free will and serve as background and context for T4DEF but it will also provide some breadth to any critical analysis and evaluation (AO2).

The libertarianism debate: free will and moral responsibility

If you asked an academic about the free will debate, they would speak of determinism, indeterminism, libertarianism that is event-caused and agent-caused, soft libertarianism, compatibilism (soft determinism), hard determinism, semi-compatibilism, incompatibilism, and also narrow and broad compatibilism – the taxonomy appears to be endless. There are also versions linked to specific academics like Dennett's Valerian model, Daring's Soft Libertarianism and Strawson's Real Physicalism. Sometimes terms are useful but sometimes they can be very confusing. It is actually possible to read an article where two philosophers debate their 'different' positions and find that their understanding of how free will or determinism work is the same, but what makes them different is how they explain such positions; that is, their positions are differentiated by the language that they use and not their actual understanding or arguments! Therefore, instead of defining specific positions by categorising or 'boxing' arguments into a taxonomy, it would be more useful to think of the approximate ideas that are floating about regarding the nature of free will.

Key quote

The traditional explanation of intelligence is that human flesh is suffused with a non-material entity, the soul, usually envisioned as some kind of ghost or spirit. But the theory faces an insurmountable problem: How does the spook interact with solid matter? (Pinker)

Key quotes

Philosophy is what you do when you don't yet know what the right questions are to ask. (Dennett)

Are we free agents? It depends on what you mean by 'free'. (Galen Strawson)

There is no such thing as free will. There is a fundamental sense of the word 'free' in which this is incontrovertibly true; and this has been known for a long time. There are plenty of senses of the word 'free' in which it is false. But the sense in which it is true seems to be the one that matters most to most people. (Galen Strawson)

Why concentrate in this way on the experience of being free, rather than the thing itself? Because the best way to try to achieve a comprehensive understanding of the free will debate, and of the reason why it is interminable, is to study the thing that keeps it going – our experience of freedom. (Galen Strawson)

Immanuel Kant pointed this out to us a long time ago, that it's characteristic of conscious decision making that you can't proceed except on the presupposition of free will; and that even if you try to deny it – if you say, 'Well, I don't believe in free will so I won't do anything – that is itself only intelligible to you as an exercise of free will. (Searle)

Two different ideas about the body and mind (the will)

First of all, we have the idea of dualism. This is the idea that there is both a physical reality and a metaphysical reality; a body and soul or a mind and body. This goes back thousands of years. The metaphysical side of mind or soul also had a tendency to link with another realm beyond life as we know it, or, after death. This notion of connection of the physical with the metaphysical was often explained through a creator God or a **Panspirit** (a universal, all-pervading spiritual force). Religions have for centuries wrestled with how this works. We have seen that for Augustine, Calvin, Pelagius and Arminius, they have tried to make sense of what the idea of a separate human soul means for human free will.

In contrast to this, we have the idea that there is no dualistic element to humanity and the metaphysical 'other' is rejected. This is often termed **materialism** (or sometimes physicalism), which in philosophical terms conveys the meaning that nothing exists beyond matter and its movements and modifications and even the thought processes have a physical explanation. This is also not new and goes back thousands of years. Democritus was an early Greek philosopher who proposed a notion of an **atomic hypothesis** – similar to modern scientific analysis – that what we have before us can be explained without appeal to anything outside of itself. The Buddha (Siddhartha Gautama) avoided metaphysical questions and viewed them as unnecessary to make sense of life. Although there are multiple expressions of Buddhism, it is held by many that Buddhism, in its most basic formula, is essentially materialistic (and atheistic) in the way it rejects metaphysical speculation. For the Buddha, one of the key characteristics of existence was that things were 'not-self' (**anatta**) or that there was no metaphysical substance to an individual or the world. The problem is that if there is no metaphysical entity, then how do we make sense of free will? Jean-Paul Sartre and Carl Rogers are examples of thinkers who attempted to explain how free will may operate under such conditions (although in his later years Carl Rogers did suggest a 'spiritual' dimension to psychology). Alternatively, philosophers, psychologists and neuroscientists today grapple with the same problem of whether or not human beings have free will.

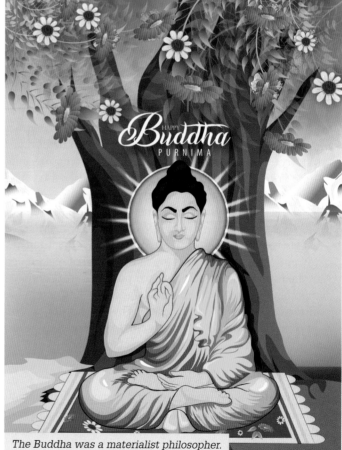

The Buddha was a materialist philosopher.

Rene Descartes and Immanuel Kant: two different dualist ideas and the implications for moral responsibility

Rene Descartes is significant because he summarised the dualist idea before him and his view remained the dominant philosophical view up until the middle of last century. His view was that we had a material body contingent upon physical laws of nature but that the immaterial mind was metaphysical and yet could still influence and cause bodily action through the brain. This would therefore allow for uncaused, spontaneous freedom of decision making and action. As Laura Weed writes, 'Free choice would not be random or down to chance and neither would it be determined or caused by the physical aspects of the world.' His theory is often called **Cartesian dualism**. The 'link' between brain and mind, however, was never clarified by Descartes. Daniel Dennett referred to Descartes' viewpoint as the **Cartesian Theatre**.

Enter Immanuel Kant. Kant is a unique case in terms of free will. Kant argued for the **autonomy of the will** and he is interesting because he established the inseparable link between morality and free will. In essence he argued that morality and free will were the keys to religious belief (the moral argument for the existence of God was the only argument Kant thought had merit). Kant saw the process of reasoning as the 'touchstone' by which all things could be judged: 'the systematic unity of the understanding's cognitions … is the touchstone of truth of rules'. Kant's *Critique of Practical Reason* is his triumph in establishing that it is through our reflections (that transcend the physical) on morality and free will that we can make a direct link to the metaphysical. Pure practical reason did not require a cause in the same way physical phenomena require causes for their explanations; for Kant, pure practical reason is 'a state from itself, the causality of which does not in turn stand under another cause determining it in time in accordance with the law of nature'. It was not a matter of 'proof' for Kant as we could not know that there is a God or that we have souls; rather, it was a case that pure practical reason justifies their existence. His philosophy is referred to as transcendental idealism and linked to this is the categorical imperative of ethical duty that entails direct, immediate moral responsibility of agents for their actions.

The implications for morality here are very strong. Freedom means control and independence; this leads to us being fully responsible for our actions. For Descartes, although he did not attempt a normative ethical methodology, his normative ethics was to pursue *la morale* (morality) and defined it as: 'the highest and most perfect moral system, which presupposes a complete knowledge of the other sciences and is the ultimate level of wisdom'. This meant a capacity for sound judgement, which Descartes referred to as 'good sense' (*le bons sens*) and 'universal wisdom'. His view was that the 'intellect' should direct a person's will as to what it ought to do as each of life's contingencies arose. Like the ancient Stoics and Epicureans, true happiness was to be sought; however, for Descartes this was more in line with the well-being of Aristotle – Descartes called it 'true health of the mind' whereby one could make 'true sound judgement' from an objective, philosophical perspective that free will affords.

Kant believed there was an objective moral law and that knowledge of this law could be gained through pure practical reason. He argued that human beings are rational and so are able to work out what is right and wrong. Acts are either morally right or wrong. According to Kant, moral value is not judged by the consequences of the act but by the actual act itself. Thus Kant had a deontological approach to ethics. If a certain act was right, then it was right in all circumstances and in all conditions. Kant referred to the highest good as the **summum bonum**. The highest good was the best possible good and he saw this as comprising virtue and happiness.

quickfire

4.39 Which Greek philosopher proposed a notion of an atomic hypothesis?

Key quotes

Before the mid-twentieth century, for a long time the dominant philosophical view of the mind was that put forward by Rene Descartes. **(Weed)**

Kant also argued that his ethical theory requires belief in free will, God, and the immortality of the soul. Although we cannot have knowledge of these things, reflection on the moral law leads to a justified belief in them, which amounts to a kind rational faith. **(Jankowiak, IEP)**

Two things fill the mind with ever-increasing wonder and awe, the more often and the more intensely the mind of thought is drawn to them: the starry heavens above me and the moral law within me. **(Kant)**

Key terms

Autonomy of the will: the idea that the will is independent

Cartesian dualism: the idea that body and mind (soul) are separate entities

Cartesian Theatre: Daniel Dennett's derisive description of any modern theory that proposes, like Descartes, that there is some central focus of the mind (like a stage) that is in control of our bodies

Summum bonum: Kant's notion that morality ('ought') indicates there can or must be ('can') a 'highest good' – the term dates back to Cicero in Roman times

Key term

Basic Argument: Galen Strawson's proposal that free will is an illogical notion because it implies that we must be *causa sui*

Key quotes

A Man can surely do what he wants to do. But he cannot determine what he wants. **(Schopenhauer)**

The causa sui is the best self-contradiction that has been conceived so far; it is a sort of rape and perversion of logic. **(Nietzsche)**

Kant also believed that free will meant that we were obligated (had a categorical imperative) to act morally and so obey the moral law. Since the will is free and independent, this means morality is meaningful. To make rational choices we must be free and to do our duty, we must be free. If our actions are not the result of free choices, then our actions cannot be regarded as the acts of a moral agent. The moral laws are viewed as acts which in themselves are of moral value. Therefore, it is not the consequences of our acts that confer moral value on them. Nevertheless, our duty is to act morally. When we act out of duty, we are acting out of a desire to be moral.

An *a priori* assault on free will: Galen Strawson's 'basic argument' against free will and the notion of moral responsibility

Many of the recent developments in the debate about free will have been imbued with the advancements made in our understanding of the material world. Professor Galen Strawson, however, is renowned for his contribution to the debate by establishing an *a priori* proof, that is, a traditional philosophical argument of logic, to deny the possibility of free will. It is referred to as the **Basic Argument** and begins with the premise that to have complete and absolute freedom, that freedom must be causa sui, a Latin term meaning 'cause of itself'. For Strawson, the argument follows that unless it could be demonstrated that human beings are 'free to choose what to do in such a way that they can be truly, genuinely responsible for their actions in the strongest possible sense', then we cannot accept the notion of free will.

The criticism of a human being's actions as being *causa sui* was not new; Nietzsche and Schopenhauer had already raised this; however, Strawson presented it officially as a coherent argument. Strawson is from the materialist fold and accepts determinism but refers to himself as a 'real physicalist'. Despite this, Strawson points out that his theory is not dependent on the free will / determinism debate; the logic holds with or without an acceptance of determinism. Strawson argues that the ways in which we have a sense of freedom is of interest, what he calls the 'general cognitive phenomenology of freedom'. He writes that it is still of interest since 'this experience is something real, complex, and important, even if free will itself is not real'. This demonstrates that even determinist philosophers, such as Strawson and Smilansky, who deny the philosophical truth of free will, still acknowledge that the illusion of free will is still there and this sense of self still remains.

Strawson argues that we have the following six illusions of self:

(1) That it is a thing

(2) That it is mental

(3) It is the subject of experience

(4) Something single

(5) Something distinct

(6) Displays character or personality.

In his latest book, *Things That Bother Me* (2018) Strawson writes: 'Philosophical materialists who believe as I do that we're wholly physical beings, and that human consciousness evolved by purely physical processes, have as strong a sense of self as anyone else.' He points out that scientists may deny free will 'in their white coats' but when they are out in the world they are 'like the rest of us … convinced of the reality of radical free will'. Strawson essentially argues, as does his former student Saul Smilansky, that it is inevitable that we live with the illusion of free will as it is part and parcel of human experience; however, this still does not make it true. Smilansky has developed his theory in a different way from Strawson. For Strawson, we can never be fully responsible for our actions; Smilansky argues that despite being an illusion, the notion of free will is not a negative at all; in fact, he refers to humanity being 'fortunately deceived'. It could even be argued to be morally necessary as it 'seems to be a condition of civilised morality and personal value'.

The renewed assault from materialism on free will: Daniel Dennett

The next group of ideas all seem to stem from what I would call an assault on metaphysics from a materialist stance. In short, quantum leaps in our understandings of how the mind works have been made possible due to advancements in science (neuroscience), technology (computing thanks to Alan Turing) and psychology.

A significant idea that made an assault on dualism was presented by Gilbert Ryle, Professor of Philosophy at Oxford. In his book *The Concept of Mind* (1949) he argued that dualism makes a '**category mistake**'. To illustrate this, he writes about a visitor to Oxford University. After seeing all the buildings individually – colleges, libraries, laboratories and faculty offices – the visitor then asks, 'Can I see the university?' Such a visitor had missed the point because they had been shown the university. To look around our anatomy, our brains and all the corresponding chemical interactions we should not then ask to be shown the 'soul' or our identity, or, to put it in simpler terms 'myself'. We have already seen this and so the question becomes irrelevant. Ryle pointed out that the belief in a soul, or metaphysical entity as being integral to a human being, as accepting '**a ghost in the machine**'. In other words, we would not look at the different parts of a car – the wheels, the engine, the chassis, the doors – and then say, 'Ok, can I now see the car?'. In the same way, the body and mind relationship needs no such explanation. This is very similar (for those candidates that have studied Buddhism) to the episode depicted in *The Questions of King Milinda* where Nagasena offers a chariot analogy as an illustration for the teaching of anatta (not self). It is interesting to note that this Buddhist text is around 2000 years old!

The impact of Ryle's arguments was that they introduced the idea that the notion of free will was a simple response to the problem of morality and moral responsibility. In other words, we can find an explanation of why we experience the 'ghost' due to our notions of morality. Some philosophers see this association of free will to moral responsibility as an '**ethical fallacy**'; others, like Kant, Peter van Inwagen and Robert Kane and many more, see the two as inextricably linked. Ryle's arguments were also significant because they marked a clear departure from dualism, and most philosophers today would accept that our understanding of what it means to be human is materialistic and almost 'mechanical'. Indeed, this 'mechanical' understanding of human beings was followed up by Daniel Dennett, Ryle's student, who was interested in philosophy but in particular consciousness and how the mind works. His interest in artificial intelligence and robotics led him to think very carefully about free will and reject what he calls the 'Cartesian Theatre'. For Dennett, everything can be explained by what he calls his Valerian model of conscious decision-making.

Is the notion of a 'soul' really just like a 'ghost'?

Key terms

A ghost in the machine: Ryle's notion of self-illusion regarding the 'free will'

Category mistake: seeing something in its entirety (the sum of all constituent parts) as belonging to a separate category, e.g. the collective buildings of a university being different from the university

Ethical fallacy: to accept that morality indicates free will

quickfire

4.40 What phrase did Gilbert Ryle use to describe a dualistic viewpoint?

Key quote

Alan Turing had the basic move that we could replace Kant's question of how it was possible for there to be thought, with an engineering question – let's think how we can make a thought come into existence. Oh, we could build a robot … so resolutely, from the third person point of view, you sneak up on consciousness from the outside. (Dennett)

Dennett formalised a theory of consciousness based upon the model of computer programming and refers to the idea of a 'self' as 'the benign user illusion of its own virtual machine'. In *Brainstorms* (1978) he suggested a combination of indeterminism and determinism to select and present choices to the agent 'some of which may of course be immediately rejected' but others that form the basis of 'predictors and explicators of the agent's final decision'. This compatibilist position recognises the integral function of considering alternatives in the neurological process. He called it the Valerian model.

A similar idea to Dennett's Valerian model can be seen in Buddhist psychology of the Yogacara school of Mahayana Buddhism that acknowledge the process of the alaya vijnana or 'storehouse consciousness' that manipulates, stores and arranges what they term bijas (literally 'seeds') and that causes (or processes) all karmic energy.

For Dennett, according to his book *Consciousness Explained* (1991) – and similar to Ryle before him – the notion of a 'captain at the helm' in control of everything within a person is simply an illusion or a 'simulated self'. Therefore, in making decisions, it is not the case that we are free because everything is determined; it is more that case that we think that we are free but it is our biological and neurological elements underlying our consciousness that have generated the perspective that we have. The reality is that it is the whole organism is the agent not one individual point within it. The problem for Dennett is what he calls 'Cartesian materialism' seems to have slipped back into scientific explanations of 'self' and 'decision making'. In the book *Conversations on Consciousness* (with Susan Blackmore) Dennett argues that to get rid of the Cartesian notion completely is to 'make yourself big'. By this he means that philosophy and science tend to scrutinise the problem of free will from a very close perspective – they always break down to the finest detail, to what he calls 'a singularity', that is, 'a Cartesian point at the intersection of two lines'. This causes a 'retreat into the punctate self'; however, we need to zoom back out again and appreciate the whole package, that is the complete human being and not some mind-projected point of 'self'. Once again there is a similarity here with the Buddhist notion of emptiness (sunyata). Its best expression is in the Prajnaparamita Hrdaya Sutra, which states: 'form is emptiness and the very emptiness is form'. So with Dennett we find a person is ultimately not a 'self' and yet this 'not a self' is the person.

The nature of the debate about free will here is the element of overall control and decision making. Many who agree with Dennett acknowledge also that since we do simulate a self through consciousness, then how can this be explained? The image of the 'captain at the helm' or 'an executive boardroom' simply is a label for a **process** that occurs at the top level in our consciousness and not some overall ontological or metaphysical reality. Dennett sees his explanation of the Valerian model as exactly what libertarians were looking for but simply explained scientifically!

Roderick Chisholm: 'agent causation' or 'immanent causation'

At the University of Kansas, Lindley lecture 1964, Professor of Philosophy Roderick Chisholm (Brown University) delivered a lecture that presented a solution to the problem of free will based on the observation that free will and determinism were incompatible. If that was the case then it logically follows that free will is also incompatible with **indeterminism** (undetermined events, chance or random occurrences), since such events are not under the control of anything. This is because to say that an arbitrary choice generated by luck is a free choice is a nonsense. Chisholm then suggested that the only explanation for this is a third option that free will must be a form of self-determination or agent-causation – as he called it 'a prime mover unmoved' and accept the principle of '**immanent causation**'. In other words, free actions may be determined or caused, but not by prior events, rather, only by a self or an agent.

Chisholm's argument was a philosophical argument and not based in neuroscientific experiment or observation. However, what it appeared to suggest for the first time was that in order to solve the problem of free will, one always had to appeal to an 'agent' of some kind; such an agent would have to be, in Robert Kane's words, 'a special "non-event" or "non-occurrent" of a kind that cannot be spelled out wholly in terms of causation by prior physical and psychological event'. In terms of philosophy, many responded by arguing that Chisholm's ideas just affirmed the intuition of an agent rather than saying anything meaningful about such an agent.

Although some felt that Chisholm's idea could only be made sense of if one accepted Cartesian dualism (since such an agent is irreducible to natural causes), some philosophers such as Timothy O'Connor tried to build upon this. Nonetheless, the idea of immanent causation in philosophical terms did not gather force. The possibility of this idea, however, has emerged again in recent years, but in response to neuroscientific evidence and not philosophical analysis. In addition, Peter van Inwagen who first defended incompatibilism later shifted his views to argue that despite Chisholm's argument being sound, the notion of a metaphysical freedom still remains a complete mystery, incoherent and unintelligible.

The implications of Chisholm's paper for morality were obvious. As a free and independent agent, this 'prime mover unmoved' would have full responsibility for its actions and no responsibility could be shirked by an explanation of determinism or a lack of control over one's actions.

Key terms

Immanent causation: Roderick Chisholm's third alternative to determinism and indeterminism that is a state of independence from both

Indeterminism: the notion of randomness, indecision, luck or chance

Study tip

Make sure that you correctly associate each relevant idea with the appropriate scholar.

AO1 Activity

Have a go at writing an imaginary debate between Kant, Strawson, Dennett and Chisholm.

Key quote

Agent-causation is a primitive, unanalysable notion; it cannot be reduced to anything more basic. Not surprisingly, many philosophers found Chisholm's theory unsatisfactory. What is wanted, they objected, is a theory that explains what freedom is and how it is possible, not one that simply posits freedom. Agent-causation theories, they maintained, leave a blank space where an explanation ought to be. (Singer)

Key terms

Readiness potential: the lag in time between the brain determining action and the consciousness being aware of it

Self-forming actions: Kane's argument that if we at times in the past freely created and changed our own character, then actions can be considered to be free

quickfire

4.41 What was Benjamin Libet famous for?

Does the body inform consciousness or our consciousness inform the body?

Psychological debates: Libet's readiness potential

Years after Chisholm's paper and alongside Dennett's development of his ideas about free will there was another significant proposal. In relation to the process of consciousness in decision making, psychology and neuroscience made an important discovery in 1985. In an experiment performed by Benjamin Libet, he concluded that the notion of a conscious will was an error because it was demonstrated that the brain has actually decided and initiated a move before the consciousness was aware of the decision being made. The lag in time between the brain determining action and the consciousness being aware of it was called the 'readiness potential'. The implications of this experiment have been used to demonstrate deterministic arguments against free will; for instance, Susan Blackmore has used this to demonstrate that there is no such thing as free will.

However, Libet's readiness potential has been criticised by Alfred Mele. Mele argued that is inconclusive because the readiness potential is simply the considering of options and deciding on action; therefore, it is possible in this time to veto an action, but the experiment cannot demonstrate any example of 'free won't'. Despite this, as we have seen with Sirigu, further research has been done in the field of neuroscience into the nature of the will (volition). However, the readiness potential did indicate that psychology and neuroscience were getting closer to explaining the relationship between volition and action in the process of decision making. In terms of morality, this meant that an alternative to an intuitive, evasive and unintelligible third-party agent could be emerging that pointed back to a more materialistic understanding of how behaviour, including ethical decisions, worked.

Key quote

One frequent version of the anti-freewill argument goes like this: modern neuroscience shows us not only that thinking is accompanied by neurological activity, but that this activity should be understood as the sole cause or explanation of all thought. If all thought is caused by fixed physical laws, then it cannot be caused by something else, such as one's choice of what to think. So freewill is an illusion. (Langford)

Modern libertarianism and moral responsibility: Robert Kane and Peter van Inwagen

In relation to the support for a libertarian free will in the strongest sense of the term, Professor Robert Kane has long been held to be its principal advocate. In his edited volume *Free Will* (2002) he begins with his definition of free will as something that is 'not beyond our control' and compares it to Aristotle's notion of our behaviour being 'up to us'. It is this idea, the notion that we have ultimate responsibility or 'up to usness' that drives Kane's view in reconsidering what is meant by 'causal relationships' being always determined. Kane suggests that Chisholm's suggestion that there are only three possibilities is too rigid and to suggest the third possibility is beyond the scope of the determinism and free will dichotomy is not necessary. Kane argues that causal relationships can **sometimes** be nondeterministic or probabilistic which **purposefully** allows for 'the power of agents to be the ultimate creators and sustainers of their own ends or purposes'. It is not true that we need 'alternative possibilities' for every action and that many acts are determined, including some from our own free will. However, because some acts in our past have clearly defined our **characters** then such 'self-forming actions' of ultimate responsibility indicate how free will works within a largely causal mechanism. He writes: 'indeterminism need not undermine rationality and voluntariness, so indeterminism in and of itself need not undermine control and responsibility'.

In contrast to Strawson and Smilansky, Kane, in his book *Free Will and Values* (1985) argues for such calls 'self-forming actions'. Kane holds that even if our character determines our actions, if we at times in the past freely created and changed our own character, then actions can be considered to be free. In 2001 in a contribution to the volume *Freedom and Responsibility* – later added to his edited volume *Free Will* (2002) – Kane compares his 'self-forming actions' to solving a mathematical equation where there occurs some 'indeterminacy' in someone's neural processes, for example disturbing background noise, that complicate the process. This means that success is undetermined because the complication of noise reduces the potential for success. However, if concentration wins the battle and the equation is solved, even though the outcome was undetermined we can still accept that we are responsible for the success through our efforts. In other words, not everything is as simplistic as causal determination, and 'self-forming actions' such as this suggest a level of ultimate responsibility for the individual. In his mammoth *Oxford Handbook of Free Will* Kane writes 'One may legitimately wonder why worries about determinism persist at all in the twenty-first century, when the physical sciences – once the stronghold of determinist thinking – seem to have turned away from determinism.'

Finally, Peter van Inwagen, takes a different position from Kane. His argument was formed on a similar basis to Roderick Chisholm – that free will and determinism are incompatible, which he referred to as the consequence argument. He also, like Chisholm, argued from this that an undetermined free will is unintelligible; however, rather than agreeing with Chisholm that it could be solved by way of some indiscriminate agent, Inwagen argued like Kant, that it was a metaphysical mystery presupposed by our practical reasoning of morality and therefore a matter of faith.

Both Kane and Inwagen see morality as functioning within the notion of freedom and in full control of the individual. Moral responsibility, therefore, cannot be explained satisfactorily through the idea of determinism; although in the case of Kane, his work suggested that we had to see the idea of 'causes' in a new light and that explanations for decisions made within a materialistic framework 'need not always be deterministic'.

Nancey Murphy's *Bodies and souls or spirited bodies?*

We now refer back to the ideas of Daniel Dennett. The idea of 'an executive boardroom' process or a 'simulated self' is ambiguous, and although it could be seen to be in line with a Buddhist teaching of not-self (anatta), it can also be seen to be a re-definition of what we mean by the term 'soul'. Dennett saw his Valerian model as exactly what libertarians were looking for. However, his idea of 'simulation' has been seen to be inadequate because although generated by biological and neurological elements underlying our consciousness, it remains a 'perspective' and not a true reality. This is why Dennett considers that in explaining free will the idea of a 'Cartesian materialism' has slipped back into scientific explanations.

The work of theologian Professor Nancey Murphy and her ground-breaking book '*Bodies and Souls, or Spirited Bodies*' (2006), has advocated that Christian theology does not necessarily require dualism and that 'embodied souls', as opposed to the traditional notion of 'spirited bodies', is a new way to understand the complexity of human beings and is more than just a case of considering their essential biological and psychological constituents. Using the most recent research from neuroscience, Murphy argues that the neurobiological complexity of a human being allows for the emergence of more complex notions than just deterministic causes or simulated consciousness. Indeed, her argument is that 'higher human capacities such as morality, free will, and religious awareness' become manifest in a human being's 'neurobiological complexity'.

Key terms

Consequence argument: the argument that free will is incompatible with determinism because there is no possibility for any control over what we can do in the future based upon what has happened in the past

Embodied souls: Murphy's physicalist explanation for the notion of 'soul' in preference to the idea of 'spirited bodies'

Key quote

One may legitimately wonder why worries about determinism persist at all in the twenty-first century, when the physical sciences – once the stronghold of determinist thinking – seem to have turned away from determinism. **(Kane)**

Key quotes

We cannot just help ourselves to the assumption that everything that happens is inexorably necessitated by some prior state of the world. (Steward)

An agent, it is said, is a persisting substance; causation by an agent is causation by such a substance. Since a substance is not the kind of thing that can itself be an effect (though various events involving it can be), on these accounts an agent is in a strict and literal sense an originator of her free decisions, an uncaused cause of them. (Stanford Encyclopedia)

This combination of indeterminism and origination is thought to capture best the idea that, when we act freely, a plurality of alternatives is open to us and we determine, ourselves, which of these we pursue, and to secure the kind of freedom needed for moral responsibility. (Stanford)

Key terms

Agency incompatibilism: the notion that determinism is false because as a system becomes more complex, forms of self-organising emerge as a result of interaction between constituent biological and neurological elements

Agent-causal theories: the idea that there is a form of 'agent' that has evolved in neurological processes

Chinese room: Searle's thought experiment demonstrating that deterministic and materialistic theories about 'free will' confuse syntax (manipulation of symbols) and semantics (meaning)

Settling: Steward's term for the process of selection and control at the very top level in consciousness that has evolved naturally

Murphy refers to top-down understanding of causation and typical of contemporary neuroscientific thought in terms of agent causal theories or 'agency incompatibilism'. This is where a complex system, at certain levels of complexity, reveal new properties that have resulted from the interaction between constituent biological and neurological elements. As a system gets more complex, more varied forms of self-organising are manifest. In support of Murphy, Professor Neil Messer in his book *Theological Neuroethics* (2017) cites Walter Glannon who points out that the psychological practice of CBT (cognitive behaviour therapy) is a classic example, reframing cognitive habits to reformulate physical states and function of the brain. For Murphy, 'embodied selfhood' is just as credible theologically as the notion of a metaphysical essence, and certainly more pertinent to what we know from neuroscience today.

Further and more recent support for what is officially known as 'agency incompatibilism' or according to *Stanford Encyclopedia* 'agent-causal theories' is the recent work of Professor Helen Steward in her work *A Metaphysics for Freedom* (2014). However, for Steward, her explanations are not imbued with theology but rather indicate an impartial scientific explanation for what we may call free will. She describes the process of selection and control at the very top level, not as causation, but as 'settling' where an agent takes action. For Steward the belief that scientific laws (e.g. causation) can accurately predict future events is in itself a matter of faith! Settling and agent exercising control makes more sense; it is through evolution that this process has occurred and is an example of survival adaptation.

In terms of moral responsibility, the notion of agent-causal theories within neuroscience firmly place the concept of a freely willed decision taken by the organism in a scientific context in a similar fashion to Kane's 'self-forming actions'. This corroboration is a powerful presentation for a modern understanding of the notion of free will that allows for ultimate responsibility of an individual.

Will the problem ever be solved?

Before we move on, it would not be a complete overview of the free will debate without mention of the philosopher John Searle. John Searle does not see any explanation for free will as satisfactory and argues that the problem of free will will always remain. This does not mean, however, as we have seen earlier in his conversation with Susan Blackmore, that Searle rejects the notion of free will. Searle is simply unconvinced that neuroscience alone can solve the problem.

Searle's objections are three-fold. The first objection attacks the idea of Dennett's simulated self; the second raises issues as to whether the scientific approach is based upon a philosophical error; the third objection is that a neuroscientific theory cannot actually justify free will without dependency on an irreducible self, due to the gap of significant content involved in explaining free actions.

(1) Searle is renowned for his thought experiment of the **Chinese room**. In the book *Conversations on Consciousness* (with Susan Blackmore) Searle explains it thus:

'Imagine I'm locked in a room, where I have a programme for manipulating Chinese symbols, and I get questions sent into the room in the form of Chinese symbols. I look up in the rule book what I'm supposed to do, and I give back answers in Chinese; so I take in Chinese input, and I produce a Chinese output; all the same I don't understand a word of Chinese.'

Searle's point is that deterministic and materialistic theories about 'free will' confuse syntax (manipulation of symbols) and semantics (meaning). You can carry out the code of Chinese without actually understanding a word of Chinese!

For Searle, an explanation of free will requires semantics; it is something more than just syntax. For Searle, they are two very different things. Even from a whole system perspective of the code there would still be no meaning or understanding. Searle's point appears to be very similar to the old ethical problem in philosophy that you cannot derive an 'ought' from an 'is'. We are back to square one!

(2) In the book *Conversations on Consciousness* (with Susan Blackmore) Searle compares neurobiological research to 'plumbing' to figure out where and how consciousness happens; however, he sees neurobiology as 'based upon a deep philosophical error' he calls the 'building block approach' whereby science seeks the 'neural correlate of individual consciousness'. For Searle 'free will is not a characteristic of all consciousness'. He states: '... the key question is not, what is the correlate of each particular conscious feature ... but rather, what is the difference between the conscious brain and the unconscious brain?' Attempting to work out how free will and conscious function would involve a detailed analysis of sequencing and synchronism of neuro-firings, or, in Searle's words, dealing 'with big chunks of the brain'! Unless an alternative to the error of the building block approach is developed, the nature of the problems associated with consciousness and free will cannot be solved.

(3) For Searle, ethical thinking and decision making in general are more complex than we might think. We may think that we choose because we take one action rather than an alternative; that is, our 'volitional consciousness' controls our actions, i.e. this one instead of that one. In reality, there are a whole set of reasons behind the immediate cause of our actions that the neurobiological level cannot account for. Searle presents this argument in his book *Rationality in Action* (2001) and refers to this notion as 'the gap'. Searle's belief is that it is the gap that contains significant content that also generates the impression of an irreducible self. This gap is real and so this 'lack of causally sufficient conditions at the psychological level is matched by an absence of causally sufficient conditions at the neurobiological level'. Until the problem of the gap is solved we cannot solve free will.

Study tip

There is such a range of material to select from that can help you explain what the relationship between free will and morality is. Make sure that you select the relevant material for the question set.

AO1 Activity

Have a go at creating a table that briefly describes the following views of free will: dualist; materialist; illusion; simulated; immanent causation; self-formulated actions; agency incompatibilism; and the gap. Associate each one with a scholar.

Key quotes

We humans are clever decision-making machines that are prone to a number of powerful illusions, in particular the illusion of a persisting inner self that has consciousness and free will. (Blackmore)

You can be mistaken about the details of your present conscious state, but you cannot be mistaken about its very existence. (Searle)

Philosophy may in no way interfere with the actual use of language; it can in the end only describe it ... it leaves everything as it is. (Wittgenstein)

Neuroscience may in no way interfere with our first-person experience of the will, it can in the end only describe it ... it leaves everything as it is. (Fifel)

Key term

The gap: not to be confused with Sartre's Gap, Searle uses this to refer to the delay in the decision-making process typical of more complex decisions that involve a whole set of reasons behind the immediate cause of our actions that the neurobiological level cannot account for

quickfire

4.42 What did Searle's Chinese room thought experiment aim to demonstrate?

Is there a 'gap' between immediate decision for action and our reasons for action?

Specification content

The worth of human ideas of rightness, wrongness and moral value, the value in blaming human beings for immoral acts, the usefulness of normative ethics.

Summary: implications of concepts of libertarianism on moral responsibility

To be morally responsible for something there needs to be an 'identity' upon which to 'pin' accountability; it is also assumed that this identity is individual in that it has acted autonomously and independently of other externally influencing factors. Hopefully we have seen that it is not just as simple as this may suggest and that there are different ways to explain the notion of libertarianism.

The following table is to help summarise how some of the different views of what constitutes an individual – which in turn influences the acceptance, rejection or re-defining of the notion of free will – can be used to respond to the Specification headings. For AO1, if a question is general, then students are free to choose from the range of thinkers below. If a question is related to T4E the relevant thinkers have been **highlighted in purple**. For AO2, students can select from the range of ideas to help them construct an argument that answers a statement on free will offered up for debate.

View of free will	The worth of human ideas of rightness, wrongness and moral value
Aristotle	We are free and responsible for developing virtues: it is 'up to us'.
Rene Descartes (dualism)	For Descartes, his normative ethics was to pursue *la morale* (morality) and he defined it as: 'the highest and most perfect moral system, which presupposes a complete knowledge of the other sciences and is the ultimate level of wisdom'.
Immanuel Kant (dualism)	Kant believed there was an objective moral law and that knowledge of this law could be gained through reason. He argued that human beings are rational and so are able to work out what is right and wrong. Acts are either morally right or wrong. Good will is the highest form of good. This is because it is not concerned about consequences or self-interest. When we act with a good will, then we act with the intention of being moral.
Galen Strawson (free will as an illusion)	Although free will is an illusion Strawson accepts that in reality the illusion of the 'self' and decision making is a powerful force in establishing a sense of morality – but one that is ultimately and completely determined and conditioned.
Daniel Dennett (free will as a simulation)	Dennett has referred to the human ideas of rightness, wrongness and moral value as comparable to belonging to a 'Moral agent club' in society.
Nancey Murphy (free will as agency incompatibilism)	Nancey Murphy reconciles spirited bodies with Christian theology. As an ordained minister in the Church of the Brethren, her understanding of the worth of human ideas of rightness, wrongness and moral value reflect this and her acceptance of an agent-causal theory of free will.
Robert Kane (free will as self-forming actions)	Aristotle's notion of our behaviour being 'up to us' presents us with the notion that we have ultimate responsibility or 'up to usness' drives. Therefore, an underlying notion of the worth of human ideas of rightness, wrongness and moral value would be required for ethical decision making.
Susan Blackmore (rejection of free will)	Susan Blackmore denies all free will; however, as a Buddhist, would accept the sense of rightness, wrongness and moral value that Buddhism teaches.
Jean-Paul Sartre (free will as existence)	Sartre believed in 'an ethics and a politics which are absolutely positive'. His understanding of the worth of human ideas of rightness, wrongness and moral value are grounded in his 'ethics of the we'; members of a society are not only individually self-aware and beings-for-themselves but also beings-for-others.
Carl Rogers (free will as integral to the fully functioning person)	Rogers argued for an understanding of free will in which in the optimum of therapy the person rightfully experiences the most complete and absolute freedom due to the fully functioning person (FFP) selecting 'the most economical vector ... determined by all the factors in the existential situation'. The human ideas of the worth of rightness, wrongness and moral value are inextricably bound up with the positive aspects of the FFP.

View of free will	The value in blaming human beings for immoral acts
Aristotle	Blame and responsibility are acknowledged; however, the onus in Aristotle's virtue ethics is on continuous learning; whilst we are accountable for mistakes, we should learn from them.
Rene Descartes (dualism)	Descartes' understanding of a capacity for sound judgement, or 'good sense' (*le bons sens*) and 'universal wisdom' directs a person's will as to what it ought to do in each of life's contingencies. Therefore human beings should have full control over, and hence full responsibility for, their actions.
Immanuel Kant (dualism)	Kant believed that moral laws were binding on human beings. It is our duty is to act morally. When we act out of duty, we are acting out of a desire to be moral. People must use their free will to live a moral life and are held accountable.
Galen Strawson (free will as an illusion)	Strawson writes in the *Impossibility of Moral Responsibility*: 'We are what we are, and we cannot be thought to have made ourselves in such a way that we can be held to be free in our actions in such a way that we can be held to be morally responsible for our actions … there is a fundamental sense in which no punishment or reward is ever ultimately just.'
Daniel Dennett (free will as a simulation)	Dennett states: 'If your brain, at the relevant time, has the competence required of a moral agent, you will be held responsible.' However, 'If through no fault of your own you lose that competence, then you are no longer morally responsible.' He argues that biological boundaries allow space for 'practical' free will, as opposed to absolute free will, and so punishment for wrong is needed for society to function.
Nancey Murphy (free will as agency incompatibilism)	Murphy's acceptance of an agent-causal theory of free will argues for the responsibility of the whole person in a top-down dynamic, inter-relationship between neurobiological processes.
Robert Kane (free will as self-forming actions)	Self-forming actions allows for 'the power of agents to be the ultimate creators and sustainers of their own ends or purposes'.
Susan Blackmore (rejection of free will)	An acceptance of no self and no free will does not mean we are not to be held responsible for our actions.
Jean-Paul Sartre (free will as existence)	Sartre wrote: 'in the end one is always responsible for what is made of one'. We are responsible for what we are and how we behave. To be free means to be fully responsible. To live life in facticity with the self-deception of being-in-itself is a free choice to make but one that is not truly free. We therefore cannot blame anyone but ourselves for our actions.
Carl Rogers (free will as integral to the fully functioning person)	Rogers' therapy means that the positive approach to life of the FFP means accepting responsibilities and adjusting life accordingly. It is inherent within the nature of an FFP that the subject would avoid any preconceived notions of immorality but simultaneously 'openness' requires one to face up to, and work through, one's responsibilities.

View of free will	The usefulness of normative ethics
Aristotle	The role models provide us with guidance in how to use our freedom. Aristotle's Nichomachean Ethics.
Rene Descartes (dualism)	Like the Ancient Greek philosophers, true happiness is to be sought in terms of well-being to achieve 'true health of the mind'. Then, one could make 'true sound judgement' from an objective, philosophical perspective that free will affords.
Immanuel Kant (dualism)	The categorical imperative has a binding force on people, irrespective of their interests. Kant saw moral principles as commands that have a truth value and they are obligatory. (1) 'So act that you treat humanity, both in your own person and in the person of every other human being, never merely as a means, but always at the same time as an end.' (2) 'So act as if you were through your maxim a law-making member of a kingdom of ends.' Kant saw the *summum bonum* (highest good) as comprising virtue and happiness.

View of free will	The usefulness of normative ethics
Galen Strawson (free will as an illusion)	Strawson writes in the *Impossibility of Moral Responsibility*: '... the conviction that self-conscious awareness of one's situation can be a sufficient foundation of strong free will is very powerful. It runs deeper than rational argument, and it survives untouched, in the everyday conduct of life.' Strawson accepts the 'power' of a personal sense of morality that is not freely followed but more determined by factors within and around us.
Daniel Dennett (free will as a simulation)	Although based on society's 'Moral agent club' a normative ethic serves to make sense of how we live and guide others in making meaningful 'choices'.
Nancey Murphy (free will as agency incompatibilism)	Christian ethics are a sound, philosophical and theological guide as they operate within the parameters of free will.
Robert Kane (free will as self-forming actions)	Normative ethics would guide self-forming actions. As we have free choice they are useful in guiding us towards the wisest choices.
Susan Blackmore (rejection of free will)	The normative path of ethics is a foundation for the spiritual journey of Buddhists to the realisation of not-self and a total lack of free will.
Jean-Paul Sartre (free will as existence)	Sartre's 'ethics of the we' imagines a situation whereby we co-exist in 'a just society in which human beings can have good relations with each other ... A society in which relations among human beings are ethical.' Although no author of a normative ethic, in his later years Sartre wrote about authenticity, gift-response, positive reciprocity, mutual recognition and authentic love. In later years he embraced socialism and Marxism.
Carl Rogers (free will as integral to the fully functioning person)	It is inherent within the nature of an FFP that the subject would follow any preconceived notions of morality whilst simultaneously being open to new ideas and be willing to amend accordingly their foundational perceptions of morality.

Sartre found his normative ethic in the 'ethics of the we' found in socialism.

quickfire

4.43 What did Daniel Dennett mean by a 'Moral agent club' in society?

Key quotes

.... man must rely upon his own fallible will and moral insight. He cannot escape choosing. (Sartre)

My choice to help another's freedom, in Sartre's view, expresses my basic project to maximise concrete freedoms in a finite world. (Flynn)

Study tip

The phrase 'choose and use' is a good way to remember the distinction between AO1 (choose = selecting and explaining relevant material) and AO2 (use – making use of the evidence in analysis and evaluation).

AO1 Activity

Try devising your own tables for the different ideas about the nature of free will.

The implications of free will on religious belief

The first thing to note is that there are some significant links to other areas of the Specification. The idea of a religious believer having free will is, in the majority of instances, integral to all the world religions in terms of an individual's fundamental relationship with God, or, in the case of Buddhism, the notion of being able to progress.

In relation to this, the world religions present, as part of their overall soteriology, specific teachings about how, in both religious and ethical terms, this is to be implemented.

Therefore, there is some varied information that follows but there is also opportunity to establish synoptic links and to access what has been learned from the study of a world religion. Rather than duplicate the information here, the following table indicates how to establish these synoptic links.

Specification content

The implications of free will on religious belief.

World religion	Synoptic relevance	Specification link
Christianity	Theme 2F: the importance of **love of neighbour** and the **role of conscience**. Particularly 2C: The **Atonement** and associated theories and 2A a **suffering God**.	**Key moral principles**: The notion that the individual believer has an **individual responsibility** to **freely choose** how to behave both religiously and ethically, in themselves, and towards others. *Teachings about the nature of God*.
Islam	Theme 2F the **five categories** of ethical action but also individual religious and ethical aspects of 2D **Salah** and 2E **Zakah**. 2A **Tawhid** but also aspects of 2F regarding **Akhirah**.	**Key moral principles**: The notion that the individual believer has an **individual responsibility** to **freely choose** how to behave both religiously and ethically, in themselves, and towards others. **The use of prayer.** *Teachings about the nature of God*.
Judaism	Theme 1B (the **Mosaic covenant**), 2B Humanity created in the **divine image**, life as a divine gift, the **sanctity of life** and the nature of humanity, 2F **Ten Sayings**, 2E **prayer**. 2A Characteristics: **omnipotent, omniscient and omnibenevolent**, etc. 3F **Holocaust theology**.	**Key moral principles**: The notion that the individual believer has an **individual responsibility** to **freely choose** how to behave both religiously and ethically, in themselves, and towards others. **The use of prayer.** *Teachings about the nature of God*.
Buddhism	Theme 1B links to the notion of Enlightenment, 1C **Patimokkha**, 2B **Pratityasamutpada, karma and rebirth**, 2C **Bodhisattva**, 2E the **Eightfold Path**, 2F the **dasa sila**, 4F **dana** and **punya**. 2A **three lakshanas**, 2D **nirodha** (nirvana).	**Key moral principles**: The notion that the individual believer has an **individual responsibility** to **freely choose** how to behave both religiously and ethically, in themselves, and towards others. *Teachings about the nature of reality*.
Hinduism	Theme 1B **personal dharma**, 1C **Ramayana** and **righteous behaviour**, 2C **karma** and **reincarnation**, 2D **Varnashramadharma**, 2F **ahimsa**, 2F **defending the poor and oppressed**. 2A **Brahman** and **atman**, 2B **Trimurti**.	**Key moral principles**: The notion that the individual believer has an **individual responsibility** to **freely choose** how to behave both religiously and ethically, in themselves, and towards others. *Teachings about the nature of God*.
Sikhism	Theme 1A **Guru Nanak's teaching against the caste system**, 2A **self, death, afterlife**, 2C **Karma, rebirth and mukti**. 2D sewa, 2E **Kirat Karo** and **Vand Chhako**. 1D **Mul Mantra** (liberating and awesome presence of God – evil thoughts can only be cleansed through God's name), 2A the **Sikh concept of God** and 4E **nature of God**.	**Key moral principles**: The notion that the individual believer has an **individual responsibility** to **freely choose** how to behave both religiously and ethically, in themselves, and towards others. **The use of prayer.** *Teachings about the nature of God*.

In the same way there are clear links with the problem of free will in the 'Philosophy of Religion' and 'Religion and Ethics' Specifications.

	Synoptic relevance	Specification link
Philosophy	Theme 1A cosmological argument, 1B teleological argument, 1E Descartes' 'God as supremely perfect being', 2ABC the problem of evil and suffering, theodicies. Theme 3A **prayer** as a religious experience and challenges to the **objectivity and authenticity**, 3A **influence of religious experience on religious practice and faith** (community and individual). Theme 3E **definitions of miracles**, 3F contrasting views on **the possibility of miracles**.	**The implications of free will for God's omnipotence and omnibenevolence; the link between God and evil.** **The implications of free will for the use of prayer.** **The implications of free will for the existence of miracles.**
Ethics	Theme 1A **Divine Command Theory**, 2A Natural Law – the premise of **'doing good and avoiding evil'** and also keeping the precepts in order to **establish a right relationship with God** and gain eternal life with God in heaven. Overlap with 2D **Finnis** and 2E **Proportionalism**. Theme 4A theories of **predestination** and 4C **use of prayer**. Theme 4C the implications of **predestination** for the **existence of miracles**.	**The implications of free will for God's omnipotence and omnibenevolence; the link between God and evil.** **The implications of free will for the use of prayer.** **The implications of free will for the existence of miracles.**

Now that we have established some synoptic links, the following sub-section is written with the aim of providing exemplar material to use and is not prescriptive. There are so many different examples that could be used from the very many different religious traditions, and areas of ethics and philosophy. Hopefully the following will help students to get the idea of how to establish the synoptic links relevant for this last section while at the same time addressing the range of implications that free will brings for religion and philosophy (including ethics). An attempt has been made to cover an example from most of the religions studied and hopefully will provide a taste of the sort of evidence and examples that can be used for both AO1 and AO2.

Since questions can be set using any phrase from the Specification, there may well be a 'general' question on the implications of free will on religious belief. Below is just a brief summary on how this can be approached but obviously there can be much more added – it is just to give you a general idea (see tables also). The topics of the implications for God's omnipotence and the link between God and evil will be dealt with separately, as will prayer and miracles.

(1) Buddhism and the implications of free will on religious belief

Buddhism is often described as a philosophy or way of life rather than a religion. The emphasis in Buddhism is on practice. Questions about belief are relatively unimportant in the sense that the way of life is driven by the goal of diminishing suffering, both mentally and physically. This is not dependent on any external agency or creator 'God'. The Buddhist path is empirical; it involves scientific testing and a practical solution. The aim of Buddhism is to exercise free will in following the path that leads to enlightenment (nibbana) by letting go of attachments that cause suffering.

The notion of free will in Buddhism springs directly from the idea of kamma (karma). The Buddhist monk Narada Thera wrote: 'We ourselves are responsible

> ### Key terms
>
> **Kamma:** the notion of individual responsibility for our thoughts that lead to actions
>
> **Nibbana:** the term for enlightenment, ultimately beyond all notions of determinism and free will

for our own deeds, happiness and misery. We build our own hells. We create our own heavens. We are the architects of our own fate. In short we ourselves are our own karma.' In addition, the Dhammapada 1:1 states: 'All that we experience begins with thought. Our words and deeds spring from thought.'

It is often said that Buddhism is all about being in control of our will through consciousness. In *The Questions of King Milinda*, the monk Nagasena compares an untrained mind to that of a 'hungry and excited ox' that is loosely tied and can easily break loose when agitated, determined by its senses. In contrast, the **arhat** has a developed mind and thought that is 'well-tamed ... obedient and disciplined' and his thoughts are firmly tied to the 'post of contemplation ... that remains steadfast and undisturbed'. The arhat is therefore in full self-control of his volitions.

Free will is central to the idea of conducting oneself appropriately, spiritual development, the cultivation of wisdom and the elimination of suffering. That is, one must choose to behave ethically in order to eliminate suffering and be able to focus on becoming wise. More than this, ethical conduct actually reduces the arising of suffering but also benefits other beings. Buddhist ethics are derived from basic observations about the world in which we live. Buddhist ethics have been referred to as a common-sense 'morality from within'.

Key quotes

It should be mentioned that any external supernatural agency plays no part whatever in the moulding of the character of a Buddhist ….. there is no one to reward or punish. Pain or happiness are the inevitable results of one's actions. **(Thera)**

This is making one's living in a way that does not involve the habitual breaking of the precepts by bringing harm to other beings, but which hopefully aids others and helps cultivate one's faculties and abilities. **(Harvey)**

Directly related to the whole idea of religion and morality is also the idea of rebirth. The ethical actions of an individual have consequences not just in this life but also beyond it. Free will and ethical activity, then, are inextricably linked to the idea of liberation, enlightenment or the Buddhist religious goal beyond this life.

The Buddhist ethical system, then, is driven by the ideas of eliminating suffering through a proactive, empirical approach to the problem and also by developing wisdom to help a person deal with suffering. Possibly the greatest strength of Buddhist ethics is its ability to be a flexible framework that can be applied to different personal situations whilst retaining adherence to the few central principles it has as guidance. Ethical practice is the start of the Buddhist path. This relates to the ancient Indian ideal of the sadhu or 'wandering holy man' and the practice of meditation (yoga). In order to practise meditation one's conduct has to be moral. The idea of free will and morality as a foundation to spiritual progress and practice is not new and certainly not unique to Buddhism.

quickfire

4.44 Where can we find the origins of freedom in Buddhist teaching?

Key term

Arhat: the worthy one who is in the final stage of rebirth and has full control of the will

Hinduism assumes free will in its understanding of karma and reincarnation.

Key quote

Then the Lord commanded us to observe all these statutes, to fear the Lord our God, for our lasting good, so as to keep us alive, as is now the case. (Deuteronomy 6:24)

(2) Hinduism and Sikhism the implications of free will on religious belief: the cycle of samsara

Hinduism and Sikhism both accept similar principles to Buddhism about the cycle of life; however, there is one key distinction. Both traditions accept the idea of a 'soul' (**atman** in Hinduism) or a 'spark' (**atma** in Sikhism) and its transmigration through the cycle of **reincarnation** depending upon the law of karma. The principles of karma are similar; however, the normative guidance for the religious life varies. Again, both systems assume the idea of freedom to choose one's path in life.

For a Hindu, moral guidance is given in relation to the **Dharma** from various religious texts and relates to both religious and social duties. In a similar way the **Rahit Maryada** (life-rules) provides the code of conduct for Sikhs and includes moral standards, practical guidance, teachings on human motives, religious and social duties and also social ethics. In both cases, the religion teaches that human beings have free will to either pursue an escape from the cycle of existence or remain in the material world through the process of reincarnation.

The implications of free will on religious belief: God's omnipotence and omnibenevolence and the link between God and evil

For both Jews and Christians the notion of God's omnipotence and omnibenevolence being compatible with free will is inextricably linked to the relationship of God to humanity and the overall plan for salvation (soteriology). Free will was given to Adam and Eve. They had the ability to choose but were also guided by God's wisdom.

In Christianity, Judaism and most world religions, God is seen as the final standard of good. God's character exhibits the highest standard of goodness. God acts consistently with that character, so that what God does is always worthy of approval (good). When God gave free choice to Adam and Eve – 'you may **freely** eat of every tree of the garden' – it is inevitable that this was a 'good' decision made by God.

Key quote

The Lord God took the man and put him in the garden of Eden to till it and keep it. And the Lord God commanded the man, 'You may freely eat of every tree of the garden; but of the tree of the knowledge of good and evil you shall not eat, for in the day that you eat of it you shall die.' (Genesis 1:15-17, NRSV)

God's goodness is something that can be relied on by his people. For instance, in Jeremiah 32:40 God says, 'I will make an everlasting covenant with them: I will never stop doing good to them.' It is believed that God's holiness means that God is separated from sin. God's nature is always to be moral and never sin. In addition, Leviticus 19:2 makes clear that God's holiness is the pattern for his people to imitate: 'You shall be holy; for I the Lord your God am holy.' The Judaeo-Christian view is that free will and morality are grounded in the nature of God himself. He is the source and standard of all that is good. Human beings have been created moral creatures in the likeness of God, and scripture provides practical guidance concerning moral living and decision making. The Old Testament prophets particularly recognised that religion and morality go together and spoke out when Israel did not practise what it preached. True religion meant to freely choose obedience to God's teachings and establish moral consistency.

Process theodicy

Free will is implicit in the classical theodicies. It is argued that the evil that exists in the world is due to humanity's misuse of the gift of free-will. God wished to create a world in which rational agents (human beings) could decide freely to love and obey God. Richard Swinburne has addressed the problem of the sheer quantity of evil, which many think is unnecessarily large. He points out that a genuinely free person must be allowed to harm herself and others. God could intervene to stop her or let her learn from the consequences. However, the latter is more in keeping with the exercise of moral freedom. What of free choice to bring about death? Swinburne argues that death is good in that it brings an end to suffering. It would surely be immoral for God to allow humans to have unlimited power to do harm. Also, actions matter more when there is a limited life.

Despite the free will argument attempting to reconcile evil and suffering with an understanding of the monotheistic concept of God as omnibenevolent and omnipotent, some have suggested an alternative solution. Robert Kane refers to this approach as 'open theism' but it is more commonly known as **Process theology** or Process theodicy. The starting point of this theodicy is to question the view that God is omnipotent and the assumption that he is capable of destroying evil. Its main proponents were A. N. Whitehead and David Griffin. The argument proposes that the problem of evil is removed by redefining the meaning of omnipotence. It is a reaction against the classical Christian theodicies in which God seems unaffected by our suffering, even immune to it and this world and its experiences are seen as relatively unimportant. The emphasis in salvation on escaping from this realm is said to illustrate this view.

In contrast, Process theology stresses this life and maintains that the most real thing about a person is the series of experiences which make up the process of their life here and now. God is seen as one intimately involved with this world and its suffering. Indeed, God is called a 'co-sufferer'. The different understanding of God's omnipotence derives from Process theology's view that creation was not ex nihilo (out of nothing). Rather, creation was the achievement of order out of a pre-existing chaos. This limits God's power, since these pre-existing materials are not totally subject to God's will. Hence God is depicted not as a powerful, almighty despot but rather as someone who creates by persuasion and lures things into being. God is in time and both affects and is affected by the world. He even depends on His creatures to shape the course of His own experiences. Such a God cannot control finite beings but can only set them goals which God then has to persuade them to actualise. Evil occurs when such goals are not realised. Natural evil is also explained. For instance, Griffin states, 'If cancerous cells have developed in your body, God cannot lure them to leave voluntarily'.

This theodicy is attempting to make sense of the reality of evil and suffering to address the negative implications that evil and suffering bring for a traditional understanding of God as omnibenevolent and omnipotent. Such negative implications have been seen in the criticisms of the theodicies presented by Irenaeus and Augustine. It is also a direct response to Mackie's argument that in order to solve the problem of evil, Christians have to accept that the omnipotence of God has to be challenged.

> **Key term**
> Process theology: the argument that the problem of evil is removed by redefining the meaning of God's omnipotence

quickfire

4.45 How do Christians justify God's omnipotence and omnibenevolence in the light of free will?

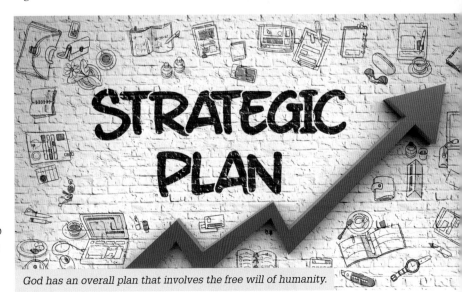

God has an overall plan that involves the free will of humanity.

Key quotes

I cry to you and you do not answer me; I stand, and you merely look at me. You have turned cruel to me; with the might of your hand you persecute me. (Job 30: 20–21)

My God, my God, why have you forsaken me?

Why are you so far from helping me, from the words of my groaning? (Psalm 22;1)

But Zion said, 'The Lord has forsaken me, my Lord has forgotten me.' (Isaiah 49:14)

quickfire

4.46 What phrase did Berkovitz use in relation to his free will argument?

The Holocaust

When thinking of human evil and suffering the Holocaust is top of the list. The unspeakable horrors and atrocities that it administered are the ultimate challenge for free will. There have been various responses by theologians to the Holocaust to try to make sense of what happened in the light of a belief in God. Eliezer Berkovitz was an Orthodox Jewish theologian who attempted to do this using the notion of free will.

Berkovitz's premise was the notion of 'wrestling with God' through reason. Reasoning is a right that religious believers have and that includes lines of reasoning that display anger and resentment. Job and the Psalmists are the classic examples. His book, *Faith After the Holocaust* attempts to address the problem of God's apparent absence during the Holocaust.

Berkovitz argued that God 'created evil by creating the possibility for evil' and that God 'had to create the possibility for evil' on the basis that there was 'the possibility for its opposite, peace, goodness, love'. In explaining the Holocaust, Berkovitz used the notion of freedom; with freedom is responsibility to act independently of God. However, Berkovitz used the idea of 'the hiding of the face' of God found in Isaiah 45:15:

Truly, you are a God who hides himself, O God of Israel, the Saviour.

For Berkovitz, God could be considered 'Saviour' as well as 'hiding' from his people. There is no inconsistency because the hiding is not due to cruel indifference to the situation or pure cold-heartedness; rather, the absence of presence is the price to pay for the bestowing of free will upon humanity. For people to have meaningful free will there needs to be a space between themselves and God. People have to decide for themselves whether or not to follow their evil or righteous inclinations. Helen Gwynne-Kinsey summarises Berkovitz's position in the Year 2 Illuminate book *Judaism*:

'This particular justification of evil is known as the free will defence, and Berkovitz makes very particular use of it in relation to the experiences of the Jewish people. God must "absent himself from history" he writes, and not intervene even when this freedom is grossly misused. Hence the Holocaust should be understood as a manifestation of evil; a tragedy inflicted on the Jewish people by the Nazis. Yet divine intervention did not occur because God had bestowed free will on human beings at the time of creation.'

Some religious believers believe that God suffers when human beings are given free will.

The implications of free will for the use of prayer

Specification content
The implications of free will on religious belief: the use of prayer.

Free will has major implications for religious belief about prayer. In Christianity it involves the notion of God's will but there are issues that certain teachings in the bible raise about requests for intervention that could be argued to be inconsistent with free will; in Islam free will and prayer are arguably more coherent and is all about obedience and devotion. Any 'requests' in Islam are centred around asking for strength to follow the guidance Allah has already given through the Qur'an.

Christianity

Jesus taught much about prayer; however, perhaps the most important teaching for Christians is found in the Lord's Prayer. The Lord's Prayer can be found in Luke (11:2–4) which is the short version; the Lord's Prayer also appears in Matthew's Gospel (6:9–13), though it is longer in form and it is the one used today.

The Lord's prayer

Luke's version reads as though the prayer was intended to be used as it stood ('when you pray, say ...'). In Matthew's version it seems that the prayer is to be used as a model. ('This is how you should pray ...'). The prayer is structured to focus on four things:

1. The relationship with God the Father.
2. God's concerns and plans for God's Kingdom.
3. The needs of humanity such as ensuring physical sustenance through daily bread.
4. The spiritual needs of forgiveness and protection from temptation.

The key phrases that seem to be relevant here to free will are:

- 'Thy Kingdom come' (all versions), and
- 'Thy will be done on earth as it is in Heaven' (in Matthew and the one used by Christians today).

Some manuscripts of Luke's Gospel have additions that reflect Matthew's version. Most scholars argue that these additions are probably liturgical additions and reflect the way that the early church used the prayer. Alternatively, Jesus could have taught the different forms on different occasions. 'Thy Kingdom come' is a request that God's rule may be effective and his authority seen. There is a sense in which God's rule was present in the lives of believers, but there is also a sense in which it was future and universal – not yet fully established. Matthew's version is used today and adds. 'Thy will be done', which is significant for free will in two ways. It is a clear indication that

1. God's will is separate from human will.
2. Despite having free will, the desire is to see 'God's will' done, i.e. the life God would want Christians to lead.

The phrase 'Give us this day ...' is a recognition that God is the provider of the basic human daily needs. It is not necessarily a 'request' to provide but more an acknowledgement that God does provide. The emphasis is on God meeting the needs that Christians have, rather than the needs they may think they have. It is also a daily request, implying a continuous dependence on God.

The lines, 'Forgive us our sins, for we also forgive everyone who sins against us' are also significant as they imply humanity has a choice in how to behave. The emphasis here is on the readiness to forgive. Just as God has forgiven humanity, so Christians should forgive others. Forgiving others is not a condition of God's forgiveness, but more a natural response from Christians, in the light of the fact

Key quote

**The Lord's Prayer
Matthew 6:9-13**
Pray then in this way:
Our Father in heaven,
hallowed be your name.
Your kingdom come.
Your will be done,
on earth as it is in heaven.
Give us this day our daily bread.
And forgive us our debts,
as we also have forgiven our debtors.
And do not bring us to the time of trial,
but rescue us from the evil one.

that God has forgiven them. The same implications for free will are present in the line, 'And lead us not into temptation'. This is significant because it recognises that humans are free to choose how to behave but is an acknowledgement of human weakness rather than a 'request' for God to intervene; guidance is different to intervention. Christians may be tempted and give way easily to sin.

The message from the Lord's prayer regarding free will appears to be that human beings are given free will but yet are still dependent upon the grace and guidance of God. However, there are other areas where Jesus teaches about prayer which do cause debate amongst Christians.

Ask, seek and knock

Luke 11:9–13 teaches that Jesus' followers should ask, seek and knock, confident that God will respond. The contrast is then made between human fathers and God the Father. If the human father gives good gifts rather than evil gifts to his children, then how much more will God give good things to his children also. In particular, the giving of the Holy Spirit is seen as a good gift from God. It is available to those who ask. Hence Christians can have full confidence and trust in God, knowing that whatever they receive from God will be good. Some Christians interpret this as indicating that prayers can be made for 'requests'; for other Christians this is a dangerous route to pursue since it is open-ended and can lead to people teaching that if they are wealthy or fortunate it is because God answers their prayers and not those of others who are poor and less fortunate in life. The teaching of Jesus could here be understood purely in terms of the Holy Spirit that is given by God and not of any divine intervention involving material gain.

Persistence

The verbs of asking, seeking and knocking are all in the continuous tense, implying that prayer is habitual. Both the parable of the Friend at Midnight (11:5–8) and the Parable of the Unjust Judge (18:1–8) contain similar teaching about persistence. In the one case, the person persists in disturbing his neighbour and not letting him sleep until he gives him the loaves he needs. In the other case, the woman persists in her petitioning to the judge until he is worn down and administers justice. God is contrasted with the sleeping neighbour and the unjust judge. If the neighbour and judge both respond, then how much more will God? God is a willing giver, but the focus is on the total determination of the characters in the two parables. They were persistent because what they were asking for was important to them. It is not teaching that persistence will always get its way but it is teaching that God responds when Christians are serious about relying on God's goodness and guidance via the Holy Spirit.

Prayer in Islam

Prayer in Islam a pure act of obedience and submission as one of the five pillars. It is therefore an exercise of free will and as such distinguishes between believers and non-believers. It is also an act of gratitude towards Allah, acknowledging total dependence upon Allah and a confirmation of complete and absolute trust. Prayer increases a Muslim's spiritual awareness of Allah's greatness and is, as such, also a form of personal spiritual development; however, it not seen as a 'connection' with Allah but rather as growth for a human being in appreciation of the deeper truth of Islam.

It would seem that prayer is solely directed from created to Creator; prayer is by no means a conversation with Allah for there can be no such personal relationship with Allah, since prayer serves as a reminder of Allah's greatness. Once again, this reinforces the nature of the act as a positive demonstration of free will to pray. However, a reminder of Allah's greatness is needed since humans are prone to

Nabawi mosque in Madinah. The tower (minaret) is the point from which the call to prayer is made by a muezzin (or Arabic mu'addin), the 'servant of the mosque'.

forget this in everyday living and therefore constantly need waking up from their dreamy distractions. It is no coincidence that the call to prayer in the morning often includes the phrase 'it is better to pray than to sleep'!

As an act of collective wills, prayer brings the community together like a military co-ordination of spiritual strength. The practice of communal prayer on Fridays builds up a (religious) community demonstrating a united will amongst the ummah. Prayer is simultaneously a public demonstration of freely chosen faith but also a private act demonstrating freely chosen devotion. Prayer typifies the action tantamount of being Muslim, that is, submission. Prostration indicates submission. A Muslim is 'one who submits'. This giving of oneself totally and freely over to Allah resigns itself to the futility of the ability to appease Allah beyond blind obedience, as Colin Turner aptly phrases it, to 'express one's total and utter impotence before One who is omnipotent'.

Key term

Ummah: term used to describe the Muslim community, from a local perspective and up to and including the worldwide community of Muslims

quickfire

4.47 Explain the two different ways Islam and Christianity explain the link between free will and prayer.

Prayer in Islam is all about complete submission of the free will to God as an act of obedience.

The implications of free will for the existence of miracles

A religious believer accepts that God exists. God's existence may be independently supported by traditional theistic arguments such as the design argument. If there is strong historical evidence that a miracle has occurred, then it seems reasonable to believe that it has, as long as there seems a suitable motive for God acting in this particular way. However, this brings with it the same issues that prayer brings in that it suggests that God intervenes in the lives of believers and as such restricts free will.

Two scholars that tackle this issue are Richard Swinburne and Maurice Wiles.

Richard Swinburne, Emeritus Professor of Philosophy at the University of Oxford, argues that natural theology establishes the probability that God would produce a revelation, which would need to be confirmed as authentic. Miracles could be the vehicle for this as long as the miracle could be judged as actual on the basis of historical investigation. The nature of God as loving and compassionate may be another reason why believers may accept that miracles occur. God's loving nature might be expected to intervene through compassion. The various world religions understand God to be loving and caring for his people. Therefore, God may be expected to intervene on occasions through miracles to show that love and care. Swinburne further suggests that additional evidence for believing a miracle occurs

Specification content

The implications of free will on religious belief: the existence of miracles.

Key quote

If the direct action of God, independent of secondary causation, is an intelligible concept, then it would appear to have been sparingly and strangely used … it would seem strange that no miraculous intervention prevented Auschwitz or Hiroshima, while the purposes apparently forwarded by some of the miracles acclaimed in traditional Christian faith seem trivial by comparison. (Wiles)

Study tip

Remember that for AO2 arguments you can draw from the examples and evidence of AO1 but it is how you use these explanations in your argument that is important. Do not just write a 'shopping list' of views. Try to comment and evaluate the quality of the views you present.

could include the miracle happening in answer to a prayer and if the prayer was addressed to a named person (e.g. Jesus, Allah). If the world is God's creation, it becomes much more likely that he would wish to intervene and respond to requests to do so. Swinburne therefore sees no inconsistency here between the existence of free will and an interventionist God.

However, some Christians feel that we then have a problem that some people are more 'free' – in the sense of on their own – rather than others?

Maurice Wiles was an Anglican priest and Regius Professor of Divinity at the University of Oxford from 1970 to 1991. His book *God's Action in the World* is a rational assessment of the logical coherency of miracles. Wiles' conclusion was that in the light of humanity's free will and the omnipotent/omnibenevolent characteristics of God, it would be a logical inconsistency to accept that miracles actually occur. In particular, one of the greatest inconsistencies of accepting miracles for Wiles was that it seemed 'strange' that some miracles accepted by the Christian faith are trivial when compared to the lack of intervention in the Holocaust or the bombing of Hiroshima. This was just inconsistent for Wiles as it logically meant that God was either 'arbitrary', 'partisan' or both of these things. It would mean that there is no rational justification and a randomness that ultimately suggests meaninglessness for miracles. It would also establish a God who prefers some over others so could not be omnibenevolent. As such, if Christians accept miracles they are also accepting a God that surely is not worthy of the title 'Almighty' nor worthy or worship. The only logical conclusion for Wiles was that similar to Aristotle's Prime Mover; that God created the world and since then does not intervene.

How God would choose to save some and not others was a key inconsistency for Maurice Wiles. For example, why allow Moses to part the Red Sea saving the Hebrews and yet allow the genocide of the Holocaust?

AO1 Activity

This section has given you an idea of the sort of materials you can use as examples to support your explanations. Now have a look at the whole Specification for Ethics, Philosophy and your study of religion to see if you can make use of any more synoptic links.

AO1 Developing skills

It is now important to consider the information that has been covered in this section; however, the information in its raw form is too extensive and so has to be processed in order to meet the requirements of the examination. This can be achieved by practising more advanced skills associated with AO1. For assessment objective 1 (AO1), which involves demonstrating 'knowledge' and 'understanding' skills, we are going to focus on different ways in which the skills can be demonstrated effectively, and also, refer to how the performance of these skills is measured (see generic band descriptors for A2 [WJEC] AO1 or A Level [Eduqas] AO1).

▶ **Your new task is this:** It is impossible to cover all essays in the time allowed by the course; however, it is a good exercise to **develop detailed plans that can be utilised under timed conditions**. As a last exercise:

1. Create some ideal plans by using what we have done so far in the Theme 4 Developing skills sections.

2. This time stop at the planning stage and exchange plans with a study partner.

3. Check each other's plans carefully. Talk through any omissions or extras that could be included, not forgetting to challenge any irrelevant materials.

4. Remember, collaborative learning is very important for revision. It not only helps to consolidate understanding of the work and appreciation of the skills involved, it is also motivational and a means of providing more confidence in one's learning. Although the examination is sat alone, revising as a pair or small group is invaluable.

When you have completed each plan, as a pair or small group refer to the band descriptors for A2 (WJEC) or A Level (Eduqas) and in particular have a look at the demands described in the higher band descriptors towards which you should be aspiring. Ask yourself:

- Does my work demonstrate thorough, accurate and relevant knowledge and understanding of religion and belief?

- Is my work coherent (consistent or make logical sense), clear and well organised?

- Will my work, when developed, be an extensive and relevant response which is specific to the focus of the task?

- Does my work have extensive depth and/or suitable breadth and have excellent use of evidence and examples?

- If appropriate to the task, does my response have thorough and accurate reference to sacred texts and sources of wisdom?

- Are there any insightful connections to be made with other elements of my course?

- Will my answer, when developed and extended to match what is expected in an examination answer, have an extensive range of views of scholars/schools of thought?

- When used, is specialist language and vocabulary both thorough and accurate?

Key skills Theme 4

The fourth theme has tasks that consolidate your AO1 skills and focus these skills for examination preparation.

Key skills

Knowledge involves:

Selection of a range of (thorough) accurate and relevant information that is directly related to the specific demands of the question.

This means:

- Selecting relevant material for the question set

- Be focused in explaining and examining the material selected.

Understanding involves:

Explanation that is extensive, demonstrating depth and/or breadth with excellent use of evidence and examples including (where appropriate) thorough and accurate supporting use of sacred texts, sources of wisdom and specialist language.

This means:

- Effective use of examples and supporting evidence to establish the quality of your understanding

- Ownership of your explanation that expresses personal knowledge and understanding and NOT just a chunk of text from a book that you have rehearsed and memorised.

Specification content

The extent to which an individual has
free choice.

Key quotes

The systematic unity of the
understanding's cognitions … is the
touchstone of truth of rules. (Kant)

If all thought is caused by fixed
physical laws, then it cannot be
caused by something else, such as
one's choice of what to think. So free
will is an illusion. (Langford)

AO2 Activity

As you read through this section try to
do the following:

1. Pick out the different lines of
   argument that are presented in
   the text and identify any evidence
   given in support.

2. For each line of argument try to
   evaluate whether or not you think
   this is strong or weak.

3. Think of any questions you may
   wish to raise in response to the
   arguments.

This Activity will help you to start
thinking critically about what you
read and help you to evaluate the
effectiveness of different arguments
and from this develop your own
observations, opinions and points
of view that will help with any
conclusions that you make in your
answers to the AO2 questions that
arise.

Issues for analysis and evaluation

The extent to which an individual has free choice

The debate here is about free will but the two key words to take note of are 'extent' and 'individual'. These two words are of great significance because the whole free will debate focuses on what we mean by 'individual' and the 'extent' of freedom this then implies.

For instance, it could be argued that if we take Sartre's view, which is one of absolute libertarianism, then, we propose that there are in fact identifiable individuals through existentialist existence and that such individuals have complete freedom. Sartre's notion of individuality, however, is a very difficult concept to grasp and in fact the 'existence' that he speaks of, and indeed the freedom, ultimately cannot be identified with being-in-itself because it is being-for-itself, which he states is 'nothingness'! However, despite this, there is strong libertarian argument that there is absolute freedom of the individual because we are 'condemned to be free'.

An interesting alternative line of argument is from Dr Susan Blackmore, a psychologist who is also a practising Buddhist. Blackmore has made the most of the evidence called 'the readiness potential' to demonstrate that it is impossible to have free will if the consciousness is not aware of movement and decisions until they have already been initiated biologically. Her argument has been questioned, however, by such as Alfred Mele, who proposed that the evidence is ambiguous because the experiment only demonstrates free wills and not free won'ts! In addition, Peter Harvey suggests that even if Buddhism has a notion of not-self (anatta) there is still the notion of an empirical self and that people have to exercise free will to develop spiritually. Despite this, Blackmore argues both that the idea of an individual 'essence' or 'consciousness' is not viable and that there is absolutely no free choice at all.

Hard-line determinist theories put forward in more recent times, such as in biological determinism, support Blackmore's claims, furthered by the argument that the development of a person is determined by their genetic inheritance and human behaviour is determined by genes and other biological attributes. This denies free will, since it implies that human beings have no internal control over their behaviour and so are devoid of responsibility for their actions. In the same way, behaviourists such as Russian psychologist Ivan Pavlov would argue that there is both biological and psychological conditioning through learning by association or reflex learning. Such arguments are perhaps more forceful when the evidence is considered to corroborate and provide cumulative support.

Very different lines of argument are presented in terms of religious views where there is great debate as to the extent of free will. Whilst Pelagius, Augustine, Arminius and Calvin are all united in agreement in the fact that 'individuals' exist as separate entities and possess souls, these theologians disagree as to the extent of this free will in the light of God's omnipotence. Each theologian puts forward arguments for this: Calvin and Pelagius are at the extreme ends of such positions in relation to total predestination and total freedom; Augustine and Arminius are moderate and see free will as part and parcel of God's predestined plan for salvation. Perhaps the notion of middle knowledge, presented by Arminius as an adaptation of Molinism, is the strongest theological case in that it does not get drawn into the debate about single and double predestination that Augustine's theology does. On the whole, it could be argued from a religious perspective that free will is a reality; however, theologically it does have problems.

An interesting recent development in the debate is worth consideration. Daniel Dennett argues that we are completely 'programmed' biologically, and that the complexity of our consciousness system causes us to 'simulate' the notion of an individual. Dennett proposes that this is in reality not the case and that there is no 'captain at the helm' or 'executive boardroom' to control things and we have to step back and see ourselves as an organistic whole. This means that there is no real individual beyond the complete whole; however, in the light of the complex processes within our consciousness we do actually make decisions and choices within the deterministic framework. Dennett's compatibilism would suggest, therefore, that there is limited freedom for individuals.

Another line of argument is from philosopher Galen Strawson who considers individuals to be completely determined; however, he accepts the notion of free will, not as truth, but as an illusion that we are forced to live with. Therefore in response to the statement, an individual appears to have as much free will as the immediate context enables, but in reality human beings do not have free will at all.

There are alternative arguments from libertarian philosophers such as Roderick Chisholm and Robert Kane. Both see it possible for an individual to have complete freedom. Chisholm suggests that the free will debate demonstrates that both determinism and indeterminism are incompatible with free will and as such the only alternative is to posit an agent since a level of control is required for decision making. This agent for Chisholm is one of self-causation or as he called it 'immanent causation'; this free agent has complete control. However, against such an argument is the suggestion that this is no different from Descartes or Kant and that 'Cartesian theatre' or 'Cartesian materialism' provides no substantial evidence as to the nature of such an agent. This is a major flaw. However, Robert Kane presents an argument that if we reconsider what is meant by 'causal relationships' then we can accept that there is indeed free will for an individual. Kane argues that causal relationships can sometimes be nondeterministic or probabilistic, which purposefully allows for 'the power of agents to be the ultimate creators and sustainers of their own ends or purposes'. If we do not need 'alternative possibilities' for every action then many acts are determined, including some from our own free will. For example, Kane argues that some acts in our past have clearly defined our characters. These 'self-forming actions' demonstrate ultimate responsibility despite working within a largely causal mechanism. He writes: 'indeterminism need not undermine rationality and voluntariness, so indeterminism in and of itself need not undermine control and responsibility'. Therefore, it could be argued that individuals do have full responsibility and free choice for their actions.

However, positing an individual identity that processes such volitions is open to Dennett's criticism of 'Cartesian materialism'. Again, in support of Dennett's organismic perspective, the works of agent-causation theories have recently suggested that there need be no agent beyond the conscious process because the agent idea is integral to the evolution of consciousness. This argument would suggest that the debate about the extent of free will for an individual is built upon the misconception that decisions are separate to the organismic whole, whereas in fact they are just part and parcel of what Steward would refer to as the conscious process of 'settling' and it is through evolution that this process has occurred as an example of survival adaptation.

Indeed, recent discussion appears to accept that we have a materialistic notion of the individual but really it is the way in which we understand this individual that determines our views about the extent of 'free will' there is! Maybe this cannot be answered?

In conclusion, it would appear that there are coherent arguments on both sides of the fence as to the extent of free will for an individual and whether this exists at all. Indeed, John Searle suggests that we can never answer the free will debate mainly because the notion of conscious decision making is so complex, and the deterministic model for consciousness cannot account for this. In response to the statement above, therefore, there cannot really be provided a definitive answer.

Key quotes

… the key question is not, what is the correlate of each particular conscious feature … but rather, what is the difference between the conscious brain and the unconscious brain? (Searle)

Philosophical materialists who believe as I do that we're wholly physical beings, and that human consciousness evolved by purely physical processes, have as strong a sense of self as anyone else. (Strawson)

AO2 Activity

List some conclusions that could be drawn from the AO2 reasoning from the above text; try to aim for at least three different possible conclusions. Consider each of the conclusions and collect brief evidence to support each conclusion from the AO1 and AO2 material for this topic. Select the conclusion that you think is most convincing and explain why it is so. Try to contrast this with the weakest conclusion in the list, justifying your argument with clear reasoning and evidence.

Specification content

The extent to which free human beings should follow a normative ethic.

The extent to which free human beings should follow a normative ethic

The issue for debate here is that if free will is established then is this challenged by a normative ethic? Does a normative ethic restrict one's freedom? Does following a normative ethic mean that we have no choice? Does 'should' mean we 'will'? These are the sorts of question that this issue raises.

To begin with, Aristotle, although a materialist, did promote Virtue Theory and although there is no established set of rules, he did argue that, in discovering the meaning of virtuous behaviour, it is role models of others which provide us with guidance in how to use our freedom. As with many of the Ancient Greek philosophers, true happiness was to be found in terms of well-being and achieving 'true health of the mind'. Then, in combination with role models, one could make 'true sound judgement' from an objective, philosophical perspective that free will affords. It could be argued therefore that *Nichomachean Ethics* can be seen as a normative ethic in itself; however, the notion of the ethic being guidance, rather than being compulsory, prevails. Therefore, one could argue that human beings should follow a normative ethic to achieve the best results for both themselves and others.

An alternative argument could be presented with reference to Kant. Kant was a libertarian thinker and believed strongly in the autonomy of the will. However, Kant believed that moral laws were binding on human beings in that it is our duty is to act morally. This is because, for Kant, when we act out of duty we are demonstrating an innate desire to be moral. In this sense, Kant would argue that people must use their free will to live a moral life and are held accountable. Nonetheless, it could be argued that this does not restrict us but merely guide us towards our duties. In other words, the binding force of the categorical imperative is obligatory due to its truth value in aspiring to the 'summmum bonum'; however, our freedom, that is autonomy of the will, means that although we should follow this, it does not mean that we will follow it. Therefore, it could be argued that the issue of 'should' we follow another 'should' (normative ethics) lays entirely at the feet of the individual freedom to choose.

The psychology of Carl Rogers is indeterminate on this issue; on the one hand, it is inherent within the nature of an FFP that the subject would follow any preconceived notions of morality, yet on the other hand they are open to new ideas and need to be willing to amend their foundational perceptions of morality as they see fit. So if there is a normative ethic then it may be useful for guidance but may not be definitive and so it could be argued that there is no ultimate compulsion to follow it. Therefore, it is not necessarily the case that we should follow a normative ethic; indeed, in some cases it may not meet the needs of the individual in aspiring to be a fully functional person.

Even determinists and compatibilists who hold views that free will is either an illusion or a simulation of 'Cartesian materialism' seem to accept the usefulness of a normative ethic. For example, Galen Strawson, although accepting that we can never be ultimately responsible for our actions, argues that there is 'power' in a personal sense of morality that, even though not freely followed, is more determined by factors within and around us. In this sense, Daniel Dennett provides support in recognising society's 'Moral agent club' and would argue that a normative ethic serves to make sense of how we live and guide others in making meaningful 'choices'. In *Conversations on Consciousness*, Dennett tells Susan Blackmore that 'I think most of us who manage to live moral lives, lives we're not ashamed of, in fact rely a great deal more on the support of our friends that we readily acknowledge.' Dennett seems to be supporting some form of collaborative, ethic norm based upon virtuous action and role models.

Key quotes

So act that you treat humanity, both in your own person and in the person of every other human being, never merely as a means, but always at the same time as an end. (Kant)

So act as if you were through your maxim a law-making member of a kingdom of ends. (Kant)

AO2 Activity

As you read through this section try to do the following:

1. Pick out the different lines of argument that are presented in the text and identify any evidence given in support.

2. For each line of argument try to evaluate whether or not you think this is strong or weak.

3. Think of any questions you may wish to raise in response to the arguments.

This Activity will help you to start thinking critically about what you read and help you to evaluate the effectiveness of different arguments and from this develop your own observations, opinions and points of view that will help with any conclusions that you make in your answers to the AO2 questions that arise.

Again Saul Smilansky argues that an illusion of self is directly related to a normative ethic that is 'useful' and that 'it is a reality' and that it 'ought to continue to be so. He argues: 'Illusory beliefs are in place concerning free will and moral responsibility, and the role they play is largely positive'. Once again, even from the perspective of a determinist that denies the truth of free will, the illusion of a free will in following a real normative ethic is seen as valid.

Sartre advocated a journey of self-definition. It is hard to see how this can be reconciled with a normative ethic other than one of self- interest – just as with Max Stirner. However, just as Ethical Egoism extends to others through the notions of co-operation with others and the Union of Egoists, likewise Sartre's 'ethics of the we' (being-for-others) acknowledges some form of norm for ethical behaviour. He writes of a society in which there are good relations and of a 'society in which relations among human beings are ethical'. Although no author of a normative ethic, Sartre wrote about qualities such as authenticity, gift-response, positive reciprocity, mutual recognition and authentic love and in later years he embraced socialism and Marxism.

From the above, it could be argued that although a normative ethic has positive values and we should follow a normative ethic, the questions that arise from this are the nature of that ethic, that is, 'which one' should be followed? Certainly, it could be suggested that many religious texts that promote ethical living would also be in the frame for consideration. The issue of 'which ethic' appears to be completely up to the individual and it is here where one could argue that conflict arises. Indeed, even for Buddhists like Susan Blackmore, the normative path of ethics is a foundation for the spiritual journey of Buddhists to the realisation of not-self and a total lack of free will. For theologians like Nancey Murphy and Neil Messer, Christian ethics are a sound, philosophical and theological guide as they operate within the parameters of free will. For Robert Kane normative ethics would guide self-forming actions. As we have free choice they are useful in guiding us towards the wisest choices.

Again, although Susan Blackmore lives without the notion of free will, she does acknowledge responsible behaviour through Buddhist principles but also the notion of responsibility for our actions. In her argument on the role of punishment in living without free will she argues that 'the criminal justice system would be stronger and fairer if it were not based on the notion of free will' because punishment is for rehabilitation, deterrence and protection of society. As is the case with Aquinas, she shifts the focus of punishment from the individual to society.

Therefore, in conclusion, there appears to be a universal agreement that a normative ethic is of value. Many seem to accept that we do tend to follow one and that it is good thing to do so. However, whether it should be fixed or flexible is another question, as is the nature of the ethic itself.

Key quote

Arguments of the 'my genes made me do it' type would become irrelevant if we agreed that every action everyone carries out is caused by their genes, their memes, and the environments they have lived in. Arguments of the 'I didn't know what I was doing' type would not hinge on whether or not the person was really responsible of his own free will, but on whether any punishment would be effective. (Blackmore)

AO2 Activity

List some conclusions that could be drawn from the AO2 reasoning from the above text; try to aim for at least three different possible conclusions. Consider each of the conclusions and collect brief evidence to support each conclusion from the AO1 and AO2 material for this topic. Select the conclusion that you think is most convincing and explain why it is so. Try to contrast this with the weakest conclusion in the list, justifying your argument with clear reasoning and evidence.

Specification content

The degree to which free will makes
the use of prayer irrelevant.

The degree to which free will makes the use of prayer irrelevant

We have already seen that free will has major implications for religious belief about prayer. This final evaluation is focusing on the idea that if we are totally free then prayers that take the form of requests are totally redundant because it would mean that religious believers are depending upon some form of intervention in their lives that extends beyond the boundaries of their free actions.

In one sense it could be argued that this is a consistent argument and that prayer by way of a request for intervention does become irrelevant. For example, the teaching in Luke's Gospel from the parables of the Friend at Midnight (11:5–8) and the Parable of the Unjust Judge (18:1–8) suggest that Christians should be persistent. Luke 11:9–13 teaches that Jesus' followers should ask, seek and knock, knowing that God will respond to them.

However, some Christians do not understand the parables in this way and see this as a dangerous route to pursue since it is open-ended and can lead to people teaching that if they are wealthy or fortunate it is because God answers their prayers and not those of others who are poor and less fortunate in life. They would argue that the teaching of Jesus could here be understood purely in terms of the Holy Spirit that is given by God and not of any divine intervention involving material gain. In addition, the teaching on persistence is not a teaching that persistence will always get its way but it is teaching that God responds when Christians are serious about relying on God's goodness and guidance via the Holy Spirit.

In addition, the Lord's Prayer, found in both Luke and Matthew, contains the phrase 'Give us this day ...' as a recognition that God is the provider of the basic human daily needs and some see this as a direct request for this to continue. Others may argue that it is not necessarily a 'request' to provide but simply acknowledging that God already does this. Such arguments would suggest that it is not a question of needs of the individual but an acknowledgement of continuous dependence on God. The same argument can be used for the ideas of 'forgiveness' and 'temptation' (trials).

An alternative line of argument could be that the gift of the Holy Spirit is all that Christians require and that this has already been given. So in relation to prayer requests, it is not the case that Christians are asking for intervention in contradistinction to free will, but that they are requesting that their 'wills' are in line with that of the Holy Spirit. Some would argue, for example, that the teaching about temptations recognises that humans are free to choose how to behave but simultaneously recognise human weakness. This line of argument would propose that guidance is different from intervention.

It appears to be the case that the degree to which free will makes the use of prayer irrelevant depends upon the purpose of prayer. In terms of the classic Lord's Prayer in Christianity, it is significant that it includes the phrase 'Thy will be done'. Some Christians would argue that this is clear indication that our free will is separate from the will of God; however, despite having free will, the desire of a Christian, therefore, is to see 'God's will' done on earth in living their lives as God would want. Therefore, the teaching of the Lord's prayer regarding free will, it could be suggested, is that human beings are still dependent upon the grace of the Holy Spirit in their actions for which they are simultaneously fully responsible.

Whatever is the case, it appears that one could argue that teachings about prayer do cause debate amongst Christians in relation to the issue of free will. For some, the 'will' aspect is irrelevant when asking out of personal interest and gain and it is a matter of 'willing' freely that which is in line with the will of God. For others, this inconsistency is apparent only and they would argue that in God's overall plan, intervention has its place, even on an individual level.

Key quote

Pray then in this way: Our Father in heaven, hallowed be your name. Your kingdom come. Your will be done, on earth as it is in heaven. Give us this day our daily bread. And forgive us our debts, as we also have forgiven our debtors. And do not bring us to the time of trial, but rescue us from the evil one.
(Matthew 6:9–13)

AO2 Activity

As you read through this section try to do the following:

1. Pick out the different lines of argument that are presented in the text and identify any evidence given in support.

2. For each line of argument try to evaluate whether or not you think this is strong or weak.

3. Think of any questions you may wish to raise in response to the arguments.

This Activity will help you to start thinking critically about what you read and help you to evaluate the effectiveness of different arguments and from this develop your own observations, opinions and points of view that will help with any conclusions that you make in your answers to the AO2 questions that arise.

Key quote

And he said to them, 'Suppose one of you has a friend, and you go to him at midnight and say to him, "Friend, lend me three loaves of bread; for a friend of mine has arrived, and I have nothing to set before him." And he answers from within, "Do not bother me; the door has already been locked, and my children are with me in bed; I cannot get up and give you anything." I tell you, even though he will not get up and give him anything because he is his friend, at least because of his persistence he will get up and give him whatever he needs.' (Luke 11:5–8)

It could be argued that prayer in Islam demonstrates coherently that prayer is not at all redundant or irrelevant. For Muslims, prayer is a pure act of obedience and submission and a complete an exercise of free will. It is not a request for Allah to intervene in their lives but an act of gratitude towards Allah, acknowledging total dependence upon Allah and a confirmation of complete and absolute trust.

It could therefore be argued that for Muslims prayer is solely directed from created to Creator; prayer is by no means a conversation with Allah but rather a reminder of Allah's greatness that reinforces the nature of the act as a positive demonstration of free will to pray. Prayer serves also the benefit of bringing together the community, such as with prayer on Fridays, and builds up a (religious) community.

In Islam, then, a public demonstration of freely chosen faith but also a private act demonstrating freely chosen devotion. There is no inconsistency in this and so free will does not make the act of prayer irrelevant. It is essentially no different from responding to a normative ethic in that it is obedience and coming into line with Allah's will, as the scholar Colin Turner aptly phrases it, to 'express one's total and utter impotence before One who is omnipotent'.

One could argue that the work of Maurice Wiles on an interventionist God, whilst relevant for 'miracles' is grounded in prayer requests. His book *God's Action in the World* is a rational assessment of the logical coherency of miracles and concludes that an interventionist God is illogical. His argument is that if we are all requesting intervention from God, then it would be 'strange' to hold to an argument that accepts that the lack of intervention in the Holocaust or the bombing of Hiroshima is consistent with a trivial answered prayer. This was not just inconsistent for Wiles, but it also meant that God could not be omnipotent or omnibenevolent since it would make God either 'arbitrary', 'partisan' or both of these things. Wiles' argument appears to be a strong defence against Christians asking for their personal prayers, based in self-interest, to be offered.

However, Richard Swinburne sees no inconsistency in an interventionist God and argues that if the world is God's creation, it becomes much more likely that he would wish to intervene and respond to requests to do so as a demonstration of love and care. For example, some Christians may accept the parting of the Red Sea as an act of both justice and compassion. However, the question still remains as to whether this seems fair. Such a question, however, could be put down to a Christian's understanding of our limited rationality in the light of God's overall plans.

In conclusion, the relevance of prayer all depends on how one views the purpose of prayer. If the purpose of prayer is one of obedience, supplication and affirmation then there appears to be great relevance to the act for free-willed religious believers. However, we can see that the notion of an interventionist God does suggest some incoherency with the notion of human free will. Gandhi once said, in conversation with a Christian minister about God 'looking after them', that 'he was not so egotistical as to think that God plans his day around him'. Maybe he had a point?

Key quotes

As such, salat is not prayer in the sense of a personal conversation with God, but rather a ritual obligation which must be fulfilled to reaffirm one's relationship with God. (Elias)

It strengthens the conscience, reaffirms total dependence upon God, and puts worldly concerns within the perspective of death, the last judgment, and the afterlife. (Esposito)

If the direct action of God, independent of secondary causation, is an intelligible concept, then it would appear to have been sparingly and strangely used. (Wiles)

AO2 Activity

List some conclusions that could be drawn from the AO2 reasoning from the above text; try to aim for at least three different possible conclusions. Consider each of the conclusions and collect brief evidence to support each conclusion from the AO1 and AO2 material for this topic. Select the conclusion that you think is most convincing and explain why it is so. Try to contrast this with the weakest conclusion in the list, justifying your argument with clear reasoning and evidence.

AO2 Developing skills

It is now important to consider the information that has been covered in this section; however, the information in its raw form is too extensive and so has to be processed in order to meet the requirements of the examination. This can be achieved by practising more advanced skills associated with AO2. For assessment objective 2 (AO2), which involves 'critical analysis' and 'evaluation' skills, we are going to focus on different ways in which the skills can be demonstrated effectively, and also refer to how the performance of these skills is measured (see generic band descriptors for A2 [WJEC] AO2 or A Level [Eduqas] AO2).

▶ **Your new task is this:** It is impossible to cover all essays in the time allowed by the course; however, it is a good exercise to **develop detailed plans that can be utilised under timed conditions**. As a last exercise:

1. Create some ideal plans by using what we have done so far in the Theme 4 Developing skills sections.

2. This time stop at the planning stage and exchange plans with a study partner.

3. Check each other's plans carefully. Talk through any omissions or extras that could be included, not forgetting to challenge any irrelevant materials.

4. Remember, collaborative learning is very important for revision. It not only helps to consolidate understanding of the work and appreciation of the skills involved, it is also motivational and a means of providing more confidence in one's learning. Although the examination is sat alone, revising as a pair or small group is invaluable.

When you have completed the task, refer to the band descriptors for A2 (WJEC) or A Level (Eduqas) and in particular have a look at the demands described in the higher band descriptors towards which you should be aspiring. Ask yourself:

- Is my answer a confident critical analysis and perceptive evaluation of the issue?

- Is my answer a response that successfully identifies and thoroughly addresses the issues raised by the question set?

- Does my work show an excellent standard of coherence, clarity and organisation?

- Will my work, when developed, contain thorough, sustained and clear views that are supported by extensive, detailed reasoning and/or evidence?

- Are the views of scholars/schools of thought used extensively, appropriately and in context?

- Does my answer convey a confident and perceptive analysis of the nature of any possible connections with other elements of my course?

- When used, is specialist language and vocabulary both thorough and accurate?

Key skills

Analysis involves:

Identifying issues raised by the materials in the AO1, together with those identified in the AO2 section, and presents sustained and clear views, either of scholars or from a personal perspective ready for evaluation.

This means:

- That your answers are able to identify key areas of debate in relation to a particular issue

- That you can identify, and comment upon, the different lines of argument presented by others

- That your response comments on the overall effectiveness of each of these areas or arguments.

Evaluation involves:

Considering the various implications of the issues raised based upon the evidence gleaned from analysis and provides an extensive detailed argument with a clear conclusion.

This means:

- That your answer weighs up the consequences of accepting or rejecting the various and different lines of argument analysed

- That your answer arrives at a conclusion through a clear process of reasoning.

Questions and answers

AO1 Theme 1 DEF

A strong answer explaining Naturalism

Naturalism is an ethical theory that proposes ethical knowledge can be reduced to, and explained through, empirical means. It argues that we can know whether something is good, bad, right or wrong by observation of the world around and our experiences. For ethical Naturalism, moral terms relate to the world as we experience it. The philosopher James Rachel wrote, 'moral properties (such as goodness and rightness) are identical with natural properties, that is, properties that figure into scientific descriptions or explanations of things'. **1**

Ethical Naturalism has the advantage of being universal. That is, what we term as 'good' is objective. We can all verify this and it means the same for everyone. Since what is 'good' can be understood by analysing the natural world around us means that our experiences have meaning because we can verify, from our experiences, that kind acts are 'good' and cruel acts are 'bad' due to the happiness or suffering that these experiences produce. For example, we all understand that to experience the kindness of another is a 'good' experience and that to experience cruelty from another is a 'bad' experience. This judgement can be confirmed by what we experience. **2**

As well as being universal, the objectivity of ethical Naturalism means that it is the world around us that establishes what is objective or real. That is, it exists independently of our subjectivity, and therefore it can be used to establish knowledge and truth. This means we can discuss ethics meaningfully and establish certain propositions about good and bad ethical behaviour. This is because the uniform, objective features of the world make ethical propositions true or false because they are based in natural facts and not conjecture. **3**

One example of a naturalist ethical theory is that of Utilitarianism. This Utilitarian approach is naturalistic because it deduces its ethical notions from the basis of the experience of human happiness. Therefore, the most useful ethical action is seen as that which brings the maximum levels of 'happiness or pleasure'. Jeremy Bentham's principle of utility was 'do that which brings about pleasure and avoids pain'. Therefore, Utilitarianism argues that everyone should aim to do the most useful thing to bring this about, that is, the actions that will bring about the maximum levels of happiness or pleasure and thereby the minimum amount of pain. Such actions that produce the most happiness are therefore good actions. F. H. Bradley extended this notion to the idea of 'duty'. He argued that we could also appreciate our sense of morality from our 'station' in life and from scientific notions such as hereditary characteristics. **4**

However, ethical Naturalism in the form of Utilitarianism is not just a personal theory. This is then extended to the 'greatest happiness principle' that further establishes its universalisability. For example, John Stuart Mill was very interested establishing an ethical society, not just individual guidance, and proposed that everyone ought to aim at the happiness of everyone, as increasing the general happiness will increase individual happiness. **5**

In summary, the most important aspect of ethical Naturalism is that objective moral laws exist independently of human beings but are grounded in the empirical nature of existence. Once this premise is established, the link is established between an objective external existence (realism) and that a meaningful (cognitivist) understanding of this, we can verify that what we experience (empiricism) informs us of our sense of ethics, or in the case of Bradley, our ethical duty. Therefore, the claim of ethical Naturalism is that we can recognise objective moral laws that exist independently of human beings and that are located firmly in the world around us. **6**

Examiner commentary

1 Excellent introduction that is focused and with a clear explanation of Naturalism. It immediately addresses the question set.

2 Focuses on one aspect of ethical Naturalism. Well explained with a clear example.

3 Development of ethical Naturalism by indicating its objectivity. This is well explained and precise.

4 This is an excellent paragraph with a clear example of ethical Naturalism being presented. The link to F. H. Bradley is also well made.

5 Further support for ethical Naturalism to support it universalisability with the example of Mill and social benefits, including the greatest happiness principle.

6 An excellent summary at the end recapping on what is contained above it in what cannot be accused of being a repetitive style.

Summative comment

This is a strong answer that is clearly structured and makes excellent use of evidence from the range of materials selected. It clearly answers the question, exploring several different aspects of the topic, differentiating with the use of specific examples.

AO2 Theme 1 DEF

A weak answer evaluating whether Naturalism is superior to Intuitionism

Intuitionism believes that we have a sixth sense of what is 'right and good' or 'wrong and bad'. People like Moore and Prichardson are key writers about it. **1**

For Prichard, moral reasoning was far superior to general reasoning when it came to ethical decisions and therefore we could tell the difference between ethical and non-ethical propositions. **2**

Naturalism, on the other hand, sees itself as the solution because it argues that we can have an objective set of moral values that can be established through empirical means. **3**

Naturalism may be seen as superior as it encourages moral discussion and debate.

Intuitionism has the virtue of corresponding with the sense that many of us have that certain actions are just 'right and good' or 'wrong and bad'. **4**

Naturalism tends to calculate decisions based upon evidence and experience.

Intuitionism is unique in that it considers the obligatory nature and how ethical awareness compels us to behave. **5**

I think that Naturalism is better because it deals with empirical facts and not just your gut feeling about something. **6**

Examiner commentary

1 'Sixth sense' tends to associate this theory with some kind of 'spiritualism' which could be misleading. It also confuses Prichard (Intuitionism) with Richardson (Emotivism). Not the best start.

2 This actually does not explain the difference between moral and general reasoning or ethical and non-ethical propositions. Is this just rote learning or does the candidate know what they mean? There is no evidence here that they do understand.

3 A good sentence but it really needs unpacking and evaluating – it has no supporting evidence – it is therefore just assertion rather than argument.

4 Again these are just assertions with no justification at all.

5 Which means ...? This candidate is not evaluating the question.

6 Whilst Intuitionism is more than just 'gut feeling', this was probably the best sentence of the answer. Pity is was not developed. No real argument here. Basic response with very little critical analysis or evaluation.

Summative comment

The candidate is simply listing a few points for and against without critically assessing them or evaluating them. AO2 needs to use the information. A simple approach of 'Intuition sees itself as superior as an explanation for morality in that ... whereas Naturalism can be mistaken because ..., etc.

AO1 Theme 2 DEF

A weak answer explaining Proportionalism

Proportionalists follow a specific rule for ethics in that we should follow our rules unless we think that they are not relevant and then use our conscience to decide. **1**

The main point about Proportionalism is that you use your conscience to reason what you think is the most loving thing to do. **2**

Bernard Moose argued that the way forward for the Roman Catholic Church in ethics was to follow his rules. The magisterium rejected his teachings but despite that they are popular today because they are a contemporary way of looking at problems. **3**

Proportionalists don't like things that are called evil because we may have to use them to come up with the greater good. For example, I may need to kill someone to save someone else's life and so this would be a good thing to do whereas we see killing as wrong. **4**

A good act may not be good in itself but applies reason to do a bad thing and make it good. A right act is following what the magisterium proposes. **5**

In summary, it can be seen that there are many facets to Proportionalism as invented by Michael Hoose. In particular, it is controversial but also makes people think about what they do. It is, however, rejected by the Pope and his gang. **6**

Examiner commentary

1 This is an inaccurate definition.

2 The candidate is getting this confused with Situation Ethics.

3 It was not Bernard Moose but Bernard Hoose; whilst this is not critical, given it is also Michael Moose in paragraph **6** does raise questions as to the understanding of the candidate. Why is it contemporary? Why was it rejected? Undeveloped response.

4 Irrelevant material mostly; the explanation of evil is confusing and whilst the greater good is relevant, there is no explanation to demonstrate understanding.

5 Totally confused and this is actually the other way around.

6 Summary is just a repeat.

Summative comment

The candidate is very confused and this is a very poor response indeed. It would be good practice to correct the answer yourselves. If you do so it may be a good structure for your own answer.

AO2 Theme 2 DEF

A strong answer evaluating whether Finnis' Natural Law is acceptable in contemporary society

In a sense, any system of Natural Law has an undeniable strength in appealing to our common human nature because it is universal in that the regulations and punishments are the same for all and this then makes it objective. Finnis' work is recognised as 'the leading proponent of Natural Law theory within the Anglo-American legal academy' according to Greenawalt. Indeed, the close relationship between morality and legal jurisdiction makes Finnis' theory applicable to all aspects of life that befall a citizen and therefore is acceptable in contemporary society. [1]

Another strong argument in support of its contemporary relevance for society is that it is grounded in reason. White argues, 'Finnis attempts to formulate a rational basis for moral action. His central thesis is that the act of making law is an act which can and should be guided by moral principles which are a matter of objective reasonableness.' Indeed, Finnis' system allows for a safe and secure community based on clear principles that can be used to carefully formulate laws. It also protects society morally since, like all Natural Law theories, it establishes clearly which acts are always bad. One of the main attractions for Finnis' Natural Law is that it does not need consideration of a God. Whilst it does not deny the importance of 'religion' as a basic good, unlike Aquinas, there is no need to ground the theory in divinity. In this way it appeals to both religious and non-religious people as a common social foundation. As Einwechter writes, 'Since Natural Law is part of the nature of things the knowledge of it is accessible to all men through reason apart from any supernatural revelation.' [2]

Another major strength is the encouragement for individuals to engage with society by embracing the common goods which are not presented as a list of 'don'ts'. Instead they encourage purpose in life, which is to be enjoyed and full of activity. The rules where there are rules seem to appeal to common sense, and the law is positive in defending human rights. This all makes for an attractive, thriving modern society. His emphasis on aesthetics, play and sociability makes a vital contribution towards the 21st-century discussions about shared values, citizenship and tolerance. [3]

However, the good of life ignores any consideration of death and the right to die and so immediately evades difficult debate about suicide and euthanasia. Indeed, Brigita White comments, 'Although, Finnis indeed posits a place for morality in the law, the type of morality Finnis has in mind is questionable.' Another question of its relevance would be the fact that it is a closed shop so to speak – we can never challenge a basic good as they are self-evident. For example, to actually not be able to go against a basic good does not recognise the fact that some ethical dilemmas are significantly complex, whereas at least a proportionalist recognises the complexity of moral issues and has the willingness to challenge the absolute application of basic goods in a practical context. [4]

In fact, this brings us on to another line of argument that would suggest that there are other, more relevant and flexible systems of ethical theory that may be better for contemporary society. These include both religious and non-religious. Indeed, our society is built upon democracy and the law, and our political system has had much utilitarian influence. People may prefer this because it is more flexible and applicable in a variety of ways and see Finnis' Natural Law as simply inflexible. [5]

There are clearly ways in which Finnis' Natural Law is acceptable in society but this does not mean that it will always work, that there are no problems, or indeed, that another alternative ethical theory may be better in serving contemporary society. [6]

Examiner commentary

1 A strong introduction with focus which immediately addresses the question set with an initial line of argument with a good use of quotations.

2 Two lots of supporting evidence are presented and both are substantiated with quotations that are relevant.

3 A focus now on the peculiarities of Finnis' system in engaging with and participating in the goods.

4 A counter argument is introduced to good effect with another quotation to support it.

5 A further argument suggests that there are alternatives to Finnis' system that may be superior and work better for society. It argues the case for utilitarian principles as a means for a legal system.

6 This is a reasonable conclusion that is insightful but it does not necessarily directly relate to the line of reasoning above it. More could have been used from the above to develop this. However, overall a good answer.

The candidate delivers some insightful support for the arguments in relation to the statement. It is a balanced answer and although by no means a full mark answer, it does have its strengths. A good exercise would be to see how you could make this a full mark answer.

AO1 Theme 4 ABC

A strong answer explaining John Calvin's Doctrine of Election

Calvin believed totally in the sovereignty of God – the all-pervasive and over-ruling providence of God, and scripture as the source of knowledge of and about God. Nothing happens by chance. In the *Institutes* he wrote, 'The will of God is the supreme and first cause of all things, because nothing happens but by his command or permission.' The sovereignty of God was an essential feature of the doctrine of predestination. As we shall see, Calvin insisted that the pure sovereignty of God's good pleasure is the origin and explanation of reprobation no less than of election. [1]

Calvin's beliefs about predestination were derived not from just his ideas about divine omnipotence, but also from reflection about human experience, interpreted in the light of scripture. He was aware that some people responded to God's grace whilst others did not. According to Calvin, scripture makes clear that some people respond to the gospel whilst others do not; for example, the parable of the Sower in Mark 4:1–20. He was also convinced that sin had corrupted both the will and the intellect. He regarded humanity as totally depraved (morally corrupt) owing to the fall of Adam and Eve. Totally depraved here does not mean completely depraved or as depraved as you could possibly be. It means tainted or depraved in all areas of the heart, mind and will. Humanity was unable to respond in faithful obedience to the invitation of God through Jesus. In other words, people cannot choose for themselves to repent and believe. [2]

Coupled with the doctrine of unconditional election was Calvin's insistence on the sovereignty of God. God is active and sovereign in his actions. It follows, therefore, that God must actively choose to redeem or to damn. Hence, the doctrine of predestination. In the *Institutes*, Calvin defined predestination as the 'eternal decree of God, by which he determined what he wished to make of every individual. For he does not create all in the same condition, but ordains eternal life for some and eternal damnation for others.' [3]

Like Augustine, Calvin was clear that there is nothing in humanity to merit any favour or mercy. Each person is worthy of God's wrath and incapable of saving themselves. He argued: 'God preordained, for his own glory and the display of His attributes of mercy and justice, a part of the human race, without any merit of their own, to eternal salvation, and another part, in just punishment of their sin, to eternal damnation.' Calvin believed that God chose to elect people regardless of their merit. In this action, he saw God's graciousness demonstrated, since God redeems individuals irrespective of their merits. For Calvin, the elect would receive a twofold grace of justification and sanctification. [4]

Larry Sharp in an article The Doctrines of Grace in Calvin and Augustine comments that 'justification is God's gift of the imputed righteousness of Jesus Christ. Through this gift of credited or reckoned righteousness we have a new standing before God, namely the same standing or position as that of Christ.' Sanctification is the process of growth in holiness and piety through life. Justification is therefore a one-time event whereas sanctification is the continual process of being made more holy. Although justification and sanctification are distinct, they are not separable. Calvin argued that there cannot be justification without sanctification; and there cannot be sanctification without justification. In the *Institutes* he writes, 'Therefore Christ justifies no one whom he does not at the same time sanctify.' According to Calvin, God made a predestined choice for all peoples, before they were even born. Certain people progress to eternal life (the elect) and some to eternal damnation (the reprobates). That number, according to Calvin, is fixed by God from eternity and no one can do anything during their lifetime to change it. [5]

Calvin saw the main purpose of predestination as the means for God to be glorified. Hence, McGrath argues that for Calvin, predestination was never a central premise but more an ancillary doctrine. However, for later followers of Calvin this doctrine became more developed and more central. One consequence that resulted was the doctrine of limited atonement. By 'limited atonement' is meant that Christ died for the sins of the elect and no atonement was provided for the reprobate. Calvin himself never used this phrase and some scholars, such as R.T. Kendall (Calvin and English Calvinism) argued that Calvin limited the extent of the intercession of Christ rather than his work of atonement. In response, others such as Paul Helm point out that in Calvin's own commentary on 1 Timothy 2:5, Calvin argues that 'the universal term "all" must always be referred to classes of men and not to persons' – that is, it is limited and does not mean 'all without exception'. [6]

Examiner commentary

1 A very good introductory paragraph that has focus and immediately addresses the question. It demonstrates good understanding and effective use of quotes.

2 A great paragraph explaining Calvin's notion of the total depravity of humanity and the biblical basis for this.

3 This next paragraph is a development of total depravity in light of the omnipotence of God.

4 This paragraph links the idea of God's omnipotence, total depravity and introduces the notion of the elect with a detailed quotation.

5 With use of scholarship and quotes the Doctrine of Election is now fully developed.

6 A good final supporting paragraph that makes good use of supporting evidence from modern scholarship. No final summary paragraph is required but what this ending does is flag up potential debates surrounding the meaning and implications of Calvin's teachings.

Summative comment

An extensive answer supported throughout by extensive use of quotations to support explanations. Selections have been made from the text in the book to arrive at this answer. Maybe it would be useful to have a go at doing the same but by paraphrasing each paragraph you choose to use.

AO2 Theme 4 ABC

A weak answer evaluating the extent to which God predestines humanity

There are two sides to this. Some argue that there is no free will and God predestines everything; and those who argue it is just all about being saved and not about free will. Religious texts can be used for either side. For example, the Bible states that 'we been predestined according to God's will ...' but also says 'Adam was free to eat from the apple tree'. Both these religious texts imply different things. 1

One scholar argues that God is so intelligent that he can think and choose as he pleases without being inconsistent. God is consistent with himself and so there cannot be any contradictions. For example, Paul says that God is a potter and made humans from clay and so if he can mould us like that he must have complete control. 2

Others argue that human beings have real choices in life and so the outcome of every event or action is not down to God but is our responsibility. However, whoever God saves is his business. 3

Then again, scholars will argue that God is supposed to be merciful and so setting up such a plan is not being kind to those who do not have the ability to save themselves and be responsible. However, religious freedom teaches that our free actions can reject God's salvation. For example, Jesus made it plain that the Pharisees 'rejected the purpose of God for themselves'. 4

As always when considering religious texts, the force of the argument will depend on whether the religious texts are taken as authoritative and whether the particular texts can be interpreted in an alternative way. 5

In conclusion there are always two sides to an argument. Both arguments are strong and it really just depends upon whether you believe one or the other. 6

Examiner commentary

1 A reasonable, if basic, introduction that sets out two sides of the argument without eloquence. However, the religious quotations are dubious!

2 This argument is trying to point out that if God is God then whatever God does cannot be inconsistent; however, it is very poorly expressed. The last sentence is ok.

3 A simple point simply made. No real development of exploration of this line of reasoning is evident.

4 Good point about Jesus and use of an example but which scholars are they referring to?

5 There is a point here but it seems to be confusing the idea of salvation through good works with predestination. There seem to be two conflated points about being able to do good and being able to reject God.

6 This is a very weak conclusion. There is nothing wrong with sitting on the fence but to do it without reasoning is pointless. The answer accepts both sides as valid but does not justify why – they may as well have advised the reader to 'toss a coin and decide'. Not good evaluation technique.

Summative comment

This answer is simplistic in its approach to the question. It would be much improved if there were greater depth of analysis and evaluation; for instance, using more accurate quotes and particular scholars. As it stands it is not that strong – especially the concluding remarks.

AO1 Theme 4 DEF

A weak answer explaining Arminius on free will (lengthy but mainly biographical)

Jacob Arminius was born in Oudewater, Holland, and this very same year John Calvin was busy establishing the Genevan Academy to set out his ideas of predestination. In addition to this, Guido de Bres wrote the first edition of the Belgic Confession at the same time, which outlined the basic doctrine of Dutch Calvinism. As Arminius grew up, arguments over Calvin's teachings interrupted those over Spanish rule. By the time Arminius was 14, William the Silent, Holland's king, was a Calvinist. [1]

Arminius became an orphan while still young. His father Herman, a manufacturer of weapons, died, leaving his wife a widow with small children. He never knew his father, and his mother was killed during the Spanish massacre at Oudewater in 1575. [2]

Arminius studied with success, starting at Leiden in 1576 and may have had seeds planted that would begin to develop into a theology that would later question the dominant Reformed theology of John Calvin. The success he showed in his studies motivated the Merchants' Guild of Amsterdam to fund the next three years of his studies. Arminius remained a student at Leiden from 1576 to 1582. Although he enrolled as a student in Liberal Arts, this allowed him to pursue an education in theology, as well. [3]

In his early life Arminius identified as a Calvinist and was a supporter of Beza who continued to promote Calvin's teachings of predestination. Arminius became dissatisfied with Calvinism and rejected Calvin's predestination for a version of predestination that he developed himself. Arminius' predestination was grounded in the theological concept of God's providence and was compatible with the notion of free will. [4]

Jacobus Arminius was also a pastor in Amsterdam and had a good reputation among his parishioners as a compassionate man and a gifted preacher. [5]

In 1618–1619 a synod was held in the Dutch town of Dordrecht (Dort) consisting of international representatives of the Reformed Protestant Churches from Germany, Switzerland, England and the Netherlands. The meetings had the main aim of uniting the disparate Reformed Churches under the Belgic Confession of 1566 which sets out systematically the declaration of faith of Calvinism. [6]

Examiner commentary

[1] This is a weak introduction as it is biographical in focus and descriptive, not immediately addressing the focus of the question.

[2] At first this answer may appear to be reasonably detailed but as we read on we will find it is on the whole just about the person Arminius and NOT about his teaching.

[3] Again this is just about what he did and not about what he taught.

[4] This is the first paragraph that focuses on the question. One would hope that this answer moves on from the irrelevance of the first three paragraphs in paragraph [5] ?

[5] The answer, unfortunately for this candidate, is no. Again, this may be interesting but it is not relevant.

[6] The Synod of Dort is relevant for the teachings of Arminius. What a shame the answer simply describes the context for the occasion rather than the theological details that it debated regarding Arminius' teachings.

Summative comment

This answer is very poor indeed because although it may be well written and fairly full of detail, it does not answer the question. Instead of focusing on the teachings of Arminius, it focuses on his life story. Interesting reading but it would get very few marks as an examination answer.

AO2 Theme 4 DEF

A strong answer evaluating how convincing religious views are on free will

How can there be an omnipotent God and yet human beings possess free will? It could be argued that with the problem of evil, Augustine laid emphasis on the fall of humanity and the inadequacy of the human condition, whereas with the nature of free will in itself, he stressed the omnipotence of God in a way that would not allow Christians to think that they were in complete control of their destiny. Augustine, in being concerned about the Pelagian controversy of free will, appears to have bridged the gap that absolves God of any responsibility for evil and allowing free will with an emphasis on God's grace. [1]

Some may argue that Augustine is inconsistent since the notion of free will in the fall emphasises humanity's freedom to disobey and this seems at odds with the idea of an omnipotent God. The Australian philosopher John Mackie clearly identified the nub of the issue when he raised his concerns about what he called the paradox of omnipotence. The essence of this is that if God is omnipotent, then to suggest there is something that God is not able to control or do then we are admitting that God cannot be omnipotent. [2]

However, it must be pointed out that Mackie's definition of God's characteristic of omnipotence is absolute power, authority and strength but something that is a constant not just in what it is but what it does. Therefore, one could argue that Mackie's own understanding of omnipotence is skewed. Religious believers can argue that omnipotence has a definitive absolute of being but also by logic an infinite range of action. In other words to say God is omnipotent does not mean God can only do omnipotent things; God must be allowed to exercise the full range of possible actions. **3**

In support of this line of argument, Augustine clearly identifies the omnipotence of God as a God who is within its power to permit freedom whilst simultaneously having an overall plan that demonstrates God's omnipotent nature. For Augustine the end of salvation maintains the integrity of God's omnipotence. **4**

Following on from this, it could be argued that through Arminius' doctrine of divine concurrence, Arminius ensures God's control in that God 'concurs' human activity by being part of it, providing the powers and abilities to act. The notion of divine providence for Arminius involves both preservation of the world but crucially governance of it whilst simultaneously allowing for human freedom. God sustains the universe by being involved in it. Neither free will nor the actions of any creature can be outside the parameter of God's providence. **5**

There could be said to be a strength of corroboration and support in the religious explanations offered in relation to the statement. Indeed, it does appear that the evidence seems to suggest that religious views on free will are convincing and have been for many; and yet, the crucial question is 'who are the many?' They are, on the whole, religious believers. It is clear that philosophers like Mackie would not be as accommodating. Therefore, the religious explanations may be 'coherent' arguments, but whether they are convincing is a different matter altogether. **6**

Examiner commentary

1 A good introduction focusing on the issues for debate. The example of Augustine is a useful one and makes a synoptic link.

2 Another synoptic link is made with the philosopher John Mackie and his point about omnipotence and free will/ evil.

3 A counter argument to this critical point is introduced to good effect and logically argued.

4 Further support for this argument is presented by way of Augustine's 'bird's cyc' view of God's overall purpose and plan.

5 A different line of reasoning is considered in relation to evidence provided by the theologian Arminius regarding concurrence of God rather than the control of God.

6 This is a strong conclusion and is directly related to line of reasoning. An insightful answer.

Summative comment

A well-argued answer that uses extensive references to scholars to support explanation. Selections have been made from the text in the book to arrive at this answer but very few quotes have been used. Maybe it would be useful to have a go at doing the same but by selecting quotes for each paragraph you choose to use.

Quickfire answers

Theme 1

1. Nothing is in the intellect that was not first in the senses.

2. Discussion about knowledge.

3. A statement or assertion.

4. The Logical Positivists.

5. That which brings the maximum levels of happiness or pleasure.

6. Kant.

7. He wanted to create a form of ethical theory that was both naturalistic and yet simultaneously into which, the idea of a metaphysical self was fully integrated.

8. It combines fact with duty, it brings the subject (individual) and object (the world around us) together, and it is a concrete (considers the whole).

9. Not really, he argued that 'there cannot be a moral philosophy which will tell us what in particular we are to do, and also that it is not the business of philosophy to do so'.

10. Hume's Guillotine.

11. The principles of *a priori* knowledge (conceptual and prior to experience) and *a posteriori* knowledge (relating to experience).

12. Good is a simple notion because it cannot be broken down; in itself, it is not relational, or dependent upon any other constituent part and neither is it a constituent part itself; it is therefore indefinable.

13. A question with a definitive answer, e.g. yes or no.

14. Moore concedes that it is possible that metaphysics might have some relevance to the question of what we ought to do, though it could have none to the question of what is good.

15. Yes, the number 4 is a self-evident truth; it may well be the case that it is not evident to some and yet evident to others. However, it still remains a truth independently of whether or not we perceive it as so.

16. The pleasures of human intercourse and the enjoyment of beautiful objects.

17. Because there is need for a gradual awakening towards a revelation of this innate intuitive awareness in the sense that when we have reached sufficient mental maturity we will have given sufficient attention to what is good or bad.

18. Prichard disagreed with Moore's consequentialism; for Prichard what we ought to do was derived through moral reasoning.

19. Moral reasoning is the recognition and assertion of one's duty by intuitive thought. In contrast, general reasoning is using the empirical evidence around us to present logical argument.

20. Because he introduced the notion of doubt, his principle of skepticism.

21. Because obligation is sometimes contrary to personal interest.

22. Mackie argued that Prichard's intuition made moral properties 'queer' in so far as they were 'entities or qualities or relations of a very strange sort, utterly different from anything else in the universe' and therefore being 'queer' it is doubtful that we could know anything about them because we need a 'special faculty of moral perception or intuition, utterly different from our normal ways of knowing everything else'.

23. Value, for Russell, is an emotive response and such questions were totally a matter for debate and personal perspective.

24. To demonstrate what ethical language does – in Ayer's words, 'to show what people are doing when they make moral judgements'.

25. Four.

26. A cry of pain.

27. Charles L. Stevenson.

28. (1) Enable disagreement about goodness. (2) Have a certain magnetism or appeal to act in its favour. (3) Not be subject to verification by scientific method.

29. No, beliefs are not about ethical convictions – they are more to do with facts that can be verified, such as the nature of light transmission in science.

Theme 2

1. He saw it as an attempt to justify Roman Catholic morality through a legal framework.

2. A universal application of the human goods identified in Natural Law through jurisprudence.

3. Laws provide a legal system within which the moral principles can operate.

4. The self-evident truths of the basic goods.

5. Practical wisdom (phronesis) and philosophical wisdom (Sophia).

6. Theoretical reasoning deals with what we have in front of us and tries to make sense of questions of explanation and prediction, very much like scientific analysis, and attempts to determine what is going to happen. It is concerned with matters of fact and explanation.

7. Practical reasoning is based upon self-evident ethical principles and deals with the normative, that is, 'what am I obliged to do to be moral?'

8. They are self-evident; they are not overlapping or a part of another basic good; they are all equally important.

9. Life, knowledge, play, aesthetic experience, friendship, practical reasonableness and religion.

10. Knowledge that is sought out because it is good in itself.

11. The important distinction is that play originates with one's own actions whereas aesthetic experience can be beyond this by simple appreciation of an object of art form, natural beauty and entails an inner experience of this.

12. Practical reasonableness is not just being aware of the treasury of distilled knowledge but it also simultaneously includes the ability to exercise that knowledge effectively.

13. Finnis argues that the term 'religion' is lame in defining this basic good because it is more to do with awareness of some cosmic order that is 'other' and that is part of being human.

14. Nine principles of practical reasonableness.

15. To be like Aristotle's phronimos (the ethical expert) and to exercise wisdom (prudential) in decision making.

16. The magisterium.

17. Aquinas' 'principle of double effect'.

18. The early proportionalists used language that sometimes had a common understanding with others, or, sometimes used specific language that had a different meaning for them, or, even sometimes, they introduced new words to discuss concepts that were already part of the debate in different wording.

19. Any two of rape, masturbation, lying and contraception.

20. The development and use of a drug called methotrexate, which targets the most rapidly growing cells of the embryo.

21. To remember that Proportionalism does not reject rules because both Natural Law and Roman Catholic theology identify clear deontological principles that are absolute. Proportionalism is part of Natural Law and Roman Catholic theology.

22. They use words like good, bad, evil, sins, value, moral evil, immoral, morally acceptable – associated with virtuous (aretaic) character; they made little or no use of right, wrong, ought, duty, obligation or a right – associated with ethical judgements.

23. As the general imperfection of the fallen world both physically and morally.

24. Because it is central to Christian ethics.

25. It is not really an ethical theory, there are misunderstandings of what teleological means, and also that some misunderstand Natural Law as deontological.

26. The German Jesuit priest Peter Knauer, although technically it was Thomas Aquinas.

27. Patriotism, according to the sociologist Stewart, is inward looking, welcoming and having pride in the positive values a country represents.

28. Reparation is focused on the victims; retribution is focused on the criminal.

29. 1965, although completely in 2002.

30. Finnis' Natural Law is neither purely secular nor purely religious. He sees it as applicable to all – universal.

31. To be able to participate in the basic goods for personal and social well-being.

32. They disagreed about how morality related to the law. Finnis saw an integral relationship; Hart saw them as separate.

33. He argues that punishment is a 'good' act. How he justifies this is complicated and debated today.

34. Hallett thought that ethical precepts and rules has been artificially established by the Church and 'smuggled in'.

35. Because it is only one aspect of moral theology for many proportionalists and not their main ethical methodology. It is also more of a general guide rather than an ethical theory.

36. Richard McCormick defined a 'conflict situation' as a situation in which 'an evil can be avoided or a more or less necessary good achieved only when another evil is reluctantly caused'. That is, according to McCormick, cases where 'there is the situation where the only alternative to causing evil or permitting evil is greater evil'.

37. Hallett's Proportionalism suggests that to balance values requires taking into account not just pre-moral or nonmoral values but also moral ones.

38. Selling frames his whole approach around becoming a good Christian and the idea of developing virtues in ethical behaviour and decision making.

39. All pre-moral values and disvalues together with any moral values associated with the event.

40. The starting point of ethical living for Selling is the person and not simply a list of commandments, therefore the aim of Christian ethics is to inquire who this person is, where they are going and what they are trying to accomplish.

Theme 4 ABC

1. Greek philosophical traditions, Judeo-Christian religious and scriptural traditions.

2. Confessions.

3. The Manicheans, the Platonists, the Church (and its scriptural tradition).

4. It rejected the need for God's grace and so diminished the power of God.

5. Born with weakened faculties (carnal concupiscence), subject to death.

6. Original Sin is inherited through the sexual act of procreation but Jesus was born of a virgin (no sexual act took place).

7. It removes Original Sin.

8. Because of concupiscence (they have an inclination towards sin).

9. Ephesians 1:4,5,11, John 15:16, Romans 8:29–30.

10. *Institutes of the Christian Religion*.

11. Divine omnipotence, reflection about human experience interpreted in the light of Scripture, the need for God to actively choose.

12. Justification means a person is declared righteous whilst sanctification means growing in holiness. Justification is a one-time event whilst sanctification is a continual process.

13. Christ died only for the Sheep.

14. The Five points of Calvinism was a direct response to the Five points of Arminianism.

15. Total depravity, Unconditional election, Limited atonement, Irresistible grace, Perseverance of the Saint.

16. Determinism has no concept of final goals whereas predestination is about final goals ordained by God.

17. Because the concept of freedom cannot be put alongside the concept of the will.

18. The locked room.

19. Criminality and violent behaviour, psychiatric illnesses, addiction, sexual orientation.

20. Classical conditioning is about learning by association or reflex learning. Operant conditioning is about learning to repeat behaviour that is rewarded and not repeat behaviour if punished.

21. Whilst both accept determinism as true, hard determinism argues it is incompatible with free choice, whist the soft determinist argues it is compatible with free choice.

22. Internal causes refer to the willingness to do an act and so the action is voluntary. External causes refer to coercion or force, so the act is involuntary.

23. Moral responsibility implies 'ought' and 'ought' implies 'can' but hard determinism maintains the person was unable to do otherwise and therefore 'could not'.

24. Leopold and Loeb.

25. He orchestrates the final destiny of each human being.

26. There should be universal salvation if God is loving and could save everyone. God is the author of all sin since all events are predestined by God.

27. Prayer can't change anything since all events are predestined.

Theme 4 DEF

28. He felt it encouraged a lax lifestyle, hypocrisy and immorality like that which he encountered in Rome. Original Sin was seen as an excuse for their immoral behaviour and so encouraged people not to even try to control their urge to sin. Sins could be confessed and be forgiven.

29. The gift of free will enabled Adam and Eve to choose whether or not to eat the forbidden fruit; but also, in eating the fruit, allowed the process of maturity to begin. Pelagius' reasoning was that humans go through a learning process, and, as they do, they grow and mature in wisdom, learning from their mistakes. Part of this process is defiance – just like Adam and Eve – in order to discover for oneself how things are. Therefore, in exercising their free will and making their own decisions, the long-term benefits outweigh the short-term pitfalls.

30. In his early life Arminius identified as a Calvinist and was a supporter of Beza who continued to promote Calvin's teachings of predestination.

31. Arminius presented his Declaration of Sentiments, a detailed written exposition of his theology and which clarified his position on predestination and salvation. It could be argued that this is more detailed than the Five Articles which are a summary of the latter.

32. They represent the classic positions in regard to dualism.

33. For Sartre, the waiter was not being his true self but merely playing out the role of a waiter as if it was his true self.

34. Electrical stimulation of the posterior parietal cortex of the brain.

35. Because, according to Professor Koch, knowing how something works does not necessarily answer the question of voluntary agent control.

36. Carl Rogers is seen as the official founder of a humanistic psychology which suggested a client-centred approach.

37. Rogers felt it was the polar opposite of defensiveness.

38. Because if he had deliberated and answered that there was no free will, that is itself only intelligible as an exercise of free will.

39. Democritus.

40. A ghost in the machine.

41. An experiment that concluded that the notion of a conscious will was an error because it was demonstrated that the brain has actually decided and initiated a move before the consciousness was aware of the decision being made.

42. Searle's point is that deterministic and materialistic theories about 'free will' confuse syntax (manipulation of symbols) and semantics (meaning).

43. The worth of human ideas of rightness, wrongness and moral value.

44. The notion of free will in Buddhism springs directly from the idea of kamma.

45. For Christians the notion of God's omnipotence and omnibenevolence being compatible with free will is inextricably linked to the relationship of God to humanity and the overall plan for salvation.

46. Berkovitz talks of 'the hiding of the face' of God.

47. Free will has major implications for religious belief about prayer. In Christianity it involves the notion of God's will; in Islam free will and prayer are totally coherent and are all about obedience and devotion.

Glossary

A ghost in the machine: Ryle's notion of self-illusion regarding the 'free will'

A priori: prior to the senses

Abstinence: the option taken not to participate in something

Act-in-itself: the simple action without consideration of intention of circumstances

Actual self: the view that we have of our self as a result of life experience

Actualising tendency: an innate directional tendency in each of us to grow, to seek new and varied experiences

Aesthetic: pleasing to the eye

Agape: Christian love

Agency incompatibilism: the notion that determinism is false because as a system becomes more complex, forms of self-organising emerge as a result of interaction between constituent biological and neurological elements

Agent-causal theories: the idea that there is a form of 'agent' that has evolved in neurological processes

Alaya vijnana: the eighth and ultimate level of consciousness, according to some Mahayana Buddhist schools of thought, where 'seeds' of thought are stored and processed

Anatta: Buddhist term often referred to as 'no soul'; the best translation is 'not self'

Apparent goods: an act that may seem good but is really not

Aretaic: Frankena's term to describe words that are to do with goodness and virtue as qualities of a person and act, from the Greek word arete meaning 'virtue'

Arhat: the worthy one who is in the final stage of rebirth and has full control of the will

Arminianism: the doctrinal teachings of Jacobus Arminius and his followers who argued for free will and that Christ died for everyone rather than just the elect

Ascetic: the disciplined lifestyle of a monk

Asylum seeker: one who is seeking refuge from a life-threatening situation

Atma: the Sikh term for soul

Atman: the Hindu term for soul

Atomic hypothesis: Democritus' notion that the universe was made up of tiny physical units

Atonement: Christian doctrine concerning the reconciliation of God and humankind, accomplished through the life, suffering and death of Christ

Autonomous: self-governing

Autonomy of the will: the idea that the will is independent

Basic Argument: Galen Strawson's proposal that free will is an illogical notion because it implies that we must be *causa sui*

Beatific Vision: the teleological end of Natural Law according to Aquinas whereby one is united with God through Christ

Behaviourism: also known as behavioural psychology, is a theory of learning based on the idea that all behaviours can be explained without the need to consider internal mental states or consciousness

Belgic Confession: a Latin document consisting of 37 articles which deal with the doctrines of God, Scripture, humanity, sin, Christ, salvation, the Church, and the end times from the Dutch Reformed Protestant perspective.

Bija: teaching about a 'seed' of consciousness found in some Mahayana Buddhist schools of thought

Calvinism: a branch of Protestantism based on the theological beliefs promoted by John Calvin. It is also referred to as Reformed Protestantism or the Reformed tradition

Capital punishment: the death penalty, execution, as a form of punishment

Carmelites: a religious mendicant order of the Roman Catholic tradition that focuses on contemplation, prayer, community and service

Cartesian dualism: the idea that body and mind (soul) are separate entities

Cartesian Theatre: Daniel Dennett's derisive description of any modern theory that proposes, like Descartes, that there is some central focus of the mind (like a stage) that in control of our bodies

Casuistry: a rational methodology that seeks to resolve moral problems by extracting or extending theoretical rules from one particular case, and reapplying those rules to new instances

Categorical imperative: Kant's view of an unconditional moral obligation which is binding in all circumstances and is not dependent on a person's inclination or purpose

Category mistake: Seeing something in its entirety (the sum of all constituent parts) as belonging to a separate category e.g. the collective buildings of a university being different from the university

Causa sui: something that is independent of cause

Chinese room: Searle's thought experiment demonstrating that deterministic and materialistic theories about 'free will' confuse syntax (manipulation of symbols) and semantics (meaning).

Claims: Prichard's term for an argument put together from general reasoning

Classical soft determinism: a theory that believes that a human action can be called free when the beings have an element of freedom despite their moral choices being completely determined by outside factors

Cognition: the mental action or process of acquiring knowledge and understanding through thought, experience, and the senses

Cognitive neuroscience: scientific study of the biological processes and neural connections in the brain

Cognitivism: the meta-ethical view that ethical sentences express meaningful propositions

Commensurate reason: justifying appropriate compensation, another term used for proportionate reason

Commutative justice: justice between individuals

Compatibilism: a theory that believes that freedom and determinism are mutually compatible in the case of some human actions. There is no logical inconsistency in believing in both

Compatibilist: the view that one theory does not contradict another (i.e. a person can both have free will and be determined)

Concrete universal: Bradley's view that the self is not isolated but is derived from dialectical relations with the world

Concupiscence: strong desire for earthly pleasures. It stems from the disobedience of the first sin by Adam and, without itself being a sin, inclines human beings to commit sins

Conditional predestination: the complex theological notion based upon the idea that free will and predestination are compatible

Conditioning: a theory that the reaction to an object or event by a person can be determined by stimuli

Conflation: the merging of two ideas

Conflict situation: a situation (dilemma) whereby available options to act ethically include bad actions

Congruence: that a person has harmony between real and ideal selves

Consequence argument: the argument that free will is incompatible with determinism because there is no possibility for any control over what we can do in the future based upon what has happened in the past

Consequentialist: any ethical theory that hinges a moral decision upon what the consequences of the action would be (the end or outcome)

Council of Carthage: Catholic Church meetings or synods held between the 3rd and 5th centuries in the city of Carthage, in Africa

Cumulative argument: a series of arguments that gain collective force and are seen to corroborate the effectiveness of each single argument in the series

Decalogue: a term for the Ten Commandments

Deontic: an evaluative term that concludes what one should do and how one should behave

Deontological: used to refer to a rule-based system of ethics

Descartes' principle of skepticism: that doubt can be resolved through challenge

Descriptive: term used as a criticism of Naturalism that it can only describe and not be prescriptive

Despotism: Bradley's understanding of absolute power or the ultimate controlling all

Determinism: the doctrine that the past determines a unique future. Every event, including human action is determined by previously existing causes

Deterrence: to put someone off a committing a crime

Dharma: the notion of moral and religious obligation

Dialectical synthesis: Hegel's view that two opposite views (hypothesis, antithesis) can be united (synthesis) through philosophical analysis. One simple example would be: hypothesis 'the universe began with the Big Bang'; antithesis 'God created the world'; synthesis 'God was the first cause and is compatible with the Big Bang'

Direct and indirect distinction: used to refer to an act that is directly intended and an indirect consequence of a direct action

Distributive justice: economic, political, and social frameworks that each society has including its laws, institutions, policies to ensure fairness and equality

Divine concurrence: God 'concurs' human activity through being part of it and providing the powers and abilities to act but does not necessarily approve

DNA: Deoxyribonucleic acid, or DNA, is the hereditary material in humans. Nearly every cell in a person's body has the same DNA and it carries genetic instructions

Donatist: a controversy about the validity of the sacraments based on the worthiness of the clergy administering it – the name is derived from their leader Donatus

Dualism: the idea that there is both a physical reality and a metaphysical reality; a body and soul or a mind and body

Duty: Bradley's explanation of ethical awareness through a process of self-realisation brought about by interaction with society and nature and acknowledgement of one's station

Dynamic power: the sense in which language is best analysed to determine meaning according to Stevenson

Economic migrant: one who seeks out a better standard of life through migration

Ectopic pregnancy: a pregnancy where the embryo embeds itself 'out of place' (ectopic), most often in the fallopian tube endangering the life of both foetus and mother

Embodied souls: Murphy's physicalist explanation for the notion of 'soul' in preference to the idea of 'spirited bodies'

Emotivism: theory that ethical propositions are simply expressions of approval or disapproval

Empirical: knowledge gained through the senses

Epigenetic: the study of changes in organisms caused by modification of gene expression rather than alteration of the genetic code itself

Epistemology: philosophy of knowledge derived from the Greek episteme (knowledge) and logos (words or discussion), i.e. 'discussion about knowledge'

Ethical fallacy: to accept that morality indicates free will

Ethical Naturalism: the view that ethical propositions can be understood by analysing the natural world

Ethical non-naturalism: an alternative term for Intuitionism

Etre-en-soi: Sartre's phrase for inanimate matter and being without consciousness, a 'being-in-itself'

Etre-pour-autrui: Sartre's new dimension in which the self exists as an object for others, a 'being-for-others'

Eudaimonia: Aristotle's term for happiness of well-being

Ex hypothesi: according to the hypothesis proposed

Executive boardroom: a phrase used to describe a central and controlling part of the neurological process that 'makes decisions'

Existentialism: a philosophical theory that understands the existence of the individual person as free and responsible for determining their own development through acts of the will

External cause: when a person's will is stopped from carrying out its predetermined choice

Facticity: the reality of 'being-in-itself'

Finis operantis: the intention behind the act

Finis operis: the act-in-itself

Fully functioning person: a congruent person that participates in the fulness of life experience

Gap: Sartre's notion of distance between a person's consciousness and the physical world that necessitates people to have free will

General reasoning: using the empirical evidence around us to present logical argument

General revelation: knowledge about God discovered through natural means such as reasoning or observation of the physical universe

Genes: a unit of heredity and is a region of DNA that influences a particular characteristic of an organism

Genome: the genetic material of an organism. A person's complete genetic code

Geometrical: to work through each of the four conditions of the 'principle of double effect' in order

Glaudium et Spes: an official document released as a result of Vatican II about the Church's mission in the world

God's grace: the love and mercy given to humanity by God because God desires humanity to have it, not because of anything humanity has done to deserve it

Hard determinism: the doctrine that determinism is true and hence no human actions are free

Heresy: a belief that is contrary to orthodox Christian theology/dogma

Heretic: a person whose beliefs are against the laws and beliefs of a specific religion

Hermeneutical: the science of interpretation

Holocaust: the term used for the murder of approximately six million Jews by Nazi-led Germany (1933 and 1945), also referred to as the hashoah (the catastrophe) by Jews

Human Genome Project: an international scientific research project with the goal of determining the sequences that make up human DNA, and of identifying and mapping all of the genes of the human genome from both a physical and a functional standpoint

Humanae Vitae: with a subtitle 'On the Regulation of Birth', a papal encyclical focused on married love, responsible parenthood, and the rejection of artificial contraception

Hume's Fork: sees the principles of a priori knowledge (conceptual and prior to experience) and *a posteriori* knowledge (relating to experience) as completely separate types of knowledge

Hume's Law: that an 'ought' cannot be derived from an 'is'

'Hurrah-boo!' theory: another term for the theory of Emotivism

Hybrid: of mixed character or composed of different elements

Ideal self: our aspiration of who we want to be

Idealism: a philosophical school associated with Hegel that proposes that there must be an identity of thought and existence as a complete whole (das Absolute)

Immanent causation: Roderick Chisholm's third alternative to determinism and indeterminism that is a state of independence from both

Immigration: term referring to the movement of population into a country for residence (short-term or long-term)

Indeterminism: the notion of randomness, indecision, luck or chance

Indifferent: another word for neutral

Infallibility: without error

Innate: part of, integral to

Interest theory: Stevenson's theory of Emotivism

Internal cause: internalised moral choice (or the person's will to do something) that is completely determined

Intrinsic evil: an act that is always evil no matter what the circumstances

Intrinsic good: an act that is always good no matter what the circumstances

Irreducible: cannot be broken down into further parts

Jesuit: someone belonging to the Roman Catholic religious order the Society of Jesus

Jurisprudence: the philosophy of law as presented by a normative legal system

Justification: the declaring of a person to be just or righteous

Kamma: the notion of individual responsibility for our thoughts that lead to actions

Liberium arbitrium: Latin phrase meaning a person has the power of making choices that are free from predestination

Libertas: Latin phrase meaning liberty

Limited atonement: the view that Christ died for the sins of the elect only and no atonement was provided for the reprobate

Logical Positivism: school of Western philosophy that sought to legitimise philosophical discussion by arguing philosophical language should be based on scientific language

Logical Positivists: famous group of philosophers interested in logical philosophy, also known as the Vienna Circle

Magisterium: the authority of the Roman Catholic Church in maintaining authentic interpretation of the Bible and sacred Roman Catholic tradition headed by the Pope and Bishops and supported by a body of scholars

Manichaeism: a belief in two equally forceful powers of light and darkness in constant battle against each other

Manicheans: those following a dualistic religious system who had a basic doctrine of a conflict between light and dark, matter being regarded as dark and evil

Massa peccati: Latin term meaning lump or mass of sin

Materia apta: Latin phrase referring to Janssens' concept of the human person adequately considered (lit. suitable form or matter)

Materialism: the idea that everything can be explained through physical processes (sometimes called physicalism)

Mauvaise fois: bad faith, but better understood as self-deception

Maxim: a general rule

Methodism: religious movement founded primarily through the work of John Wesley, whose preaching centred upon the theology that God's grace was given to all

Middle knowledge: a theory developed by Luis de Molina, a Spanish Jesuit priest that argues God is aware of every computation of possible choices

Migrant: one who moves from one country to another

Monotheistic religions: Monotheism literally means the belief in only one God. The major monotheistic religions are Judaism, Christianity and Islam

Moral event: the term preferred by Professor Joseph Selling to describe an ethical 'act' because it conveys the idea that there is more to an ethical action than just the act-in-itself

Moral reasoning: application of intuition

Nationalism: the term used to describe an insular view of a nation and an aggressive attitude towards other nations

Natural evil: used to refer to events in the natural world that cause evil and suffering, e.g. disease and natural disasters

Naturalistic Fallacy: Moore's view that it is a logical error to explain that which is good reductively in terms of natural properties such as 'pleasant' or 'desirable'

Nature: inborn or hereditary characteristics as an influence on or determinant of personality

Neant: Sartre's understanding of human essence as empty of being-in-itself or 'nothingness', not having being, it is supported by being

New Morality: a reference to the situationism/consequentialism of Fletcher and followers

Nibbana: the term for enlightenment, ultimately beyond all notions of determinism and free will

Non-metaphysical moral realism: an alternative term for Intuitionism

Non-sensuous moral ideal: Bradley's term for Kant's general theory of duty

Normative ethics: the study of how people ought to act morally

Normative: to do with 'norms' of behaviour used in ethics to describe theories stating what we should do or how we should behave

Nurture: upbringing, education, and environment as an influence on or determinant of personality

Obligationism: an ethical view proposed by Charles Curran based in duty as part of his theology of compromise

Occam's Razor: entities should not be multiplied beyond necessity!

Omnibenevolence: the quality of being all-loving, sometimes stated as being all-good

Omnipotent being: a being with unlimited power

Omniscience: the state of knowing everything

Ontic evil: physical natural evil such as the fact of death, disease, pain and suffering

Original Sin: the sin committed by Adam in the Garden of Eden. More particularly, it refers to the doctrine that sin is inherent to human nature as a result of the Original Sin by Adam

Origination: the bringing-about of decisions and actions in such a way that these are not effects from a chain of cause and effect, they are in control of the person

Panspirit: the idea that there is an ultimate and universal, all-pervading spiritual force

Papal encyclical: a declaration of official teaching from the Pope

Papal infallibility: the belief that whatever is declared by the Pope through the Magisterium is inspired by God and infallible

Parietal cortex: one of the four major lobes of the cerebral cortex in the brain containing grey matter that transforms visual information into motor commands

Patriotism: the term used to describe pride in one's country

Pelagian controversy: the debate concerning the means by which people obtain righteousness

Peripatetic axiom: philosophical view found in Ancient Greek philosophy that 'Nothing is in the intellect that was not first in the senses'

Phronesis: practical wisdom

Platitude: a moral comment that has been used too often to be meaningful, cliché

Platonists: those asserting, with Plato, that the phenomena of the world are an imperfect and transitory reflection of the eternal reality of the ideal forms

Polemical: philosophical argument of or involving strongly critical writing or speech

Predestination: for some it refers to the determining of individual human destiny by God. It does not necessarily deny free will. Others see predestination as a predetermination by God of all actions and events removing free will of any kind

Preliminaries: gathering of claims

Pre-moral evil: a potential feature of a moral act, e.g. anger, deceit – some proportionalists extend this to all types of imperfection, that occurs as a result of any action

Premotor cortex: one of the four major lobes of the cerebral cortex in the brain that initiates movement

Prevenient grace: God's grace that precedes each human moral decision, associated with the Holy Spirit

Prima facie duties: first impression; accepted as correct until proved otherwise

Primae facie: accepted until demonstrated otherwise

'principle of double effect': a term to describe an ethical method of interpretation first identified in Aquinas' treatment of killing in self-defence

Process theology: the argument that the problem of evil is removed by redefining the meaning of God's omnipotence

Proportionalism: an approach to Natural Law that focuses in particular on the fourth condition of the 'principle of double effect' as outlined by Thomas Aquinas

Proportionate reason: reasoning that ensures evil that occurs is compensated and subsumed by a greater good

Proposition: statement

Propositions about attitude: views or value judgements about statements of belief

Propositions about belief: statements of fact or verifiable by empirical means

Protection: to protect the common good of society as a whole

Providence: the theological idea that God is closely involved in monitoring and guiding the created world

Pseudo-concepts: something treated as a concept but can only be mentally apprehended and not empirically verified

Punctate self: to identify a precise point at which we can define the 'self'

Rahit Maryada: the Sikh code of ethical conduct

Rational choice theory: the legal theory that people are reasoning agents who freely weigh up means and ends, costs and benefits, and therefore make freely willed rational choices when committing an illegal act

Rationalistic moralism: the theory that morality is purely accessible through reason and has no need for God

Readiness potential: the lag in time between the brain determining action and the consciousness being aware of it

Real goods: an act that is truly good

Realism: view that an object exists in reality independently of our mind (mind-independent)

Reasoning wrongly: to follow the wrong line of reasoning based on error

Reflet: Sartre's subtle distinction of the reflecting process that is a 'mirror' of the self-conscious but yet in itself has no essence; in his own words, 'that precise obligation to be a revealing intuition of something'

Reform: to change one's character from criminal to law-abiding

Refugee: one who has sought refuge from a life-threatening situation and been granted asylum

Reincarnation: transmigration of a metaphysical soul from one body or form to another that takes place at the point of death

Remonstrance: a word specifically used of the forceful protest of the Arminians of the Dutch Reformed Church in 1610 to the Staten-Generaal in the Netherlands

Reparation: to make amends to the victims of crime

Retribution: to 'pay back' the criminal that which they are due

Revisionists: those scholars who support Proportionalism

Salvific reality: the realisation that the teleological end of life is salvation

Sanctification: the state of proper functioning; living according to God's design and purpose

Self-evident: a proposition that needs no verification and remains a truth independently of whether or not we perceive it as so

Self-forming actions: Kane's argument that if we at times in the past freely created and changed our own character, then actions can be considered to be free

Self-realisation: Bradley's view that the self wanders through a philosophical course of discovery, interacts with society and nature and, ends with a realisation of one's identity and ethical role within the world

Settling: Steward's term for the process of selection and control at the very top level in consciousness that has evolved naturally

Simulated self: Daniel Dennett's notion that our neurological process of generating the 'self-illusion' is like a computer simulation

Sophia: philosophical wisdom

Soteriology: a quest to discover what the requirements for salvation are

Sovereignty of God: the teaching that all things are under God's rule and control. He is sovereign both in principle and practice

Station: Bradley's term to acknowledge the location, role and function of a human being in the social and natural world

Sui generis: unique, from the Latin 'of its own kind'

Summa Theoligica: Thomas Aquinas' main theological writing

Summum bonum: Kant's notion that morality ('ought') indicates there can or must be ('can') a 'highest good' – the term dates back to Cicero in Roman times

Sunyata: the Buddhist notion, related to anatta, that existence is ultimately empty of self-being (svabhava)

Synod: an assembly of church clergy of a particular church

Systematically arranged theology: theology arranged primarily for teaching purposes

Systematically derived theology: theology derived from first principles

Tabula rasa: literally means 'a clean slate' and refers to the peripatetic axiom

Tautology: saying the same thing twice over in different words

Taxonomy: the overall scheme of classification of ideas

Teleological: used to refer to an ethical system that has a final goal or 'end'

The argument from queerness: Mackie's view that Intuitionism is too odd to accept

The elect: those people chosen to salvation, by the grace of God

The Fall: the descent from perfection to sin recounted in Genesis 3

The gap: not to be confused with Sartre's Gap, Searle uses this to refer to the delay in the decision-making process typical of more complex decisions that involve a whole set of reasons behind the immediate cause of our actions that the neurobiological level cannot account for

The Protestant Reformation: a sixteenth-century European movement aimed initially at reforming the beliefs and practices of the Roman Catholic Church

The reprobates: those people, untouched by God's grace, left to be consumed by the defect of concupiscence

Traditionalists: those scholars who support the Magisterium, traditional authority of the Roman Catholic Church

Transcendental idealism: Kant's complex philosophy found in the Critique of Pure Reason (1781, 1787) that rejects the notion of objective empiricism and argues that our experiences of things are only 'sensible forms of our intuition'

Ummah: term used to describe the Muslim community, from a local perspective and up to and including the worldwide community of Muslims

Underivative: is not dependent on or derived from something else, a simple concept

Unequivocal: used to refer to something that is beyond doubt

Universalisability: Mill's utilitarian principle that that everyone ought to aim at the happiness of everyone, as increasing the general happiness will increase individual happiness

Univocal: used to refer to a word that has only one possible and unambiguous meaning

Unlimited atonement: Christ's atoning death was for all humanity

Unreflective consciousness: Prichard's explanation that intuition is not determined by philosophical reflection

Utilitarianism: theory first systematically outlined by Jeremy Bentham stating that we ought to aim to produce the greatest amount of pleasure and the least amount of pain

Valerian model: Daniel Dennett's explanation that neurological processes incorporate decision making by computing alternative choices

Value balancing: the process of balancing different moral and pre-moral values according to Garth Hallett

Value maximisation: the process of arriving at a final ethical decision according to Garth Hallett

Values and disvalues: a proportionalist way of calculating elements of a moral event

Verification principle: methodology of the Logical Positivists that only statements that are empirically verifiable (i.e. verifiable through the senses) are cognitively meaningful

Veritatis Splendor: a papal encyclical published in 1993

Volition: the 'will' or mind process that initiates action

Index